10/08

A Journalism
of Humanity

A Journalism of Humanity

A Candid History of the World's First Journalism School

Steve Weinberg

UNIVERSITY OF MISSOURI PRESS

COLUMBIA AND LONDON

Library of Congress Cataloging-in-Publication Data

Weinberg, Steve.
   A journalism of humanity : a candid history of the world's first
journalism school / Steve Weinberg.
          p.   cm.
   Includes bibliographical references and index.
   Summary: "Founded by Walter Williams, a newsman who
lacked a college education, the University of Missouri's School of
Journalism is regarded as among the best in the world. Weinberg
uncovers the history of the school's first 100 years, revealing the
flaws as well as the virtues of the Missouri Method"—Provided
by publisher.
   ISBN 978-0-8262-1796-7 (alk. paper)
   1. University of Missouri—Columbia. School of Journalism—
History.   I. Title.
   PN4791.U55W45 2008
   070.4071'177829—dc22
                                                      2007043025

∞ This paper meets the requirements of the
American National Standard for Permanence of Paper
for Printed Library Materials, Z39.48, 1984.

Designer: Kristie Lee
Typesetter: The Composing Room of Michigan, Inc.
Printer and binder: The Maple-Vail Book Manufacturing Group
Typefaces: Adobe Garamond and Times

The University of Missouri Press acknowledges the generous
contribution of the Missouri School of Journalism, Office of the
Dean toward the publication of this book.

The book's title comes from "The Journalist's Creed," composed by Walter Williams, founder of the University of Missouri Journalism School. Toward the end of the creed, which is posted in newsrooms and individual offices around the world, Williams wrote, "I believe that the journalism which succeeds best, and best deserves success . . . is a journalism of humanity, of and for today's world."

Contents

Preface   ix

One
Journalism Education?
Who Needs Journalism Education?   1

Two
The Founder: Walter Williams   4

Three
Inventing the First Journalism School,
Out of Nothing, in the Middle of Nowhere   13

Four
Not Merely a Student Newspaper:
The *Missourian* and the Missouri Method   31

Five
Bricks and Mortar during Peace and War   55

Six
Battling for Hegemony as Journalism Education Spreads . .   66

Seven
More Than Print: Adjusting the Missouri
Method for the Broadcast Era   98

Eight
Translating the Missouri Method to Faraway Places:
From China to the Beltway 117

Nine
The Dilemmas of Scholarship in a Vocational Setting:
Master's Degrees and PhDs 132

Ten
Reaching Out to the Profession: Midcareer
Journalism Education 174

Eleven
The Missouri "Mafia" 212

Twelve
Present and Future: The Dean Mills Era 222

Sources and Acknowledgments 257

Index 263

Preface

Rilla Dean Mills, dean of the University of Missouri School of Journalism since 1989, approached me about reporting and writing this centennial history—the first of its kind because the school he directs was the first of its kind.

That Mills approached me instead of a different author says much about him. First, Mills is well aware that I have spent my career primarily as an investigative journalist. In fact, I moved to the University of Missouri campus in 1983 to accept the executive director position at Investigative Reporters and Editors (IRE). IRE is a membership organization that includes some of the most talented investigative journalists from around the world; it is one of many professional groups with headquarters at the Missouri Journalism School.

Second, Mills is also well aware that, although I respect him as a human being, we have disagreed about his management style and his management decisions.

What sort of dean would approach an investigative reporter and faculty dissenter to write the history of the institution he directs, then agree to a promise, in writing, of editorial independence? The answer: a dean who is unafraid of an unvarnished institutional history.

Mills knows, in addition, that I am a loyal alumnus of the Journalism School (BJ 1970, MA 1975) and the father of a more recent graduate (Sonia, BJ 2002). I believe that, despite its shortcomings, the Missouri Journalism School has made a positive contribution in the realms of newspapers, magazines, radio, television, photography, advertising, public relations, and online information. He quite likely understood that I would not savage my alma mater; I hope readers agree that I have written a candid but ultimately constructive history.

From the start, I calculated that the primary audience for this book would be current and former Missouri Journalism School students, staff, and faculty. Despite that premise, I harbored no intention of writing a book that would appeal only to insiders. I hope it will appeal also to anybody else who cares about journalism—as an academic enterprise and as a conveyer of knowledge.

I examine the Journalism School in the context of its home university, the city of Columbia, the county of Boone, the state of Missouri, the nation, and the world. The school is located in Columbia, Missouri, to be sure, but its rich history transcends mid-Missouri by thousands of miles in every direction. In addition, I examine the Journalism School in the context of professional education, as well as the context of the employers it feeds with practitioners of the journalistic craft.

Some sections of the book will strike readers as negative. I cannot alter certain realities. For example, the Missouri Journalism School has always been part of a university with a reputation for racism and sexism. It should come as no surprise to readers that a university that failed to admit an African American student until 1950 and failed to hire an African American professor until 1969 spawned a Journalism School that sometimes acted just as shamefully.

While I hope the book will be judged as thorough, it is not intended as encyclopedic. Many famous and infamous students, staff, and faculty have spent time on campus. Most of them will not receive even a brief mention, however. To chronicle the exploits of every deserving member of what has become known as the Missouri "Mafia," bound together by their devotion to what has become known as the Missouri Method, is impractical. Even compiling an accurate list of all faculty, all staff, and all students since 1908 has proved impractical. I realize that every faculty member and every staff member, including those who came and went quickly, touched the lives of at least a few students. I also realize that every student touched the lives of at least a few faculty and staff. But given the size of the cast—tens of thousands—I must focus on the relatively small percentage who had the most significant impact on the largest number.

My own attachment to the Missouri Journalism School, continuing one way and another since 1966, obviously has influenced—consciously and subconsciously—some of the passages you are about to read. When I possess firsthand knowledge of people and occurrences, I have allowed that knowledge to inform the narrative. I am acutely aware that my firsthand knowledge is open to interpretation by others with different values and vantage points.

Now, an explanation about the organization of the narrative. Many institutional histories rely on relentless chronology. That tactic demonstrates a certain logic. On the other hand, rigid chronology can end up being stultifying—and confusing when numerous streams and themes are flowing through an institution simultaneously.

This book relies heavily on chronology through Chapter Three. Until the death of Walter Williams in 1935, the history of the Missouri Journalism School is straightforward. It revolves around Williams himself, the *Missourian,* and, to a lesser extent, instruction in advertising—the business side of journalism. After Williams's death, numerous individuals shared authority for the school's direction. Furthermore, advances in technology brought photojournalism, radio news, television news, the diversification of the magazine world, public relations practices to accompany advertising in a mix newly termed strategic communication, online journalism, and then convergence journalism.

After Chapter Three, the book becomes more thematic and less chronological—although, within the themed chapters, chronology is observed as faithfully as practical and unifying narrative threads do appear. Those narrative threads include the continual struggle of the *Missourian* to survive financially, the search for an appropriate magazine vehicle to teach students, the difficulty of keeping up with technology in broadcasting and photojournalism, the feeling among those in the advertising/public relations sector that they are second-class citizens in a school called "journalism," the tension between vocational training and academic scholarship, as well as sexism and racism.

Dean Mills arrived at the Journalism School in 1989. He is mentioned throughout the text. But I have saved most of what has happened at the Journalism School since his arrival for the final chapter.

I encourage readers to use the Index if it seems somebody or something ought to be mentioned but cannot be found in the most logical chapter. For example, not everything about KOMU-TV is found in Chapter Seven, even though that is the primary chapter about television instruction at the Missouri Journalism School.

Steve Weinberg
October 2007

A Journalism
of Humanity

One

Journalism Education?
Who Needs Journalism Education?

It is fortunate that Walter Williams carried the genes for dreaming big, because only somebody with that ability would have tried to start a journalism school when and where he did.

From the time of Williams's birth during 1864 until the opening of the University of Missouri Journalism School during 1908 as the world's first, employment in the realms of newspapers, magazines, advertising, and public relations received little respect—often not even from those practicing the craft. Reporters, editors, and those who worked on the business side of periodicals tended to drift into their jobs without training, with little formal education, and with scant interest in measuring the reactions of consumers. If somebody broached the idea of a journalism school, the reaction among practitioners was almost always negative. As for academics, they tended to sneer at journalism; they certainly never entertained a serious thought of it becoming part of the academy. If journalists needed to learn the craft, they could do so on the job, according to the conventional wisdom.

It apparently never occurred to those spouting the conventional wisdom that it made little sense. Obtaining the broad knowledge necessary to understand the workings of a complicated and often inexplicable world required all the education a brain could absorb. Communicating that understanding usually called for practice, practice, and more practice with a talented mentor. Before the Missouri Journalism School opened, few such mentors existed. Those who did often lacked the time at work to serve as a mentor. It seemed logical to Williams from an early age that a university could broaden an individual's all-around knowledge more efficiently than could any other institution, and that mentors could be hired by a university to teach the vocational elements.

Prior to the University of Missouri becoming the first campus to open a full-fledged journalism school, it and a few other campuses dabbled in journalism education—usually on the initiative of an English professor or business professor or agriculture professor or one of the institution's public relations employees or an actual journalist serving in an adjunct role. Such isolated courses, unsurprisingly, barely made a dent in the ignorance and callowness of practicing journalists.

In his *American Journalism: A History, 1690–1960,* Frank Luther Mott, unquestionably a great scholar, devotes only a dozen pages scattered among nine hundred to college education. The first reference does not appear until page 405, a clear indication that the training of journalists through higher education occurred only as an afterthought during the nineteenth century and into the twentieth.

Four years after the Civil War ended, with Confederate general Robert E. Lee having assumed the presidency of Washington College (later known as Washington and Lee University), scholarships became available to students stating they intended to enter the newspaper world. Lee, apparently motivated by what he considered irresponsible coverage by Civil War newspaper correspondents and a desire to see journalists play a role in rebuilding the South, said he would offer up to fifty full-tuition scholarships on the condition that each recipient "would labor one hour a day in his profession of journalism," educate himself in a liberal arts curriculum, and apprentice with a talented editor. However well intentioned Lee's offer was, the scholarships made no appreciable impact on advancing journalism education.

During the 1870s, Whitelaw Reid, a college-educated gentleman who earned journalism credentials on Civil War battlefields and in postwar Washington, D.C., used his rank at the *New York Tribune* to speak against the conventional wisdom. Reid suggested a "school of journalism, to be appended to the regular college course, as one of the additional features of university instruction, like the school of mines or medicine or law." Reid wanted editors specifically to receive a liberal arts education as part of a journalism-school curriculum. After all, editors on any given day needed to muster knowledge about a dozen topics or more. Reid, however, found little enthusiasm for his proposal within newsrooms, including his own.

In 1873, the Kansas State Agricultural College offered a journalism course. Cornell University followed in 1876. The University of Iowa and Ohio State University each initiated a journalism course during 1892. The first curriculum in journalism that can be documented arose at an unlikely venue—the Wharton School of Business, University of Pennsylvania. Joseph French Johnson, formerly financial editor of the *Chicago Tribune,* planned a sequence of journalism courses at Wharton in 1893. The plan lacked staying power, withering as a new century arrived.

What could have been the initial four-year curriculum for journalism students began to appear during 1904 at the University of Illinois. Frank W. Scott expanded offerings from a lone course known as Business Writing/Business Correspondence in the Rhetoric and Oratory Department. Scott added Newspaper Writing to the mix. He proposed "to give, on the side of theory, an insight into the history of the newspaper and the aims and ideals of modern journalism, and on the side of practice to give exercise under criticism, in the more practical forms of newspaper writing." But the four-year curriculum failed to gain official sanction until 1910.

The University of Missouri dabbled in journalism education starting in 1878, because of an English professor named David Russell McAnally. Born during 1847 in Tennessee, McAnally arrived in St. Louis with his family at age four. After a brief teaching career, McAnally joined the *St. Louis Globe-Democrat* in 1875 as an editorial writer. He moved to the University of Missouri faculty during 1877. Besides chairing the English Department, McAnally taught the history of the journalistic craft and offered instruction to students wanting to learn newspaper-style writing.

McAnally remained on campus eight years before returning to the *Globe-Democrat* editorial page. No other professor stepped in to keep journalism instruction alive. For those wanting to institute journalism education, the prospects looked grim.

Two

The Founder

Walter Williams

Born in 1864—twenty-five years after the nearby University of Missouri initiated higher education west of the Mississippi River—the future dean was the last of eight children spread over twenty-four years from the marriage of Marcus and Mary Jane Littlepage Williams. Sibling seven was eleven years older; Marcus Walter Williams received lots of attention from his adult and near-adult sisters and brothers.

The middle name given to that eighth child honored John Walter, a Sunday school teacher of the baby's older sister Susan Ann. The family referred to the baby as Marcus or Marcus Junior, but he later decided to use his middle name. The baby's birthplace was Boonville, Cooper County, Missouri, about thirty miles from where the world's first journalism school would later be established.

On the day of Williams's birth, the Civil War raged. Within a few months, blood would be shed in Cooper County, as Union forces, southern sympathizers, and guerrilla bands clashed. Walter's parents tried to keep the family away from harm and somehow remain optimistic.

With all that nurturing, Walter graduated from Boonville's high school at age fifteen. Walter wanted to attend the University of Missouri, but he knew that would strain the family budget. Still a young teenager, slight of build, unathletic, with a squeaky voice that would not change even after reaching puberty (it changed, in fact, only after a near-fatal bout with typhus in 1905), Williams felt he needed a paying job to help his family. Mature beyond his years, he thought about careers open to intelligent young men, including his parents' ferry, pottery,

4

and carpentry businesses; the law, the path followed by two older brothers; the ministry, an alternative suggested by the family's Presbyterian pastor; or politics. Fascinated with newspapers, a voracious reader interested in current affairs, Williams as an immediate palliative applied for a position at the *Boonville Topic,* an easy walk from his family's residence.

Williams could consider himself fortunate to grow up in a state with a rich and rather progressive newspaper realm dating back to 1808. The progressive outlook included at least a few newspaper editors and publishers who understood that journalists could benefit from organized training.

During 1869, for example, in its second issue, the *Boone County Journal* published an editorial under the headline "A School of Journalism." Edwin William Stephens, the apparent author of the editorial and a future colleague of Williams's, wrote, "Why should we not have a school for editors? At least instruct the student in the true theory of editorial duty. Precisely how such a school should be conducted, it would be very difficult to say. . . . But there is manifestly not only room, but a real demand for it. We have an abundance of good newspaper writers, but a paucity of skillful editors."

Also during 1869, St. Louis journalist Norman J. Colman, publisher of *Colman's Rural World,* suggested that journalism be included as "a course of study" at the state university. Appointed to the University of Missouri Board of Curators, Colman tried to persuade his colleagues during his sixteen-year tenure to establish a journalism program, commenting, "Like all other professions, the Editorial has grave and responsible duties devolving upon it—but unlike others, certain prescribed qualifications have not been required before entering upon the discharge of professional duty."

In 1869, Colman served as president of the Missouri Press Association, which had begun meeting two years earlier. With the group's backing, Colman helped organize a lecture series about journalism at the University of Missouri College of Arts and Science during 1873. But nothing substantial grew from the lecture series.

Still, the possibility would not die. During 1879, when the Missouri Press Association met in Columbia, William F. Switzler of the *Columbia Statesman* told the group he saw a logical association between newspapers and the university: "The state press and the state university are powers with the people. Each is an important factor of their freedom and prosperity, and of their future greatness and glory. . . . Each is an educator—the press directly—of those who now govern the country, the university primarily of those who will hereafter govern it. . . . Editing a newspaper is as much a profession as practicing law or medicine . . . a department of journalism ought to be established, and I have no doubt at no distant day will be established, in our own and other universities."

The year of Switzler's address, Williams, at age fifteen, became a newspaperman in Boonville, starting as a printer's devil, an apprentice position that involved dirty work around the typesetting equipment and the presses. He enjoyed the tasks given to him, eventually receiving opportunities to report, write, and edit. Williams put aside plans to pursue other careers and kept postponing university attendance. The individual who would essentially invent university-level journalism education would never attend a university as a for-credit student.

At age twenty, Williams switched newsrooms but not towns, moving to the *Boonville Advertiser* as editor in chief. Two years after switching Boonville employers, Williams began to expand his professional horizons outside his hometown, attending his first Missouri Press Association meeting, where he spoke on "Journalism from a Business and Social Standpoint." During 1887, he represented his state's newspapers at the National Editorial Association convention in Denver.

Just three years after joining the Missouri Press Association, at age twenty-five, Williams became president. He devised a vision for the newspapering "profession," a word he used often in contravention of the conventional wisdom. The vision consisted of editors from all over the world meeting, sharing information, and cooperating in building the profession, while halting attacks on one another.

Despite the fervor of Williams's vision, that same year he left newspapering to accept an offer from Missouri governor David R. Francis to serve as a bookkeeper at the state penitentiary in Jefferson City. Williams would increase his pay, and he planned to write on the side. Even with the financial incentive, his departure from journalism surprised many who thought they knew Williams well. In the *Columbia Herald* of March 7, 1889, Edwin Stephens commented, "Walter Williams, the bright young editor of the *Boonville Advertiser,* has accepted a clerkship in the Missouri state penitentiary at eighteen hundred dollars. We hate to see as talented a man as Williams leave the field for which he is so well fitted . . . to accept a clerkship and, like the rest of us, go off after lucre. But we wish him well and hope he may soon return to the craft."

Perhaps Williams had been influenced by a desire for regular office hours that would allow him to court Hulda Harned. Williams had been living as a bachelor at a Columbia residential hotel. He began pursuing Hulda after glimpsing her at a social event. He learned that she had studied art and literature at Hardin College in Mexico, Missouri. She reciprocated his interest. The couple announced their engagement within weeks, and Williams began saving money to build a house for them on Hitt Street in Columbia, about five minutes by foot from the University of Missouri campus. She continued living with her family on a near-ly inaccessible farm near the town of Vermont, not far from Boonville.

Unsurprisingly, given Williams's devotion to journalism, the position inside state government turned out to be a bad fit. Even the romance with Hulda could not erase the yearning for printer's ink. Within three months, Williams depart-ed state employment. In a letter to a friend, he said he had been victimized by partisan political infighting. That probably played a role, along with objections from politicos to Williams's freelancing, as well as Williams's ineptness with bud-get numbers. But the essential truth was this—Williams missed journalism.

Despite a salary reduction from eighteen hundred dollars annually to thirteen hundred dollars, Williams joined the *Columbia Herald,* a weekly purchased by Stephens in 1870 when it still carried the name *Columbia Journal.* Born during 1849 into what became a well-known Columbia family, and a University of Mis-souri graduate at age eighteen, Stephens, a devout Baptist, at the suggestion of his successful merchant father entered newspapering instead of becoming a min-ister.

By the time Williams joined the *Columbia Herald* staff, the commercial pub-lishing plant also handled book printing, court reports, and compilations of state statutes, employing about one hundred individuals. Williams decided to stay in mid-Missouri despite offers based on his precocious accomplishments from the *Cleveland Plain Dealer* in Ohio and the *St. Louis Republic* closer to home.

That decision to remain in mid-Missouri allowed Williams to complete his courtship of Harned. They married in 1892, with the ceremony occurring at the Harned family residence. The family of Hulda and Walter eventually included a daughter, Helen, plus two sons, Walter Winston and Edwin Moss.

Working obsessively partly from professional passion and partly to support his family, Williams improved the look and content of the *Herald.* By 1895, a news-paper rating service called it the best country weekly in the nation. Never again would Williams be seriously tempted by a job outside journalism. "The position of country editor will compare favorably with that held by any prince or poten-tate," Williams said. "He has a larger audience than all the preachers in his town. He has more influence than the banker or the lawyer. He has lots of fun, and if he loves his profession as all good editors do, nothing could prompt him from it."

Becoming increasingly active professionally outside his newsroom, Williams started a publication called the *Missouri Editor* in 1894. When journalists out-side Missouri subscribed, Williams and business partner Stephens saw an opportunity to spread their professional gospel as well as perhaps earn significant money. So they changed the name to the geographically broader *Country Editor.*

In Stephens, Williams found a colleague a decade older to rely on in his many ventures, including the quest for journalism education. Stephens rarely tired of lobbying his Missouri Press Association colleagues to work for formal journalism instruction at the university level, preferably at the University of Missouri.

Plans for formal journalism education continued to meet resistance, no matter how much Stephens and Williams proselytized. The belief that newsroom training had always proved sufficient would not die. A *Kansas City Star* editorial said that while a journalism school "may be pushed in Columbia, the establishment will never receive an order from any newspaper office for one complete journalist ready to work." The *St. Louis Globe-Democrat* weighed in: "The country printing office is really our only school of journalism. . . . There is no other place where preparatory general training for the duties of the profession can be obtained, where a young man can learn to be an all-round journalist."

At the *Paris (Missouri) Appeal,* editor H. J. Blanton recalled "with some degree of amusement the annual resolution E. W. Stephens would lay before the Missouri Press Association. . . . I could not forget the fervor with which Walter Williams always moved its adoption. Just to humor these popular members, all of us would vote for the resolution, then go out behind the barn for a hearty chorus of laughter at the idea of training for journalism anywhere except in the office of a country newspaper."

Thus, as the twentieth century approached, the words *journalism* and *education* linked together still sounded like an oxymoron to most who heard them. Yet Williams refused to become discouraged about instituting journalism education, perhaps because of the faith he applied to all matters, personal and professional. Religiously devout, Williams served as editor of the monthly regional newspaper published by the Presbyterian Church. In Columbia, Williams's Sunday school teaching shifted from a traditional classroom setting to the church auditorium when attendance reached nearly four hundred.

Although Williams never obtained formal education beyond high school, he educated himself impressively, and lots of people noticed. Missouri governor Lon V. Stephens, a fellow Boonville native, appointed Williams to the University of Missouri Board of Curators during 1899. At the same time, Stephens accepted Williams's suggestion to appoint two of Williams's friends as well. Williams seemingly had created a power base on the Board of Curators—perhaps with a new push for a journalism school in mind—and he became deeply involved in the governance of the campus.

The University of Missouri was beginning its rise to prominence with Richard Henry Jesse as president and an earlier governor, David R. Francis, having provided a financial infusion for higher education. Jesse employed almost no staff and thus became increasingly reliant on Williams's volunteer counsel. As Jesse became increasingly indebted to Williams, the president would do more and more to help Williams achieve his dream of establishing a journalism school.

Not even a university president and a determined curator could push aside every obstacle, however. Frustration grew year after year, especially in the mind of a journalist like Williams accustomed to publishing newspapers that achieved something akin to instant gratification. The bureaucracy and politics of higher education seemed impenetrable and interminable.

Nonetheless, Williams believed he sensed sentiment turning in his favor. Some within journalism grasped the need for preparation—if for no other reason than to understand advancing technology. Typesetting equipment and sophisticated presses altered the production process. Photography became common in many newsrooms, and cameras were not standardized.

In addition, a large proportion of readers had come to expect news reports divorced from the partisan political agendas of publishers, which meant reporters and editors needed instruction about effective techniques of information gathering and presentation. Even if newsroom supervisors possessed the qualifications to offer such instruction, the deadlines inside newsrooms made extensive on-the-job teaching impractical. The growth of newspapers throughout Missouri continued, offering more venues that could potentially send employees to a campus. In 1900, a count showed ten morning dailies, sixty-one afternoon dailies, and about eight hundred weeklies across the state.

While Missourians dithered about a journalism school, it appeared the first one would open at Columbia University in New York City instead—because, somewhat ironically, of a wealthy visionary with a strong Missouri connection. Joseph Pulitzer, owner of the *New York World* and the *St. Louis Post-Dispatch,* had proposed to endow a journalism school at Columbia University in 1892. Since then, Pulitzer, a deliberate, fretful man, had drafted plan after plan for the school he wanted named in honor of his family.

During August 1902, Pulitzer tried to summarize his oft-stated visions with the utmost clarity by writing a memo at his estate in Bar Harbor, Maine. Concerned about his health, he also worried about his legacy: "My idea is to recognize that journalism is, or ought to be, one of the great and intellectual professions; to encourage, elevate and educate in a practical way the present, and still more, future members of that profession, exactly as if it were the profession of law or medicine. . . . To differentiate between journalism as an intellectual profession and as a business must be a fundamental object. . . . I have selected Columbia because it is located in New York, because it is centrally located and accessible to all students, journalists, reporters, lecturers and the leading editors. . . . Why not teach in it things which every right-minded journalist must aspire to know, an easy opportunity of acquiring which would raise professional tone and pride? Why not teach, for instance, politics, literature, government, constitutional principles and traditions (especially American), history, political economy, also the history and the power of public opinion and public service, illustrated by concrete examples, showing the mission, duty and opportunity of the press as a moral teacher? Besides this, teach if possible the practical side—news gathering, news editing, news writing, style, composition, accuracy, everything, even to the make-up of a newspaper. It all could be taught."

Columbia University accepted two million dollars from Pulitzer in 1905, more money than Walter Williams had dreamed of. But it took until September 1912 to open the Columbia University journalism school. By then, Pulitzer had died.

Back in Missouri, at the other Columbia, the matter of creating a journalism school finally and formally reached the University of Missouri Board of Curators on December 18, 1906. The minutes summarize a report from a three-person committee of Williams; J. Carleton Jones, a Latin professor who also served as College of Arts and Science dean; and Albert Ross Hill, director of the university teachers college. When President Jesse appointed the three men, he almost certainly knew what their decision would be, thus fulfilling a debt to Williams while pursuing his own agenda of expanding the main campus of the state university. The minutes say in part:

"(1) That a college or school of journalism be established as a department of the university, coordinate in rank with the departments of law, medicine and other professional schools.

"(2) That the School of Journalism be provided with adequate laboratory equipment for practical journalistic training.

"(3) That the course of study be at least four years in length and that the entrance requirements be at least equal to those of the Academic Department. That the curriculum be so coordinated as to insure cooperation between this school and the Academic Department including many courses now offered in Arts along such lines as English, foreign languages, history and the social sciences, etc., some general courses in journalism that might count toward a degree in Arts, together with some strictly professional courses intended only for those who wish to secure a professional degree or certificate from the School of Journalism."

As the reality of a journalism school became imminent, speculation resounded across the state about who ought to serve as the dean. Should it be a prominent journalist from the metropolis of St. Louis or Kansas City? A prominent journalist from outside Missouri? Somebody with administrative experience and a high-level degree already serving on the university faculty, but not a journalist?

To plenty of observers, Williams did not seem like a logical choice, given his lack of a university education. Knowing about the doubters, but also knowing that his name had entered the discussion, Williams wondered whether at age forty-four seeking the position made sense for his career, especially because it would mean surrendering his editorship of the *Columbia Herald*. What about security for his family, especially if the journalism school failed to attract an adequate number of students? What if the state legislature and the university failed to provide adequate funding after a year or two? What if opposition from news organizations would not cease—would graduates from the school end up without jobs?

Williams sought advice from Frank Thilly, a Cornell University philosophy professor who had previously taught at the University of Missouri. Should I accept? Williams asked. He continued, "It would not be financially advantageous. I am not a college graduate. I am on the Board [of Curators]. The field is new and unorganized. The risk of failure is considerable and might be larger for me. I would change from one official relation with the university to another, and the attitude of the faculty and, to some extent, of the students might affect unfavorably my chances for success. Finally, it would bring about a recasting and reshaping of my life plans."

So why even consider saying yes, given the actual and potential drawbacks? "The work has large chance for good," Williams ruminated to Thilly. "It is in the interests of my profession. It would give opportunity to do some literary work that I cannot otherwise accomplish. There is fascination in the creation of a new school, on the broad lines existing nowhere else. I might be of service to the university, the state and journalism. Somebody must do the work. Am I the right man?"

Thilly said yes. So did others whose advice Williams sought, including his brother Billy, a judge; and Champ Clark, a Missourian who had been elected speaker of the U.S. House of Representatives in Washington, D.C.

President Jesse made the offer to Williams. He accepted and reluctantly resigned his position on the university's Board of Curators. He left the *Columbia*

Herald, the newspaper he had nurtured. Despite needing to support a family, Williams refused to accept the four-thousand-dollar salary offered to him as dean, worrying about a budget shortfall before the school started operating, as well as expressing concern at too large a gap between the dean's pay and amounts budgeted for the rest of the faculty. Instead, he began the deanship with a salary of thirty-three hundred dollars.

With the deal sealed, Williams now had to create the world's first freestanding, degree-granting journalism school. No template existed for the task.

Three

Inventing the First Journalism School, Out of Nothing, in the Middle of Nowhere

As Walter Williams invented the world's first journalism school during 1908, he could not have imagined that, one hundred years later, the plan he devised would be known as the Missouri Method. Nor could Williams have known that his invention would be so durable it would need only occasional tweaking during its opening century—much as the authors of the U.S. Constitution could never have predicted the durability of their seminal document.

The school opened officially on July 1, 1908. It would have made sense to devise the curriculum, find classroom space, recruit students, and hire faculty and staff over a period of a year or two, accepting the first class for the fall of 1909 or 1910. Williams, however, decided classes would commence during 1908. While dealing with the details, he found time to set out his philosophy for those who felt a journalism school could never be justified as an intellectual endeavor within a university setting.

In the first of a series of bulletins published by the Journalism School, *Training for Journalism as a Profession,* Williams wrote: "Journalism as a profession attracts each year more men to its ranks. Nor is the supply of capable, well-trained journalists equal to the demand. Opportunities for large public service are greater in journalism than in any other vocation and will be increasingly so as the public comes to depend more and more upon the press for information and guidance. The salaries paid for newspaper work have increased in recent years. The efficient newspaperman has an assured income from the very beginning of his work. Higher salaries come with large ability and special training. One American journalist has a salary greater than that of the president of the United States. The fascination of journalism, the sense of power, of creative work, of possibilities for usefulness, the position which journalism has taken in the world, appeal to the ambitious man who would make the most of himself. There is constant call for reporters, editors, special writers, correspondents, publishers, ad-writers, men in all departments of journalism, in city and country, on daily, weekly and monthly journals. It is to supply this demand, in the interest of the state, to furnish well-equipped men for leadership in journalism, with high ideals and special training, that the Department of Journalism at the University of Missouri is established. It is to train for journalism—not to make journalists. In thus training for journalism the university in large degree serves the state."

What were the advantages of a college degree in place of an extended apprenticeship such as Williams himself had served? The answer seemed simple to Williams, despite his positive experience as an apprentice: editors and publishers, seemingly always on deadline, rarely halted to explain what they were doing and why, much less to think about how anything could be done better. The impact of the Missouri Method derived from Williams's plan to create a real-life daily newspaper serving an entire small city, a newspaper where the faculty editors existed to explain the what, why, and how to the student reporters. This innovative vocational training would alternate with classroom instruction in the liberal arts and the sciences.

Williams borrowed what made sense from professional schools in other fields. Schools of law, medicine, agriculture, engineering, and teacher education had become realities within his lifetime, in some instances replacing apprenticeships. Furthermore, each of those professional schools combined the lecture/classroom method with hands-on practicums in real-world settings—such as hospitals, courtrooms, factories, and schoolhouses. So why not journalism? The classroom instruction would combine liberal arts courses, skewed toward future journalists when practical, with journalism-specific courses. The practicum would consist of a daily newspaper aimed at readers throughout Columbia and Boone County. Starting a real-life newspaper staffed by students and directed by faculty, in competition with already existing commercial enterprises, had never been tried. Williams would need to figure out how to obtain and pay for the equipment, too—an expensive proposition.

Albert Ross Hill, who had succeeded Jesse as the university's president, told the general faculty that the campus "is the first in America to establish and organize a school of journalism. I believe it is possible for the school to give dignity to the profession of journalism, to anticipate to some extent the difficulties that journalism must meet and to prepare its graduates to overcome them; to give prospective journalists a professional spirit and high ideals of service; to discover those with real talent for the work in the profession, and to give the state better newspapers and a better citizenship. I hope the faculty of the School of Journalism, upon whom rests the responsibility for all this, will prove worthy of the trust imposed in them."

To be accepted, student applicants needed to have a high school diploma or to pass a specially designed examination. During his or her first two years at the university, the student's credit hours would include at least six of mathematics, logic, or psychology. Soon after, the Journalism School began requiring five credits of economics, five credits of philosophy, and five credits of either political science or sociology. Later specifications included ten credits in speaking a foreign language bolstered by an additional course in reading the language, a semester of either physical science or biological science with a laboratory course included, a semester of American government, six credits of English literature, and six of English composition.

The original degree program consisted of one hundred and twenty total credits, including ten practical journalism courses adding up to twenty-five credits completed mostly during the junior and senior years. Later, the number of journalism credits increased to thirty, one-fourth of the total. The numbers speak for themselves—Williams hoped to send broadly educated liberal arts graduates with journalism trade skills into the job market.

It is impossible now to re-create the flurry of activity in Williams's life during the summer of 1908. The requests for interviews piled up, as the new journalism school and its proposed newspaper attracted lots of attention. *Harper's Weekly* editor George Harvey, who during 1908 presented a Yale University lecture advocating specialized journalism education, ran a story on June 27, 1908, about Williams's plan. Numerous commentators, including those at the *Kansas City Journal,* used the occasion to praise the choice of Williams as dean. Other commentators, while having nothing against Williams personally, wondered why anybody believed journalism could be taught effectively in a university setting.

It certainly came as no surprise when publishers of the local Columbia newspapers, as well as generally supportive compatriots at places such as the *St. Louis Star,* opposed the creation of a university newspaper soliciting advertising dollars from merchants. Publishers of the *Columbia Daily Tribune, Columbia Herald,* and *Columbia Statesman* protested to the University of Missouri Board of Curators.

The *Tribune* had started during September 1901 as Columbia's first daily newspaper. Founder Charles M. Strong served as editor and publisher, operating from a downtown headquarters. In early 1902, Strong sold a 50 percent interest to Ernest L. Mitchell. A couple of years later, Strong left Columbia, with Mitchell becoming sole owner. The newspaper gained little attention and little praise until 1905, when Edwin Moss Watson bought it upon the unexpected death of Mitchell. Watson's brother-in-law, Henry J. Waters, helped close the financial end of the sale.

Watson, born in Callaway County during 1867, had grown up in Columbia and gravitated toward journalism early, working for newspapers around the country—including the *Columbia Herald,* where Edwin Stephens instructed him—before and after graduating from the University of Missouri in 1890. A faithful, vocal member of the Democratic Party, Watson did take a hiatus to earn a law degree and serve as Columbia's city attorney, but he could not stay away from newspapering. He never opposed creation of the Journalism School per se. In fact, he assisted the Missouri Press Association campaign.

During 1908, though, Watson grasped the adverse financial implications for his enterprise: "The *Missourian* has a liberal advertising patronage, and is in the field for such business as generally comes to a newspaper. It is submitted that this is competition. The state pays for the paper, for printing, and employs the publishers. If students were merely trained in journalism, there could be no possible objection to the *Missourian,* but in all fairness should the state go into the newspaper business against private individuals?" Other Missouri publishers agreed with Watson; broadsides appeared in the *St. Louis Star, Mexico Ledger,* and *Hannibal Morning Journal.*

Williams countered the complaints at a Missouri Press Association meeting in Fulton: "Our school seeks to do for journalism what schools of law, medicine, and agriculture have done for those vocations. Previous to the existence of those schools, training in those fields was obtainable only in the lawyer's office, the doctor's office, and on the farm. But now professional schools have taken the place of such individual training. They have attained their development by the application of the laboratory or clinic to their instruction programs. The School of Journalism is to be conducted on the same plan. . . . The needs of the first year compel the adoption of a plan which was unfortunately seized upon as the 'state competing with private enterprise.'" Partly because of his influence within the Board of Curators, Williams held complaining commercial publishers at bay.

Somehow, in what can fairly be termed a near miracle, Williams managed to piece together an entering class of students, faculty, staff, teaching space, and an outside printing contract (until a plant could be built) by the time the fall term at the University of Missouri opened on September 14, 1908.

By 4:30 p.m. on September 14, two veteran St. Louis newsboys were hustling the premiere edition of the *University Missourian* newspaper. Subscriptions cost two dollars for the school year. Single copies sold for two cents. An editorial cartoon in that first issue is headlined "Our Six Columns Will Help." The illustrator is identified only as "Sanders," who sketched a child's right arm wrapped around a tiger. The child is wearing a sash with the words *University Missourian.* Page 1 contains four stories: legal and financial troubles are causing Columbia Theater to close; the city jailer has been accused of serving tainted meat to increase his profits while the inmate population decreases; a two-time widower, having received two proposals from women to wed and chosen one, is being sued by the other for an alleged breach of promise, a charge he denies in a *Missourian* interview; and a blind man is receiving a cornea transplant from a rabbit, according to a United Press story from New York.

The editorials on the first day explain the purpose of the Journalism School and its newspaper. Albert Ross Hill is featured not only as the new University of Missouri president but also as a friend of the Journalism School. A historical feature discusses the *University Missourian* magazine founded in 1871 by Eugene Field, a newspaperman who later became well known as a poet before dying in 1895. Page 3 relates more about journalism training in a university setting, introduces the new faculty, and contains a letter from University of Missouri alumna Mary Irwin McDearmon of St. Louis; she wishes that in light of the impressive journalism course offerings, she could return to campus. A graphic shows the university's enrollment. Advertisements appear from an optical company, a chocolates shop, a tailor, a printer, and a downtown clothing store offering suits and overcoats. Photographs appear liberally, including pictures of guest editorial authors.

The newspaper continued to distinguish itself during its first month, especially considering the inexperience of most of the student reporters and editors. A feature about newsboys appears under the headline "Those Piercing Yells Come From Boys With University Missourian." A news story explains how the popularity of the automobile is depressing sales prices for horses. University of Missouri freshmen are hazed in print, as upperclassmen poke fun at them. A speech by President Hill warns that among the dangers of life at the university are "overemphasis of student and social activities and intellectual artificiality or dishonesty."

From the start, the newspaper did not aggrandize Walter Williams; he is not mentioned significantly even once during the first two weeks. That counted as a positive. Some days, though, frustration overtook the editors, who worried that a newspaper produced within a university setting would exercise self-censorship. Unfortunately for the cause of truth, the *Missourian* editors shied away from publishing controversial information. Charles G. Ross, one of the initial editors, wrote to a confidante on October 8, 1908, "There is no real news in Columbia that would interest you; indeed, there is no real news of any kind. If there were a bit of real live news, I suppose the *Missourian* would be throttled."

Despite Ross's skepticism, the newspaper had no trouble filling its pages. Soon, the *Missourian* started publishing on Saturdays. Then, because of intense interest in college football, Sunday editions began appearing during the season. Circulation on a normal day numbered around one thousand. A student-written editorial stated, "The School of Journalism has passed the experimental stage and the University Missourian will give this year practical demonstration of the school's success. As a newspaper it will give the news truthfully, graphically and fearlessly." The dilemma of how candidly to cover the university—given the newspaper's partial dependence on campus administrators—never disappeared entirely.

The dilemma of whether the *Missourian* should appear in the morning or afternoon never entirely abated, either. The discussion revolved around which time slot would best serve educational purposes, would please the largest number of readers, and would least anger publishers trying to earn a livelihood without the advantage of university backing.

The state legislature proved to be responsive to the publishers after the University of Missouri president and the Board of Curators failed to do the bidding of the *Tribune*'s Watson as well as the publishers of Columbia's other newspapers. The legislature's next payment to the university included a provision that "no part of any money appropriated be used directly or indirectly for the support, maintenance, or publication of any newspaper which solicits, receives or accepts paid subscriptions or which prints or publishes advertising."

The wording sounded like a death knell. The Board of Curators, politicized and seemingly resistant to Williams's influence, expressed reluctance to battle with the legislature. The curators seemed to be saying that the *Missourian* must halt publishing, along with a College of Agriculture magazine and an Alumni Association magazine. Williams knew that saving the *Missourian* would be difficult. But he knew he must succeed.

His plan required him to take the lead in organizing the University Missourian Association, incorporated in Boone County—essentially a brilliantly conceived legal dodge. The creation of a separate association would avoid direct financial and administrative linkages to the university. The nine-member board of directors would be elected annually by journalism students. That student board would appoint the newspaper's managing editor and the advertising manager. If any money remained from operations at the end of each fiscal year, it "shall be placed in a fund for the improvement of said publications, which fund shall be handled separately by the treasurer under the direction of the board of directors."

A local lawyer filed the incorporation documents at the Boone County courthouse during July 1909. Williams's plan kept the *Missourian* publishing as if nothing had happened. The *Tribune*'s owners never entirely accepted the commercial aspects of the *Missourian*. From time to time over the decades, the disagreement would flare into public view.

Given the labor-intensive task of producing a daily newspaper, each faculty member hired in the Journalism School's early years needed to demonstrate versatility, whether duty called in the newsroom or in the classroom. The catalog for the first year shows Newspaper Making as the laboratory course that produced the *Missourian,* with News-Gathering as a related course; Newspaper Administration and Comparative Journalism, both taught by Williams; Newspaper Jurisprudence, taught by Law School dean John D. Lawson; Newspaper Publishing (emphasizing business operations rather than the editorial side); Magazine and Class Journalism (covering pretty much all forms other than general-circulation daily newspapers); Correspondence (stressing special features such as reporting during wars); and Office Equipment (covering mechanical operations such as presses and type).

Some aspects of journalism suffered from secondary status for a while; the Missouri Journalism School could not serve as all things to all students immediately, given its small faculty, limited budget, and uncertain future. For example, making the *Missourian* look appealing did not fall into any course right away. Photojournalism as thought of today did not exist. "Newspaper illustration" might have been the most apt term in the early 1900s, but how to teach it effectively seemed elusive.

Herbert Warren Smith (BJ 1911) joined the faculty in 1913 to teach what he called "illustrative art." Smith installed the school's photoengraving plant. Eventually, the engraving camera acquired a screen, allowing the *Missourian* to publish halftones to augment line engravings. In 1922, Smith moved to the *Dallas Morning News,* and he remained in Dallas until his death.

In 1923, Horatio Booth Moore began teaching using a new term, *photo illustration.* The technology progressed slowly, but it seemed the Journalism School could always rely on a faculty member to stay informed about photography, even if that person could not be termed "cutting edge." The ascendancy of cutting-edge photojournalism would have to wait until the 1940s.

As Williams filled the gaps with new faculty, he set the tradition early that they did not need doctorates or even master's degrees to teach successfully, bucking common practice on the rest of the campus. The decision carried consequences for the Journalism School; professors and administrators in other disciplines felt at liberty to demean the Journalism School as a mere vocational enterprise, unworthy of academic equality.

When tenure for journalism faculty and promotions from instructor to assistant professor to associate professor to full professor became issues, Williams and future deans would not always prevail. Tenure and promotion were not entirely internal Journalism School decisions and never would be. As a result, biologists or historians or advanced degree holders from other academic disciplines serving on campus tenure committees could cause havoc within the Journalism School, and they sometimes did. Williams believed that the positives of hiring faculty directly from newsrooms, advertising agencies, and public relations firms, even if those men and women lacked advanced degrees, clearly outweighed the negatives.

Teaching journalism courses during the first year, in addition to Williams, were Silas Bent and Charles Ross, both formerly of the *St. Louis Post-Dispatch.* A childhood friend of Harry Truman, Ross qualified as a prodigy. He reportedly read thousands of books by age fifteen, graduated from high school early, and entered the University of Missouri in 1901. Ross had worked for Williams at the *Columbia Herald* while also a University of Missouri student. When he joined the Journalism School faculty, Ross was only twenty-three years old.

In addition to the small faculty recruited for the first year, Williams found money to hire a small staff—Warren H. Orr as circulation manager of the *Missourian,* E. R. Evans as advertising manager, and Cannie R. Quinn as Journalism School stenographer.

After a year of teaching, Bent returned to newspapering in Chicago, in part because he and Williams did not mesh well. Bent's big-city wit, irreverence, and party-going fitted poorly with Williams's preference for a more sober demeanor among his faculty members.

The most important fallout from Bent's departure turned out to be not his loss but rather the gain of Frank Lee Martin. A *Kansas City Star* staff writer, Martin met Williams during 1905 when the reporter traveled to Columbia to learn about a rumored typhoid fever epidemic; Williams, victimized by the fever, became an interviewee, then a social acquaintance, and finally a mentor. Apparently never comfortable in a metropolis as large as Kansas City, Martin liked the atmosphere of Columbia; so did his new wife, Martha Marie Hall, a receptionist at the *Star*. Because the future of a new journalism school seemed uncertain, Martin arrived to teach on a leave of absence from the newspaper. He never returned to the newsroom.

Martin, about six feet four inches and gaunt, was born in York County, Nebraska. He graduated from the University of Nebraska in 1902. His future as a newspaperman looked promising. His intelligence, earnestness, and modesty were reflected in his easy smile. As a young Journalism School teacher, Martin stressed accurate and otherwise sound reporting, a strongly developed individual sense of public service, and mastering the current job before thinking about moving up.

He pushed student journalists to meet as many people as possible inside and outside government, those with high-ranking offices and those with no offices. "You can never tell when one of these friends might tip you off to an exclusive news story," Martin told his students. He tolerated teaching straight-ahead news writing, with the five Ws and the H (who, what, when, where, why, and how) stated within or near the opening paragraph. But he especially enjoyed teaching feature writing, in part because the *Star* had emphasized narrative journalism more than most newspapers.

Some students found Martin irritating in his mannerisms and plodding in his classroom presentations. His dry humor confused some of them, as when he introduced guest speakers by ostensibly making light of their accomplishments, or when he said with a straight face to his students that they had flunked the class just after receiving a wristwatch from them.

Overall, though, students seemed to respect him as a professional and found him approachable as a person. His most common nickname was Hon, derived from his insistence that politicians and other so-called dignitaries be referred to in print as *Mr.*, not with the traditional *Honorable*. Knowing the depth of their teacher's devotion to that stylistic rule, his students devised a prank during a field trip with Martin to explore Missouri-related feature stories. The students wired the next town on the agenda that the "Honorable Frank Lee Martin" would be arriving with the group. He was so introduced.

As for Ross, students tended to like him immediately and without qualification, although at first he wondered what he had done to earn their respect. Just three years out of college, he felt nervous before meeting his newspaper correspondence class for the first time. When a drop of warm water fell from one of the overhead pipes in the Academic Hall classroom, landing on Ross's forehead in view of the students, he said, "This might be an omen. I hope it is the last time I am in hot water with this class."

Dale Wilson, one of Ross's early students, recalled him as "a broad-shouldered man with deep-set eyes that made his cheekbones seem prominent. He was tolerant with students but sometimes irritated by fellow faculty members from other departments—'They're always complaining about being misquoted.' On one of my first reporting assignments Ross sent me to interview Dr. Charles Elwood, head of the sociology department, who had just returned from England. He had been teaching at Oxford. Elwood talked slowly and I took full notes. . . . The story made page one in the *Missourian*. Next day Ross stopped me in the hall. 'Elwood phoned that he was accurately quoted,' he said. 'That's the first time any blankety-blank professor has done anything but gripe over a story.'"

Needing classroom materials, Ross, Martin, and Williams decided to write books that filled the gaps. Williams and Martin produced *The Practice of Journalism,* with E. W. Stephens Company as publisher. Ross, who advocated objectivity in a purer way than did Williams and Martin, composed a competing book, *The Writing of News,* coming from out-of-state publisher Henry Holt. In 1916, Charles E. Kane (BJ 1915), a new faculty member, tried to make sense of the growing journalism literature. The University of Missouri Bulletin series featured Kane's research under the title *The Journalist's Library: Books for Reference and Reading.*

Williams persuaded guest lecturers to visit campus, providing expertise lacking on the faculty, plus giving the students variety. Despite personal inconvenience—Columbia, Missouri, would never constitute a convenient travel destination for those residing out of state or in the state's two large bookend cities—guest lecturers made the journey. They included Norman Hapgood of *Collier's Weekly;* Walter Wellman, Washington correspondent for the *Chicago Record;* and Henry Schott of the *Kansas City Star.* Williams also persuaded professors from elsewhere on the campus to serve as guest lecturers after conceiving short courses familiarizing fledgling journalists with the terminology of the disciplines they would write about. Williams enlisted faculty from education, agriculture, medicine, engineering, mining, music, athletics, art, drama, and law to participate.

Initial enrollment included fifty-three freshmen calling themselves candidates for a bachelor's degree from the Journalism School. Eight more enrolled in journalism courses but did not designate themselves as degree candidates; three others were College of Arts and Science students specifically requesting journalism courses. Women constituted six of the sixty-four students. The students came from seventeen states across the continent, with one Canadian in the mix. From the start, the Journalism School demonstrated geographic diversity unmatched elsewhere within a state university concentrating on educating Missouri residents. That geographic diversity enriched the learning experience.

To the extent that a typical day during the early years of the Journalism School can be reconstructed, it probably looked something like this:

Classes commenced at 8 a.m., as the bell in Switzler Hall on the campus Quadrangle chimed. Opened in 1872, Switzler was the oldest of the academic buildings. Williams had persuaded university officials to rename the former agriculture classroom building in honor of William F. Switzler, who had directed the *Columbia Statesman* newspaper.

In one room a professor lectured about writing editorials to persuade readers about a timely issue involving government, commerce, or the campus. In another classroom, agricultural journalism constituted the topic, with students from the College of Agriculture as the audience. In the newsroom, students gathered to produce a new day's edition of the *Missourian*. At nine a.m., according to the university schedule, a new round of classes began—advertising in one room, journalism history in another—and a new wave of student reporters and editors assembled for daily newspaper assignments. In the copyreading class, students sat around a big table in easy reach of the teacher; each student received a story to check for grammar, spelling, flow, and accuracy.

After ten a.m., as newspaper deadlines crept closer, most of the work at the school was of a practical nature, the formal lectures put aside until the next day. Pencils glided over paper, typewriters clacked out a beat, telephones rang. Students in the reporting classes, interacting with the teacher in charge, received short-term deadline assignments as they would from the city editor of a metropolitan daily. Editorials and feature stories came from other classes dealing especially with those formats. Students oriented more toward the business side of newspapering solicited and composed advertisements under the direction of an experienced supervisor.

No matter how busy he was with his duties as dean, Williams played a day-to-day role in the *Missourian*. He selected typefaces, helped conceive the style guide setting out consistent writing and editing practices, and scanned every sentence after publication, marking the pages with praise and criticism for distribution to students and faculty. Williams also stayed in touch with nonjournalists around Columbia so he could process their feedback. He presided over a Tuesday men's lunch group called the Round Table Club, with the joking title of "dictator." When he knew he would be absent, he told the other members to elect another dictator for the day.

After a year of Journalism School operations, Williams could point to the first graduate—Charles Arnold of Ashland, Missouri. He had earned a bachelor's degree from the University of Missouri in 1907, then remained in Columbia to serve an apprenticeship at the *Columbia Herald* with Williams. Williams persuaded Arnold to enroll for a second bachelor's degree, one that would give the young man a special place in the history of journalism education. Arnold then succeeded Williams as president and manager of the *Herald*. In 1914, Arnold moved to Pittsburgh, spending the rest of his career at the University of Pittsburgh teaching journalism and handling public relations for the campus.

As classroom offerings grew with student enrollment, Williams intended the course content to improve the quality of the *Missourian*. New courses included photography, engraving, literary reviewing, and advertising sales. Williams apparently worried little at first about large enrollments for each course, as he focused on expanding the range of offerings. One of the most ardent advertising students in a school not known for that specialty at first, Joseph Edwin Chasnoff, earned his degree in 1911 and almost immediately joined the faculty. He interacted tirelessly with potential advertisers, selling the advantages of reaching consumers through a daily newspaper.

Students discussed their supervisors endlessly, as employees discuss their supervisors in every workplace. Williams as professor seems to have generated the most discussion of all. No ivory-tower or closed-door administrator, Williams placed himself on display in the classroom daily. He conceived the course called History and Principles of Journalism (shortened to "H and P" by just about everybody), which became a legend, for better and for worse. Those who disliked the class said jokingly that "H and P" stood for "Hell and Purgatory." Williams believed the class would set the tone for the entire student body, representing to them and the outside world what the school stood for.

Sounding a theme in lecture after lecture to his students, Williams said, "Other professions deal with phases of life. The law thrives upon the quarrels of men. When peace comes there will be no need for lawyers. Medicine thrives upon the disease of mankind, and when hygiene has done its best or worst, we shall have no need for the doctor. Theology deals with man's relation to God and spiritualistic ills. When we all get as good as we should be, we shall not need the preacher. Journalism is more. It deals with the body politic. . . . Heaven has no room for lawyers or doctors or preachers, but we will want to know what the other angels are doing, so there will be a morning and afternoon newspaper in the New Jerusalem."

The dean used materials from his Sunday school teaching in his nominally secular class, providing a journalistic twist to the Word. About Moses, Williams said, "In a single slight book of the five which Moses edited, a book the contents of which would not occupy a half page in today's newspaper, Moses, the first great editor, gave more criminal news, and that more graphically than today's newspaper would dare report—the disobedience of Adam; the drunkenness of Noah; the falsehoods of Abraham; the iniquity of the whole city of Sodom; the vileness of Shechem, the son of Hamori; the wickedness of Judah with Tamar, the woman in black, who sat by the roadside." About Luke, Williams said, "His story has the characteristics of the best reporting—clearness, vividness, truthfulness, facts in due proportion, human interest."

Williams found common purpose between journalists and ministers. He told an audience of clergy, "It is for you, gentlemen, preferring achievement to complaint, to aid journalism as good journalism seeks to aid every righteous cause. Commend and help, when commendation and help are merited. Condemn and refuse to support when condemnation and refusal are deserved. As you strengthen the faith of the journalist, his faith in man, his faith in God, which are fundamental to his highest success and usefulness, you help through him the community which supports his journal and which his journal serves."

Students who experienced Williams as a classroom teacher tended to admire him as a human being and a dean, but not always as a lecturer. One graduate recalled how Williams emphasized the importance of accuracy, fairness, and terseness while composing news stories, "but in his teaching he forgot the terseness. H and P was boring. The dean talked very slowly, a habit he had acquired when he had a speech impediment. . . . His lectures were platitudinous, but his personality was inspiring and he commanded respect." A second student recalled that Williams "often paused in mid-sentence until one wondered when he was going to continue. This was his manner when he served as toastmaster, too. But it seemed to bring emphasis to the point he was making." A third student noted that Williams "was an autocrat. He would get carried away and preach instead of teach."

Paul J. Thompson (BJ 1914) ended up teaching journalism at the University

of Texas from 1919 until 1959. "History can be taught separately from principles, and principles can be taught separately from history. It was typical of Dean
Williams' interests that he linked the two subjects, and he successfully taught
them together," Thompson recalled. "Those of us who were exposed to the History and Principles course thought the dean was setting up ideals which no human being could attain. Yet he seemed so certain about those ideals that they
were accepted by all of us. There is no doubt that we were greatly influenced by
his lectures."

Thompson especially enjoyed learning editorial writing from Williams. "Our
class . . . was very small; also, it met in a very small room in old Switzler Hall.
There was something about the intimacy of our relationship as teacher and students in that class which made his discussions more impressive. He talked about
the policies and services of the great *La Prensa* of Buenos Aires and the influence
of the *Times* of London. He mentioned many great editors and newspapers—
many of the editors being those of the past, though he did not overlook the great
journalists of the present. Without openly condemning the yellow journalism
that was rampant in many areas of the United States at that time, he was able to
give the members of his class a conception of journalism that enabled us to separate the good from the bad after we left his classroom and entered the ranks of
practicing newspapermen."

As the editorial writing professor, Williams became involved in local issues but
reputedly refused to use his influence to bend coverage in any direction. Thompson recalled that the institution of building codes, the city manager form of government, and the construction of a water-softening plant were matters favored
by Williams. Williams nonetheless "requested full and objective coverage of all
opposition" to the proposals, Thompson said.

Whatever Williams's shortcomings as a classroom teacher, he made up for
them with his intellectual mentoring and career advice. As the school labored to
win attention and then approval, Williams worked tirelessly on behalf of the students, as evidenced by a letter to the publisher of the *Fulton Gazette*. In addition
to seeking a print outlet for the students, Williams hoped the publisher would
help instruct about the line between legitimate editorial content and public relations: "Would it be worthwhile, as an advertisement to the *Gazette,* for you to
pay the traveling expenses of one of our senior students in journalism, who would
write two columns or more for the University Missourian about you? I am planning to send some of the senior class in journalism out to neighboring towns for
serious interviews upon subjects that make for Missouri's larger prosperity. It
seems to me a story of the *Gazette,* its building and its owner, his views on coun-

try journalism, etc., would be a fine contribution to Missouri history of the best type. Unfortunately, we have no appropriation to meet such expenses and I am selecting a half-dozen public enterprises like the *Gazette,* thinking the advertising features would be worth their meeting the cost of the student's journey."

Williams used his connections from journalism, church, and fraternal groups to help place students overseas, at the *Japan Advertiser* in Tokyo (to which at least two dozen Missouri journalism degree holders would gravitate) as well as at numerous Chinese news organizations. Internationalism became a cornerstone of Williams's life, and thus of the Journalism School, which at times seemed like an extension of himself.

After the Journalism School ended its initial academic year, Williams traveled to Montreal, sailing from there to Liverpool, England, then returning to Montreal on September 13 before trekking back to Columbia. His travel companions were Ethelbert F. Allen, a Kansas City real estate speculator and civic leader, and Campbell Wells, a Platte City banker who served as a University of Missouri curator. All three of the men belonged to the fraternal Masons organization.

After they returned, they printed three hundred copies of a seventy-seven-page booklet titled *From Missouri to the Isle of Mull.* It is not about journalism education except for three pages devoted to an Institute of Journalists meeting in Plymouth, where Williams spoke to many of the three thousand members about professional training. Despite the brevity of the visit, Williams felt comfortable including social commentary in the booklet, an indication of the seriousness and passion he carried everywhere. An example: "Ireland is the saddest country. In Palestine where the people are poor and suffering there are smiling harvests and the land laughs in the sunlight. In Spain where wretchedness is the common heritage of the peasant folk, the skies are gorgeous with coloring and the climate holds continuous jubilee. But in Ireland the hillside and the meadow, the bare backs of the mountains and the blackened bogs seem to sympathize with the Irish people. Land and inhabitants alike appear in tears. . . . Ireland is her own worst enemy, ably assisted by England."

The overseas network developed by Williams allowed him to indulge his penchant for finery as well as for travel. After Hollington K. Tong (BJ 1912) returned to China, Williams paid the shipping costs to obtain a Chinese-made rug. Tong arranged for a friend of his who owned a rug factory to produce the custom piece. After the rug made the complicated journey from China to mid-Missouri, Williams began a new conversation with Tong about obtaining Tibetan silk artworks for use as wall decorations.

Williams corresponded with Alfonso Johnson, another former Missouri Journalism School student, who had accepted employment in Japan. The dean asked the younger man to order two silk shirts from Johnson's favorite shirt maker, "white or nearly so, suitable for use with tuxedo dinner coat. I had a couple made, but the bosoms are too short. They should be somewhat longer, else they do not meet properly the rest of my clothing. Have them made in the best and latest style and of the best quality of silk, and add an extra pair of cuffs to each."

Williams relied upon and helped female students and male students alike. Initially, many other journalism schools did little if anything to encourage women students. Williams could come across as paternalistic with women students, but he took them seriously as potential professionals. Malvina Lindsay wrote of him in the *Washington Post,* "Women journalists particularly owe him a great debt. Before the coming of schools of journalism, newspaper offices were largely closed to them on the basis of any dignified, professional status. Most editors accepted them only as sob sisters, muckrakers or stunt reporters. Their writing was expected to be flashy and maudlin. But through their training in schools of journalism and through Dean Williams' personal sponsorship of them and belief in them, they were graduated into professional respectability and new fields of opportunity are opened to them."

Among the six students graduating from the Journalism School in 1910, Mary Gentry Paxton of Independence, Missouri, became the first female degree holder. Paxton, later identified by the last name Keeley, could not attend college as she wished right after high school graduation, due to the death of her mother and her father's reluctance to finance her education. She eventually attended Hollins College in Virginia for a year, but family matters intervened once more. Next came the University of Chicago for a summer. By then, Paxton had decided she wanted to practice journalism. Her adviser at Chicago said the big-city campus offered nothing along that line, but the University of Missouri was about to open a journalism school.

"In the middle of the school year, in 1908, I was sitting on the doorstep [in Kansas City] waiting for this school of journalism to start," Paxton recalled. Summoned to Columbia on short notice for the opening of classes, Paxton found herself in a Jesse Hall basement room with a few fellow students, all strangers to her at that juncture, plus the three-person faculty of Williams, Ross, and Bent. Hill, the university's president, walked in. "The president, being a forthright man, said he was glad to see us but could not talk about schools of journalism because he didn't know anything about them," Paxton remembered. "I have the impression that he really thought that we were all there ever would be and we might not be around the campus long. Right after he sat down, I was petrified when the dean called on me, since I was the only woman . . . I could only rise and stammer that I did not know any more about journalism schools than the president did. That brought a laugh."

After graduation, Paxton obtained a reporting job at the *Kansas City Post.* "I was the first woman reporter in Kansas City and was a curiosity. The *Star* wouldn't take a woman. They had a contempt for journalism schools." When Paxton walked into the newsroom six days after graduating, she saw a fellow she already knew from the Journalism School. Referring to the city editor, the fellow said, "If there's anything [he] hates worse than a cub reporter, it's a woman reporter. You'll get fired." The fellow was wrong.

One of Paxton's 1910 classmates, Robin Gould, did not pursue a lifelong journalism career. Still, he talked so fondly about his Journalism School experience that his descendants developed a fondness for the institution. More than ninety years after Gould's graduation, his family created an endowment to be used at the dean's discretion for faculty research or other needs.

The name of Walter Williams carried weight with lots of employers. Everett C. Norlander attended the Missouri Journalism School but never finished. He traveled to Chicago, seeking a job at City News Bureau, but received a rejection from manager Walter B. Brown. "As I was leaving I remarked that I had just left the University of Missouri School of Journalism in the hope of breaking into the newspaper business in Chicago," Norlander recalled. "From then on it was a different story. 'Sit down,' said Mr. Brown. 'How is Dean Williams?' After answering as best I could the eager questions he asked concerning the School of Journalism, I was hired and began working the following morning."

Special efforts by the dean on behalf of students came to seem normal. After graduation from the Journalism School, Lee Shippey, from Higginsville, Missouri, sold an article to *Collier's* magazine, but the editor demanded photographs related to the topic. Shippey knew that Williams possessed such photos in a personal collection, and he wrote with a request to borrow them. A week passed without a reply. Upset, Shippey called the dean long-distance but had to leave a message. When they finally connected, Shippey complained, "You're awfully hard to catch. I wrote you days ago and got no answer. And now I've had to take most of today to get you by telephone." The dean expressed his regrets, adding, "I'm telephoning from the hospital. My son is very ill." The next day Shippey received the photos special delivery. "When the evening paper came out that day I saw that Dr. Williams' son had died."

R. R. Allbaugh, an alumnus who became publisher of a Laramie, Wyoming, newspaper, saw Williams close up regularly while a student, and the patina of greatness never wore off. As a senior, Allbaugh received a job from Williams publicizing the Journalism School. "My work started with a daily visit to the dean's office at 4 p.m. sharp. He would suggest a story or stories that might be helpful to the school . . . and the university. . . . After our daily talk, it was then up to me to go out and get the material for said yarn and write it up. These stories went out on his personal letterhead to the paper or papers he suggested. And you can well bet this material got the attention he so well deserved."

Allbaugh called Williams "one of the finest and greatest men I have ever known. . . . He usually wore dark suits and was a very immaculate dresser, ever so tidy and neat. His voice was on the soft, quiet side, beautifully modulated, and was so commanding that you didn't want to miss a single word that this outstanding gentleman had to say. . . . He was not a robust, athletic type of man in any sense of the word; [I] doubt if he ever played golf or engaged in any athletic type of play. His complexion was actually on the pale or white side, and along with his white hair made him a very commanding figure when seated at his desk or just walking in his slow, even pace. He simply stood out from the crowd. I'll never forget the man's hands. He had long beautiful fingers, very white, too, and probably the most expressive hands I have ever seen. He almost talked with those white fingers when he moved his hands in that quiet, beautiful manner of his. His letter writing: I saw many of his letters and most were in the one or two-paragraph length, and truthfully he could say more in those two long paragraphs than many of us can say in a page-long epistle. What a command he had of words."

One problem Williams could not fix—low salaries offered at lots of newspapers, advertising agencies, and public relations firms. The dean heard from alumnus Foster Hailey, who later became a foreign correspondent and editorial writer at the *New York Times*. The letter arrived from the newsroom of the *New Orleans Item and Morning Tribune*. Hailey had started at thirty dollars a week but mentioned another alumnus starting at fifteen dollars, "a starvation salary." While working quietly behind the scenes to improve newsroom salaries, Williams could sound upbeat about the current reality. He wrote a former student that "the ordinary news reporter will always be an ordinary news reporter, but the interpretative reporter will have a bigger opportunity and more salary. . . . I look for fewer journalists in the future and better ones, a higher standard and more permanence of tenure, at more adequate salaries. A decided tendency in this direction is observable."

For once, Williams was not all that prescient.

Four

Not Merely a Student Newspaper
The Missourian *and the Missouri Method*

The *Missourian* has always stood out in discussions of the Journalism School, even one hundred years after its founding and after the school added the dominant television station in the market, a well-regarded radio station, magazines, and Web sites.

The newspaper's name changed a few times in the early going, but otherwise the enterprise differs little from Walter Williams's creation. (It became the *Daily Missourian* in 1916, the *Evening Missourian* in 1917, the *Columbia Evening Missourian* in 1920, and the *Columbia Missourian* in 1923. A Sunday newspaper replaced the Saturday edition in 1958. The shift from evening to morning publication took place in 1968. In 2007, the *Missourian* started appearing seven days a week, with original content online every day, too.)

In 1912, Williams identified thirty-two universities with some sort of journalism instruction. But none had established a general-circulation daily newspaper staffed by students and directed by faculty in competition with already existing commercial newspapers. None ever would, either, even as the number of universities offering journalism instruction climbed into the hundreds.

Although the newspaper provided a unique cornerstone of the Missouri journalism program, from the start it sucked up scarce budget resources. Sometimes advertising and circulation revenue combined to put the newspaper at the break-even point, but never on a guaranteed basis. Journalism School personnel labored to prevent the deficits from compromising the value of the newspaper as a teaching tool. For example, newspaper management sometimes rejected advertise-

31

ments on grounds of taste, turning away income in the process while upholding standards. On December 13, 1912, managing editor Harry D. Guy informed the manager of the Columbia Theater, "In view of the fact that the play produced in your theater last night was not of such a character that self-respecting people could witness it, the *University Missourian* wishes to notify you that it herewith cancels the existing contract in relation to advertising . . . until the management of the theater can furnish proof that the attraction offered is of sufficiently high standard to warrant patronage."

With or without certain advertising accounts, the newspaper slowly expand-ed its page count. On September 8, 1915, an editorial informed the readership of "the largest and most complete regular edition of the paper ever issued. Every department of a metropolitan newspaper was represented—telegraph news of the foreign war, foreign and domestic news of general interest, feature articles of local interest to Columbia and Boone County, a serial story by a leading Amer-ican novelist, a sporting page of local and national events, a farm page, a society column and the local news of Columbia and Boone County." The newspaper, originally four pages, became eight pages on most days. Sometimes the page count reached twenty.

Inadequate physical facilities caused the publishing portion of the newspaper to assume a gypsy-like quality. The difficulty of finding willing, affordable, ca-pable outside printers was overcome with completion of the first University of Missouri building dedicated to the Journalism School. During 1920, the Jour-nalism School moved the printing plant into Neff Hall. Students wrote and edit-ed copy in what later became Neff Auditorium, where a hole had been cut through the floorboards. The students would place ready-to-publish copy into a bucket, then use a rope to send the filled bucket to the printers one level down.

In 1924, the school purchased its first large press from a manufacturer in Bat-tle Creek, Michigan. With in-house printing flexibility assured, special sections abounded, commemorating anniversaries and extraordinary events such as foot-ball homecomings and the naming of a new university president. News of major import might lead to an extra edition of the newspaper; one announced the re-sults of the 1920 national elections, and another the death of U.S. president War-ren G. Harding. The *Missourian Magazine* became part of the mix in 1924 as a weekly supplement. It served readers additional local fare and gave students new opportunities to publish.

A new building with up-to-date equipment pleased Williams. But he still needed to find money for newsprint, equipment repair and replacement, wages for pressmen, and salaries for the faculty editors. Williams conceived a plan to place the newspaper on relatively sound financial footing, then asked the advice of three graduates who lived nearby and had developed business expertise: Frank W. Rucker, advertising manager for the *Independence Examiner,* later a Missouri Journalism School faculty member and author of a 1964 Williams biography; Harry E. Ridings, advertising manager for Greenlease Motor Company in Kansas City; and J. Harrison Brown, advertising manager for A. P. Green Fire Brick Company in Mexico, Missouri. They agreed to the incorporation of the Missourian Publishing Association, which sold stock to alumni at one hundred dollars per share.

The corporation promised to repurchase the stock when it possessed sufficient money. Any profit would be devoted to newspaper operating expenses. Sixty investors sent their cash. With money available, the *Missourian* could afford to subscribe to the United Press for coverage of national and international news, supplementing local coverage by student reporters.

Williams did his best to oversee newsroom staffing. Some of his hires demonstrated remarkable longevity. Eugene W. Sharp earned his BJ in 1923, then returned to his hometown of Oklahoma City to begin employment. Williams wrote him in Oklahoma City on short notice during September 1923 about the possibility of filling in for Elihu Root Childers, who had been granted a year's leave. Childers taught courses about the country newspaper, agricultural press, office management, principles of typography, advertising, and trade/technical journalism. Sharp accepted the last-minute invitation, became entrenched in the newsroom, managed to earn his MA in 1926, and taught at the *Missourian* through 1969, when he accepted emeritus status.

Normally a good judge of character, Williams sometimes made difficult judgments. When the respected Alfonso Johnson left his position as *Missourian* business manager during 1924, Williams agreed to hire E. A. Soderstrom (BJ 1921) as the replacement, but only reluctantly, despite Johnson's endorsement. Johnson commented, "I am leaving my work in the hands of one who made a great record in school and has since done good work on Houston Harte's San Angelo, Texas, paper. I know that Mr. Soderstrom will carry on the work to your satisfaction and will make the *Missourian* even bigger and better."

When Soderstrom asked for a raise more quickly than Williams thought appropriate, the dean and J. Harrison Brown corresponded about the request for the boost to thirty-six hundred dollars annually. Williams felt disinclined to say yes; Brown argued that the raise should be granted. In a memo to Williams, Soderstrom noted he had played a role in a profit of eight thousand dollars during 1925; had increased circulation from about twenty-eight hundred to an all-time high of thirty-two hundred; and had helped start a magazine affiliated with the newspaper. Soderstrom won the raise, then became so indispensable that he remained in the job until 1952.

Soderstrom had to deal with precarious finances, as did a succession of editors and deans. During the economic depression, Frank L. Martin wrote alumnus Ralph H. Turner at the United Press Kansas City bureau on September 25, 1931, "Would it be possible for a man in your bureau in Austin, Texas, or Denver, or both, to file our football story, play-by-play account, of the Missouri-Texas or Missouri-Colorado game?" The *Missourian* "would arrange for the leased wire and . . . pay all expenses of tolls." The newspaper, like so many other enterprises, was facing "hard times. We are trying to cut all the corners we can, and the expense of sending a man to Austin and to Boulder is high."

Sara Lawrence Lockwood, who as an assistant professor was the first highly visible female teacher at the Missouri Journalism School (and later would be the second wife of Walter Williams), increased the reach of student reporting and writing beyond the newspaper itself. She accomplished that goal by publishing between hard covers, with herself as editor, the 177-page *Written by Students in Journalism: Selected Articles Written by Students in the School of Journalism, University of Missouri, as Part of Their Class Work During 1926–1927.*

The Missouri Method extended to the teaching of photography, advertising, and public relations courses. The photographers tended to find kinship with the reporters and writers. After all, everybody agreed that first-rate photographs enhanced the newspaper, and photojournalism students considered themselves especially efficient news and feature information-gatherers, as encapsulated in the adage "a picture is worth a thousand words." As a result, tension between the news people and the picture people seems to have been minimal, or downright nonexistent.

The same blanket statement cannot be made about the relationship between news faculty and advertising faculty. Sure, the *Missourian* needed advertising, but the news faculty worried that the revenue tail might end up wagging the information dog, that concerns about offending advertisers might compromise gutsy coverage.

Advertising and public relations students often constituted at least half the enrollment of the Journalism School. Advertising courses had been offered from the first year. The initial public relations course, as far as research can discern, arrived in 1946, taught by veteran professor Thomas Cecil Morelock, who was doubling as the director of public information for the entire campus. About half the journalism programs across the United States taught public relations as part of the curriculum. Pedagogical reasons aside, the Journalism School needed advertising and public relations students for the tuition dollars they provided. Still, despite the unifying efforts of Williams, the divide between the news and advertising cultures within the Journalism School could not always be bridged, especially after his death.

Intellectually, Williams could justify including all parts of the enterprise within the same curriculum, rather than placing advertising and public relations in the business college—the other dominant model across the nation. Ideally, reporters and editors should understand how advertising salespeople help keep a newspaper afloat; salespeople should understand how news is gathered and disseminated without fear or favor.

That mutual understanding remained in place for many decades, at least on the surface. Advertising students completed required courses in news reporting and writing. Some of them griped, but probably not as much as did news and feature students required to complete a course in advertising history and principles. Anxious to see their bylines in the *Missourian,* students chafed at the advertising course requirement when it delayed entry into the newsroom. In retrospect, many news and feature majors conceded that they learned valuable lessons for the real world. Advertising professors Milton Gross and Robert Haverfield, both Missouri Journalism School graduates who became longtime teachers at their alma mater, often broke down the resistance through their encyclopedic knowledge and obvious concern for students as individuals, not merely anonymous faces in a large lecture.

Williams seemed blind and deaf at times to how the different cultures viewed and heard one another. The reporting, writing, and editing purists could reasonably express dismay at a Journalism School awards gathering that included a "Banquet of the Nationally Advertised." Every course at the meal, plus every edible item and household product in a gift bag handed to those attending, carried a sponsor's identity. The program notes said the event had been "made possible by the cooperation of more than fifty of America's foremost users of printed publicity. Both the food served and the favors given consist of nationally advertised products." An example: "Budweiser and ginger ale at the banquet table and Bevo in the basket are offered as samples of the products of the Anheuser-Busch Company, St. Louis." Some journalists wondered how Williams could endorse what they saw as a sellout of principles.

Because Williams and his successors as dean have been news-oriented, the advertising and public relations students, staff, and faculty frequently have felt more discomfort about the cultural divide than have the reporting, writing, and photo-

journalism students, staff, and faculty. Those in the advertising and public relations realm have tended to voice the complaint that they feel like "second-class
citizens" of the Journalism School.

Even so, the deans managed to win enough respect that advertising and public relations graduates have frequently given back to the school. Paul Synor (BJ
1942) created memorable advertisements after his graduation, including those
featuring Tony the Tiger, Charlie the Tuna, and Morris the Cat. As Synor aged,
he thanked his alma mater with a $2,500,000 bequest for student scholarships.

Another clash of cultures revolving around the Missouri Method involved the
publication of editorials in the *Missourian*. Many newspapers have traditionally
published editorial opinion. Missouri Journalism School students hoping to gain
employment as editorial writers naturally wanted relevant experience while enrolled. In its early decades, the editorial page sometimes featured hard-hitting
pieces on local issues.

Walter Williams promoted and taught editorial writing vigorously. After his
death, the course shifted from professor to professor, depending on staffing.
James W. Markham brought in experts from other parts of the university to provide background for student editorial writers on issues such as atomic energy and
the role of religion in society.

Long before the term *environmentalism* became common, the editorial page
campaigned to reduce the use of soft coal and increase the use of cleaner natural
gas. Improved garbage disposal, more intelligent automobile traffic routing,
clearer street signage, better allocation of city water and light department revenue, and municipal health regulations aimed at low-quality milk constituted
some of the editorial-page campaigns.

As a generalization, hard-hitting editorials became less common in later
decades. Maurice Votaw, holder of the first master's degree from the Missouri
Journalism School (1921), returned in 1949 to teach at his alma mater. When
editorial writing fit into the course offerings, Votaw often served as the combination professor/editor. Dean Frank Luther Mott allowed student-generated political endorsements to appear in the newspaper and generally expressed no hes-
itancy about the editorial opinions. "Then," Votaw recalled, "the next year [Earl]
English became dean and he was very hesitant about our coming out in support
of anyone. He thought it wasn't right for the paper, even though once the material goes to the press room, the university has nothing more to do with the *Missourian*. . . . But English felt that since the faculty and students were university,
that it wasn't quite proper to say this man should be elected or this rule should
be abolished or anything like that."

In 1971, Roy Fisher succeeded English as dean. Fisher had served as the managing editor of the *Chicago Daily News.* "He was accustomed to taking sides in every campaign," Votaw noted. Editorial writing at the *Missourian* became Fisher's domain for a while. He supervised students, sometimes generated the editorials himself, and generally approved every word of every editorial before it appeared in print.

Fisher's successor, James Atwater, from a *Time* magazine background, allowed editorials to appear in the *Missourian* without actually teaching the course, but he felt so uncomfortable that he or his designated agent vetted them regularly, and sometimes killed them. Because of budgetary constraints within the Journalism School and a decreasing demand for editorial writers in professional newsrooms, the course in editorial writing atrophied until it disappeared. Some faculty, staff, and students have argued that a newspaper devoid of locally written editorials has been emasculated and fails a public service test.

Free speech controversies involving the Journalism School sometimes occurred outside the editorial page. During 1949, syndicated columnist Westbrook Pegler visited the Journalism School by invitation. Some students and townspeople protested the choice of Pegler as a speaker because of his reputation as a rumormonger and political partisan. During the introduction of Pegler, Dean Mott said, "Anybody who thinks that Journalism Week programs are set up as a mutual admiration society is badly mistaken. We try to provide a realistic view of American journalism as it is and anyone who dislikes that view has a right to dislike and say so, but no sensible person will question the value of the presentation of varying opinions, varying modes of writing and varying personalities on this platform. The man I am about to present is a stormy petrel of American journalism. Many readers, myself among them, disagree with many things he has written. We have invited him to this platform not because we agree with his opinions but because he is a distinguished writer and we think you ought to see and hear him. Even those of our friends who hate him most violently ought not to think the students of the Missouri School of Journalism are a set of precious darlings wrapped in cotton wool who are likely to be contaminated by the sight of the face and the sound of the voice of Westbrook Pegler."

As with editorials, the emphasis on controversy-inducing investigative journalism at the newspaper (and eventually at KOMU-TV and KBIA-FM) ebbed and flowed. The quantity and quality of investigative journalism have depended primarily on the presence of faculty members with the skill and the will—as well as an attitude about reporters comforting the afflicted while afflicting the comfortable.

It has sometimes proved awkward for the newsroom to investigate the university and the state legislature, given the direct and indirect budget linkages with those institutions. For example, during November 1986, student reporters Penny Brown and Mark Robichaux exposed what seemed to constitute wasteful spending by the governor's appointees to the Board of Curators. One story opened like this: "In October 1985, University of Missouri curator Edwin Turner chartered a flight at university expense to visit the UMC College of Veterinary Medicine and attend a Mizzou football game. One month later, he chartered another flight to visit the UMC School of Journalism and attend another football game. Together, the two trips cost the University nearly one thousand dollars. Had he driven the one hundred twenty miles from his home in Chillicothe, Missouri, and been reimbursed at the University's standard twenty-one cents per mile, the two trips would have cost a total of one hundred dollars." Turner, a hardworking curator donating countless hours away from his business and family to oversee the University of Missouri as an appointee of the governor, obviously would have preferred a different emphasis in the story.

Some powerful sources and subjects objected to what they perceived as unfair or incompetent coverage. On January 27, 1981, for example, Dean Fisher received a letter from University of Missouri basketball coach Norm Stewart. Stewart complained about *Missourian* sports editor Randy Covitz (BJ 1972), who had seven years' experience at a Memphis newspaper before accepting the Journalism School job.

Stewart, idolized by many basketball fans, alleged Covitz had been carrying a grudge for at least a year about lack of access to basketball players in the locker room after games. In the January 26 edition of the *Missourian,* Covitz "made note of the fact that we had closed our dressing room to the media for the second straight game," Stewart said. "It did not say why. Both of these games were road games. We charter aircraft. This allows us a savings and also cuts down on time spent away from the classroom. . . . I am passing this along to you and asking these questions: What is the purpose of reporting? Is it to carry out your own personal wishes, desires and maybe frustrations? Is it an opportunity to carry out personal vendettas through power of the pen? . . . Shouldn't it be administered by someone who is big enough to remove personal feeling and trite expressions from their decisions?"

Fisher responded to Stewart that Covitz would be leaving the *Missourian* and that Tom Brooks would become the new sports editor. "When Tom gets installed, let's have lunch together one day with Tom and try to reach some reasonable agreement on how these matters should be handled." Covitz's resignation letter to Fisher reflected dissatisfaction: "Obviously the past year has left me bitter. I had been here all of six months when it was determined for me that my services were no longer wanted. I was given little guidance, no direction, only some second-guessing and Monday morning quarterbacking."

The ferreting out of waste, fraud, and abuse did not occur in a vacuum. Competition played a role. Sometimes, given its inexperienced but massive reporting force, the *Missourian* would outshine the *Columbia Daily Tribune* on sensitive stories. Other times, especially during the late 1970s and early 1980s under the editorship of the talented, charismatic Carolyn White, herself a Missouri Journalism School alumna, the *Tribune* would outshine the *Missourian* on in-depth projects. The *Tribune's* investigative zeal gradually diminished after White's departure in 1982.

To bolster the *Missourian's* investigative efforts, faculty member Ernest Morgan took the lead in organizing a public affairs reporting emphasis at the Journalism School. For academic credit, students could choose to spend a semester in Jefferson City or in St. Louis with faculty supervision. A laconic Texan with fourteen years of newsroom experience and a late-in-life doctorate from the University of Texas, Morgan inspired students with his high standards from the time he joined the faculty in 1969. Morgan heard so often that he resembled Clark Kent, the mild-mannered fictional journalist who could transform himself into Superman, that he hung a Superman poster in his office.

The training in Jefferson City and St. Louis, supplementing instruction in the classroom and the main newsroom, meant that, for the most part, students launching in-depth projects knew the appropriate techniques and found themselves well grounded in legal and ethical precedents.

Dale R. Spencer, a lawyer-journalist, taught media law courses for decades until his unexpected death in 1989. Born in 1925, Spencer worked as a teenage newspaper reporter in Pocatello, Idaho, joined the military during World War II, ended up in Columbia, earned a BJ in 1948, joined the faculty in 1950, earned a master's degree in 1955, began teaching journalism law courses in 1958, earned a law degree in 1968, wrote a textbook titled *Law for the Newsman,* and worked mightily for Journalism School–Law School joint degrees.

Spencer's death at age sixty-three came as a surprise because he kept himself in excellent physical shape by swimming, bicycling, running, and walking. Sandra Scott (later using the name Sandra Davidson) shifted from the University of Missouri Law School faculty to teach Spencer's course. In addition to her Journalism School classroom teaching, Davidson, holder of a PhD in philosophy as well as a JD, has represented the *Missourian,* KOMU, and KBIA when legal disputes have arisen, as Spencer had done before his death.

Law and ethics often collide during reporting and editing, leading to further culture clashes but also providing valuable teaching moments. Professional ethics has been taught well at times and poorly at other times at the Journalism School. During the 1970s and into the 1980s, Donald P. (Don) Ranly devoted as much as one-third of the course Principles of American Journalism to ethics instruction. John Merrill, in his Philosophy of Journalism course, also covered ethics in intellectually challenging ways. Too frequently, though, discussions of ethics in the classroom and newsroom seemed to devolve into little more than "what is legal is permissible," or what faculty loosely called "situational ethics," which seemingly could be reduced to the formulation "do what you need to do as the situation warrants."

In the late 1980s, the Journalism School attracted Edmund B. Lambeth and Lillian (Lee) Wilkins to the faculty. Two of the brainiest, best-known journalism ethicists in the nation, attuned to investigative reporting as well as other forms of the craft, Lambeth and Wilkins prepared students more thoroughly than ever before. No longer did situational ethics reign, as Lambeth and Wilkins taught deeper principles that work in real-life dilemmas. Their clear writing in professional journals, monographs, and textbooks spread their views on ethics far beyond campus classroom lectures.

Lambeth had just spent four years as director at the University of Kentucky Journalism School. When he moved to Columbia in 1987, he brought with him the National Workshop on the Teaching of Ethics in Journalism, begun at Kentucky with a grant from the Freedom Forum. As Lambeth explained, "The five-day workshop trained junior as well as senior professors in the teaching of this specialty. It was a course made increasingly relevant, and even urgent, by the aggressive new emphasis on investigative reporting."

Wilkins, while teaching at the University of Colorado, attended the workshop during its first year. When Wilkins (BJ 1971) returned to Missouri nearly twenty years later as a professor, she created a media ethics course for graduate students.

While law and ethics instruction ebbed and flowed until the arrival of Lambeth and Wilkins, narrative writing instruction—so vital to doing in-depth journalism well—remained pretty much a constant. G. (for George) Thomas Duffy influenced thousands of feature writing students during his twenty years in the *Missourian* newsroom and Journalism School classrooms. Born in 1911, Duffy

joined the faculty during 1961, after thirty years as a reporter and editor, mostly in East St. Louis, Illinois, his place of birth. Frequently outspoken, the university professor without a college degree almost immediately became a cult figure for some students, and a gruff, feared teacher to avoid for others.

In 1964, student Alice Samuels wrote about Duffy positioned behind his desk
"at the *Columbia Missourian* as if on a pedestal. . . . Duffy . . . didn't put himself
on that pedestal. His students placed him there. . . . Tom Duffy is the person you
look up to with respect when he tells you to go back to the county courthouse—
go back, trudging in the freezing cold with a heavy coat and snow boots—to look
something up in a file that you thought you could get by without looking up.
When he causes you to miss your lunch hour because a story has broken, you are
proud that he called on you to get the scoop."

Samuels related how in May 1964 about fifty graduating seniors gathered in
an apartment with a sign lettered "Duffy's Tavern," an allusion to his sometimes
excessive alcohol consumption. Normally a reticent man who shunned social
contact, Duffy agreed to join them. Samuels noted how "for the first time, that
professional newsman's face looked like that of a small cherub receiving his first
paint brush and palette. . . . He was touched. But more than that he was proud
and happy. . . . The students talked of how they felt they had learned more from
Duffy than they ever imagined they could gain from one person."

Hoping to expand his heartfelt teachings beyond the students in his classroom, Duffy in 1969 arranged with local publisher Lucas Brothers to print a
modest-looking but substantive book titled *Let's Write a Feature*. He gathered the
examples from his classroom and newsroom rather than from famous feature
writers. "Beginners are more at ease with beginners and the learning process becomes easier," Duffy said. He believed in lots of assignments: "You learn to write
feature stories by writing feature stories." In class, he would hand a student a
name from the Columbia telephone directory, usually chosen at random. The
student would be given twenty-four hours or forty-eight hours or maybe a week
to research and write a compelling profile. "It's not the story of the chair, it's the
story of the person who made it," Duffy would say, almost as a mantra.

Heath Meriwether counted himself a Duffy disciple. Meriwether grew up in
Columbia during the 1950s. His father operated a print shop near the Journalism School. By age sixteen, he was covering sports for the *Columbia Daily Tribune*. Meriwether never thought about attending any university but Missouri. The
Journalism School "provided the perfect combination of classroom attention to
the craft of writing and discussion of journalistic issues and hands-on reporting
for the *Missourian*. My *Missourian* editors—Tom Duffy, Gene Sharp, and Phil

Norman—treated every J-School student as they would a professional reporter. Their expectations pushed us to treat our stories as if each one were a page-one scoop." Between his junior and senior years, Meriwether interned at the *Miami Herald*. Eventually, he would run the Miami newsroom.

Duffy retired in 1981 at age seventy. He continued living in a downtown apartment one block from the Journalism School, mostly reclusive, until his death during 1984. Many of his students had no idea that he had been married, fathered a son, and become a grandfather. It might be a legend that lots of former students named their children after Duffy, but one did for sure—Rodney David Gibson (BJ 1963), the father of Thomas Duffy Gibson.

Despite his emphasis on feature writing, Duffy talked little about magazines. In fact, magazine journalism served as a stepchild to newspapering at the Missouri Journalism School decade after decade.

Winston Allard, born in 1909, joined the faculty in 1945 and served as an early exception to the lack of emphasis on magazine journalism. Allard, with degrees from the University of Oregon and the University of Iowa, inaugurated a class in which students won a higher grade if they succeed in selling their stories to magazines. Student Guy Wright sold a story about his mustache, and mustaches in general. Naomi Scott sold a feature to *Blue Book,* which billed itself as "a magazine for men by men." She signed her name Norman Scott, and the check arrived at her apartment in that name. The successes of Allard's students provided grist for a *Newsweek* account of March 7, 1949, with Allard pictured at his desk. The feature said that, since 1945, Allard's students had sold more than fifteen thousand dollars worth of stories.

Allard taught a separate book reviewing course. About a dozen reviews of two hundred words each found their way into a weekly syndicated column laid out by linotype professor Paul Fisher and mailed to about eighty Missouri newspapers.

Donald G. Romero joined the Journalism School faculty during 1958 after more than twenty years as a magazine editor and writer. Like Allard, Romero emphasized writing for real-world magazines, and his students made sales to national publications including *True, Modern Maturity,* and *Mother Earth News.*

Despite his real-world experience and lively classroom lectures, Romero made few inroads into the predominant newspaper culture at the Journalism School. No student-staffed, faculty-directed magazine achieved the wide recognition of the *Missourian*. A local magazine had been distributed with the newspaper off and on since the 1920s, but more off than on. After a spell with no magazine, the Journalism Students Association suggested a revival in 1961, with no short-term success. In 1971, Commerce Bancshares Incorporated of Kansas City donated twenty-five hundred dollars to the Journalism School to help pay for a statewide feature magazine. Professor Paul Fisher, a typography expert, served as adviser and oversaw publication of feature stories written by the students.

Missouri Today died after a couple of issues, but the magazine spirit had finally entered the Journalism School culture permanently. Perhaps one of the most carefully planned transitions occurred during 1971–1972, when a new magazine distributed with the *Missourian* became known as *Vibrations*. Dean Fisher paid close attention; in one memo, he told the staff he hoped for a magazine that would be "offbeat, controversial, irreverent, and sassy" without offending community standards.

In 1976, Don Ranly, who earned his doctorate at the Journalism School after leaving the Catholic clergy during the Vietnam War, became director of the magazine program. Ranly pleaded for growth of the magazine faculty, given an enrollment of 152 students as of 1979, about 20 percent of the entire Journalism School. Ranly himself enhanced the magazine faculty not only because of his administrative skills but also because of his spellbinding lectures, devotion to making the oft-dreaded editing course a transcendent learning experience, and passion for semantics, a topic too readily ignored in a craft devoted to words.

John David Marsh (BJ 1986) recalled how Ranly "demanded excellence. He cajoled, he brought out the best in you, and he commanded your respect and attention in every interaction through his incredible wealth of knowledge, understanding, and that mellifluous voice of his. Among all the accolades I have ever received, I still hold in the highest esteem a compliment he gave me on my graduation day. While I was standing in front of my parents after the ceremony, he told me that an article I had written for the *Missourian* Sunday magazine, just published, was one of the best pieces he had read in a long time." Nearly twenty years later, Marsh commented, "I was thrilled. Still am."

Ranly continued as director of the magazine program through 2004, when he began a phased retirement from the faculty. By then, *Vibrations* had morphed into *Vox,* a Thursday city magazine distributed with the *Missourian* as well as on its own all over Columbia. When Jennifer L. Moeller (later Jennifer Moeller Rowe) joined the magazine faculty in 1998, she provided a steady presence at *Vox* as editorial director.

As of 2008, the magazine faculty numbered ten, each with professional experience in reporting or writing or design or publishing or some combination of those skills. Administrative assistant Kimberly (Kim) Townlain and chair Jan Louise Colbert, Ranly's successor, handled day-to-day chores so efficiently that the faculty enjoyed more time than expected to build bridges to the magazine industry commensurate with long-standing ties between the *Missourian* and the newspaper industry.

Despite the weekly magazine's relative independence from the *Missourian,* its iterations could not escape the vicissitudes of the venerable parent newspaper. Editor in chief after editor in chief put his imprint on the newsroom while struggling to manage the turnover each semester and provide content of such high quality that maybe, against overwhelming odds, the newspaper would challenge the *Tribune's* circulation dominance and also achieve permanent profitability.

From Walter Williams's death in 1935 until the early 1970s, men from the Williams era kept a steady course in the newsroom. The end of the old regime at the *Missourian* can fairly be pegged to the early 1970s. Because of the Vietnam War, Watergate, and other examples of irresponsible government conduct, complete with cover-ups, journalists in general had become less naive, more skeptical. The increasing reach of large corporations and their high-handed behavior toward consumers ratcheted the stakes for journalists up even higher. Investigative reporting was becoming institutionalized in numerous newsrooms for the first time in the history of any national media. Journalism was becoming more socially acceptable as a career. With the popularity of the book *All the President's Men* by *Washington Post* reporters Bob Woodward and Carl Bernstein, followed by the movie of the same name starring Robert Redford as Woodward and Dustin Hoffman as Bernstein, journalists even became desired party guests in some milieus. Veteran journalists could scarcely believe what was occurring.

At the *Missourian* during 1973, managing editor William B. Bickley (BJ 1934, MA 1935), one of those Williams-era journalists, died unexpectedly. He was sixty. An accomplished copyeditor and rewrite man, Bickley exuded quiet confidence. He had worked his entire journalism career within the cocoon of Boone County—five years at the university's alumni magazine before joining the faculty in 1941—and was not inclined to alter the *Missourian's* regimen. One of Bickley's esteemed faculty editing colleagues, Robert M. Neal, had died even younger, at forty-nine. Neal took his life during 1951, apparently depressed because of long-time ill health. Bickley had labored mightily to fill the educational gap left at the newspaper and in the classroom by Neal.

During Bickley's long tenure, complaints arose about insufficient staffing of the city desk and the copy desk, a problem related to budget shortfalls and thus largely beyond the managing editor's control. Decade after decade, the complaint about an unwieldy student/faculty ratio at the *Missourian* never faded away.

Bickley's death caused turmoil; faculty member Dale Spencer, who taught copyediting and law courses, stepped in as acting managing editor. The void at the top resulted in lobbying of the journalism dean, Roy Fisher. Seeing an opportunity, city editor John Philip (Phil) Norman made his case to Fisher for increased coverage of agricultural issues, which had dropped off drastically in the previous decade. Furthermore, rumors circulated that Norman might be appointed to fill Bickley's role.

Born in 1916, Norman joined the Missouri Journalism School faculty in 1955 from the realm of small newspapers and earned a late-in-life master's degree in 1958. In conjunction with Norman's eventual promotion to full professor, Editorial Department chairman Keith P. Sanders made the case that lack of scholarly research should not become an issue. Norman's teaching and service ranked high. Furthermore, he worked within a national network of journalists—led by the Associated Press, United Press International, and the three major television networks—to improve election-night coverage.

Norman "represents an unusual case," Sanders commented. "He does not fit the stereotype most people—including, I suspect, most other faculty members—have of a full professor. His folksy sense of humor stands him in good stead; he is one of the few persons I know who is liked by virtually all who know him."

During a time of transition in the newsroom, Norman could be counted on for stability. But change at the *Missourian* arrived in the person of an outsider. Daryl R. Moen had not attended the Missouri Journalism School, earning his degrees from the University of Wisconsin–Eau Claire and the University of Minnesota. That outsider status made him a surprise choice given the inbred nature of the Journalism School faculty in general, and the even more inbred nature of the *Missourian* faculty. Science writing professor Joye Patterson communicated to a friend, "The new editor for the *Missourian* arrived this week. He's twenty-nine, six years of editing experience. There is, as you might expect, a wait-and-see attitude prevailing."

Before moving to Columbia in 1974, Moen worked at small-circulation newspapers in Wisconsin and Illinois. "I actually found out about the job from a newsprint salesman," Moen recalled. "When I arrived, Bill Bickley [was] dead . . . and the paper had drifted leaderless for a long time. Each department editor basically ran his or her own show. That meant there was little coordination, no one to mediate disputes or start new programs. First, it was a shock for some of the editors to have a boss. It was also a shock to me to have so many reporters and editors. . . . When I walked into the newsroom, the students were so packed in that I had to push and shove my way across the floor to get to my office. . . . I was impressed with the quality of the students and most of the faculty, but I was not impressed with the quality of the stories we were putting into the paper."

Moen visited with local government and business leaders to educate himself about issues. "I was welcomed enthusiastically, but I kept hearing the same refrain—your students make too many errors," Moen said. "That led to the thing of which I am most proud. I wrote and got the faculty to accept the accuracy check policy still being used. At the time, it wasn't easy. This was the Watergate era. Journalists were full of themselves. The idea that we should let any source know what we were going to print before we printed it was anathema to most of the profession, including many *Missourian* editors."

Moen found his plans for the newspaper complicated by precarious finances. "Roy Fisher insisted that the paper go offset and managed to get a new press and equipment in the backshop," Moen recalled. "We still had Linotypes when I arrived. The forced march into new technology saved the *Missourian* from being swallowed by high production costs."

Coverage of one pressing issue especially bedeviled Moen: "When the first campaign began to get the city to vote on a can deposit ordinance, the *Missourian* faced a severe economic threat from the grocers, who opposed the ordinance. The manager of Nowell's . . . and their attorney . . . came in one day to talk about the ordinance. At that time, we still ran editorials like a real newspaper. When I indicated that we would be coming out in favor of the deposit ordinance, they made it very clear that we were risking their advertising, and the advertising of other grocers. I knew that if they pulled their advertising, the *Missourian* might not survive, but the threat made me angry. I looked at [the lawyer] who had made the statement about the advertising, and said, 'I don't react well to threats. I am happy to talk to anyone about the merits of the deposit ordinance, but if you came down here to threaten the *Missourian,* then this meeting is over.' And it was. They got up and left. After a couple minutes of reflection, I figured I had just ruined the paper. I ran up to Dean Fisher's office and told him what had happened. I was fully prepared to resign. Fisher listened to the story, mulled it over a few seconds, then looked at me and said, 'You did the right thing.' And that was that. He wrote the next editorial we ran endorsing the deposit ordinance. Fortunately, neither Nowell's nor any of the other grocers followed through on the threat, probably, in part, because the *Tribune* also endorsed the ordinance."

Moen began to build his own team. "We were fortunate to have some faculty openings right away," he said. "We brought in Brian Brooks to run the copy desk and George Kennedy to run the city desk. Later, we recruited Ruth D'Arcy to run the features department. Those three hires are among the most important I participated in because they all had long-lasting impact on the paper and the school."

Barbara Luebke followed Moen from the DeKalb, Illinois, newsroom in 1974. She recalled walking into the *Missourian,* at the age of twenty-five, seeing about one hundred student reporters, and thinking, "What have I gotten myself into?" She ended up enjoying the atmosphere, though. She was amazed by the quality of the students, "defined by their dedication, their drive, their commitment to journalism, not communication in the generic sense of today."

Luebke chafed at the secondary role of women on the faculty. "There was definitely an old boys' network at the Journalism School and in the *Missourian,*" she said. "The few women faculty at the time met regularly for dinner and conversation, and sooner or later the conversation centered on the sexism. We felt it in the sense of entitlement that our male colleagues had, especially about administering the school." When desirable administrative openings occurred, Luebke said, "the women's group was quite unhappy about the lack of even pretending to have an open search. For a variety of reasons, however, no one else was willing to challenge the boys. I became the sacrificial lamb. I knew I did not stand a chance, but I put myself forward to make a point. Yikes! How young and naive I was." Nonetheless, Luebke felt the good outweighed the bad, and eventually she earned her doctorate at the Missouri Journalism School before leaving to teach elsewhere.

Moen served as managing editor for nine years. He remained on the Journalism School faculty after stepping aside, broadening his emphasis to design and graphics, as well as writing and reporting, teaching a range of courses. He wrote or cowrote influential textbooks in each realm he taught.

Brian Brooks, a Missouri Journalism School alumnus already on the faculty, followed Moen as managing editor. "I wanted the job. I asked for it and got it," Brooks said. He found "lots of students and not enough editors" in the newsroom. "We hired some terrific city editors while I was there . . . two of the three had been on teams that had won the Pulitzer."

As suggested by Brooks's comment, the newspaper sometimes attracted city editors who had already earned renown within journalism and who intended to make Missouri their permanent home. Frequently, however, *Missourian* city editors and copyeditors fell into the category of relatively inexperienced and transient. They left newsroom positions elsewhere for reduced salaries and long hours because they wanted to earn a master's degree or a doctorate from the Journalism School.

Brooks enjoyed emphasizing the positive recognition the *Missourian* sometimes earned for its news coverage. "I recall with great delight sitting at a luncheon table at the Missouri Press Association awards with David Lipman, then managing editor of the *St. Louis Post-Dispatch*, and David Zeeck, then managing editor of the *Kansas City Star*. When it came time for presentation of the award for best investigative reporting, Lipman claimed the third-place award, Zeeck accepted the second-place award, and I accepted first. That was a great moment. To think that student reporters could do that was amazing."

Brooks, like Moen, remained on the Journalism School faculty after stepping aside as managing editor. Also like Moen, Brooks broadened his professional horizons, adding computer expertise to his credentials.

With the managing editorship open again, the Journalism School considered hiring nonalumnus Ben Johnson as the first black editor in chief of the *Missourian,* and apparently of any Missouri newspaper. He and his wife, Mary Bullard-Johnson, had already moved from Detroit to Columbia to direct the Journalism School's newly created Multicultural Management Program. Born in Louisville, Kentucky, Ben Johnson attended college at Wayne State University in Detroit and Lincoln University in Jefferson City, Missouri. After service with the U.S. Marines, Johnson ended up at the *Detroit Free Press.*

The search failed to yield a clear-cut favorite among the applicants. In a July 21, 1987, memo from search committee chair Byron T. Scott to Dean Atwater, Johnson and another finalist both received recommendations, with reservations. Eventually, Johnson received four search committee votes, the other finalist (a female) received three votes, while yet another candidate (also a female) received one vote. At that juncture, the newspaper had never been directed by a black or a female.

Scott's letter said that Johnson possessed "significant and proven managerial background, a good orientation to the current problems of the paper and an enthusiastic and energetic plan for attacking those problems. His superiors at Knight Ridder were unanimous in their evaluation that Ben is ready. In addition, he has insight into the racial and minority tensions that surfaced [within the Missouri Journalism School] this spring. Barriers to Johnson's candidacy include a reputation for contentiousness, a frequently expressed attitude that he is chauvinistic (not supported by direct evidence), his lack of a graduate degree and his expressed commitment to the job of two to three years. Several committee members were told that there will be newsroom resignations if he is appointed. We did not consider that pertinent to our deliberations, however. The persistent rumor, denied at all levels, that his appointment as managing editor would be tied to finding a significant job for his wife, also was discussed." The other finalist received the offer but decided against moving to Columbia. Johnson ended up with the job.

Johnson's tenure at the *Missourian* led to increased awareness of minorities and dispossessed citizens in general, resulting in protests from at least a few racist individuals in Boone County as well as praise from readers.

During early 1988, Johnson signed petitions to repeal the municipal container deposit ordinance and to recall Mayor Rodney Smith. City editors Virginia Young, Sherry Ricchiardi, and Stanley E. (Stan) Abbott complained to Johnson, then wrote a memorandum to Dean Atwater and Associate Dean Kennedy: "We were outraged to learn today that Ben Johnson signed petitions. . . . We teach our students—in fact, we lectured on it just this week—that journalists should avoid not only conflicts of interest but the slightest appearance of conflicts of interest. We went to great lengths to explain how displaying bumper stickers or wearing campaign buttons could alienate someone they're interviewing, and damage their credibility with readers. Ben's defense of his actions floors us even more than the actions. To paint the petitions as a neutral act that simply got the matters before voters is ludicrous. . . . How can Ben edit a deposit story or a recall story and not be suspect when he changes the copy? How can we write news stories on these subjects that are not deemed suspect by readers? . . . How can you expect us to work for him?"

Abbott, Ricchiardi, and Young demonstrated the high quality of city editors on the staff before, during, and after Johnson's newsroom leadership. Abbott, who arrived at the Journalism School in 1982, had spent fifteen years at the *Anchorage Daily News,* where he had supervised reporting that won a Pulitzer Prize. Joining him in the *Missourian* newsroom was his wife, Jeanne Abbott, who had grown up in Columbia and worked as one of his reporters in Alaska. Ricchiardi had written superb features for the *Des Moines Register.* Young had written and edited breaking news and investigative projects at the *Columbia Daily Tribune.*

On the same date as the memo to Atwater and Kennedy, Ricchiardi and Young addressed Johnson directly: "We were appalled at your response to our reporter, Scott Wyman, during the interview about the petitions you signed. His question about a conflict of interest was not 'stupid-assed.' It was incredibly appropriate. . . . We don't believe he or any other student deserves to be treated with such disrespect. Our students take enough abuse during the regular course of their reporting duties for the *Missourian.* They don't deserve it from newsroom faculty. We feel you owe this young man an apology."

George Kennedy replied to Ricchiardi, Young, and Abbott the same day, noting that he had talked to Johnson about signing the petitions. Kennedy reluctantly conceded that some journalists believe they should be able to exercise their rights as citizens without undergoing professional criticism. He cited political endorsements by the Newspaper Guild, editors who participate in United Way campaigns, *Tribune* publisher Hank Waters's organizational involvements, plus "Brian Brooks' membership in a downtown civic club and his support of university athletic recruiting and of fraternity activities, all of them actual or potential subjects of *Missourian* coverage." Addressing cooperation with Johnson, Kennedy said, "I for one expect that editors here as on any newspaper will have disagreements, sometimes serious ones, and continue to be able to work together. Each of you will have to answer for yourself whether you can do that."

With Atwater about to leave the deanship, on July 7, 1989, Kennedy wrote the incoming dean, Dean Mills: "Ben has faced resistance, both passive and active, from a number of his newsroom colleagues. I suspect that he was hurt more than he wants to show and that the hurt, added to his insecurity, which he also works at concealing, has had a lot to do with his swings from lack of firmness and even lack of effort to over-aggressiveness. . . . If he is to be saved as managing editor or editor—and I still think that is possible even though I am less optimistic than I was two years ago—we will have to figure out some way to provide . . . support and guidance."

On December 6, 1989, Mills made an offer: Johnson's title would shift to editor, with the editorial page as his domain. His academic rank, salary, and benefits would not change. He would teach five courses per calendar year. When the negotiations snagged, the Journalism School asked Johnson to leave by the summer of 1990.

With Johnson gone, Mills became publisher of a newspaper that would eventually reinvent itself drastically during his long tenure as dean. In 1990, Mills could not have dreamed just how drastic that reinvention would be, or just how hard he would need to labor to keep the *Missourian* alive.

Every Journalism School dean, in fact, found himself fending off attempts to kill or emasculate the *Missourian,* in part because the Waters family at the *Columbia Daily Tribune* never stopped complaining about the Journalism School's negative impact on its livelihood.

The irritation flowed both ways. As some Missouri Journalism School alumni accumulated fortunes in the media realm, they discussed schemes for neutralizing the Waterses' efforts. Alumnus Houston Harte, a successful Texas newspaper owner, even explored buying the *Tribune,* then combining its operations with those of the *Missourian.* On *San Angelo Standard-Times* letterhead, Harte recorded details in a May 10, 1943, memo for the files.

Harte talked to Columbia businessman R. B. Price, who "thought [the *Tribune* sale] would be a fine thing for the university and a good thing for the town." But Price wondered whether the Waters family would sell at an affordable amount. As Harte related, "He says the *Tribune* is profitable under its present management, that the owner is about forty-five years old and wants to live in Columbia." Harte studied the Columbia market, with its then population of approximately twenty thousand and its twenty-five or so annual conventions. He liked what he saw, musing that a strong advertising department at a university-owned *Missourian-Tribune* combination could provide a twenty-five-thousand-dollar annual profit for the Journalism School "to be spent on the right kind of instructors."

Harte's stealth initiative ended up buried. It became clear to a succession of Journalism School deans that they needed to bolster the business side of the *Missourian,* so that the editorial staff could continue to function. During the 1950s, 1960s, and into 1973, business manager Doral Flynn wrestled with the *Missourian's* precarious future, never giving up but never finding a magic formula for guaranteed survival. He died at a Missouri Press Association meeting in January 1973.

Scrambling to replace Flynn on short notice, Dean Fisher made an unexpected choice by going to J. Robert (Bob) Humphreys (BJ 1949) and giving him a new title, general manager, with expanded authority. Humphreys had returned to the University of Missouri in 1970 to earn a master's degree and start a new job track, leaving behind a career on the news and business sides of radio in Oregon.

"I told Fisher when he offered me the [general manager] job that I didn't know anything about print production, that I was strictly a radio man and advertising sales guy," Humphreys recalled. Fisher replied that veteran printers Reed Coday and Jim Brown would handle the production flow while Humphreys grew into the rest of the duties. When Humphreys asked advertising professor Milton Gross, also associate dean of the Missouri Journalism School, for hints on serving as general manager, Gross replied, "Just run it like you own it."

As "owner," Humphreys needed to deal quickly with improving the printing function. "Our letterpress was on its last legs and the offset press had limited capacity," Humphreys recalled. "Don Reynolds, president of [a newspaper chain] and a Missourian Publishing Association board member, asked how much it would cost to add press capacity rather than have another firm do our printing. He later sent me a check for ten thousand dollars to add a new press unit."

Humphreys relied heavily on existing staff, such as Barbara Gilpin. Her book-keeping skills helped Humphreys understand the newspaper's financial situation, which had seemed mysterious when he assumed the job. Like so many unsung staff members throughout the Journalism School, Gilpin operated in near anonymity as far as most faculty and students were concerned—an unfortunate reality within many large, diverse institutions.

Knowing his limitations as a one-man band, Humphreys hired a full-time advertising salesperson, rather than relying entirely on students. Rick Wise (BJ 1974) filled the position. He enjoyed calling on business owners around Columbia, hoping to obtain their advertising dollars. At a Columbia appliance store, Wise recalled, "There was always a poker game going on right at the front counter. I would play a few hands, maybe get an ad, maybe not—probably depending on if I won any hands or not—then go on my way. I remember if a customer came in the door and [the store manager] had a good hand, he would tell them 'wait just a minute if you don't mind, I've got an awfully good hand here and I can't fold.'"

After selling an advertisement, Wise worried about getting it placed in type properly. The men in the *Missourian* printing plant qualified as "characters" who did not always take well to a young, upstart ad salesperson. "You had to approach them in just the right way to get some of your ads set up. Sometimes screaming worked, sometimes bribes, sometimes pity, you never knew for sure. You just kept trying whatever method you had available until one worked. They were a lot of fun actually, and very colorful."

Humphreys wanted those advertisements, and the news, to reach more readers. So he built on a situation negotiated by his predecessor Flynn and advertising professor Ruth B. Bratek. They had agreed to a request by local grocer Jack Nowell to distribute ten thousand extra copies of the Wednesday newspaper to increase the reach of the supermarket's advertisements. Those copies ended up at the homes of nonsubscribers. Humphreys decided to institute a free tabloid sent through the U.S. Postal Service to twenty thousand households. To keep costs manageable, Humphreys applied for a bulk mail education rate. When he received permission to send the twenty thousand tabloids at a reduced cost, two competitors challenged the *Missourian* at the Postal Service, and prevailed.

The *Columbia Daily Tribune* was one of the challengers. The other challenger demonstrated the changing media landscape in Columbia, an alteration that boded ill for the *Missourian*. It carried the name of Winsor Newspapers and owned small dailies in Boonville, Missouri, and Canton, Illinois. The Boonville printing plant, about thirty miles west of Columbia, also produced the *Mid-*

Missouri Weekly Shopper, delivered to about forty thousand homes by an independent contractor starting in 1972.

John Thomas (Jack) Swartz (BJ 1970) represented Winsor Newspapers in Columbia. He helped mount the successful legal challenge to the low-cost mailing permit obtained by the *Missourian.* Eventually, in 1982, Swartz moved to the *Missourian* at Humphreys's urging. Swartz brought with him the local Eastgate grocery store advertising, then helped build a critical mass of additional supermarket advertising that bolstered the *Missourian's* finances for a while. Furthermore, Winsor Newspapers left the Columbia market about a year later.

With the academic side of the advertising curriculum at the Journalism School needing leadership, in 1987 Humphreys became chair, as an associate professor with tenure. By then, Edward Heins had become the *Missourian's* general manager. A towering man physically, with an unforgettable voice that sounded as if it emanated from the bottom of a wooden rain barrel, Heins could seem intimidating. He arrived at the Journalism School in 1979 after an unusually varied career within journalism, having served as editor on small dailies in Wisconsin and Iowa, as a wire service bureau chief, and as managing editor of a large daily. Then, for five years before joining the Missouri faculty, Heins served as president of a company in Cape Girardeau, Missouri, disseminating a free circulation newspaper filled with profitable advertising.

Heins exhibited aggressiveness as he attempted to stabilize the *Missourian's* finances. "Many retailers decided they would no longer split their advertising between newspapers," Heins recalled, describing the Columbia market in 1979–1980. "Many were picking the newspaper with the largest reach and dropping smaller publications. In Columbia, at that time, the choice was the *Tribune* because of its larger paid circulation."

Dean Fisher knew that, in Cape Girardeau, Heins had challenged the paid general circulation daily newspaper with a free newspaper distributed three days a week, timed to the advertising cycle—Sunday, Tuesday, and Thursday. "Our approach in Cape Girardeau was to publish a full-service newspaper, with news, and tailor the distribution to coincide with the area the city retailers had deemed to be their retail trade zone," Heins recalled. "Our free-distribution newspaper went to every household in that area." That meant Heins's newspaper achieved greater penetration where the retailers wanted to go than did the traditional competition.

Heins set out to do the same with the *Missourian.* "First, we surveyed the major advertisers and had them draw on a map the area where the bulk of their customers lived. Even at that time, Columbia merchants drew customers from far outside the city limits. The retailer-drawn retail trade zone included about forty thousand households. Of course, that was nearly seven times the paid circulation of the *Missourian*. But, of more consequence, it was more than twice the paid circulation of the *Tribune*."

An unexpected angel appeared, Heins said, as he struggled to establish carrier routes for the retail trade zone. The angel was Joe Forsee, a former Missouri Journalism School faculty member. "He took time off from his job as executive of the International Circulation Managers Association to actually walk the routes for us. He was living in Washington, D.C., but was from Ashland and helped while he was home on vacation."

To differentiate the free weekly from other shoppers, Heins worked with newsroom editors to set up a series of new beats for students. Those led to the creation of original editorial content for the shopper. The timing worked well for *Missourian* editors, because rising enrollment in newsroom courses had made it difficult to find attractive beats for all the reporting students.

Now Heins was ready for the big test—whether the new product would halt the trend of advertisers making "all-or-nothing" buys, the mind-set that had led to increasing domination by the *Tribune*. The big test focused on Nowell's, the only Columbia grocer that had continued to split advertising between the *Tribune* and the *Missourian*. Nowell's supermarkets ranked as Heins's number-one advertising account.

With the free-circulation weekly in place, Nowell agreed to drop his *Tribune* advertising circular and do all his business with the *Missourian*. Nowell told Heins that if the test failed, all of the supermarket's advertising revenue would shift to the *Tribune*. The *Missourian* passed the test, eventually wresting other grocery advertisements from the *Tribune* as well.

Unsurprisingly, the forays upset the *Tribune* ownership. At one point during the early 1980s, Tribune editor-publisher Hank Waters III used his friendship with University of Missouri chancellor Barbara Uehling to push harder than usual for a scale-back at the *Missourian*. Waters's initiative took root for a while. Under pressure from the university administration, Dean Fisher responded by ordering advertising salespeople to stay away from *Tribune* accounts and shelving a campaign to boost circulation. Uehling eased the restrictions during 1982 after the *Missourian* showed a 1981 deficit of fifty-four thousand dollars. The pressure from Waters would continue to return in one form or another, however, as Dean Mills would soon learn.

Five

Bricks and Mortar during Peace and War

While the long-term existence of the *Missourian* has sometimes seemed tenuous, the edifices housing its newsroom—as well as the news operations of KOMU-TV and KBIA-FM—provide a sense of permanence. Buildings alone obviously do not constitute a journalism school. Yet when current and former students, staff, and faculty talk about the Missouri Journalism School, so many of the memories—positive and negative—are associated with Jay H. Neff Hall or Walter Williams Hall or Gannett Hall or Lee Hills Hall, with the KBIA studio on the top floor of Jesse Hall, or with the KOMU building six miles south of Columbia on the highway leading to Jefferson City.

Specific spaces within each building tend to evoke special memories among those who studied, taught, and handled staff matters inside. One such space is a basement room for classes that became known as the Neff Hall "pit." John T. Schneller (BJ 1980) joined the faculty in 2001 after a long career at the *Columbia Daily Tribune*. He commented that when middle-age or older graduates return, "the one thing they seem to remember most is the pit. In retrospect, the pit was almost something of a religious experience—a special, and, I dare say, sacred place that was separate from the rest of the physical world. Kind of its own isolation chamber . . . remind[ing] me of the kivas, which I believe were subterranean places the Hopis used for spiritual gatherings."

Beginning reporting/editing classes used to meet in the forbidding recessed room; even if the beginning students experienced the good fortune to learn in a more pleasant space, faculty members teaching the course would gather below-ground to coordinate the numerous sections. Phil Norman, sometimes coordinator of the course, issued bulletins to the other instructors. The heading at the top of the bulletin read, "The Pit."

It is conceivable that the Journalism School never would have gained its own space without generous alumni donating large sums to help accommodate the expanding number of students, faculty, staff, and course offerings. The university perhaps would not have spent the tens of millions of dollars necessary for buildings dedicated only to journalism.

Ward Neff (BJ 1913) donated money to honor his father, Jay Holcomb Neff, an Indiana lawyer born in 1854 who moved to Kansas City, served as mayor there, and entered trade publishing. When Jay Neff died in 1915, Ward Neff inherited his father's livestock-related newspapers and magazines. Ward Neff had disliked attending journalism classes in the makeshift set-up at Switzler Hall, so he decided to rectify the situation.

Neff announced the gift of money for a building to Walter Williams during a breakfast in Kansas City during 1918. State government dallied, however. Impatient for the ground breaking, Williams wrote Henry F. Childers of the *Troy (Missouri) Free Press,* hoping he would intervene with specific legislators: "May I invoke your potent aid in a matter of large importance to the School of Journalism?" Williams then told Childers the particulars of the legislative appropriation the Journalism School would need to supplement the Neff gift, including fifteen thousand dollars for laboratory equipment.

After Williams prevailed, construction proceeded pretty much on schedule. The building opened for classwork in 1920. A bronze tablet in the building corridor explained that Jay Neff's life "exemplified the high ideals of journalism: truth, fairness, generosity, devotion to duty, unselfish public service." Williams wrote to Ward Neff that "the young women students of the School of Journalism have taken in hand the furnishing of the women's room in Jay H. Neff Hall, and have obtained by a fashion show, a fashion supplement to the Missourian and their own personal gifts a sufficient amount to accomplish their desire. The men students have in mind furnishing the conference room."

Because of the *Missourian*'s needs, Neff Hall housed more than classrooms and faculty offices. The main floor included a newsroom, a copyediting area, a telegraph/telephone room, and a library. Julia Sampson, who had joined the University of Missouri library staff in 1913, took charge of the book collection, which she expanded and watched over until 1946.

Befitting the Neff family's background, the school's curriculum expanded to include agricultural journalism and rural newspapering. The year after Neff Hall opened, the university counted 210 journalism majors and another 90 nonmajors enrolled in journalism courses, up 25 percent from the previous year. The students arrived from thirty states and five foreign nations.

Neff Hall never outlived its usefulness, but it needed a companion much sooner than anticipated because of growing enrollments, an expanding library, and new technology. The proposed Walter Williams Hall received a state legislative appropriation and a federal government supplement approved by the university's Board of Curators during 1935. The design reflected the architecture of Neff Hall, and the new building was connected to Neff Hall through an archway. Walter Williams Hall opened for use during 1937. The pressroom and related operations for physically producing the *Missourian* occupied the basement. A plate-glass wall allowed students, staff, faculty, and visitors to watch the production process from the corridor without endangering themselves or interfering with the skilled laborers.

Faculty and staff sought help with physical improvements whenever possible, because funding from within the university and from the state legislature always seemed to fall short. On November 23, 1959, for example, Clifton C. Edom, director of photojournalism, wrote Melville Bell Grosvenor, editor of *National Geographic* in Washington, D.C. They had met in person earlier that month. "All of us on the Journalism School staff long have recognized the need for teaching color photography," Edom said, "and the need for a press which would print color halftones in our daily and Sunday paper. . . . Upon occasion, we have attempted to overprint a color block, or have attempted a duotone. While we have done pretty well considering our facilities and equipment, no one knows better than we that this is a poor substitute for a three or four-color halftone. With this in mind, you can well imagine [the] elation that you were interested in the possibility of lending a hand. As you requested, we are making an immediate study, and will soon submit facts and figures as to how much it will cost to modernize our press so that we can have full color reproduction."

In 1961, the newspaper transferred to a visually unimaginative but functional new building called the Annex, an addition to the north end of Neff Hall, facing Elm Street. The boxy architecture, the loading dock for newsprint, and the adjacent parking lot presented visitors approaching from the north with an ugly first impression of the Journalism School. A state bond issue helped finance the approximately $420,000 cost.

By then, the building designed in 1953 for KOMU-TV had become a second home for broadcast students, who needed to own an automobile, borrow an automobile, or hitch a ride with an acquaintance to report for their shifts. From the highway, the building looked eerie, especially given the nearly eight-hundred-foot-tall tower/antenna piercing the Boone County sky.

Next in the progression of buildings came Gannett Hall, squeezed into the little remaining space on the north end of the often-photographed, visually pleasing campus Quadrangle. The building connected with Neff Hall. A donation from the Gannett Foundation, an offshoot of the most pervasive United States media conglomerate, combined with a state legislative appropriation, paid for most of the three-story building. Television and radio students, staff, and faculty especially appreciated the up-to-date technological work area. In conjunction with the availability of Gannett Hall, the Journalism School lost its use of an old house at 305 Watson Place that had been the site of a classroom plus staff and faculty offices. The University of Missouri demolished 305 Watson Place soon after.

In 1995, the opening of Lee Hills Hall gave the *Missourian* a modern newsroom, with the press operation remaining in the Annex. The construction of Lee Hills Hall expanded the University of Missouri campus north of Elm Street into the municipal downtown for the first time, a decision that did not sit well with some traditionalists as well as town-gown antagonists. To ameliorate opposition, the building was designed to blend with the red brick campus—the lighted lantern and facade echoing Jesse Hall—while also achieving compatibility with off-campus structures nearby.

Before construction of Lee Hills Hall could proceed, the Journalism School, characteristically, had to beg the university administration for funds. Such pleas often contained the pained suggestion that the university treated its world-famous academic unit with less favor financially than warranted.

Dean Mills wrote Chancellor Haskell Monroe on October 9, 1989, about the status of campus support for the proposed building. "If my figures are correct, the new School of Law raised only two million five hundred thousand dollars in private funds for its new fifteen million dollar building, less than twenty percent. The College of Veterinary Medicine is raising approximately three million seven hundred thousand dollars of the projected fourteen million nine hundred thousand dollar cost of its new building, or about twenty-five percent. As you know, the School has been offered a two million dollar grant from the Knight Foundation toward construction . . . to receive the grant, we must come up with two million dollars in matching funds from the state and private sources. The . . . study ordered by the campus recommends a seventy percent increase in space . . . to accommodate the *Missourian* and the other academic and professional activities that have given us a national reputation." Mills pointed out that with the Knight Foundation money and another one million dollars expected from private donors, the university and state would need to provide only half the projected budget of six million dollars.

Lee Hills, frail but alert, attended the building's dedication on April 18, 1995. Born in Granville, North Dakota, during 1906, Hills started reporting in 1921 for the weekly newspaper in Price, Utah. He attended the University of Missouri from 1927 until 1929 but did not graduate because of family financial pressure to accept a job at the *Oklahoma City Times*. From 1932 to 1942, he worked in the newsrooms of Scripps-Howard dailies—Oklahoma City, Indianapolis, Memphis, and Cleveland. He found time to earn a law degree in 1934. Hills switched to the Knight newspaper group by joining the *Miami Herald* in 1942. He rose to the top of the masthead there and at the *Detroit Free Press* before switching to the corporate headquarters of Knight, later Knight Ridder.

Even with the constant addition of new buildings, most of the time it seemed as if the facilities would never match the need. After 1908, the Journalism School's enrollment tended to grow steadily, with demand sometimes outstripping available space. The big exceptions were the war years. World War I and World War II notably altered the look, feel, and substance at the Missouri Journalism School.

World War I nearly brought an end to the Journalism School. At the start of the 1916–1917 academic year, enrollment totaled 305. A year later, that number had dropped to 173. Much of the decrease consisted of students who had come from rural areas. They returned home to help on family farms that produced much-needed food for the nation. Soldiering served as the other drain. Walter Williams wrote a colleague that journalism professors Herbert Warren Smith and Charles G. Ross "are drilling in the faculty company. They make distinguished-looking soldiers." Ross, who disliked teaching women because he believed many of them would waste their professional training after marriage, found himself discontented with so few males to instruct. Ross also found himself increasingly intolerant concerning committee work and other nonteaching duties. He left the university to join the Washington bureau of the *St. Louis Post-Dispatch*.

Journalism education bounced back after the war, at first with difficulty, then more readily. A wave of early Journalism School graduates who had already distinguished themselves returned to teach briefly or for the long haul. Henry F. Misselwitz (BJ 1922) accepted a reporting position at the *St. Louis Post-Dispatch*.

In 1923, he returned to Columbia on a story assignment—the lynching of a black man by a white mob. Misselwitz could not save the man's life, but he did conduct an interview with him just before members of the lynch mob killed him. Misselwitz had placed himself in the midst of danger. That impressed Dean Williams, who hired him to teach reporting.

With enrollment surpassing prewar levels, in 1925 Williams spoke to the American Society of Newspaper Editors in Washington, D.C., addressing the question "Are Schools of Journalism Getting Anywhere?" He delineated the multiple values of a four-year journalism degree, which included numerous liberal arts courses. The Journalism School required the mixture so "that [a student] may know, that he may know where to find, and most of all that he may know how to think. Ours is a tip-toe profession," Williams said. "Intellectual alertness, the thinking mind, is necessary therefore. Intellectual curiosity and the ability to know how to gratify that curiosity are essential."

Williams expressed certainty that journalism schools already had made a positive difference. He called on top editors and publishers to do their part: "The poor pay and the uncertain tenure of newspaper workers, particularly of reporters—upon whom, in [the] last analysis, the newspaper depends—often make the continued practice of the profession of journalism unattractive. . . . The newspaper publisher must learn to pay more money for real reporting even at the expense of money for faster presses. Men are more important than machinery in the profession of journalism."

By World War II, with Williams dead, the faculty found its way without his leadership to alter graduation requirements for those called to military service. They also cut back course offerings, especially for graduate students, to keep the enterprise afloat despite a decimated teacher corps. On January 1, 1943, Missouri Journalism School administrators announced that "the extraordinary demand for newspaper and radio workers in the present labor situation has caused the school . . . to change its rules for the duration of the emergency to admit second-semester freshmen." With students being sent into newsrooms and advertising agencies before finishing the normal course load, faculty promised to "keep in touch with employers in order to study the professional progress of the student in actual employment." To receive a degree from the university, the students would need to complete normal coursework after the war.

Faculty, students, and graduates of the school faced all sorts of dilemmas because of World War II. For example, Mort Walker, eventual creator of the nationally syndicated Beetle Bailey comic strip, arrived at the university to study journalism in 1942, but the army draft plucked him away after the first semester of his sophomore year. During his military service, Walker earned an engineering degree on army time.

"After service, I returned to MU with over three years of credits but no prerequisites for J-School," Walker recalled. "I enrolled anyway, being a bit of a rebel. I was a straight A student, editor of the school magazine . . . and a member of Sigma Delta Chi when Dean Frank Luther Mott—people with three names always impress me, I should get another one sometime—called me into his office and yelled 'What are you doing in journalism school?!!' 'Getting educated, sir,' I replied. Evidently that wasn't the right answer because he kicked me out. . . . I gathered all my credits and graduated as soon as possible . . . came to New York, got a job as editor in chief of three national magazines of Dell Publishing Company and became the top-selling magazine cartoonist of the year. I was invited the next year to speak at Journalism Week, and got my revenge."

When the Missouri Press Association met during the war years, everybody noted the large number of editors, publishers, and other media employees in the armed forces. As a result, the school's Journalism Week topics aimed at Missouri Press Association members examined subjects such as the impact of gas rationing on the collecting of news and the coverage of sports competitions.

Betty Ann Peterson Neill (BJ 1944) recalled, "During the war years that I was a student, there were few of us in school. I had wonderful reporting beats—the [university] president's office, Boone County Courthouse—all in one semester. [Actually, a] quarter then, due to a multitude of military people on campus for special training. As a result, my transcript is full of fractions." The Journalism Students Association newsletter relied on a staff of eleven, all females.

The *Journalism Alumni News* of January 1, 1943, featured twelve former students covering the war for newspapers, magazines, and wire services. Among them, Frank L. (Sonny) Martin (BJ 1936), son of the former dean, wrote from war zones for the Associated Press. The same issue of the newsletter noted the deaths of five journalism students during military maneuvers in various parts of the wartorn globe.

Notices like this became commonplace in the *Missourian:* "T. C. Morelock, associate professor of journalism, will leave tomorrow for New York City, where he has accepted a position with the foreign branch of the Office of War Information. Morelock, who has been in charge of copy reading and editing courses at the School of Journalism, will do similar work for the OWI, which sends a heavy file of news abroad to all parts of the world. Morelock's family will remain in Columbia for the present. Dean Frank Luther Mott . . . has recommended to the Board of Curators that Morelock be granted a leave of absence for the duration of the war." Morelock, born in 1896, had joined the journalism faculty in 1924 after earning his BJ two years earlier. He earned his Missouri journalism master's degree in 1927.

As of January 1945, eight Missouri Journalism School faculty members had taken leaves of absence because of their involvement in the war effort. The shortage became even more severe when Frances Dabney Grinstead (BJ 1921, MA 1928) departed after nineteen years on the faculty because she had published a successful novel and wanted to write fiction full-time. She later taught journalism at the University of Kansas. Then veteran classroom teacher James Edward Gerald (BJ 1928, MA 1932) departed for the University of Minnesota, where he earned a PhD and taught for the rest of his career, also writing influential textbooks and monographs on journalism law, ethics, and social responsibility.

In his memoir, Mott noted that during World War II "the whole pattern of our operations had to change abruptly. . . . The war and its aftermath brought startling changes in our courses and requirements, in our student body, and in the atmosphere of the school. We had to shift quickly to an accelerated curriculum to enable boys going into the service to finish, whenever possible, before the army called them. And then suddenly we found our classes made up of more than three-fourths girls, instead of the customary one-fourth. This was the 'paper doll' era. Only eleven men were graduated in our class of 1944, along with forty-seven women. But as soon as the war was over, the men came flooding in, hundreds upon hundreds of them, eager and in a hurry to make up for lost time, waving the GI Bill of Rights in their hands. Our two modest buildings and our struggling laboratories were crammed to their limits and past. My own lecture course in History and Principles of Journalism was literally homeless for a week at the beginning of the fall term of 1946. Too large to find even standing room in our own auditorium, the class met a time or two in the basement of the Methodist Church. But, understandably enough, we were not welcome there, and I tried unsuccessfully to get into a movie theater. Eventually, we occupied the concert hall of the old music building, where I lectured three times a week to the accompaniment of pianos above us and flutes, saxophones and drums behind us. The next year, with an enrollment of about five hundred, we met in the university auditorium. These were busy, harried months when we were doing the best we could for twice as many students as we had facilities for."

Mott assisted the World War II effort by teaching journalism for the army school at Biarritz, France, during 1945. He served among two hundred fifty professors from about one hundred universities invited by the army to provide class-es for military men waiting impatiently to return home. Two more or less full-scale universities sponsored by the U.S. Army began operating despite a short start-up time: Biarritz in France and Shrivenham in England. The military men admitted had at minimum earned high school diplomas. A term ran eight weeks, with two weeks off before the next term began. Mott instructed about two hundred students during the first term. They published a newspaper as a laboratory exercise, and not so incidentally as a way to bring news to the entire military university.

His military-related mission done in France, Mott entered Japan during 1947 with the designation "War Department expert." Specifically, Mott was serving as a consultant to the Press and Publications Department of the Civil Information and Education Division of the Supreme Command, Allies of the Pacific. "Mine was a double task—I was expected to advise Japanese newspaper management about the ethics and business of journalism under a democratic ideology, and to counsel Japanese university authorities in regard to education for journalism," Mott said.

While overseas, Mott heard a lot, saw a lot, and learned a lot about the hazards faced by Missouri Journalism School graduates in World War II. One of the most dramatic accounts involved John Benjamin Powell, class of 1910, a faculty member for a stretch starting in 1912 and a pioneer in Western-style journalism imported to the Far East. The Japanese military made Powell a prisoner of war on December 20, 1941, after overrunning Shanghai, where he was working as a journalist. Torture administered by the Japanese over seven months led to Powell losing his feet. He returned to the United States in 1942 as part of a prisoner exchange, spending long stretches in hospitals and never achieving full health again. Mott hoped to bring Powell to the University of Missouri campus for a lecture series. Powell, however, could not travel comfortably enough to make the journey. He died on February 28, 1947, at age fifty-nine, having just completed a speech to University of Missouri alumni at the Sheraton Hotel in Washington, D.C. He expired of natural causes while sitting at the head table after completing the talk.

None of the deadly, highly publicized wars after 1945 (Korea, Vietnam, the Persian Gulf, and others) affected the Missouri Journalism School nearly as much as had World Wars I and II. The decade of the 1950s emphasized postwar celebration, especially the focus on the Journalism School's fiftieth anniversary. The organizers of the celebration emphasized the bricks-and-mortar solidity of the expanding school as well as the renown of the school's graduates.

It is revealing to examine the school's most prominent graduates as chosen by the fiftieth anniversary celebration committee, which itself included some high-powered graduates, especially from the advertising and public relations realms. These individuals, with graduation dates included or omitted as in the original list, were:

Herman R. Allen, 1934, education editor, *Newsweek*
John J. Archibald, 1949, sportswriter, *St. Louis Post-Dispatch*
Orland K. Armstrong, 1925, staff writer, *Reader's Digest*
Robert A. Asbille, 1948, copy editor, *Des Moines Register and Tribune*
Charles Barnard, managing editor, *True*
George Warren Beshore, 1948, associate editor, *Capper's Farmer*
Albert Best, 1949, Sunday editor, *Detroit News*
Hal Boyle, 1932, feature writer, Associated Press
Raymond Brandt, 1918, Washington correspondent,
     St. Louis Post-Dispatch
Laura Lou Brookman, 1921, contributing editor, *Ladies' Home Journal*
Norma Lee Browning, feature writer, *Chicago Tribune*
Wright Bryan, 1927, editor, *Cleveland Plain Dealer*
John Cauley, 1932, Washington bureau, *Kansas City Star*
Carl McArn Corbin, 1936, editor, *New Orleans States-Item*
John Crichton, 1940, editor, *Advertising Age*
Sam Cook Digges, 1937, general manager, WCBS-TV, New York City
Arthur Edson, 1934, feature writer, Associated Press
Chester Feldman, 1949, associate producer,
     I've Got a Secret television show
John Donald Ferguson, 1915, president, *Milwaukee Journal*
F. M. Flynn, 1924, president and publisher, *New York Daily News*
William Froug, network program supervisor,
     Columbia Broadcasting System
Rex Goad, 1927, manager, news department,
     National Broadcasting Company
Foster B. Hailey, 1924, foreign correspondent, *New York Times*
Lee Hills, 1929, vice president and executive editor, *Detroit Free Press*
Dorothy Belle Flanagan Hughes, mystery novelist
Malvina Lindsay, 1913, columnist, *Washington Post and Times-Herald*
Elmer Lower, 1933, director of operations, CBS News
Mary Margaret McBride, writer and commentator
Marion Duncan McQueen, vice president, D'Arcy Advertising Company
Vernon C. Myers, publisher, *Look*

Everett C. Norlander, 1919, managing editor, *Chicago Daily News*
Saul Pett, 1940, feature writer, Associated Press
Robert Riggs, 1927, Washington bureau, *Louisville Courier-Journal*
Dorothy Roe, women's editor, Associated Press
Walter D. Scott, 1936, vice president, National Broadcasting System
Roger Straus, 1938, president, Farrar, Straus and Cudahy,
    book publisher
Jack Sutherland, 1948, White House correspondent,
    U.S. News and World Report
Joyce A. Swan, 1928, executive vice president,
    Minneapolis Star and Tribune
Lyle C. Wilson, 1922, vice president and general manager,
    United Press International

For those who like pomp, the elaborate, self-congratulatory fiftieth anniversary celebration must have seemed like nirvana. The Journalism School produced an "official first-day cover" envelope engraved with the phrase "50th anniversary, University of Missouri School of Journalism." The not-to-be-missed word *First* was highlighted typographically in front of the word *School.* The keepsake also featured a drawing of the Quadrangle columns and of the Journalism School buildings, along with a variety of other symbols (printing press, television camera) next to a bust of Thomas Jefferson and his words "Liberty of the Press, Guardian of All Our Liberties." The commemorative postage stamp with a face value of four cents said "Freedom of the Press."

The postage stamp, while impressive, actually represented something of a disappointment. The Missouri Journalism School, with help from university President Elmer Ellis, had lobbied the U.S. postmaster general and related committees for a stamp more specific to the school and the university. When obstacles arose to obtaining a stamp with such specificity, U.S. House of Representatives leader Clarence Cannon and U.S. Senator Stuart Symington became involved on the Journalism School's behalf. To some practitioners of journalism, seeking help from politicians who needed to be reported upon without prejudice (negative or positive) seemed unwise, and probably unethical. In any case, the Journalism School campaign failed to procure the desired wording and design but emerged with at least something to show. Walter Williams would have loved it.

Six

Battling for Hegemony as Journalism Education Spreads

In 1930, Walter Williams, at age sixty-five, became University of Missouri president. By then, he had remarried after nine years as a widower. The wedding occurred in 1927. The bride: Sara Lawrence Lockwood (BJ 1913).

Lockwood's parents had moved from Rock Port, Missouri, to Columbia during the 1890s, when Sara was five, and she attended public schools in Columbia. Lockwood had eight siblings, seven brothers and a sister; all of them attended the University of Missouri, and six received degrees. After her graduation from the Journalism School, she, with Williams's help, obtained a job as the first female reporter at the *St. Joseph Gazette*. She had hoped Williams would help her with a job placement in Japan, but he refused to assist an unmarried young woman to find work in the Orient.

Upon learning of Lockwood's return to Columbia a couple of years later to care for her ill mother, Williams found employment for her as an administrative assistant at the Journalism School. Lockwood organized a library for the students and a clipping file for the *Missourian* staff, thus alleviating the persistent institutional memory problem related to constant student and faculty turnover. She also occasionally graded class papers and wrote freelance pieces about the school.

What probably only a few knew was that Williams, while his first wife was still alive, made what Lockwood interpreted as a sexual advance. Confused about how to react to her idol's aggressiveness, she left Columbia after a year, reporting at newspapers in Tulsa and Philadelphia. Later, as a widower, Williams visited her in Philadelphia, asking her to consider marriage. She said she was engaged to marry another man. Williams left Philadelphia disappointed and perplexed.

Her engagement eventually broken, Lockwood set aside her uneasiness about Williams and returned to Columbia during June 1921. She joined the Journalism School faculty at an annual salary of twenty-six hundred dollars, the same amount she had earned at the Philadelphia newspaper. Lockwood taught reporting; women's page editing; trade journalism; column writing; literature and drama reviewing; and feature writing, among other courses. In summer 1924, she taught a four-week "travel course" for female journalism students; they visited "state institutions" at St. Joseph and Chillicothe. They also visited the Oklahoma oil fields, writing daily stories and features for newspapers that agreed in advance to consider publication. An innovator, Lockwood initiated a weekly magazine distributed with the *Missourian*. It lasted until 1930, when Depression economics killed the project.

Away from the job, Lockwood began a romance with widower Williams, old enough to be her father. Understandably confused about her feelings for Williams, her former mentor, Sara again left Columbia, to report at a Honolulu newspaper and collect her thoughts. He courted her from afar and visited her in Hawaii. She was covering the police beat, and the dean spent evenings at the station house waiting for her to complete her stories. The unusual courtship culminated in marriage on October 22, 1927, in Salt Lake City, at the home of Lockwood's cousin. The newlyweds arrived back in Columbia on a football weekend. The crowd filling the football stadium learned about the marriage over the loudspeaker system.

Journalism School graduate and woman-about-town Mary Paxton Keeley recalled that students became upset with the marriage because Lockwood insisted that Williams dismiss his secretary, Cannie Quinn. The students showed their displeasure by refusing to give the couple a wedding gift. Keeley commented that Sara wanted to "own" her husband and so "tried to alienate him from all his old friends." For Keeley, Williams lacked the sex appeal that other women mentioned. "I could never understand the physical attraction that he seemed to have for women. I could never think of him as being a very attractive man; I mean, he was the homeliest man I ever saw. He was so homely that he was attractive, and he had a wonderful personality and voice to make up for his homeliness."

Sara Lockwood Williams left the faculty after marrying Walter, using her skills to write a journalism school history and freelance articles, serve as president of professional communications sorority Theta Sigma Pi, and research a master's thesis about the *Columbia Herald* during the time the paper was under Williams's editorship. She also became a part of Columbia society; when she entertained prominent women at tea, local newspapers took note.

When Walter Williams assumed the presidency of the University of Missouri in 1930 during a financial crisis, he did not intend to serve merely as a caretaker. Williams became the eleventh president of the university as student enrollment totaled about twelve thousand, with about five hundred faculty and staff. The university faced especially acute difficulties because of the national depression, volatile relations between some faculty members and outgoing president Stratton D. Brooks, as well as public relations problems caused by a sociology class questionnaire about sex. Williams remained journalism dean, but Frank Lee Martin handled many of the day-to-day duties and certainly was ready to wield full authority after more than twenty years on the faculty.

Martin originally reacted to Williams's appointment as university president with understandably mixed emotions. Martin wrote J. B. Powell on July 22, 1930, that Williams's new role "has met with universal approval and has solved a situation very satisfactorily for the university as a whole, but naturally it has been a blow to the School of Journalism. With the aid of what Mr. Hoover terms 'best minds' among the alumni, we will try to keep the school progressing."

As Martin became de facto dean, the Journalism School faculty looked like this: Williams, teaching History and Principles of Journalism and earning an annual salary of sixty-five hundred dollars; Martin, Theory and Practice of Journalism, five thousand dollars; Thomas C. Morelock, *Missourian* and editorial classroom duties, three thousand dollars; Eugene W. Sharp, *Missourian* and editorial classroom duties, twenty-seven hundred dollars; Emery Kenney Johnston, advertising courses, twenty-eight hundred dollars; Thomas L. Yates, advertising courses, twenty-two hundred dollars; Edith C. Marken, *Missourian* and classroom copyreading duties, twenty-one hundred dollars; Frances D. Grinstead, general journalism instruction, nineteen hundred dollars; and William H. Lathrop, photoengraving laboratory, sixteen hundred dollars. Almost every one of them had earned one or two degrees from the Missouri Journalism School. But retaining graduates to join the faculty proved difficult, because of high demand for them elsewhere.

Although the Journalism School had not split into departments, an informal split categorized faculty by news and editorial, rural journalism and country publishing, feature writing and magazine production, and advertising and business. Eight University of Missouri faculty members from outside the Journalism School taught courses within the school under Martin's loose supervision.

While essentially running the Journalism School, Martin served as semiofficial entertainer for business occasions. A family friend recalled Martin serving liquor even during Prohibition. Williams normally knew what Martin was doing; the two men often ate lunch at Harris' Restaurant on Ninth Street, then strolled to Columbia Savings Bank to visit with other university and community leaders.

Martin enjoyed hunting trips, which allowed him to combine business and pleasure. On November 22, 1935, Martin responded to a letter from Edward W. Sowers of the *Boonville Advertiser* about whether freshly shot duck could be obtained to serve at a dinner. "Since you have asked me about the duck hunt," Martin answered humorously, "I want you to know that it was no trivial expedition. The senator from this district and I killed two snipes and one duck. In order that the record may be kept straight, however, I must say that the duck was a cripple and we ended his life by hitting him over the head with an oar."

Williams wanted to resign as University of Missouri president in September 1934 because of ill health, but the Board of Curators refused to accept the resignation. His failing health caused Williams to miss an increasing number of functions. On April 24, 1935, for example, the *Columbia Missourian* published this boxed item: "Walter Williams, president of the University of Missouri, though unable to attend the activities of Fine Arts Day, sent the following message of greeting, which was read today at the luncheon . . . 'Man does not live by bread alone, or by chemistry, or mathematics. To live a full rounded life, he must need have knowledge and appreciation of the things of the spirit, of painting and sculpture and architecture, of the fine arts that open the soul's eyes to the larger visions of beauty and satisfaction. It is through all these—and more—the fine arts, that we approach more nearly the finest of all the fine arts, the art of living the most abundant, radiant life. It is in large measure for this reason that we offer students in all divisions of the University of Missouri an opportunity to add to the larger life, to open further the windows of man's soul to visions of loveliness, to offset the all too frequent emphasis upon the trivialities of the so-called practical life which in the truest sense is neither practical nor life.'"

Finally grasping the extent of Williams's illness, the Board of Curators accepted his resignation. During July 1935 the board named him dean emeritus of the Journalism School, expecting that Martin would serve as dean in both name and fact.

While dying at home, Williams said farewell to his wife as well as to his daughter and son from his marriage to Hulda—Helen (Mrs. John F. Rhodes) of Kansas City and Edwin Moss Williams, a 1925 Journalism School alumnus living in

New York City while employed as sales manager of United Press Association. Son Walter Williams Jr. had died previously, while a University of Missouri sophomore.

Walter Williams's funeral took place on July 31, 1935, at the First Presbyterian Church, followed by burial in Columbia Cemetery. The funeral featured Williams's favorite hymn, "A Mighty Fortress Is Our God."

Unsurprisingly, expressions of regret inundated the Journalism School dean's office and Sara Lockwood Williams's study. The University of Missouri Bulletin for February 10, 1936, carried the title *In Memoriam, Walter Williams, 1864–1935*. Roscoe B. Ellard, Missouri Journalism School professor, edited the eighty-page booklet. It includes a foreword by Frederick A. Middlebush, who succeeded Williams as university president. Next came memorial poems by Vernon Meyer (BJ 1935) and Roberta Mansbarger (BJ 1931); obituaries from national and local newspapers; plus additional obituaries, editorials, and columns from around the state, nation, and world, with China most heavily represented internationally.

Not quite two months after the funeral, Sara wrote a personal letter from her home at 102 South Glenwood Avenue to F. M. McDavid, a Missouri state senator also serving as the university Board of Curators president. "You know of course that my house and my life are in great confusion," Sara said. "We were such constant companions; our married life was so ideal that the terrible aloneness now seems almost unbearable. I realize this is selfish, but that doesn't ease the hurt. His was such a full life. I have never known anyone who gave more or gained more from living. He was so useful, so joy-giving, so noble and generous, such a marvelous dreamer who could make dreams come true. How wonderful to have lived as he did, and what power his influence will continue to have through generations to come. He was my mentor, my inspiration and my confidant for more than twenty years. These eight years of living with him have been supremely happy, crowded years. He tried to build up happy memories. He studied to give me every advantage and joy possible. I know I have had in eight years what many people never have in a lifetime."

Sara assumed an informal advisory role in the school's operations. As early as October 30, 1935, the *Missourian* announced that the widowed Mrs. Walter Williams would travel to China to teach at Yenching University in Peking (now Beijing) at the invitation of Vernon Nash (BJ 1914, MA 1928). On March 3, 1937, the *New York Herald Tribune* reported that Sara Williams had just returned from Yenching and would be teaching a course titled Opportunities for Women in Journalism at Washington University in St. Louis. She remained active in Missouri Journalism School activities until her death in 1961.

Nash played a role not only in Sara Lockwood Williams's life but also in keeping fresh the memory of Walter Williams's contributions to journalism. Nash had worked a couple of years on small newspapers, spent three years as a Rhodes Scholar, accepted a job in 1919 with the Kansas City YMCA, then in 1924 joined the faculty of Yenching University as a journalism instructor. Nash received help on that foreign campus from Hin Wong, the first Chinese student to graduate from the Missouri Journalism School (1912), and from Eva Chang (BJ 1924), the first Chinese woman graduate.

Through all those job changes, Nash never forgot the impact of Walter Williams on his education. So he agreed to direct the Walter Williams Memorial Journalism Foundation, working closely with Dean Martin. The fund-raising outlook seemed grim; the goal of a one-hundred-thousand-dollar endowment felt distant and perhaps impossible during a national economic depression. Solicitations stated that donations would be used "to carry on the ideals set forth by Walter Williams. . . . The Foundation will foster the development of higher professional journalism standards, promote the development of better understanding between peoples at home and abroad through the medium of journalism, strive for the maintenance of a free press and disseminate the teachings and precepts of Walter Williams and such others as shall advance the interests of journalism ethics and welfare." The foundation never completely fulfilled its mission, becoming at most a marginal presence within the Journalism School culture.

Ultimately, Williams's best-known legacy became the "Journalist's Creed." Professors assigned students to memorize the creed, word for word, punctuation mark by punctuation mark. It hangs on walls in newsrooms and home offices throughout the world.

It reads like this:

"I believe in the profession of journalism.

"I believe that the public journal is a public trust; that all connected with it are, to the full measure of their responsibility, trustees for the public; that acceptance of a lesser service than the public service is betrayal of that trust.

"I believe that clear thinking and clear statement, accuracy and fairness are fundamental to good journalism.

"I believe that a journalist should write only what he holds in his heart to be true.

"I believe that suppression of the news, for any consideration other than the welfare of society, is indefensible.

"I believe that no one should write as a journalist what he would not say as a gentleman; that bribery by one's own pocketbook is as much to be avoided as bribery by the pocketbook of another; that individual responsibility may not be escaped by pleading another's instructions or another's dividends.

"I believe that advertising, news and editorial columns should alike serve the best interests of readers; that a single standard of helpful truth and cleanness should prevail for all; that the supreme test of good journalism is the measure of its public service.

"I believe that the journalism which succeeds best—and best deserves success—fears God and honors Man; is stoutly independent, unmoved by pride of opinion or greed of power, constructive, tolerant but never careless, self-controlled, patient, always respectful of its readers but always unafraid; is quickly indignant at injustice; is unswayed by the appeal of privilege or the clamor of the mob; seeks to give every man a chance and, as far as law and honest wage and recognition of human brotherhood can make it so, an equal chance; is profoundly patriotic while sincerely promoting intentional good will and cementing world comradeship; is a journalism of humanity, of and for today's world."

No dean after Williams would match the founder in terms of longevity, renown, or influence at the Missouri Journalism School. But each earned credits in his own right, starting with Martin.

Williams's biographer Frank W. Rucker, who knew Martin personally, said of him: He "was steeped in the tradition and idealism of the school. He was a man of good sense and great loyalties, the maker of great reporters. He was a wonderful friend, teacher and administrator, guiding the school through the difficult years of the Great Depression."

Like Williams, Martin was peripatetic and deeply involved in journalism education. In the year of Williams's death, for example, Martin traveled to Washington, D.C., to attend the American Agricultural Editors Society convention, then continued to New York City for a meeting of the Missouri-Yenching Journalism Foundation and a gathering of the American Association of Schools and Departments of Journalism, which he served as president.

Martin enjoyed passions outside journalism, including duck hunting and the St. Louis Cardinals major league baseball team. During 1935, Martin wrote George R. Staples, a Journalism School alumnus newly named as Cardinals publicist, "I can't tell you how much I thank you for the season ticket for the Cardinal season which reached me today. . . . Mrs. Martin and I expect to make use of the ticket often during the year." The next year, the situation became complicated when Staples felt abused by ticket requests from Journalism School faculty and staff other than Martin. On May 29, 1936, Staples sent a letter to Martin on Cardinals stationery regarding a request from *Missourian* business manager E. A.

Soderstrom for press passes: "Whenever possible we send our passes to the editors of papers. We find that when passes are sent to the business managers they are nearly always prone to put the entire matter on a space rate basis as Mr. Soderstrom does in his last letter, in which he says—apparently referring to the United Press baseball stories carried by the Missourian—'I am sure if we charged you space rates for it, it would amount to several times the cost of the few tickets we use.' It is true that we send out news stories about the ball club to editors, but we expect these stories to stand up for their own news value. . . . We have never made it a practice to try to use our passes as a club on editors of daily newspapers to get them to run our stories."

Various faculty and staff besides Martin provided continuity many years beyond Williams's death. One of the most important was Edith M. Marken (BJ 1924), an overqualified administrative assistant from Hampton, Iowa. She worked on small Iowa newspapers, then became secretary to the Beloit College president. Williams persuaded her to return to the Missouri Journalism School during 1929. Martin relied on her heavily. After Martin's unexpected death in 1941, Marken remained to help orient Frank Luther Mott, the first dean hired from outside Missouri. Later administrative assistants proved just as vital to the workings of the school, including Hazel Murdock, Mary Frances Potter, Bettie Koelling, Rene Collins Rau, Pansy Riley Cure, and Patricia A. Cloyd.

During the Williams-Martin years, the Missouri Journalism School stood out as the best by nearly every measure. An exception must be made, however, for the Journalism School's shabby treatment of African American applicants. Prior to the 1960s, most American institutions dishonored themselves by mistreating members of minority groups, especially African Americans. The shame of universities is especially poignant because they are filled with administrators, faculty, and staff educated enough to realize that no entire race is inferior to any other race. By design, the University of Missouri and all its academic units, including the Journalism School, discriminated against African American applicants for employment and for admission as students. While the Journalism School from its opening admitted students who looked "different," including those from China and Japan, African Americans remained outside merely because of their skin tone.

On December 11, 1935, University of Missouri president F. A. Middlebush received a memo from the registrar's office. It said: "On November 2 we received a request from N. A. Sweet of St. Louis for a catalog of our School of Journalism. We presumed that this might be a prospective student and wrote our usual form letter stating that the catalog was being sent and asking him to furnish us with an official transcript of his high school credits and of any college work he might have had so that his admission might be arranged. I have just received through Dean Martin a transcript of the record of Nathaniel A. Sweet showing four years of college work done in Lincoln University." The registrar asked Middlebush if the standard reply "to Negroes seeking admission to the university" should be sent to Sweet, then commented "perhaps I should add that since he was graduated from Lincoln University in 1928 and since Lincoln was not accredited as a standard four-year until 1934, he may find difficulty in gaining admission to any recognized graduate school."

The Journalism School largely escaped public calumny for its racist policies until 1939, when Lucille H. Bluford applied for admission to the master's degree curriculum. Bluford, twenty-eight years old at the time, served as managing editor of the *Kansas City Call*. She had earned an undergraduate journalism degree from the University of Kansas. Registrar Stanley W. Canada minced no words with her. Writing Bluford about the revocation of her acceptance letter to the university, Canada said that "when your credits were accepted by correspondence it was not known by the university authorities that you were of the colored race. If such fact had been known then you would have been immediately advised . . . that you could not be admitted."

Bluford sued the university in Boone County, Missouri, Circuit Court. Rather than advocate admission for Bluford, the obviously proper action, Frank Martin took a less admirable stance. He advocated opening a separate journalism school for African American students at Lincoln University in Jefferson City.

On February 17, 1940, Martin confided to a friend, "Most of my time recently has been spent trying to prevent a member of the black race from entering the School of Journalism." On April 16, 1940, former Journalism School faculty member J. B. Powell, living in China, wrote Martin, "I happened to see a clipping . . . about your 'affair' with Miss Lucille Bluford. I hope the Japanese don't get hold of it and exploit it out here to our detriment. . . . Both the Japanese and German press services have been picking up everything detrimental to American life, particularly relating to racial and social conditions and circulating to the press here."

Martin replied that the "Bluford case is still hanging fire after an ordeal in the Boone County Circuit Court where I had to engage in battle almost single-handed. No decision has been rendered. I am hoping, however, that the decision here will be favorable, and then if her attorney carries it to the Supreme Court we will have another School of Journalism operating in Lincoln University at Jefferson City and thus end the litigation. It is all an attempt in these modern times of so-called great liberalism to engage in a fight for social equality. This girl, as you can easily imagine, has no interest whatsoever in attending the University."

On January 28, 1942, Kenneth E. Olson, Northwestern University journalism dean, wrote to James Edward Gerald, who was serving as the acting Missouri Journalism School dean following Martin's death the previous July. Discussing a court order meant to compel Bluford's admission to the University of Missouri or offer her an alternative at Lincoln University, Olson explained that he had agreed to serve as the technical adviser to Lincoln only after Martin's refusal to fill that role. "It has been a headache," Olson commented.

Bluford never gained admission to the University of Missouri. The Journalism School awarded her an honor medal during Journalism Week in 1984, trying to atone, far too late, for its sins.

In 1948, as racial discrimination continued in less virulent form after a world war that started to break down cultural barriers, Dean Mott used the phrase *nigger in the woodpile* during a class lecture. Student Elias Holtzman objected. While he conceded that the phrase had been sanctioned by lexicographers, more than common usage was at stake, Holtzman said. "You spoke of truth and ethics in your lecture, and you almost took a philosophical turn. . . . In the same lecture, you spoke of the harshness of a certain word, 'propaganda,' and from previous lectures I understood you to be an advocate of decency—in print, in expression and in life. Yet do you consider the expression 'nigger in the woodpile' basically true and ethical or even decent? . . . It carries unfavorable implications to a People."

As a result of Holtzman's letter, Mott apologized. But then another student, John Riley Hahn, wrote, scolding Mott for apologizing. Hahn said he hailed from cotton country, that he knew many Negroes, that he had never known a Negro who would object to being called a nigger, and that professors should not be censored for language they use in a classroom.

A group photograph of the journalism faculty in 1951 shows no minorities, two white females, and fourteen white males. Change came only grudgingly, and without fanfare.

On February 4, 1956, Robert Spencer Carr wrote to Dean Earl English from Clearwater, Florida. Carr's wife, Catherine McCarthy, had graduated from the Journalism School in 1925. Carr said he and other residents wanted to sponsor a "Negro" to attend a journalism school outside the South. On February 9, 1956, English answered: "So far, we have not had undergraduate Negroes in our School of Journalism. We have, however, graduated at least one with a master's degree. We work very closely with Lincoln University at Jefferson City, which has a very fine department of journalism." English said he felt unconcerned about how a Negro would be treated by faculty and fellow students at the Journalism School. Problems might arise, English said, while the student was reporting in the community for the *Missourian* or for KOMU. "I know we will have to face this problem sometime, but I am not looking forward to it with any pleasure."

During the mid-1950s, James Allen Saunders apparently became the first black student to receive a Missouri journalism degree, a master's dated 1955. Saunders, from Charleston, Illinois, studied advertisers' attitudes toward metropolitan newspapers with a black audience. In 1966, Flora J. Higgins, from St. Louis, apparently became the first black female graduate of the Missouri Journalism School. She had entered the university as an engineering major but decided to change her emphasis. After graduation, Higgins worked as a manager in the Washington, D.C., office of corporate giant AT&T.

Bert N. Bostrom, in his history of the journalism honorary society Sigma Delta Chi, noted, "Recruitment and placement of minority journalists had no priority with Sigma Delta Chi from its beginning through the mid-1960s. The society's leadership admitted later that it simply didn't give any attention to what was a developing problem until publication of a report by the National Advisory Commission on Civil Disorders, which explored the causes of violent racial unrest during 1967 in various cities, especially Los Angeles, New York, Newark and Detroit."

The need to treat all student, staff, and faculty applicants fairly came into sharper focus as journalism schools around the nation hoped to challenge Missouri's dominance.

The end of an era and the rise of the new educator generation received an exclamation point with the death of Willard G. Bleyer during 1935, the same year as Williams's death. Bleyer, a University of Wisconsin professor, influenced the theory and practice of journalism education during its first twenty-five years almost as much—perhaps as much—as did Williams. Some of the up-and-coming journalism schools seeking hegemony had hired faculty and administrators directly influenced by Williams and Bleyer.

The departure of Roscoe B. Ellard from the Missouri Journalism School faculty provided an early indicator of a possible shift in hegemony. Ellard informed Martin on October 10, 1940, that he was joining the Graduate School of Journalism at Columbia University. Ellard told Martin he did not solicit the offer and would be departing reluctantly, given his three degrees from MU, going back to 1913, and his ten years on the faculty. Money played a role in Ellard's decision. Columbia University offered Ellard eight thousand dollars for the nine-month academic year plus extra pay for summer teaching—several thousand dollars more annually than he received at Missouri—plus research support beyond what Missouri provided.

Because Columbia University is in New York City, its journalism program—which during its history has sometimes led to bachelor's and master's degrees, sometimes to a master's only, and more recently includes a PhD option—receives media attention out of proportion to its influence and quality. The location of the Pulitzer Prizes for newspapers and the arts at Columbia University afforded the journalism school endless free publicity; later, the National Magazine Awards and the Alfred I. DuPont–Columbia broadcasting awards did the same. The founding of *Columbia Journalism Review* on the New York City campus brought additional national attention. Although the Missouri Journalism School became home for national awards and professional publications, none carried quite the cachet of those at Columbia University.

Archives at the Missouri Journalism School yield occasional unfavorable comments about Columbia University's program. On January 15, 1940, for example, Dean Martin wrote to alumnus Henry H. Kinyon about a mutual acquaintance considering sending his son to Columbia University. Martin said the acquaintance might be laboring under "a misconception of graduate work at Columbia University. While it is called the Graduate School of Journalism, the year's work consists solely of basic professional work, which we give here at the University of Missouri and is not post-graduate work. I don't know whether you will want to say it to him or not, but there is a whole lot more to a course in journalism, such as we are attempting to give here, than a young man gets directing a college publication. It would be a good deal like students going out from this institution with all their journalism work on the *Missouri Student*."

The evolution of accreditation for journalism schools helped everybody involved make some sense of the struggles for hegemony. For several decades after the opening of the Missouri Journalism School, attempts at establishing an accreditation system foundered. The American Association of Teachers of Journalism began setting curriculum standards, as the American Association of Schools and Departments of Journalism did later. The two groups combined their efforts in 1923 through the Council on Education for Journalism. The council's principles and standards statement issued the next year suggested at least one hundred and twenty academic credits for a bachelor's degree, with liberal arts courses making up the bulk of the hours and a foreign language considered advisable.

On April 12, 1930, in Washington, D.C., the American Society of Newspaper

Editors received a report from its Committee on Schools of Journalism, chaired by George B. Armstead of the *Hartford Courant.* The statistical portion of the report is divided between the twenty-one institutions belonging to the American Association of Schools and Departments of Journalism and the thirty-five offering courses but not part of the association. Of the twenty-one members, Missouri had enrolled the most journalism majors in the senior class, 138. Columbia University placed second with 82.

Although Armstead expressed appreciation of journalism professors in portions of his remarks, his tone was largely critical—he wanted undergraduates to absorb the liberal arts, leaving the vocational aspects to graduate schools. In response, H. H. Herbert, a University of Oklahoma professor serving as secretary of the American Association of Teachers of Journalism, offered thinly veiled criticism of newspaper editors: "Another serious criticism of journalism students is their superiority complex, shown in an unteachable attitude in the newspaper office and in an inflated idea of their usefulness to the paper that employs them. Some editors think that somehow the schools add to, rather than diminish, the sum of egotism found in journalism graduates. To editors who have undergone the travail of attempting to sort out good from bad among the stream of recruits flowing into their offices, it is apparently treasonable for teachers to allow their students to become anything but humble apprentices."

Systematized cooperation between journalism schools and newspapers began during the early 1930s through the Joint Committee of Schools of Journalism and Newspaper Groups. That effort languished for a few years but revived by the end of the decade primarily because of Kenneth E. Olson, journalism dean at Northwestern University and then president of the American Association of Schools and Departments of Journalism. In 1939, the first steps toward meaningful accreditation were made through a joint effort spearheaded by journalism educators in conjunction with a variety of newspaper organizations—the American Society of Newspaper Editors, American Newspaper Publishers Association, National Newspaper Association, Inland Daily Press Association, and Southern Newspaper Publishers Association. The joint effort adopted the name National Council on Professional Education for Journalism.

By the late 1940s, accreditation of journalism schools had become common, thanks to a successor group called the American Council on Education for Journalism, sponsored by school and newspaper associations in conjunction with the Carnegie Foundation, which provided annual financial support from 1946 to 1950. The governing board consisted of five newspaper journalists, one from each of five professional organizations, plus five journalism educators.

Missouri Dean Frank Luther Mott wrote, "A system of quantitative and qualitative measurements, with inspections by committees, resulted in a list of thirty-eight accredited schools and departments of journalism, announced in 1948. Five more were added the next year. Journalism schools tended to expand curricula to include most of the standard forms of communication. Advertising courses had long been common; magazines and industrial periodicals received attention; photojournalism won an assured place; radio and television grew in importance. Journalism research, sometimes in graduate programs and sometimes in institutes performing tasks for the industry, developed in many schools." The National Association of Radio and Television Broadcasters joined the accreditation process in 1952; the Magazine Publishers Association joined in 1957. The number of accredited programs kept rising.

As accrediting expanded, it began to occur by sequence. In 1948, Missouri could claim six accredited sequences, more than any other journalism school. By sequence, the nation's accredited schools offered a total of twelve curricula in advertising, seven in advertising-management, six in agricultural journalism, eight in community journalism, four in home economics journalism, four in management, five in magazine publication, thirty-one in news-editorial, two in pictorial journalism (photojournalism), thirteen in radio journalism, one in science journalism, one in communications/public opinion, one in informative writing.

The direct involvement of newsroom journalists in the accreditation process at the standards level and during visits to campuses affected the battle for hegemony. Newsroom journalists brought the discrepancies between vocational instruction and academic theory into especially sharp relief. How much did journalism educators need to consider the employability of their students in newsrooms, advertising agencies, and public relations firms immediately upon graduation? How much should journalism education approximate the conditions of newsrooms, advertising agencies, and public relations firms? Was it more important for a new graduate to write headlines proficiently or to understand the inner workings of a state legislature and the latest ways of treating cancer? Would adding meaningful education in social sciences allow journalism schools to prepare reporters and editors to practice interpretive reporting, thus providing context to the news? What, if anything, could be done about the numerous editors and publishers and advertising agency executives who shunned journalism school graduates no matter what the curriculum, preferring well-educated liberal arts majors?

After leaving his teaching position at the University of Iowa to join the Missouri Journalism School faculty, Earl English served as executive secretary of the accrediting committee agreed upon as the standard-bearer. The appointment surprised him. "I was a newcomer as a college professor, only six years out of high school teaching, and hardly well-known enough to be chosen for the accrediting job. I had attended some of the national conventions, however, and had served as chairman of the National Council on Research," English recalled. "Most important for me in assuming the work was the fact that I had just completed my doctorate program at Iowa in experimental psychology with emphasis on psychophysical methods. I was enthusiastic over my classroom and laboratory experiments with quantitative methods, so that the assignment to isolate measurable standards in journalism education seemed like an exciting opportunity."

English devised more than three dozen items "intended to reflect the factors that have a bearing on journalism training," as he explained it. He compiled the data on a single chart for all journalism programs seeking accreditation, allowing everybody involved to see the relative rank for each criterion. In addition, English persuaded the accrediting organizations that approval or disapproval should be awarded sequence by sequence, rather than for each school as a whole. The sequence-specific accreditation led to minority criticism that it would cause splintering within journalism education.

In his unprecedented position, English visited forty-five of the forty-six journalism programs seeking accreditation during the mid-1940s. Writing in *Journalism Quarterly* during 1949, English shared impressions through generalizations. Here are a few.

Facilities: "Journalism instruction does not fare very well in the general character and suitability of the building or space occupied by the forty-six schools. Too often, the instruction is centered, it seems, in a temporary structure or in the oldest and most beat-up building on the campus."

Students: "Both educators and non-educators who visited more than one or two schools became aware of the apparent wide differences in the quality of the journalism student bodies from school to school. Some schools do attract better students than others."

Faculty: "An evaluation of faculty was, it developed, the most important consideration in the visiting reports, although I'm afraid our comments appeared unreasonably brief at times—confined for the most part to staff generalities—for, to a man, the committees hedged at specific criticism of individuals, aware, of course, of the danger of personal indictments based on very brief periods of observation."

Throughout the accrediting discussions, the greatest controversy arose over the standard that journalism majors should graduate with 25 percent of their courses in journalism and 75 percent outside the major. Within the accreditation world, all media-related courses became categorized as professional courses and thus could not be applied to the 75 percent liberal arts tally. Northwestern University, Boston University, Stanford University, the University of Wisconsin, and the University of Michigan all decided to pull out of the accreditation process. The Missouri Journalism School stuck with the accreditation process.

The vocational nature of accreditation put an emphasis on job placement. Strong job placement in turn allowed the Missouri Journalism School to fare well in the hegemony sweepstakes. For the most part, placement efforts could legitimately be called extraordinary, starting around 1910 with the personal touch of Walter Williams. Until the year Williams died, he played a direct role in student job searches. His attitude permeated the faculty.

In 1953, Earl English commented that the school received about six times more requests to hire students than it had students to supply. In other words, the potential jobs came to the students, rather than the students having to visit locale after locale.

Robert W. Haverfield (BJ 1942), an advertising professor, doubled as placement director, defining the position more thoroughly than anybody before or since. He joined the faculty in 1948 after military service followed by an advertising position at the Missouri Power and Light Company. Married to Betty Luker, a fellow Missouri Journalism School graduate, Haverfield enjoyed talking about his biological family and his extended family of former students. An inveterate name-dropper, Haverfield unknowingly inspired a game played during his classroom lectures. Student Kevan Neff recalled the name-drop bingo competition. "Draw a small grid of boxes and insert the names of any ad agency personality, such as Dick Christian," Neff explained in retrospect. As Haverfield's lecture progressed, the players "marked the names off on a card. When you got three in a row, you [were supposed] to stand up and yell . . . bingo."

Well-organized, and with devoted staff assistance led by Nellie Jeffries, Haverfield systematized what became known as the Journalism Placement Center. Even during years that disappointed, Haverfield generally looked good by the standards of other journalism schools. For example, in his December 1971 accounting, Haverfield said, "The Journalism Placement Center experienced a serious lag in the number of recruiters visiting the Missouri campus this past year, but nevertheless can report a fairly successful year for the school's graduating seniors. Fortunately the companies and media interviewing were those with the ability and needs to hire members of the class of 1971. Several interviewers told students that although they had reduced the number of schools visited substantially, they still had this school on their list."

Haverfield's statistics showed fifty interviewing teams on the campus during 1971, with seventy-one seniors obtaining employment as a direct result of the visits. Furthermore, alumni thinking about switching jobs could view 321 listings in a twice-monthly placement bulletin. Forty-four alumni found new employment as a result of bulletin notices. In addition, Haverfield said his office played a role in finding summer internships for sixty-two students, each of them earning academic credit.

By then, the nature of the Journalism School's job placement effort had changed drastically from the early decades. Students were no longer going out into a print-oriented world, as a succession of placement directors and staff—culminating in a new century with Jill McReynolds as chief academic adviser and energetic, efficient Phousavanh Sengsavanh as chief liaison with potential employers—found out. Broadcast majors abounded and were followed by a proliferation of majors in what became known as "convergence journalism."

Walter Williams can be considered a conceptual genius in the context of journalism education. Unsure whether to accept the deanship of the world's first journalism school in 1908, he said yes, then stayed deeply involved until his death in 1935. He and his second wife, Sara Lockwood Williams, lived in a stylish Columbia residence about a mile from campus. In 1929, they hosted journalism faculty members and spouses at their home. As an alumna of the Missouri Journalism School and later both a staff member and a faculty member there, Sara played a significant role in the development of the curriculum. Walter Williams stands in the center of the sidewalk; Sara is the first woman to the right of him. (Courtesy University Archives, Lewis Hall, University of Missouri–Columbia)

Mary Gentry Paxton, later Mary Paxton Keeley, found herself the only woman in the first full-fledged Journalism School graduating class, in 1910. She carved out a distinguished career as a journalist and journalism educator. (Courtesy University Archives, Lewis Hall, University of Missouri–Columbia)

The Journalism School had to carve out space in University of Missouri classroom buildings designed for other academic majors. Switzler Hall, on the campus Quadrangle, served as the borrowed, temporary home for journalism classes. The "journalism" sign imposed upon the ivied facade was temporary, meant to identify the building for off-campus visitors to Journalism Week in 1911. (Walter Williams, Scrapbooks, 1901–1902, c. 1910, 1930–1931, Western Historical Manuscript Collection, Columbia, Missouri)

The Journalism School occupied its own building for the first time in 1920. Ward
Neff, a 1913 alumnus and agricultural newspaper publisher, provided the money
for Jay H. Neff Hall, in honor of his father. At the north end of the University
of Missouri Quadrangle, Neff Hall would foster memories among thousands of
students, staff, and faculty. (Courtesy University Archives, Lewis Hall, University
of Missouri–Columbia)

Walter Williams Hall, the Journalism School's second building, connected to Neff Hall, creating a handsome and hallowed archway. Walter Williams along with his faculty and staff proved masterful at raising money for buildings, because it seemed the University administration and the state legislature never provided adequate funding. Funding difficulties continued after Williams's death in 1935. Not even his service as president of the university could change the equation significantly. (Courtesy University Archives, Lewis Hall, University of Missouri–Columbia)

Among the best-known gifts received by the Journalism School were two stone lions from China. The unveiling occurred in 1931. By then, Frank Lee Martin (the tall man on the right), who joined the Journalism School faculty in its second year, pretty much ran the operation day to day, with Williams (on the left) serving as university president despite his lack of a college education. (Maurice E. Votaw Papers, 1909–1978, Western Historical Manuscript Collection, Columbia, Missouri)

After Frank Martin's death, Frank Luther Mott became dean in 1942. Shown here having his portrait painted, Mott was the first outsider to serve as dean and the first nationally known scholar. But he never altered the hands-on Missouri Method of learning. (Courtesy University Archives, Lewis Hall, University of Missouri–Columbia)

KOMU-TV (Channel Eight) started broadcasting in 1953. Just as the Columbia *Missourian* became the first student-reported general circulation newspaper in competition with a private-sector venture, KOMU was the first such student-reported television news outlet. The location of the newsroom, about six miles south of Columbia, separated television students, staff, and faculty from those on campus. But the Journalism School managed not to balkanize completely because of the expansion. Ed Lambert is on the right. (Courtesy University Archives, Lewis Hall, University of Missouri–Columbia)

Earl English, who had followed Frank Luther Mott from the University of Iowa to Missouri, succeeded him as dean in 1951. Mott remained on the teaching faculty. English, like Mott, had earned a doctorate, but he also knew better than to undermine the Missouri Method. English played a gigantic role in the establishment of uniform standards for university-level journalism education, so that accreditation recognized something identifiable. In addition, English was coauthor of a widely used high school journalism textbook. (Journalism School Collections)

Eugene Sharp served as one of many dedicated, talented *Missourian* editors, KOMU editors, and, later, KBIA-FM editors supervising students semester after semester in newsrooms with gigantic turnover. (Journalism School Collections)

In addition to their hands-on media experience, journalism students completed about three-quarters of their university credit hours in the arts and sciences. As a result, the Journalism School library, which started out in Walter Williams Hall, received lots of patronage. (Journalism School Collections)

Roy Fisher, left, and James Atwater, right, reversed the pattern of the dean as academic scholar established by Mott and English. Fisher arrived from the editorship of the *Chicago Daily News* in 1971. After Fisher left the deanship, in part because of his fierce advocacy for additional resources that upset university administrators, Atwater arrived from the Time Incorporated magazine realm. The search to replace Fisher did not go smoothly at first, so Elmer Lower (BJ 1933), a former president of ABC News, served as dean during 1982–1983. (Journalism School Collections)

Gannett Hall extended the Journalism School presence on the university's Quadrangle. Named for the widespread news and information corporation, the building reached completion at the end of the 1970s. (Courtesy University Archives, Lewis Hall, University of Missouri–Columbia)

Lee Hills Hall extended the Journalism School campus across Elm Street into the edge of downtown Columbia. Lee Hills, who attended the Journalism School, became an influential newspaper executive. The building opened in 1995, with the *Columbia Missourian* newsroom occupying the top floor, *Missourian* business operations occupying some of the middle floor, the photojournalism sequence occupying the basement, and magazine sequence faculty offices throughout. (Department of Publications and Alumni Communication, photo by Rob Hill)

Rilla Dean Mills took over as the Journalism School's top executive in 1989, moving from the California university system. His main accomplishments included building up the advertising–public relations curriculum until it became known as strategic communication; assembling a more diverse faculty; and conceiving new research initiatives accompanied by funding from the Donald W. Reynolds Foundation for a massive expansion of the Journalism School physical plant on the university's Quadrangle. (Journalism School Collections)

Seven

More Than Print

Adjusting the Missouri Method for the Broadcast Era

As journalism schools competed for the brightest students, those that could afford radio and television news equipment greatly expanded their appeal. At the Missouri Journalism School, the broadcast news curriculum was established using the print curriculum as the touchstone—offering experience in real-world settings while competing with for-profit enterprises. The Journalism School broadcast saga became especially poignant when first its television station and later its radio station established market dominance, something the *Missourian* never achieved.

The first radio news course entered the curriculum during 1936, in conjunction with local station KFRU. The Journalism School hired its own graduates to supervise radio students. Georgia Bowman (BJ 1937) gained professional experience at radio station WLW in Cincinnati before returning to Columbia as the radio faculty member. When she departed to become radio chief for the American Red Cross in St. Louis, Kenneth Harrison (BJ 1941) replaced her, arriving from the radio bureau of United Press in Chicago.

The makeshift arrangement with KFRU improved during 1947, when the Journalism School created a radio sequence with professor Edward C. Lambert in charge. In 1948, the St. Louis media company that owned KFRU sold it to Mahlon Aldridge, its on-site manager, and the Waters family, owners of the *Columbia Daily Tribune*. Despite the *Missourian-Tribune* rivalry, Aldridge asked Lambert to remain as KFRU news director to supervise the student reporters and producers. Lambert agreed.

Born during 1910 in What Cheer, Iowa, Lambert worked on newspapers right after high school and again after graduating from Iowa State Teachers College. It was not until he started teaching high school in Aurora, Illinois, that Lambert began learning firsthand about radio. Along the way, Lambert earned his master's degree from the University of Iowa. After U.S. Navy service during World War II, he moved to Columbia to direct the journalism program at Stephens College, a women's school. He moved to the Missouri Journalism School within a year. While teaching and simultaneously serving as KFRU news director, Lambert earned his doctorate from the Journalism School in 1952. His dissertation topic seemed prescient: "The Organization and Administration of Television Programming for School Systems and Institutions of Higher Learning." Earl English and Frank Luther Mott served on his dissertation committee.

Radio's broadcasting dominance would not last. The first license obtained in Missouri by a commercial television station, KSD in St. Louis, carries the date 1947. Kansas City's WDAF began broadcasting in 1949. Earl English, new to the journalism faculty, found it difficult to comprehend the lack of curiosity about television throughout mid-Missouri, with the exception of Lambert's inquiries. So English decided to explore the possibilities on his own.

"No valid source of information, no authority, on the desirability and feasibility of introducing television into a university community under the restrictions imposed by the Federal Communications Commission seemed available," English recalled. As a result, he decided to invite Allen B. DuMont to Columbia. A businessman from New Jersey who had invented the cathode ray tube and founded the first television programming network, DuMont surprised English by responding affirmatively. But even DuMont's enthusiasm during a public session in Columbia failed to generate a sense of adventure within the University of Missouri outside the Journalism School. Administrators seemed especially worried about the cost of establishing a television station.

As a result, mid-Missourians interested in television programming had to use a strong antenna to bring in a signal from St. Louis or Kansas City. English would not give up, however. On August 15, 1949, Chester Burger, an assistant news editor at CBS Television Network in New York City, sent English a detailed letter about how to design television news courses at the Missouri Journalism School. That advance planning became part of the University of Missouri's application to the Federal Communications Commission for a television operating license.

With a bow toward Washington, D.C., Lambert in a 1952 speech said about the proposed KOMU-TV, "First of all, it will seek to carry out the university's long-established intention of bringing a complete practical education and the intellectual and cultural offerings of the campus within the reach of every citizen of the state. Secondly, the television station will seek to provide laboratory facilities of the highest type for students who are interested in learning the highly skilled work of the various phases of video. In this commercial station the students will be able to study for their chosen work in a typically professional atmosphere."

The University of Missouri received its license on January 15, 1953. The federal agency authorized a station of 316,000 watts; the university started at 48,000 watts, jumping to 251,000 watts during 1955. That signal could carry into twenty-seven Missouri counties within a seventy-five-mile radius of Columbia.

During the wait for a ruling from Washington, D.C., the Board of Curators had requested an opinion from the Missouri attorney general about the legality of operating a commercial television station instead of a strictly educational one. After all, the *Missourian* had brought complaints from commercial newspaper publishers. The attorney general found no legal problem as long as the education of students served as the principal reason for operating a station.

With the federal license and the approval of the state attorney general in hand, the university sent out bids for construction of the tower and studio and for the purchase of equipment. The tower along Highway 63 reached a height of 774 feet. Philip E. Berk, who served as news director from 1953 until his death in December 1962, tried to keep construction and programming acquisition on track so the station could begin broadcasting. A staff came together quickly, with Lambert serving as program director. George Kapel, imported from Worcester, Massachusetts, became station manager, and Duane M. Weise moved from Syracuse, New York, to run the engineering operation. Two advertising salesmen and two programmers rounded out the lineup.

The first broadcast aired on December 21, 1953. Roger Allbee, a University of Missouri senior majoring in English during 1953, recalled watching the television screen inside Memorial Union on campus as KOMU aired its first signal. Allbee enrolled in a course that required him to assist at the station. He enjoyed the chores. After graduating from the university in 1954 and serving two years in the army, he returned to Columbia to work at KOMU, remaining there into the twenty-first century.

The schedule of programs had to be created from nothing. As it shaped up for the on-air debut, KOMU filled Thursday nights from 6:30 to 7:00 with the show *RFD 8*. The University of Missouri Agricultural Extension Division prepared the program. Topics included fence construction, poultry house remodeling, and pig raising. Agricultural advertisers expressed reluctance to spend money on the new venture until Ralston-Purina of St. Louis stepped up to buy time.

The program *Showcase* aired from 4:30 to 5:00 p.m. on Sundays from 1954 through 1957. Locally produced, it offered a look at university teaching, research, service, and student activities. The program *Not in Our Stars* aired from 5:30 to 6:00 p.m. on Fridays, featuring talks by University of Missouri psychology professor Fred McKinney about human behavior.

Quite a bit of the locally originating daytime programming aimed at a female stay-at-home audience. For example, home economist Marian Reid and hostess Lorraine Ellis discussed recipes, conducted interviews, and offered other items of interest to women. In the public affairs arena, *Missouri Forum* served as a localized version of the network offering *Meet the Press*. It aired at 5:30 p.m. on Sundays with Lambert as moderator. The Missouri governor tended to appear on a regular basis. Among the highlights of the nightly news coverage were a 1958 murder trial in Cole County that included an early experiment with cameras in the courtroom and a three-part series about Columbia's urban renewal efforts.

The National Broadcasting Company (NBC) served as the primary network connection for the new television station, but KOMU also carried programming from the Columbia Broadcasting System (CBS), American Broadcasting Company (ABC), and DuMont. At the end of 1954, KOMU and CBS terminated an agreement allowing the local station to carry that network's programming. NBC decided to court the station with program offerings that would make it the sole network connection. The conundrum became whether the KOMU sales staff could find advertisers for the proposed shows. Not just any advertiser would fit into any time slot. Compromises based on the need for money and the desire to observe ethical guidelines abounded. For example, on June 14, 1955, sales manager John O. Conwell announced that KOMU would begin accepting beer advertising on locally produced shows, but not during news programming.

Classroom-type educational programming did nothing to achieve improved profitability, but it did fulfill an implied obligation for KOMU to serve as something more than a typical commercial station. KOMU offered academic credit courses through the University of Missouri, starting with John G. Neihardt's *Epic America*. During a forty-seven-lecture series, Neihardt read from his epic book *A Cycle of the West,* interpreted his words, and explained the events that inspired the poems. Next came *State Government and Administration,* taught by political science professor Robert Karsch, followed by *International Relations,* taught by political science professor Louis Kahle.

At the high school level, KOMU offered a physics class in cooperation with the University of Missouri Adult Education and Extension Service. The filmed course aired five days each week, with 162 half-hour sessions in total. Students completed assigned readings, written reports, and tests graded at the university. High schools wanting to participate provided a classroom with a television set, plus an adult to monitor the room as well as coordinate the reading and writing assignments. The course helped high schools without qualified physics teachers or laboratories to expand their offerings.

Too few people handled too many chores during the early years. Janice Ann Mosley, later Jan Tomas (BJ 1959), recalled that during 1958, "I was the only newswriter for Phil Berk. He picked me up every day and brought me back to the campus after the broadcast."

Money looked like a problem at KOMU for a while, thus limiting news coverage and quality entertainment programming. For the 1956 budget year, the station operated at a deficit of about twenty thousand dollars. English sought help from a consultant, writing on June 12, 1956, that the loss put the school "in a rather difficult position with our critics," given the station's charter to operate as a self-sustaining entity. The Board of Curators and the Journalism School administration did not want to incur deficits regularly, especially given the *Missourian's* drain on the budget.

The Missouri Method is by definition expensive, especially at a broadcast station where news-gathering equipment is costly and becomes outmoded quickly. KOMU needed to stay ahead of the rest of the nation's television newsrooms, or its graduates would become less employable. But nobody on the campus wanted the Missouri Method as practiced at KOMU to cripple the Journalism School financially.

When the university administration periodically explored the possibility of selling KOMU, the Journalism School faculty and staff opposed that scenario. For example, on September 28, 1970, the Journalism School sent the university administration a resolution stating that the campus should "continue commercial operation" of the station. Broadcast majors constituted 18 percent of the journalism enrollment at that juncture. "KOMU-TV, like the *Missourian,* is unique," the resolution stated. "No other university offers students professional training on general media under faculty supervision. . . . If it is sold, it is gone forever; its loss would be a tragic blow to the educational process and to the stature of the university." Talk about a sale halted in the short term.

Eventually, professional management on the business side erased the deficit. The managers increased profitability while almost always refraining from interference with news coverage. Thomas R. Gray, who became KOMU's general manager during 1974, played a major role in the establishment of financial stability. He replaced Robert Dressler, who was experienced in television and a pleasant person but not always successful at negotiating the complexities of the university bureaucracy.

Gray, on the other hand, knew almost nothing about television at first, but lots about the university bureaucracy. A nonjournalist with a 1962 economics degree from the University of Missouri, Gray, employed in the campus administration building, had become responsible for maintaining the paperwork required by the Federal Communications Commission. As KOMU grappled with leadership and budget problems during the early 1970s, campus administrators asked Gray to step in.

Kent Collins (BJ 1970), who later joined the Journalism School faculty, serving as news director and then as Broadcasting Department chair, said, "We would have lost KOMU had it not been for Gray's good-old-boy style of leadership . . . his business acumen took hold. The station got progressively more successful financially, feeding the Journalism School's [broadcast] newsroom. When he took early retirement in 1998, the place was amazingly successful—great news ratings, excellent public service, terrific involvement in the community, and revenues that support the educational mission."

Given the complexity of its split commercial/educational mission, KOMU needed a guiding light on the news side as well as on the business side. As Lambert eased toward retirement, Rod G. Gelatt assumed that role more avidly and for a longer stretch than any other faculty member. While a member of the University of Iowa faculty, Gelatt had visited Columbia during 1962 for a professional conference; he was impressed by the hands-on approach as well as by the facilities that made the approach workable. He met Phil Berk, KOMU news director and then the only broadcast faculty member other than Lambert. A few months later, Gelatt heard that Berk had died of a heart attack. Writing Earl English about whether he would consider a candidate for the vacancy, Gelatt received an encouraging reply. After meeting in Columbia with the dean and Lambert, Gelatt had heard nothing, until a reporter called to ask for a photograph. Why? Gelatt asked. "Because you're the new news director of KOMU," came the reply. (As Gelatt settled in, Berk's widow, Joan, wrote a 1964 master's degree thesis at the Journalism School titled "KOMU-TV: The First Ten Years.")

Others had been hired with similar informality, including Richard (Dick) Cannon for the photojournalism department. "Earl [English] had met him on a fishing trip and was impressed, apparently, with Cannon's camera skills," Gelatt

recalled. "I took these two experiences to mean that while Earl was a strong sup-
porter of academics, in building a faculty to teach journalism skills he put significant store in a prospect's professional abilities. At the time, the PhD was not
a prerequisite, nor was I at any time urged to seek one."

Broadcast faculty tried to keep the students grounded in reality, with sometimes tempestuous short-term results that tended to mellow as the novice talents
matured. Frances L. Gorman (BJ 1965) remembered her disappointment at how
few female students received on-air opportunities. "Much of my time was spent
typing labels for the news film, and I poured and served coffee for the guests on
[the interview program] 'Missouri Forum.' Though it frustrated me that I was
not given the option of being on the show, I did get an opportunity to visit with
many interesting guests." Gorman, who changed her name to Madden after marrying, found satisfaction during the early 1990s when her daughter Sarah attended the Journalism School and received a wider range of opportunities.

Betsey Barnett Bruce (BJ 1970) attended the Missouri Journalism School
partly because her father had done so, but mostly because KOMU attracted her.
"In 1969, there were only four women in the broadcast news sequence," she recalled. "I remember Dr. Lambert telling me women were 'economic luxuries' in
newsrooms. That was like waving a red flag in front of a bull. . . . When it came
time to sign up for a KOMU show, I avoided the news/public affairs show because it appeared the female students rarely did anything beyond greeting guests
and getting them water. So I signed up for the soil and water conservation show,
where I could produce and appear on camera. . . . I made a connection during
Journalism Week that [yielded] my first television job." Bruce became a prominent television journalist in St. Louis, where she spent her entire career.

Richard Ransom (BJ 1989), who became a television news anchor in Memphis and Milwaukee, said that the Journalism School broadcast faculty "didn't
bullshit you. We have interns all the time at my current station who think they
will be stars and start in big markets, making big money right out of school. They
are not getting a reality check from their professors. . . . Mizzou lets you know
from day one that you must have a deep passion for this business, that you have
to be willing to start in places like Peoria and Tupelo making a laughable salary."

Daniel E. Garvey used the reality of laughable salaries to make sure students
understood that they needed to enter broadcast journalism because of passion
rather than a desire for quick wealth. A rare PhD (Stanford University, 1971)
amid the broadcast faculty, Garvey impressed students with his mixture of scholarly instruction, practical experience at the network level (ABC and NBC), plus
irreverence. Deborah Hacker, later Deborah Serra (BJ 1975), recalled Garvey

asking students why they had decided against becoming plumbers, which would have allowed them to make steady money and help members of society in obvious ways. Hacker, along with a few other broadcast students, convened discussions at a downtown Columbia restaurant named Harpo's. Garvey "went with the flow and would allow class 'field trips' for the continuation of lunch bunch activities," Hacker said. In 1976, Garvey left the Missouri faculty for California State University–Long Beach, where he spent the remainder of his career.

Amid the comings and goings, Gelatt provided stability at the station, including his service of eleven years as KOMU news director. Gelatt worked with students to develop a "philosophy that broadcast news can cover any story, no matter how complicated or sensitive . . . creating a sense of trust and confidence among news sources with whom the newsroom associated frequently."

As a classroom teacher, Gelatt attempted to instill "appreciation of the power of language . . . the impact of pictures, the overall influence of television in our lives, and a need to be sensitive to the effects of what we do on the customers." As Broadcasting Department chair, Gelatt felt proud about hiring more women and minorities, establishing rules for electing future chairs, and interviewing potential students who appeared talented but lacked the requisite grade-point average, then advocating for their admission when warranted.

Anchoring a newscast served as an incentive for students wanting a dose of glamour to complement the hard work of reporting, editing, and producing. Students received anchor assignments only if they demonstrated certain skills.

Gelatt, who appeared on-air as the anchor almost every night while also employed as the news director during the 1960s, recalled, "When I got into this relatively new business called television news, the word 'anchor' hadn't yet cropped up. If you were on the air, you were a newscaster—same as in radio, from whence most TV news people came in those days. Typically, whoever was the news director also was the main guy reading the news, from a script, and most were, indeed, guys, white, not particularly handsome. As I said, they were news directors, not hired for their looks."

Only after Gelatt departed as news director and a new general manager came aboard did the situation change. "The great awakening was that news directors are not by birth the best people on the air; they should be sought out and hired based on their skills as journalists and people managers and administrators," Gelatt said. "Anchors should be hired on the basis of their talents—the ability to speak clearly, look sincere, sound knowledgeable, read well aloud, inspire confidence, appear trustworthy, and come across as someone the average citizen would gladly welcome into his or her living room or bedroom. But because viewers might tire of just one person doing that, the coanchor was born. And the Lord said, let it be a woman to share a big desk with the man. And let them smile and appear friendly, but not too friendly. And thus Small Talk was born. All the while, of course, there were the weather person and the sports person, still mostly white males, although a few comely weather girls began appearing in front of maps and charts."

Eventually it became obvious that KOMU should hire outside professionals as anchors. "While we expected the person to have some teaching responsibilities—largely in the sense of overseeing students in the newsroom and serving as copyeditor—the academic credentials were less important decisions than the individual's skills as an anchor, or as a news producer," Gelatt said. "We've hired both former students such as Angie Bailey and Sarah Hill, who would go out into the world and make a solid track record for themselves, and folks who had never been to Missouri before. . . . We've groomed some of our students—those with quite obvious anchor skills—and put them into the anchor chair on weekends or to fill in when one of our hired professionals is away at 5 p.m., 6 p.m. or 10 p.m. . . . In the old days, students rarely got on the air. For one thing, there just weren't many openings; there were no weekend newscasts until I started them sometime in the mid-1960s. There was a noon newscast anchored by a teaching assistant, and the teaching assistants did the cut-ins on the *Today Show*. . . . We did not offer any instruction in on-air performance, other than informal critiquing on a one-on-one basis. It wasn't until Lillian Dunlap came onto the faculty [around 1990], offering her considerable skills as a speech instructor, that she and I put together a much-needed course focusing on speaking and reading skills, ad-libbing for spontaneous live reports, and interviewing techniques."

KOMU newscast anchors came and went, in some cases making only a momentary impression. Corrice Collins was an exception. After becoming dean in 1971, Roy Fisher shook up the status quo by hiring the young black man from the Jackson, Mississippi, market as the anchor. Some of the professional journalists at KOMU worried that Fisher had unintentionally set up Collins for failure, given his lack of a journalism degree and his limited newsroom experience.

Max Utsler, a Journalism School broadcast faculty member, recalled that "many folks thought mid-Missouri would never accept a black anchor. They were wrong. Corrice became one of the most popular personalities in KOMU history. When the Channel Eight all-star basketball team would travel mid-Missouri playing high school faculties or town teams, Corrice was easily the most popular figure. Kids and young and old ladies would line up to get Corrice's autograph and talk to him. He was the anchor at the time the ratings and revenue began to grow." Collins eventually departed for newsroom jobs in Kansas City and later Chicago.

Race relations are rarely simple, in the Journalism School and elsewhere. Collins's anchoring worked out well. But a race-based misunderstanding at KOMU made national news during 1987. Faculty member Francelle (Fran) McBride asked colleague Mark A. Pardee why a show he produced, *People You Should Know,* did not feature African Americans. Pardee, who is white, replied in a joking tone to McBride, who is black, "Do you know any watermelon dealers I should know?" The KOMU colleagues had worked together since 1983, having returned to the Journalism School after earning their BJ degrees and working briefly at metropolitan television stations. McBride said later she had taken no offense personally. But some black students who heard the exchange felt otherwise.

As Dean Atwater recalled, "The students brought their complaints to me and the other leaders of the school. Looking into the incident, we found something far more disturbing, at least to us, than a heavy-handed and inexcusable joke. We discovered that many minority students, as well as black alumni, felt the school was insensitive to their needs and that some faculty members had made statements they found offensive."

Rather than bury an embarrassing situation, the *Missourian* published a story about the Journalism School's race-based troubles. *Editor and Publisher* spread the word to journalists around the world. A *Christian Science Monitor* story reached lots of nonjournalists. State legislators raised questions about the handling of the incident. A faculty-staff committee wrote a document titled "Notes on Sensitivity." The document included a policy statement applying to the *Missourian,* KOMU, and KBIA newsrooms. The admonitions included avoidance of stereotyping, the importance of seeking out rarely heard minority sources, and the need to edit out extraneous mentions of race, gender, religion, or age. A Fair Practices Committee came into existence at the Journalism School to hear complaints and mediate. The three faculty members on the committee received their mandate from the school's elected Policy Committee.

The seriousness of the racial tension at KOMU led the Journalism School administration to move more aggressively to hire African American faculty. Lillian Dunlap arrived at the end of the 1980s. She had worked as a television journalist in Indianapolis from 1980 to 1985, taught in Malaysia at the university level, and completed studies toward her doctorate before joining the Missouri Journalism School faculty. A popular classroom teacher and skilled newsroom coach, Dunlap remained for a decade before joining the Poynter Institute for Media Studies in St. Petersburg, Florida.

Greeley Kyle arrived, too. Before joining the Journalism School faculty in 1994, Kyle practiced investigative reporting at WMC-TV, Memphis. After thirteen years of reporting, he decided to earn an advanced degree and teach. He said he researched "excellence in journalism education. All the research I looked at pointed to Missouri as the premier journalism school in the world. And since I've always worked at number-one radio and television stations, I wanted to work at the number-one journalism school."

Despite the reputation among minority journalists that mid-Missouri could feel uncomfortable, Kyle said he felt at home. "Here, I can create in others the passion and purpose that drove me into the profession," he said, "and I can do it with the cream of the crop, many of whom are destined to be the leaders of tomorrow's journalism. This way I can attempt to make the world a better place today, tomorrow, and for generations to come."

A muscular former football player, Kyle looked imposing when standing at the front of a classroom. Students quickly realized, however, that they were learning from a spellbinding teacher with a compassionate soul who cared about every one of them as individuals.

When the Journalism School decided to expand its broadcast ownership to a radio station, naturally faculty, staff, and student diversity became a consideration. The founders of the radio station, however, were all Caucasian. In mid-Missouri, diversity rarely comes quickly or easily.

The university applied for a license in 1966 to build a noncommercial educational radio station. At the time, Stephens College was operating an evenings-only educational FM station. Columbia was home to two commercial AM stations, KFRU and KCGM. The Missouri legislature budgeted about twenty-six thousand dollars of the proposed KBIA-FM operating costs if the Federal Communications Commission approved the plan. The university agreed to supply money from its budget to supplement the legislative appropriation. Later, the U.S. Department of Health, Education, and Welfare contributed funds because of the educational mission.

The Federal Communications Commission said yes to the construction request during August 1967. After that, planning stalled because of budget shortfalls. Eventually, the budget would rely mainly on underwriting support from foundations and for-profit businesses and from listener memberships. The main studio ended up on the fourth floor of Jesse Hall rather than within the Journalism School complex, partly because equipment and engineering support already existed due to a University of Missouri instructional broadcast operation. Campus politics played a role as well. KBIA had been promised by the university's central administration as a resource for academic departments in addition to the Journalism School. The newsroom operation of KBIA did receive space in the Journalism School complex. The split physical setup sometimes led to communication problems between the studios.

During December 1971, the University of Missouri Board of Curators approved W. David (Dave) Dugan Jr. as the station's first general manager. Dugan had earned degrees at Dartmouth College and St. Bonaventure University and accumulated twenty years of broadcast experience, including eight years as a CBS correspondent based in New York City, traveling to the hot spots of civil rights, space exploration, and national political events. Many of his reports aired on the evening news, with Walter Cronkite as the anchor. While in New York City, Dugan had entered higher education part-time, working at Columbia University on a summer program designed to recruit, train, and find jobs for minority journalism students.

After Dugan began making his mark at the Journalism School, M. E. Luehrs of Luehrs Broadcasting Company in Trenton, Missouri, commented that "through the years, many of us have felt that the Broadcasting Department is a second cousin to the print media department. . . . Largely through Dave's effort, we feel that the Broadcasting Department has been upgraded." Journalism School broadcast faculty member Roger Gafke noted that Dugan's arrival presaged "a really first-class broadcast news operation that included working intensively with the students on development of excellent journalism and career development. We said that getting students well placed after graduation was our final exam as a faculty. The period was Camelot!"

In retrospect, Dean Fisher agreed. He noted the irony of a lifelong newspaperman presiding over a massive broadcast expansion. Because the *Missourian* could not accommodate all the students required to serve as reporters and editors, broadcast majors found themselves excused from newspaper duty. In a joking manner, Fisher told a Missouri Press Association gathering that "we built the broadcast sequence in order that serious [newspaper] journalists would not be encumbered by crowds of broadcast dilettantes."

Gafke (BJ 1957), a Columbia native originally employed at the local commercial radio station KFRU, became KBIA-FM's first news director in 1972. Gafke had joined the faculty during 1968. After his discharge from the Air Force, Gafke had settled in downstate Illinois, first as a newspaper editor, then as a radio station news director. Gafke returned to Columbia for three reasons: "First, I was asked by Dean English. Until his request to join the faculty and help expand the radio news program, I had never thought of a faculty role for me. The position of faculty was somewhere 'up there,' a position that I had not considered. Second, as I thought about the request, I realized that I had taught Sunday school, swimming lessons, served as a part-time teacher at the Belleville college during my Air Force duty, asked the Southern Illinois University communications department for interns for my newsroom, etc. I thought that perhaps there was a teacher inside me. Third, I concluded that since I was going to continue to be involved in daily journalism . . . the worst that I was doing was moving to Columbia to practice journalism, and if I needed to escape, I could find another job from there."

Gafke's KBIA reporters doubled as journalism students, working for class credit—the Missouri Method in action, just as at the *Missourian* and at KOMU-TV. Student after student recalls Gafke's quiet, confident leadership, which led them to labor hard for him, willingly. The first KBIA broadcast aired during April 1972. Listeners heard classical music, news, and public affairs programs. The public affairs programming included examination of a hospital bond issue and the city council agenda. News programming included reports from student journalists in Columbia, Jefferson City, Washington, D.C., and European cities.

Roger Karwoski, who started at KBIA during 1972 and remained into the new century, noted that National Public Radio began in 1970, so it and KBIA "kind of grew up together." NPR had only a small reporting staff, relying heavily on its affiliates such as KBIA.

Initiative in news gathering waxed and waned at KBIA. It flowered under the direction of Jack Hubbard, who had worked for United Press and for public television and who left the Missouri Journalism School for CBS News. The flowering of KBIA continued under Margaret (Meg) Howard; Mike McKean (BJ 1979), who reported for radio in Houston, Texas, before joining the faculty of his alma mater; and Lena Sadiwskyj, with experience at the Canadian Broadcasting Corporation.

During the McKean-Sadiwskyj years at KBIA, the daily news and feature program *Between the Lines* captivated listeners. But when McKean assumed other responsibilities within the faculty and Sadiwskyj left first for the KOMU newsroom and then for a commercial television news job in another state, KBIA's reporting suffered.

During the final half of the 1990s, KBIA's news and feature programming lost respect among previously admiring journalists. On October 25, 2000, Bob Priddy (BJ 1963), news director of the Missourinet reporting service based in Jefferson City, complained to the journalism dean, "I was embarrassed last week as I drove one thousand miles back to Missouri from Albuquerque, New Mexico," Priddy said. "It was Tuesday and I was rushing back to Missouri . . . after hearing the news of the [Governor Mel] Carnahan plane crash Monday night. I had National Public Radio on for most of that trip. I heard reports from people at KWMU in St. Louis and from people at KSMU in Springfield. But I heard nothing that originated from people at the world's first and I think greatest school of journalism and from the University of Missouri's NPR affiliate. . . . I don't know if I'm offended, but, doggone it, I'm close. I've just . . . checked the courses offered in the School of Journalism and that only adds to my distress. . . . It is abundantly clear that the School of Journalism has no real interest in teaching radio as a career opportunity for students or as a valuable journalistic voice in our communities." Dean Mills replied tellingly, "I, too, am pained by the lack of quality local coverage of KBIA. . . . I know it is not enough to say that we're working on it—though we are."

Even as Priddy complained, the broadcast faculty was locating the personnel and the funding to reinstitute radio classroom instruction and KBIA laboratory coursework. The turnaround came in part because Michael W. (Mike) Dunn, KBIA general manager, allocated new resources, as he had so often in the past. Dunn had moved to the University of Missouri in 1986 from a combined radio administrative and teaching position at Central State University in Oklahoma City. Using imaginative business practices, he helped revive the University of Missouri Concert Series so that it fed a revenue stream to KBIA. By booking high-quality classical and popular music and dance acts for the concert series, Dunn could offer attractive tickets for KBIA listeners who made significant financial contributions.

Kent Collins said Dunn pushed the broadcast journalism faculty to upgrade news gathering in the new century, then found money in the budget to pay most of the salaries for a faculty member and two professional staff members to supervise KBIA students. "The faculty decided to get back into the radio journalism business because National Public Radio was a big success. KBIA—read that as Mike Dunn—was a big success," Collins said. "Meanwhile, commercial radio news nationwide was declining. It made sense that we make a move to reinstate radio news instruction. We realized early that there is a significant convergence play in radio news, that radio is going to play a big part in the new media world, probably not as broadcast, but as the sound of news on the Internet."

Quality journalism sometimes came with a cost. Faculty editors at the *Mis-*

sourian had lived with occasional pressure from University of Missouri administrators and other would-be censors in positions of authority since 1908. KOMU and KBIA editors tended to face censorship challenges more frequently because of the stations' greater reach and more immediate impact compared to the local newspaper.

During May 1970, for example, students roiled the University of Missouri campus with protests against the U.S. government's continuing warfare in Vietnam and Cambodia. On May 7, KOMU student journalists Philip B. Blumenshine and Richard Olenyik entered Jesse Hall, the campus administration building, hoping to see Chancellor John Schwada, the leading target of protesters.

Blumenshine, with television camera in hand, began shooting film of the hallway entrance to Schwada's office. Suddenly, Schwada appeared, asking Blumenshine about the purpose of the filming. Blumenshine explained the need for footage to illustrate a story about the protests. Olenyik then entered the conversation, telling Schwada that protesters had cheered when a rally leader suggested attending, uninvited, an already planned reception at the chancellor's campus house the next evening, May 8. Olenyik asked whether Schwada knew about that plan. No, Schwada replied, asking to speak off the record about the upcoming reception. Olenyik explained his reporter status to Schwada, saying he wanted a public comment or no comment at all.

At that juncture, according to Olenyik, "Schwada became indignant, asked my name, and said he was dissatisfied with Channel Eight's coverage." Blumenshine reentered the conversation by asking Schwada how the television station could offer balanced coverage if the chancellor spoke off the record. Schwada said he would stand by a "no comment" rather than offer a quotation for airing. Olenyik started to walk away but heard Schwada calling him back. The chancellor "asked my name again and demanded that we not say anything about tomorrow's reception on our newscast. I again said simply 'thank you' and left. . . . When Schwada demanded that we not run anything on the reception, he made an obscure threat to me. Although he did not say what, he said that if the reception story was aired, something would happen at KOMU."

Blumenshine showed up outside the reception at the chancellor's house with his KOMU camera. Schwada asked him to stop filming. Blumenshine returned to KOMU with the film. He learned the next day from Glenn Griswold, the station manager, that Schwada had complained and also asked for the film. Griswold did not give the film to Schwada but did remove it from the news desk, placing it in his desk drawer. Rod Gelatt, KOMU's news director, persuaded Griswold to remove the film from the desk and hand it over. Later, Gelatt met with Schwada, who withdrew his demand and agreed to trust Gelatt's news judgment. The film "had not even been processed," Gelatt recalled. "No one knew what was on it, or even if anything was on it." Gelatt did know that the footage was all silent; none of Schwada's words could be heard.

The incident entered public consciousness on May 10, when the *Columbia Daily Tribune* published a story based in part on information obtained from Blumenshine. Journalists and nonjournalists alike from across Missouri and across the nation complained about Schwada's interference. In the end, Schwada never confiscated the film or did anything meaningful to halt its airing. Gelatt decided to air the film five days after Blumenshine shot it, telling the audience that while the film contained little of news value, it had become newsworthy because of the controversy.

On May 21, after an hour-long meeting with Schwada, Gelatt wrote a report to Dean English. Some of the discussion had centered on the film itself and on whether KOMU reporters had invaded Schwada's privacy at his campus residence. Gelatt emphasized to English that the long-term implications of censorship trumped short-term disagreements. Gelatt had asked Schwada "whether I, as news director, am regarded as being any more or any less than the news director of any other television station, and whether I am to be charged with operating the news department as best I can with every intention to do so fairly . . . or whether he, as chief administrator of the campus . . . will influence what is reported." Schwada did not answer directly, Gelatt said, but commented "that his position makes him responsible for the station's operations and that, as with a publisher or manager or owner of another station, he can determine policy."

In late June, Blumenshine wrote a complaint to the Federal Communications Commission, questioning whether the federal agency should renew KOMU's operating license. Blumenshine accused Schwada of attempted news suppression, argued that the University of Missouri failed to invest adequately in the physical plant, alleged mediocre news and entertainment programming, and raised the danger of market concentration given the university's role in publication of the *Missourian.*

Dean Fisher expressed determination to halt incursions by university administrators into news gathering. During course sign-up by students, "Dean Fisher ordered a halt to registration for any class that required students to work in the Channel Eight newsroom, until the administration formally agreed that the Journalism School would have full control of the news operation," Gelatt recalled. "It didn't get a lot of public attention, but Fisher won."

On December 5, 1972, Fisher and the faculty discussed coverage by KOMU-

TV of violence occurring during a strike of Public Service Employees Union Local 45. After the discussion, Fisher wrote University of Missouri system president
C. Brice Ratchford regarding a request to KOMU from university general counsel Jackson A. Wright. The lawyer wanted to use television film of picketing on
university property in a court proceeding.

Acknowledging that the university curators are the licensed owners of KOMU,
Fisher nevertheless emphasized that the Journalism School "has a continuing academic and journalistic responsibility" regarding reuse of the film. "Professional
and ethical considerations" of journalists needed to take precedence over the university's "proprietary rights" in this instance, Fisher said. Complying would compromise "academic freedom and journalistic responsibility." Fisher told Ratchford that the university should refrain from even requesting material unless it had
"sufficient reason to believe that a crime has occurred" and "that the information
sought is essential to a successful presentation of evidence."

Ratchford replied that the university indeed needed the film to "establish the
facts relating to the alleged violations of the court injunction. We are sensitive to
the concerns of the faculty. . . . We assure the faculty that we would be reluctant
to make any request that might compromise the objective position that the media news departments should maintain on all matters of public concern." Speaking more generally, Ratchford noted that such situations would probably arise in
the future: "They impose upon us, as upon no other university, a challenge to
demonstrate how a free press and a responsible university can relate effectively to
one another. . . . We urgently need to establish a stated policy which will assist
us in meeting this objective."

The next dean, James Atwater, had to deal with unhappiness from campus
chancellor Haskell Monroe concerning Channel Eight reporters arriving late at
events. "Late 8" missed a City Council presentation connected to the university's one hundred fiftieth anniversary, Monroe complained on September 23,
1988. Rod Gelatt, the broadcast faculty chair, responded to Atwater, saying he
knew about the lateness problem and would try to alleviate it. The class sched-
ules of KOMU reporters did not always mesh well with staged events, Gelatt noted. "I hope we can get across the notion," Gelatt said, "that Channel Eight is not
a public relations arm of the university, and it could lose even more credibility if
it appeared to be an agent for the chancellor or president or any other administrator."

Amid the obstacles to coverage, including pressures from university officials,
KOMU and KBIA managed to air lots of first-rate journalism, including inves-

tigative stories that would have made any newsroom proud. A 1990 investigation by student David Raziq for KBIA uncovered patient abuse and Medicare fraud at a local nursing home. A 1999 investigation by student Mark Greenblatt for KOMU implicated a state government official in an inhumane puppy-mill scheme.

The KOMU newsroom added computer-savvy faculty for the new century, especially Jennifer Lee Reeves, who had worked for seven years at commercial television stations after earning her BJ at Missouri. Reeves's husband, Randy, also a Journalism School alumnus, joined her on the faculty as a KOMU newsroom supervisor. As all the Journalism School newsrooms began collaborating as part of the convergence movement, Jennifer Reeves took the lead in designing what she called the Smart Decision Election Guide to inform voters about local political candidates through well-researched Web postings.

During coverage of the September 11, 2001, attacks on New York City and Washington, D.C., with an emphasis on the local aftermath, KOMU felt pressure from influential outside interests in what became an ugly dispute. Soon after September 11, KOMU news director Stacey Woelfel ordered on-air journalists to refrain from wearing American flag lapel pins, worrying about perceived fairness and balance in presenting the news regarding international terrorism. Woelfel's order angered some state legislators, who placed patriotic fervor ahead of responsible news gathering. Woelfel refused to back down, Dean Mills supported the decision, and KOMU as well as the Journalism School won accolades from professional journalists across the nation.

Woelfel's professionalism surprised nobody who knew him well. He had graduated from the Missouri Journalism School in 1981 (along with his twin brother) and worked at an Orlando, Florida, television station before returning to KOMU in 1986. By then, a young generation of newsmen and newswomen had begun to influence the culture at KOMU, including Mackie Morris, who had transformed himself from a newspaper sports reporter and editor, and Patricia Gorman Spaulding and her husband, Harvey D. (Dan) Spaulding, who followed a more direct television newsroom route, moving to KOMU from WFRV-TV in Green Bay, Wisconsin. Woelfel made his own mark on the newsroom by hiring first-rate journalists such as Gary Grigsby and Holly Edgell, content to teach wave after wave of students while remaining almost anonymous outside the KOMU studios.

After becoming news director, Woelfel led with quiet confidence. Showing respect for his predecessors at KOMU, Woelfel named an editing bay for each former news director: Phil Berk, Duke Wade, Rod Gelatt, Clark Edwards, Leigh Wilson, Jack Hubbard, Dick Nelson, Dan Spaulding, Kent Collins, and John Quarderer.

As of 2008, Woelfel had served longer as news director than anybody else in KOMU history. Woelfel "has brought us from typewriters to a state-of-the-art computerized newsroom," said Collins, his faculty supervisor. "He has maintained ratings and ethical leadership in the market despite the development of strong competitors and the flood of cablevision alternatives." Furthermore, Woelfel had worked successfully to double the daily newscast time each day, matching a doubling of broadcast student enrollment during his tenure.

The controversy about Woelfel's September 11 decision did not die down quickly. But then again, nobody expected use of the Missouri Method to avoid controversy, whether in Columbia or anywhere else the Journalism School offered courses—including Jefferson City, Washington, D.C., New York City, and a growing number of foreign nations.

Eight

Translating the Missouri Method to Faraway Places

From China to the Beltway

Walter Williams's overseas travels before 1908 and after led to all manner of linkages between the Missouri Journalism School and international journalists, in China and Japan especially and, to a lesser extent, in the Philippines, Germany, Mexico, and Guatemala. Missouri as the center of international journalism education assaulted logic, given the remote geography and largely homogeneous demographics of the state. But Williams willed it to happen.

William Southern, editor-publisher of the *Independence (Missouri) Examiner*, recalled a trip to Guatemala with Williams. The men had attended official lunches and dinner banquets. Necessarily flexible when traveling in different cultures, Williams nonetheless refused to surrender certain bedrock principles, such as attending church. When Williams saw the Guatemala program for the weekend, he penciled through all the Sunday activities, then found the only Protestant religious service held in English to attend.

Decades after Williams's death, an alumnus of the Missouri Journalism School was driving a nearly impassable roadway on assignment in Guatemala's southern highlands, a journey punctuated by questioning from military patrols about whether the reporter had encountered guerrilla troops. Suddenly, by the side of the road, the journalist noticed something that looked like a historical marker. He stopped to examine it more closely. Translating to himself as he read, the journalist saw these words: "Walter Williams Highway, 1925. The government of the republic, in tribute to the memory of the North American citizen Walter Williams, president of the University of Missouri and founder of the first school

117

of journalism and the World Press Congress, who with his presence on the inauguration of this highway in 1925 cordially fostered relations between the great people of North America and our own, is disposed to designate it in his name in recognition of his merits."

It sometimes seemed as if Williams had been everywhere at the same time. In addition to traveling overseas every year during an era when such travel took far more effort and far more days than it does in the twenty-first century, Williams encouraged journalists and scholars from the rest of the world to visit mid-Missouri. Williams wanted them to see how the pioneering school operated, and he wanted American students and faculty to benefit from the experience of those who practiced the journalism craft far away.

Given his evangelical instincts, Williams shared his knowledge of international journalism. After his nine-month global journey during 1913, he wrote *The World's Journalism,* published during 1915 as part of the School of Journalism Bulletin series begun in 1912. That year, 1915, marked the initial meeting of the Press Congress of the World as part of the Pan-Pacific International Exposition in San Francisco. Journalists from eighteen nations attended. Later meetings, stimulated by Williams, occurred in Honolulu during 1921 and Geneva during 1926.

Thomas W. Parry Jr. (BJ 1923) reminisced about the 1921 congress; he had become involved as a student assistant to Williams. In a 1935 letter to Williams, Parry wrote, "Do you remember the summer I spent in Columbia trying to learn shorthand from Miss Rosenthal by night and taking dictation by day? I am sure the members of the World Press Congress had the most difficult set of names of any men in the world, and I have often wondered if they recognized their own names when they received the letters which I had typed. I may have been the most miserable secretary in your experience, but I assure you I enjoyed the prestige of that job even more than the remuneration—and you know how welcome was the remuneration."

The Press Congress of the World gatherings demonstrated Williams's influence, idealism, and ability to make unlikely events happen. The official literature of the congress, featuring Williams as president, stated that improvements in journalism could be achieved "through acquaintanceships formed between journalists at world conferences; through discussions of journalistic activities and enterprises proposed at its meetings, opening the way for a better understanding between the journalists of all nations."

Nothing obvious accounted for Williams's internationalism or special relationships in China and Japan. Perhaps words such as "circumstance" and "fate" are as good an explanation as any.

The linkage between the Missouri Journalism School and Hollington K. Tong, class of 1912, became one of the most pervasive and long-lasting. Born into a Christian home, Tong received a first-rate education in Shanghai but temporarily gave up his ambition to attend a university when his father died unexpectedly, leaving the family in financial straits. After employment as a high school teacher and a journalist, Tong established accounts to make sure his family would live comfortably for at least a few years, then borrowed money for an education in the United States. He attended Park College, a religious institution in the Kansas City metropolitan area, pursuing further studies at the Missouri Journalism School and Columbia University in New York City. Returning to China, he practiced journalism in Shanghai and Peking before entering the realms of politics and diplomacy for the remainder of his long life. He influenced policy while serving on the staffs of the legislative Senate, National Oil Administration, Ministry of Foreign Affairs, and Commission for the Improvement of the River and Canal Systems of Chihli Province. Tong moved to Taiwan in 1949 after the Chinese communists took control of mainland politics. Tong never lost contact with Williams, or with Williams's successors as dean.

Among all the Chinese graduates of the Journalism School, Tong probably labored most heartily to keep communications flowing among the group. On March 23, 1940, he and ten other men who had attended the Missouri Journalism School gathered in Chungking, arranged for a group photograph, then sent it with a letter to Dean Frank Martin. At the time, Tong served as vice minister of the Kuomintang Central Publicity Board. One non-Chinese man attended the gathering—Maurice Votaw, who taught journalism in China before closing out his career at the Missouri Journalism School later in life.

After Tong began establishing linkages among Chinese students, Chinese mid-career journalists, and the Missouri Journalism School, Edgar Snow strengthened the bond. Snow began taking journalism classes at Missouri in 1925 at age twenty, after studying at a Kansas City junior college. Restless with wanderlust, Snow left Columbia after a year. Making the arduous journey to Shanghai, with a letter of introduction from Williams, the fledgling journalist found his way to the *China Weekly Review.*

The *Review* had been founded early in the century by Thomas Franklin Fairfax Millard, a University of Missouri graduate known as the dean of American newspapermen in the Orient. On Williams's recommendation, Millard had hired former Journalism School faculty member John B. Powell in 1917 to provide editing help. Snow met Powell upon his arrival, began reporting, and ended up writing from and about China until his death in 1972. Because no other English-language journalist demonstrated so much daring and attained such access to those involved on all sides of the struggle for power in China, Snow gained fame in the United States through his newspaper dispatches, magazine articles, and books.

Snow's contribution to the long-term linkage between the Missouri Journalism School and Chinese journalism—while impossible to quantify—is significant. New generations of journalists in both countries have not forgotten: in 1980, the Missouri Journalism School became involved in the Edgar Snow Fellowship program, through which China sent ten promising young journalists to the Columbia campus annually to earn master's degrees.

On July 19, 2005, Peking University honored Snow in a ceremony timed to the centennial of his birth. The Missouri Journalism School cosponsored the celebration. Professor Esther Thorson represented the Journalism School by giving the keynote speech, while faculty members Betty Winfield and Wayne Wanta plus doctoral student Ernest Zhang presented research related to Snow's accomplishments.

While Snow achieved high visibility, the lower-profile Maurice Votaw forged linkages between the Chinese journalism elite and the Missouri Journalism School in so many ways for so many decades that his influence is difficult to grasp fully. After earning the first master's degree awarded by the Missouri Journalism School, Votaw wrote Williams on July 5, 1921, from the University of Colorado, where he was teaching reporting classes. Votaw revealed that he wanted to find a professorship overseas and hoped for the dean's blessing.

On January 10, 1922, Williams received a letter from the assistant foreign secretary, Department of Missions, Protestant Episcopal Church headquarters, New York City. The correspondent wondered if Votaw would make a good teacher at a journalism school within one of the church's foreign universities. Williams presumed, correctly, that an opening had occurred at St. John's University, Shanghai, where he had visited a month earlier. "The beginning courses in journalism there have been conducted by Mr. Don D. Patterson, a graduate of the School of Journalism of the University of Missouri," Williams replied, and Votaw would serve well as a replacement: "He has the missionary spirit, is a real teacher and I can commend him unreservedly. He is small of stature, though not dwarfish, and lacks impressiveness of personal appearance. This does not interfere with the success of his work."

Despite receiving Williams's recommendation, Votaw believed that the dean resented the appointment to the St. John's faculty, because Williams did not initiate and control the process. Williams "got great prestige from having sent all the Missouri graduates to the Far East"—Japan and China—until that point, Votaw noted. "He reminded me several times, 'You went without my permission!'"

The "Patterson" mentioned by Williams was Don Denham Patterson (BJ 1917) from Macon, Missouri, who worked at the *Kansas City Star* and Associated Press before joining the *Weekly Review of the Far East* in Shanghai. Powell served as his boss, completing the linkage to the Missouri Journalism School. The review's letterhead described it as "a weekly journal devoted to the economic, political and social development of the Republic of China. . . . Closer relations between China's 400,000,000 people and the people of other nations means greater prosperity for the whole world."

Patterson would return to Missouri in September 1922 to teach advertising at the Journalism School. The return meant booking passage on a ship for a two-week journey to Seattle, then traveling overland to Missouri. Patterson's wife, Ruth, and son reached Columbia ahead of him; she carried a white duck tuxedo made in China for Williams at a cost of fourteen dollars. Ruth Patterson also transported Chinese linens ordered by the dean. Williams requested a Peking rug, too, ten feet by twelve feet, for his office. "It should have a body color of deep blue and a simple border in tones of brown and tan and yellow. The body should be without any center ornament, one solid color," the always particular Williams said.

After settling in as Patterson's successor, Votaw wrote Williams on March 1, 1923, from St. John's University, Shanghai. The teaching felt mostly satisfying. "I am meeting a much better response because of you," Votaw said. "Just the fact that I was a student of yours makes Chinese journalists listen to me air my views and acquiesce. . . . It makes my heart feel good, also, to hear praise of you from the mouths of foreign journalists."

During 1929, Votaw wrote Williams about whether to leave Shanghai for a permanent job in the United States. Votaw wanted a face-to-face conversation during a visit to Columbia for his mother's seventieth birthday, but he knew Williams would be attending a conference in Hawaii. "Were I to return to America after having been teaching in a Chinese university for seven to ten years, what would I be fitted for? Most likely daily newspaper work would be pretty much of a strain, and I have no doubt that magazines and publications would be besieged by job seekers. Then, too, I have grown rather fond of teaching. . . . Really, I have developed a most persuasive tongue from showing the rising youth of the nation what they should and should not do. . . . But as for journalistic teaching positions in America, I am so far away that any communication about prospective places is rather hopeless. So, out of your great wisdom and experience, do you have any advice for me?"

Despite Votaw's worries about remaining in China, he stayed and stayed and stayed. Moving beyond the classroom, the intrepid Votaw traveled to the Soviet Union and throughout China, writing about communists and noncommunists, filing for newspapers in Baltimore and Toronto, contributing to Reuters news agency dispatches. Partly for safety and security reasons, Votaw left journalism to accept a job with the coalition government from 1939 to 1948 in Chungking. While in Chungking, Votaw dodged Japanese bombs, disseminated communiqués through the Ministry of Information, and helped the American Red Cross spread medical supplies as well as relocate refugees. Votaw left mainland China during 1949 amid communist-generated hostility toward Americans, never to return.

Returning to his alma mater as a faculty member, Votaw quite naturally noticed differences between students on the Missouri campus and those he had taught in Shanghai. "In China the teacher ranks up very high," Votaw said. "If you would tell [students] to do something, they would do it without arguing. . . . Whereas American students quite often, if they think you are giving them too heavy an assignment, they'll tell you . . . 'Oh, I don't think I can get that done.'" Votaw commented on student dress. Young women wearing slacks to class upset him: "One summer one girl appeared in shorts. Dean English saw her and called her in" and asked her to refrain. But such enforcement did not last. The long hair of female and male students bothered Votaw, too, especially because those students seemed unclean.

About student attitudes toward newspapering, Votaw commented, "Ordinarily the Missouri boys and girls I had in class were not nearly as hard working as the students from other states and from foreign countries. . . . Why? Because any high school graduate . . . can get into the university. . . . Many of them were satisfied just to get ordinary grades, because they were involved in all kinds of other stuff. . . . They'd be late in handing in their editorials and I'd take off points for being late. Some of them didn't like that."

In addition to the Votaw linkage, the breadth and depth of the Missouri-China relationship during Williams's lifetime can be partially grasped by reading this account published in the *New York Sun* on June 23, 1930. Under the headline "Wins Fellowship in Journalism / Graduate of Yenching to Study at Missouri," the story said, "David C. H. Lu is the first graduate of Yenching University at Peiping, China, to whom a fellowship has been awarded by the Missouri-Yenching Association. Every year the schools of journalism at the University of Missouri and Yenching each award a fellowship which carries with it the privilege of studying and teaching in the other. Last year the first fellow from Missouri, Samuel D. Groff, went to Yenching. . . . The School of Journalism at Yenching was modeled after that at Missouri. Fifty American newspaper publishers contributed sixty thousand dollars to maintain it for its first five years and Vernon Nash, a graduate of the School of Journalism at Missouri and a former Rhodes Scholar, was chosen to head the school.

"Mr. Lu was born in New York City in 1906. When he was eleven years old he went to China for the first time, remaining there for 10 years to attend schools in Canton. As a junior he went to Yenching University for the purpose of studying journalism, but those courses having been at that time suspended temporarily, he majored in English instead. In 1928 he took his courses in journalism at a summer school in Shanghai maintained jointly by the colleges of eastern China. He graduated from Yenching in 1929, and during the last year has served as Peiping correspondent to Chinese and foreign newspapers under the supervision of Hin Wong, professor of journalism at Yenching."

Another example of the linkage centered on James C. H. Shen, born during 1909 into a Shanghai family of five children. He borrowed money from relatives to earn a bachelor's degree from Yenching University during 1932, then worked as a reporter in Shanghai for two years to save money to attend the University of Missouri, navigating immigration regulations successfully. He earned his Missouri Journalism School master's degree in 1935, returned to China to practice journalism, then entered the government, where he rose to become vice minister of foreign affairs. Eventually, Shen became ambassador to the United States from Taiwan during the Nixon administration.

Before Shen returned to China, Frank Martin helped arrange a short-term position at the *Washington Post.* On June 23, 1935, Shen wrote Martin, "I have been getting along fine on the *Washington Post* so far. The ice has been broken, so to speak, and the big editors have ceased wondering how a Chinese boy, looking just like one of those laundry boys in Washington's Chinatown, could have courage enough to try a metropolitan paper."

Sometimes the Missouri connection seemed elliptical but turned out to be significant. William F. Woo, editor in chief of the *St. Louis Post-Dispatch,* was the son of Ky Tang Woo from China and Elizabeth Hart from Kansas City. Ky Tang came to Missouri to study at the Journalism School because he met University

of Missouri graduates covering the Chinese civil war during the 1930s. After arriving in Columbia, Ky Tang met Elizabeth. They fell in love, eloped to Illinois
where interracial marriages could be licensed, graduated from the university, and
moved to Shanghai, where both worked for the China Press. They divorced, but
only after the birth of William. He graduated from the University of Kansas and
started a journalism career that took him to the top of the *Post-Dispatch* newsroom hierarchy in 1986. While serving as an editor, he played a role in hiring
dozens of Missouri Journalism School graduates.

The linkage between the Missouri Journalism School and other nations led to
elaborate gifts that became part of campus lore. Chinese journalists in conjunction with the Chinese government gave the Journalism School two stone lions of
fifteenth-century vintage. The lions had symbolically guarded a temple in Nan-
king and represented Chinese American friendship.

Williams unveiled the gifts with fanfare, seeming to suggest that they had
come to the school unsolicited when in fact he had solicited them avidly. Votaw,
who lived in Shanghai at the time of the presentation, provided the backstory:
"Have you seen the stone lions at Neff Hall? They came from the temple at the
birthplace of Confucius. . . . A lot of things had been given by alumni in Japan
to the School of Journalism, so Missouri alumni in China decided we'd like to
do something. We approached Dr. H. H. Kung, who then was minister of rail-
ways. He was a descendant of Confucius. He presented those and the Chinese
had them transferred to Shanghai. Then we got free passage across the Pacific to
Seattle on an American boat, but the railroad wouldn't give us free passage so we
had to pay the freight from Seattle to Columbia. It cost each of us about ten dollars, as I remember. There were about ten of us. . . . The originator, the one who
first suggested it, was J. B. Powell, who was a Missouri graduate, and who ran the
China Weekly Review in Shanghai."

After Williams's death, Powell presented the Journalism School with a silver
bowl, given to him by a Chinese journalism association to commemorate fifteen
years of service. On September 26, 1939, Dean Martin expressed gratitude to
Powell: "I want you to know that it will be placed in our historical library and
retained there forever, together with other objects and documents of a similar nature. . . . When we built Walter Williams Hall, we found an admirable place to
keep historical journalism material of this nature, which we have been accumu-
lating for thirty-one years now. . . . We find that it is much used and often visited, not merely by our own students, but by those who come to visit the university."

The America-Japan Society of Tokyo gave the journalism school a seven-foot granite lantern to symbolize friendship between nations, a friendship achieved partly through international journalism. As part of the presentation ceremony in Columbia, the Japanese ambassador to the United States took his place in an academic procession from Jesse Hall to Neff Hall. A customary nineteen-gun ambassadorial salute signaled the start of the procession. The president of the Journalism School student body unveiled the lantern, assisted by the three other student officers.

Not all gifts arrived from the Far East. During 1925, the British Empire Press Union gave the Journalism School a stone from St. Paul's Cathedral, London. The symbolism is that the cathedral "looks down upon the birthplace of English literature, the English newspaper press and the English publishing business." The stone had been quarried in England around 1724. A meridian plate on top of the stone, prepared by the U.S. Coast Geodetic Survey, shows the distances from the school to major cities around the world. University of Missouri and Journalism School officials used the presentation to generate massive publicity, staging a formal ceremony to accept the gift.

Students and faculty found ways to visit the gift-giving nations. In 1933, Professor Roscoe Ellard led nineteen students enrolled in his foreign correspondence class on a world cruise, leaving New York City's harbor for a voyage to Cherbourg, France, a motor trip to Paris, a flight to London, a journey by ship to Marseilles, continuing to Port Said and Cairo, Bombay, and Shanghai before returning to London.

Frank Martin wrote to Karl Bickel at United Press about Ellard's class, characterizing the journey as "a trip around the world to study newspaper conditions and world problems. I am particularly interested in their having an opportunity to meet leaders and eminent journalists in various parts of the world, and they will, of course, call upon those in charge of the United Press bureaus in the various cities. I do not know whether you have a full-time correspondent in Bombay, but even if he is a part-time correspondent, I thought we might enlist his aid in seeing that the party has an opportunity to get in touch with the newspapers and other places of interest in that city."

As word spread within international journalism circles about the University of Missouri, as ease of travel increased, as admission procedures became attuned to applicants with school transcripts from outside the United States, the number of nations represented in the classroom grew. In 1952, the entire university enrolled seventy-five students from nations other than the United States, with eighteen classified as journalism majors. Those eighteen arrived from China, Formosa, Japan, Korea, Turkey, Germany, Argentina, and Canada.

In 1957, the Journalism School hired Newton I. Townsend (BJ 1948, MA 1949) from the newsroom of the *Topeka (Kansas) Daily Capital.* Townsend supervised a program, paid for with a U.S. State Department grant, intended to train midcareer journalists from other countries. The initial class included seven students from Korea and one each from Bolivia, Pakistan, Iran, and Formosa. They spent eight weeks in classes, eight weeks working for Missouri newspapers, and eight weeks traveling throughout the United States.

As the internationalization of the Journalism School student population and faculty grew, trends and waves began to emerge. Perhaps the biggest wave involved Korea. Faculty member Won Ho Chang became the bridge to the Journalism School for Korean students from 1972 until his retirement thirty years later. Chang earned a college degree in Korea and then moved to the United States, where he earned a journalism degree from Oregon State University and a master's degree from the University of Southern California. While living in Los Angeles, Chang, among other pursuits, worked as public information officer for the *Herald-Examiner* newspaper. Before moving to Missouri, Chang completed a doctorate at the University of Iowa.

Chang's students in Columbia included Jaeyung Park, a well-known Korean journalist at the time of his arrival at the University of Missouri during 1997. He earned a master's and a doctorate at the Missouri Journalism School, then returned home to direct the Korean Media Research Center. Chang built bridges in the other direction, too, helping American journalism students settle in Korea. Chang is credited by David J. Marcou (BJ 1984) for "arranging my first job in journalism, for South Korea's Yonhap News Agency, without which I never would have met, photographed, and had letters from Mother Teresa, and without which I would never have married my son's mother and fathered Matthew."

After Chang retired, others at the Journalism School formalized the international visiting professionals program he had inspired. Journalists from overseas audited courses and participated in a weekly seminar. International journalists sponsored through prestigious, difficult-to-attain Fulbright and Muskie fellowships became a yearly fixture at the Journalism School.

Every dean hired by the Journalism School enjoyed overseas travel and the international viewpoints of students earning degrees in mid-Missouri. As a result, each built on Williams's internationalism to expand the geographical opportunities. For example, the Journalism School established a London semester in 1972, catering originally to graduate students wanting to spend a semester, for academic credit, away from the main campus.

David Nichol, already in Europe for the *Chicago Daily News,* became the first

London-based adjunct faculty member. After Nichol's departure in 1978, finding a knowledgeable, available British journalist to supervise the London semester part-time proved to be a challenge. Some of those hired worked out well, such as John Whale, who signed on in the late 1970s with credentials including two books about journalism and a decade of writing about the arts and politics for the *Sunday Times of London,* plus nine years at Independent Television News, two of them as the network's Washington, D.C., correspondent. Others worked out less well, including a journalist who lasted just one semester given his abusiveness to students, staff, and junior faculty, some of it perhaps stemming from overconsumption of alcohol.

The Journalism School also offered graduate students opportunities to earn academic credit under the supervision of adjunct faculty members in Jerusalem, Brussels, Honduras, and El Salvador, plus Hong Kong in affiliation with the *Asian Wall Street Journal.* Those programs became difficult to justify on a permanent basis, given the unpredictability of enrollment and the agony of hiring part-time faculty with the appropriate talents. Sometimes students expressed disappointment that an overseas offering disappeared quickly and quietly.

In the mid-1980s, Dean Atwater placed the Journalism School back on the path of Williams's evangelical internationalism. It was a move that came naturally—Atwater had been stationed overseas for *Time.*

The internationalism of the Missouri Journalism School expanded with vigor after the arrival of Dean Mills in 1989. Because of Mills's experience as a Moscow correspondent for the *Baltimore Sun* and his fluency in Russian, his emphasis on the then Soviet Union and its Eastern European neighbors surprised nobody. Mills went beyond his personal interest, however, by altering the administrative structure of the Journalism School so that a specific staff would coordinate existing international programs and scout for new ones. That seemingly minor change in the administrative structure would launch all sorts of unanticipated changes. The influx of international students and the far-flung assignments of faculty members led, among other things, to an explosion in the amount and nature of academic research at the so-called vocational school.

Although Washington, D.C., is not a foreign country, it is certainly an exotic locale with its special byways and a language called government-ese. The Missouri Journalism School developed a strong link there early. That link came with the departure of faculty member Charles Ross. Walter Williams wrote a friend on August 13, 1918, "Mr. Ross left us this month to go to Washington, where he will hold the position of Washington correspondent of the *St. Louis Post-Dispatch,* which, as you know, is one of the prizes of American journalism." That

Ross-related influence remained in force through his tenure as press secretary to President Harry Truman.

In 1968, the Journalism School established a permanent, salaried presence in Washington, D.C., with the hiring of Ed Lambeth. As Lambeth explained in retrospect, "During the tenure of Earl English as dean there was a significant influx of bachelor's degree holders from around the United States and overseas who wanted significant professional experience in the master's degree programs to which they applied. The Missouri Journalism School, with a very few exceptions, was known during the 1960s and earlier as primarily a BJ-granting institution, with the MA available to a few profession-bound students and others seeking either an MA for junior college or a PhD for university teaching and research careers. There also were the occasional students who wanted the MA degree to teach high school journalism."

Responding to the situation, English "established graduate programs in Washington, D.C., and Brussels, the site of the emerging European Community," Lambeth said. "In 1968, the civil rights movement and social programs such as the war on poverty were magnets that drew conscience-driven students into the field of journalism. So the attraction was a pressing one. At that time, our Freedom of Information program had a Washington office, then directed by Sam Archibald, who had been staff director of the [Representative John] Moss subcommittee on freedom of information. He was Dean English's recruitment aide during the search for a founding director of the Washington Reporting Program." Lambeth, a Washington correspondent with Gannett Newspapers, received the appointment.

A native of Birmingham, Alabama, Lambeth earned his bachelor's and master's degrees at Northwestern University's journalism program. He reported for newspapers in Binghamton, New York, and Milwaukee before joining the Gannett Washington bureau in 1962. While designing and directing the Washington semester, Lambeth also reared two children as a young widower and earned a doctorate in political science from American University. At first open only to graduate students, the Washington semester emphasized writing news stories and features from the nation's capital for newspapers agreeing to publish the mostly localized pieces. The articles published in Missouri newspapers raised the visibility of the Journalism School around the state. The articles in newspapers located outside Missouri raised visibility around the remainder of the nation.

The students felt like instant Washington correspondents, more or less. Many accepted journalism jobs in the nation's capital after graduation. Others accepted jobs at the newspapers for which they had served as correspondents. Some years, the high-rent (by Missouri standards) facilities in the National Press Building, three blocks from the White House, could not accommodate all the students who wanted to enroll. During fall semester 1974, for example, fourteen students attended, with another fifteen turned away.

Lambeth departed Washington in 1978, when he decided to teach journalism in a more traditional setting at Indiana University. Steve Weinberg (BJ 1970, MA 1975) left the *Des Moines Register* newsroom to replace him. After five years, Weinberg moved to the main campus to direct the group Investigative Reporters and Editors and teach part time. Roy Fisher left the deanship to replace Weinberg as director of the Washington semester. When Fisher retired, Wes Pippert took over in 1989, moving from United Press International, where he had covered the nation's capital as well as capitals around the globe, with a specialty in Middle East politics and cultures.

As the Washington semester evolved, it opened to undergraduates as well as graduate students and offered alternatives for students from all sequences—print and broadcast news as well as advertising and public relations. One day each week, the students left their professional assignments to gather at the National Press Building in an office rented by the University of Missouri. There, they listened to guest speakers, many of them Missouri Journalism School graduates, discuss reporting, editing, lobbying, campaign consulting, and working inside Congress or the executive branch or the judiciary or the military. When practical, the students met the speakers in their workplaces to soak up the atmosphere. Household names among the list of speakers include Helen Thomas and Sam Donaldson.

During 2006, the Journalism School added another professional in Washington, as Jeffrey Dvorkin moved from National Public Radio to direct the Committee of Concerned Journalists partnership with the school and to fill the Goldenson Chair in Community Broadcasting. During 2007, however, Dvorkin resigned, citing divergent philosophies within the Committee of Concerned Journalists. Dvorkin did not remain on the Journalism School faculty.

To complement the numerous opportunities offered to students participating in the Washington semester, the Missouri Journalism School began a program in Jefferson City, Missouri's state capital, and established an urban reporting center in St. Louis.

Dean Fisher had decided that the Journalism School should show the way for newspapers, magazines, and radio and television stations to improve coverage of news from the state capital. Phill Brooks, reporting from Capitol Hill for National Public Radio as part of the Journalism School's Washington semester, received a visit from Fisher about joining the faculty to initiate a radio reporting program in Jefferson City. Brooks said yes, then lined up Missouri radio stations that would accept student-reported, student-produced features about the legis- lature, governor, executive branch agencies, and state courts. When Fisher de- cided that Missouri newspapers should be served as well as the radio news oper- ations, he asked Brooks to teach print students along with broadcast students.

"I wasn't sure I was qualified and was even less sure that print and broadcast coverage were compatible," Brooks recalled. "After all, our Columbia-based news- rooms were competitive and had no collaborative agreements at all. In the school, there very much was a broadcast versus print mentality. You allied yourself with one or the other—most definitely not both."

Fisher would not relent. "Roy kept persisting and eventually won me over," Brooks said, "leading to our school's first fully converged print, radio, and tele- vision newsroom. . . . It was only after Roy left as dean that I began to appreci- ate the wisdom of his arguments to me—that medium is less important than knowledge about the issues a journalist is covering."

Accomplishments piled up quickly. In a May 6, 1975, memo, Brooks said, "The House of Representatives Judiciary Committee chairman has credited our coverage of apparent open meetings laws violations by the [university] Board of Curators for what appears to be the curators' subsequent decision to abide by the law. . . . It led to an investigation by the lieutenant governor . . . and the intro- duction of legislation to specifically include the university in the open meetings law."

Brooks remained in the job as of 2007, making him the most experienced member of the state capital journalism corps. Many of Brooks's former students later found employment as state capital correspondents. His reputation for curt- ness scared some students, but most adapted to his high standards and the can- did commentary that accompanied that style. Laetitia (Tish) Thompson, a broadcast major, studied with Brooks during 2000. In retrospect, Thompson said admiringly that Brooks is "a truly insane genius. . . . I spent three semesters [in Jefferson City], mostly without earning credit, learning how to cover state gov- ernment, and it has singlehandedly helped me more than anything else I learned at Mizzou. Phill made me cry almost every single day, but no one else has since. No one scares me, no one intimidates me, no one can simply write me off, be- cause Phill gave me nerves of steel."

To head the urban reporting center in St. Louis, Fisher hired Spencer M. Allen, a veteran radio and television journalist. The first group of students reported their stories about the past, present, and future of cities during the fall 1972 semester, operating from a room on the University of Missouri–St. Louis campus. Despite the opportunities for real-world training in understanding urban dynamics, the St. Louis semester expired during one of the periodic Journalism School budget cuts mandated by the university administration in response to lower-than-desired legislative appropriations and tuition income.

The Missouri Journalism School established its presence in New York City as the twenty-first century opened, with a summer program designed primarily by Mary Kay Blakely, a magazine faculty member, the author of three book-length memoirs plus dozens of features for national publications as a staff writer and a freelancer. Blakely had moved to Columbia from New York City in 1997 but used her connections to the New School University in Manhattan so that Missouri journalism students could attend lectures there while interning elsewhere in the five boroughs for most of the week.

A supervised New York City presence harked back to the 1970s, when Missouri Journalism School students could spend a semester in the city with science writer-editor David Hendin. Joye Patterson, the talented, self-effacing science journalist on the faculty at the time, persuaded Hendin to supervise students in New York City despite the lack of payment for him in the Journalism School budget. Hendin, who had earned his bachelor's degree in biology from the University of Missouri followed by a master's degree from the Journalism School in 1970, had succeeded quickly after moving to New York. He wrote a column called "The Medical Consumer" syndicated around the nation, plus gained employment at the Newspaper Enterprise Association as the organization's science editor. When students studied with Hendin during a New York City semester, they received assistance from him in publishing their writing. What began modestly became another example of the Missouri Method at work, transported to New York City. Patterson also arranged an internship in Washington, D.C., for graduate students at the weekly magazine *Science News*.

But as the Missouri Method expanded across the globe, pressure was building on the home campus to bolster the academic research component of the Journalism School. That pressure threatened to compromise traditions dating back to 1908.

Nine

The Dilemmas of Scholarship in a Vocational Setting
Master's Degrees and PhDs

The multiplicity of distant programs with faculty from the Columbia campus in residence set the Missouri Journalism School apart from the rest of the university: the international sites in London, Brussels, Jerusalem, Sydney, Buenos Aires, Moscow, and additional locales, depending on the decade and the political climate; the Washington, D.C., semester supervised by full-time faculty; the New York City opportunity guided by a faculty member sent there for the summer; the Jefferson City and St. Louis news bureaus. All that academic glamour contained a downside, however. For pedagogical and budgetary reasons the Journalism School needed to fit as comfortably as possible within the larger university, but its renown and its perceived vocational training caused uneasiness within the academic community from the beginning.

It is easy to understand the discomfort and even dismay of faculty members with PhDs in academic disciplines across the campus as they saw the appointment of a founding dean without a college education or heard about faculty without doctorates or teaching experience hired directly from newsrooms and advertising agencies and public relations firms.

The discomfort and dismay set in early as faculty from other disciplines realized that the new Journalism School would not immediately offer a master's degree or a doctoral curriculum. Furthermore, the Journalism School stood out even among professional/vocational colleges within the university. After all, law faculty had earned law degrees and medical faculty had earned medical degrees in addition to their bachelor's degrees. Each of those professional schools had established itself on the campus in 1872, allowing their faculty to think of the Journalism School as an upstart interloper.

The tension that arose within the university setting did not surprise those in the fledgling Journalism School. Because no university was offering a graduate-level journalism degree in 1908, it was obviously impossible to hire anyone with such a degree for the journalism faculty. For the most part, however, women and men with advanced degrees in other subjects did not possess the practical experience to teach the Missouri Method effectively. The conundrum did not dissolve quickly or easily.

Ultimately, tacking a master's degree onto the bachelor of journalism curriculum proved relatively easy within the university's rules. Maurice Votaw received the first master's degree in 1921. Born in Eureka, Missouri, Votaw moved to Columbia during 1915 with his family, entered the Journalism School, and received his bachelor's degree at age nineteen. After graduating, he reported briefly for a newspaper in McAlester, Oklahoma, then spent a year teaching journalism at the University of Arkansas. He returned to Columbia with a plan to earn a master's degree in journalism. Professor Frank Martin listened, agreed, and eased the path for Votaw. Two graduate-level journalism courses existed then—Newspaper Making and Journalism Research. In addition, Votaw completed history courses at the university. He wrote his thesis about the content of educational magazines.

Williams did not vehemently oppose creation of graduate study within the Journalism School, but he harbored doubts. At one point, Williams commented, "It is as true today as it has been since 1908 and the beginning of journalism schools that, though students may write many dissertations on libel, one libel suit filed against the paper they are editing teaches a whole student body a great deal more about libel than any number of dissertations it might write."

Establishing a doctorate within the Journalism School proved more controversial than creating the master's degree. Faculty and administrators in other disciplines wondered if journalism carried enough intellectual heft to award a PhD. In 1931, the Journalism School faculty recommended a PhD plan that included "six semesters of advanced courses without serious interruption, together with a dissertation. Before being admitted to the preliminary examinations, the candidate must give evidence of ability to translate French and German on sight." University of Missouri officials eventually approved the plan.

In 1934, the Journalism School awarded its first PhD to Robert Lloyd Housman (BJ 1922, MA 1925). Housman's doctoral research traveled in two directions: "Early Montana Territorial Journalism as a Reflection of the American Frontier in the New Northwest" and "Confidential Survey of Administration, Problems, and Function of the *St. Louis Post-Dispatch*."

Before earning his doctorate, Housman decided he wanted to settle into the academic world. During 1925, as Housman was about to complete his master's degree, a journalism teaching position opened at the University of Montana. Walter Williams wrote the dean there, A. L. Stone, with information about four candidates known to him. Of Housman, Williams said, in part, "He is scholarly, accurate, dependable, a brilliant writer and I think would make an excellent teacher. He is a Jew, though not over-aggressive." Housman overcame whatever anti-Semitism might have existed in his case. He obtained the job at Montana, where he remained eighteen years, eventually serving as the school's director.

Perhaps unsurprisingly in a nation beset by anti-Semitism, other references to the Jewishness of students arose in correspondence. In 1940, Dean Frank Martin recommended student Stanley Zabowsky for an internship at the *Hannibal Courier-Post*. "Mr. Zabowsky is not Jewish as his name might indicate, and is of presentable appearance," Martin told his contact.

Even though its graduates were making their mark throughout academia, the Missouri Journalism School seemed nearly invisible in scholarly circles for a long time. The small number of dissertations that emanated from the school following Housman's struck scholars elsewhere as more descriptive than theory-based, as more about journalism than evidence of thinking about journalism, the result of persistence rather than intellectual heft.

Perceptions about scholarship at the Journalism School began to change after the appointment of Frank Luther Mott as dean in 1942. With Walter Williams and Frank Martin both dead, the university administration saw its first opportunity to appoint a Journalism School dean who had not been present at the creation. Mott, with both a doctorate and award-winning books on his résumé, looked like someone the university's nonjournalism faculty would accept as a fellow scholar.

Born in 1886 near What Cheer, Iowa, where his family published the newspaper, Mott later helped his father at the Audubon, Iowa, newspaper, before entering Simpson College in Indianola, Iowa, and eventually transferring to the University of Chicago, where he earned a bachelor's degree in 1907. He then joined his father in editing the Marengo, Iowa, newspaper. On his own, Mott edited the *Grand Junction (Iowa) Globe*. Relentlessly curious and drawn to the classroom as well as the newsroom, Mott earned a master's degree in 1919 from the University of Chicago and a doctorate in 1928 from Columbia University.

Mott taught at Marquand School for Boys at Brooklyn while in New York City. Then he returned to his childhood and adult professional passion, becoming journalism dean at the University of Iowa in 1927. He served as editor of the scholarly *Journalism Quarterly*. By the time of his appointment as dean at Missouri, Mott was fifty-six years old and had served as president of the American Association of Schools and Departments of Journalism. He had also won a Pulitzer Prize for his multivolume history of American magazines.

Howard Rusk Long (BJ 1930, MA 1941) came to know Mott well. First as manager of the Missouri Press Association, then as a young University of Missouri faculty member, finally as a confidant of sorts, Long bonded with Mott. In 1968, Long published a slim book, *Frank Luther Mott: Scholar, Teacher, Human Being*. Long called Mott "the greatest scholar I have ever known."

By temperament, Mott did not fit well into a deanship, especially given what Long termed his "obsession that he would not live to finish his great work, [his] history of American magazines. In my opinion, his acceptance of the deanship at the University of Missouri was a deliberate choice between the professional advancement his accomplishments already had earned for him and the fulfillment of his dream. The offer from Missouri was the great professional prize of his day. There were factors of salary and prestige that no responsible man could overlook."

After absorbing Mott's memoir, *Time Enough: Essays in Autobiography*, Long commented, "There are two observations to be made about this exercise in self-revelation. The first of these is that if Frank Mott said an unkind word about any person with whom he had been associated during his life, I did not find it. It occurs to me that the device of preparing a series of essays was adopted for the express purpose of leaving himself free to eliminate from the record the unpleasant incidents of his life. That administrative work in an institution of higher learning brought few real pleasures to Frank Mott and many days and weeks of unpleasantness is no secret. In his personal life there were the usual sorrows, and his professional life certainly encountered its share of frustrations and disappointments. But of these things he wrote not at all."

Long criticized Mott on one count—for failing "to place in proper perspective the role of his wife, Vera Ingram Mott." Long considered Vera "a scholar in her own right." Mott responded to the criticism, according to Long, by agreeing that "he had not done justice to Mrs. Mott, and then explained it had been her wish to be left out of the published work, except for casual references, when they seemed appropriate."

All in all, Mott came across more dramatically as a speaker than as a memoirist. "There was a bit of the ham in Frank Luther Mott," Long said. "He recognized it himself, made no apologies for it, and exploited at every opportunity this side of his personality as an outlet for the intellectual energy which seemed always during his waking hours to be at the boiling point." Mott also became known for what Long called "small affectations," such as bow ties and unusual academic hoods worn at campus ceremonies, including "a flaming red and white creation."

Although he encouraged research within the Journalism School faculty, Mott did not advocate as aggressively as he perhaps should have for more comprehensive graduate-level journalism education. He worried that editors and reporters in newsrooms across the United States would consider such courses irrelevant and maybe even effete, thus reducing their confidence in journalism education.

In the magazine of the American Society of Newspaper Editors, under the headline "Education for Journalism: A Four-Point Creed," Mott wrote, "I have long refrained from public discussion of education for journalism, its problems and its philosophy. When I entered this field thirty years ago, schools of journalism were very often under attack, and I felt strongly that we teachers were likely to come out second best in a debate with the editors who did not like us, and that our best answer was to show what the schools could do. I thought our real defense was not in words but in accomplishments. So fixed in my mind has this thought become over the years that I had some hesitation when asked to write this piece. . . . But . . . I find a satisfaction in setting down here for my friends at ASNE in four succinct paragraphs my philosophy of education for journalism. And to make it look more like a 'creed,' I shall number the paragraphs."

In paragraph one, "Liberal Arts and Sciences," Mott said that his father had commented repeatedly that "a newspaperman must know everything." Mott's father also provided this quotation from Benjamin Franklin: "The author of a gazette ought to be qualified with an extensive acquaintance with languages, a great easiness and command of writing and relating things clearly and intelligibly and in few words. He should be able to speak of war both by land and sea, be well acquainted with geography, with the history of the time, with the several interests of princes and states, the secrets of courts and the manners and customs of all nations." Given those influences on him, Mott said, "I have always been fully committed to thorough grounding in the liberal arts and the sciences for anyone preparing for a career in journalism."

In paragraph two, "Specialized Training," in a sentence that sounds like Mott was writing in 2008 rather than six decades earlier, he said that "in this technological age no educational system does its full duty if it does not provide specialized training calculated to prepare the student to make his maximum contribution to society. In other words, he must be trained to know, and also to make use of what he knows. . . . The old-timers used to say that newspaper techniques could be taught only in a newspaper office under non-institutional control. This was pure nonsense, but the old-timers clung to it honestly because they had not been trained in journalism schools and they knew they were pretty good. . . . That does not contradict the principle that basic techniques properly correlated with courses in the arts and sciences in a good journalism school is, after all, the best preparation."

In paragraph three, "Selected Curriculum," Mott commented that "one of the chief services that a school of journalism offers is that of providing a curriculum," mixing just the right courses "after much study and experimentation."

In paragraph four, "Study of Journalism," Mott wrote of his desire to "inculcate in students a respect for their chosen profession. We are not training hucksters. . . . We believe the ethical standards of the journalism of the future will be set mainly by our graduates."

Mott did not hold back on his own research, no matter what he thought about the quantity and quality of the work other researchers produced. While serving as Mott's guide during a quest to meet journalists in all 114 Missouri counties, Long realized that the awards heaped upon Mott for his research had failed to tame the dean's insecurities.

"In our rolling classroom, I suffered with Frank Mott through the revision of his [book] *American Journalism* and received my first insights into the professional jealousies of the scholarly world," Long said. "Dr. Mott was particularly sensitive about the unfavorable implications in the review of the first edition prepared by a man he had known while working on his research in the Library of Congress. There was some overlap in their interests and the other chap had beaten him into print, no small incident in itself. The comparatively small number of minor errors in the first edition were a source of chagrin. Actually the book was remarkably clean and most of the bugs Mott had already discovered for himself. But long after this work was accepted as in a class by itself, an occasional letter of correction would come to his office in Neff Hall, directly from his critic or forwarded by the publisher. Each such communication became a hair shirt to be brooded over, checked against the sources, and discussed with his intimates until torn to shreds."

As Mott improved *American Journalism* with each new edition, Long decided it deserved to be called a classic. "Frank Mott, I am convinced, had read everything in print remotely related to the subject of journalism, and his ability to reach into the recesses of his mind for the appropriate reference to this book or that article represented what he was known to refer to as 'full and ripe scholarship.' Early in his career he began to compile lists of important books on journalism, not the best necessarily, he said, but the one hundred books on the subject which appealed to him most. . . . With each new edition, there were always some changes. New books were added and there were usually a few reappraisals of books previously included or omitted."

The book list became the basis of Mott's Journalism School research-oriented course, the Literature of Journalism. He taught it weekly, with his home on Cliff Drive as the meeting place and Mrs. Mott serving tea with refreshments. Shelves on three walls of the home classroom held about six thousand books. He limited enrollment to master's and doctoral students, who tended to speak highly of the course's rigor.

Karen Kuntz List (BJ 1970) earned a master's and doctorate away from the University of Missouri, entered academia at Pennsylvania State University, instructed classes at the University of Wisconsin and University of Rhode Island, then returned to the Journalism School to teach history. List evaluated Mott as a teacher for a publication timed to the centennial of his birth.

She concluded that Mott succeeded in the Literature of Journalism course at his home "because he was a scholar in the true sense of the word. . . . Mott had read all of the books [on his shelves] and everything else remotely related to journalism and early on had begun to compile a master list of those books that appealed to him most. That list became the basis for the literature course. The unstructured class consisted of three or four students' presentations each week. Each began with a biographical sketch of a journalist, then a critical analysis of his work. Mott's presence weighed heavily because he either had written about those early journalists himself or was in correspondence with those still living. His memory was encyclopedic, and it was not unusual for him to interject 'I may be wrong about this, but if you look at page three hundred ninety-two . . . ' He was not wrong. He was also likely to jump from his chair, delve into a file and retrieve a letter or memo from the journalist being discussed."

Mott's immersion in the literature of journalism "inspired his students," List discovered. "Many went to great lengths to impress him, working harder than they ever had worked before, some presenting their material without notes, as he did. The catch was that Mott expected that. He thought everyone should be as involved in journalism history as he was, so he accepted superior performance as his due. To the slackers, he showed no mercy."

In a large class like History and Principles of Journalism, taught to perhaps five hundred students over two semesters, "Mott was not at his best," List commented. "One of his contemporaries said that he was just too much for the typical undergraduate, and that H and P was a dreadful ordeal." Except for the H and P lectures, Mott delegated instruction to teaching assistants, who kept track of attendance and graded "the infamous ten- to twelve-page objective tests filled with multiple choice, true/false and matching questions from [Mott's book] *American Journalism*. 'Who was the first reporter to be kissed by Lincoln?' students were asked. And they were prepared to indicate on which side Greeley parted his hair."

Mott admired Greeley so thoroughly that he made a study of the legendary editor's characteristics; in the lecture hall, Mott might transform himself into Greeley—the squeaky voice, the fretful conversation, the flapping arms, the shuffling walk. After William Howard Taft began teaching H and P, Mott would come out of retirement for the Greeley lecture. Mott "had suffered a heart attack, and Taft worried that as he hopped across the stage illustrating Greeley's 1872 stagecoach trip west, he might collapse. But his enthusiasm carried him through," List said.

One of Mott's exercises in H and P stayed with students, in spite of their overall negative evaluation of the class. Frank Mangan (BJ 1948) recalled his first day in the class during 1946. "Dean Mott began by stressing the importance of getting our facts correct, honing our powers of observation necessary to become real journalists. In the middle of Mott's lecture, an angry young man in the audience leapt onto the stage shouting obscenities and pummeling the dean. Turns out that this display was a setup so that Mott could later ask his students to write a news story describing exactly what happened. But the plot thickened when a returning GI . . . figured that Mott's life was in danger, jumped up on the stage, and began beating the hell out of the attacker. At first, the students didn't know what to think. Then it all sunk in and the audience roared. Mott got up off the floor, brushed himself off, and had a good laugh, too."

Mott did not generally make himself accessible to students, holing up in a library or at home. Still, his generosity toward students could astound. Donald R. Flynn (BJ 1952) ran out of personal funds at the end of 1951, the middle of his senior year. He began withdrawing from his classes. Mott called him in to talk. Embarrassed, Flynn admitted his financial problems. Then, according to Flynn, Mott said, "I don't know you very well, do I? I don't know you at all." That was true, Flynn replied, telling Mott they had crossed paths only in the History and Principles lecture, "but of course the classes were large, and we hadn't had a chance to get acquainted." Then, to Flynn's surprise, Mott advised against quitting and offered the student fifty dollars. "It was a great deal of money to me then . . . but it was more than money . . . it was encouragement," Flynn wrote Mott later. Mott never asked for repayment. Five years later, Flynn, while employed at a Topeka, Kansas, newspaper, repaid the loan anyway.

Students tended to respect and like Mott as a human being, if not necessarily as a classroom instructor. On Mott's sixty-fifth birthday, the History and Principles students arranged for a telegram to arrive during class time. After reading the telegram and receiving an ovation from the students, Mott addressed personal remarks to the class: "I am not retiring, I am not resigning. . . . At least twenty-five years ago, I began a historical study of American magazines. Three volumes of this work have been published and three more remain to be written and published. I don't think anybody else will do it if I don't."

Mott's opinions as expressed in class sometimes caused trouble. On December 24, 1946, George Seldes, who was serving as editor of the newsletter *In Fact* after having completed a noteworthy newspaper career, wrote to University of Missouri President F. A. Middlebush. "For many years now, students of journalism at the University of Missouri have reported to me on remarks made by Professor Frank Luther Mott, ranging all the way from biased criticism to falsehood and libel," Seldes said. "More than a year ago, I wrote you about a published statement by Professor Mott, which was libelous. I received a note from your secretary saying you were away, but would reply. When I received no reply, I wrote you again, and you did not [so] much as reply to this serious charge. I am now informed that the other day Professor Mott in a lecture in his History and Principles of Journalism class again attacked me, saying that my book *The Facts Are* should be called 'The Facts Aren't' and paying special attention to my report on the press attacks on George Washington."

Seldes wondered why Mott had singled him out for criticism. "My statement was documented. It quoted the most reliable source in America, the dean of historians, Charles A. Beard. . . . Dr. Mott is entitled to his opinion of me and my books. He has all the rights of a critic. But he has no right to lie about me or my books, or to libel me, or to be unfair or unjust or dishonest."

Middlebush replied on December 27: "If you feel that you have a legitimate basis for a libel suit against Dean Mott or any other member of the staff of the University of Missouri, the courts are open to you. Needless to say, this office does not attempt to be such a tribunal." Seldes wrote again to Middlebush on January 2, 1947: "I am amazed by your reply. You have a professor at your university who has lied about me. Whether or not I have a libel suit depends on a thousand legal technicalities, and besides, I have not the money to sue him or anyone else who has libeled me in the six years I have been publishing my week-ly exposing falsehood in the press. The reason I wrote you is because I was un-der the impression that there was such a thing as ethics in the teaching profes-sion, and that universities were devoted to the spreading of truth, not dirty little remarks and personal prejudices." Seldes never received satisfaction.

When serving as an administrator instead of a classroom teacher, Mott need-ed to make difficult decisions about hiring and might have missed the special qualities of some candidates. In 1946, Mott decided against hiring a young ap-plicant named Scott M. Cutlip, who was specializing in public relations. Upset at what he called the first job rejection of his career, Cutlip wrote an anguished letter to Mott on August 9, 1946. Six years later, while teaching at the Universi-ty of Wisconsin, Cutlip helped write what would become a big-selling public re-lations textbook. As a Wisconsin professor, and later as journalism dean at the University of Georgia, Cutlip played a leading role in establishing public rela-tions as an academic discipline. The Missouri Journalism School would come late to meaningful public relations instruction; Cutlip might have altered that short-coming.

Like deans before and after him, Mott had to reckon with the desire of African Americans to become part of the student body, staff, and faculty. If Mott advo-cated for nondiscriminatory treatment of African Americans, no evidence has surfaced, and he does not appear to have served as an enthusiastic advocate for better treatment of women in the Journalism School.

It appears, however, that Mott became the first dean forced to publicly con-front the treatment of homosexuals within the Journalism School. The big pic-ture regarding homosexuality is difficult to determine, because it is impossible to know which students, staff, and faculty publicly identified themselves as gay. Mott's specific dilemma involved Emery K. Johnston (BJ 1922, MA 1928), who had served on the advertising faculty for twenty-four years when his sexual ori-entation became widespread public knowledge.

Based on vague references in archives, it seems quite likely that some Journal-ism School faculty, staff, and students suspected Johnston's homosexuality. But given his skills as a classroom teacher, administrator, and researcher, it mattered little, as long as he kept his private life separate from his faculty duties.

Johnston's situation changed during May 1948, after his arrest by police. The *Columbia Missourian* headline read, "Three Men Fail to Raise Bail, Remain in Jail on Morals Charge." The *Columbia Daily Tribune* headline the same day said, "Johnston Is Off University Teaching Staff / Is Relieved of Duties Pending Ac-tion by Board of Curators." Police told reporters that an investigation of an "al-

leged homosexual ring" involving perhaps thirty-five students, Columbia busi-
nessmen, and out-of-towners had begun several months earlier. The specific
charge against the fifty-year-old Johnston: sodomy. He shared the local jail with
his roommate (a thirty-nine-year-old Columbia businessman) and a Rolla man
employed training World War II veterans in farming techniques.

Johnston pleaded not guilty. University officials did not wait for a trial to determine innocence or guilt. Within a week of Johnston's arrest, he no longer
could call himself a faculty member. His lawyer, Edwin C. Orr, blasted the university's curators as "cowardly."

In November 1948, Johnston changed his plea to guilty just before a sched-
uled trial, apparently to spare other homosexuals embarrassment and perhaps loss
of their jobs. At the sentencing hearing, Mott and other Journalism School personnel testified to Johnston's excellent professional standing; they urged against
a prison term for Johnston. The judge granted four years of probation.

During 1948 and 1949, University of Missouri administrators tried to ferret
out other homosexuals on campus. The hunt turned ugly. Willard L. Eckhardt,
a law professor, asked the university president for permission to resign as chairman of the Committee on Discipline. He found little time to teach, and no time
for academic research, Eckhardt said. "The investigation of homosexual activities among students took all other available time, including evenings, Sundays
and holidays. Individual cases took twenty hours or more . . . talking to the students concerned."

After Johnston's departure, there is no evidence that open discussion about the
sexual orientation of students, staff, and faculty in the Journalism School occurred for decades. That began to change during the 1980s, as the gay rights
movement encouraged students, staff, and faculty to end their secretiveness.
Without fanfare, the Journalism School admitted openly gay students and hired
and promoted openly gay staff and faculty.

Mott's ardor for the quality of education at the Journalism School never lessened, but his satisfaction in the dean's role diminished noticeably. Although still
vigorous, Mott stepped aside. Earl English, another former University of Iowa
scholar, succeeded Mott as dean in 1951. Mott continued on the faculty as a
teacher and researcher until his death during 1964. He read a lot, wrote for publication, baked delicious apple pies, and corresponded regularly with former students and faculty.

Again, by hiring English, the Journalism School attracted a dean with a doctorate and a desire to give scholarly research greater emphasis among a faculty

drawn mostly from newsrooms, advertising agencies, and public relations positions.

A typography expert, English was born during 1905 in Lapeer, Michigan. He received his bachelor's degree from Western Michigan University in 1928, working part of the time as a printer and reporter for the *Kalamazoo Gazette.* English taught journalism in the public schools of Peoria, Illinois, for seven years, doubling as the track-and-field coach. During that stretch, he married Ceola Bartlett. They eventually became parents to two daughters. He loved hunting and fishing, making trips all over the Midwest and around the globe to see what he could catch. Fine cigars and sports cars pleased him, too.

High school students across the nation came to recognize English's name after Iowa State College (later University) Press published his *Exercises in High School Journalism,* which went through six printings in seven years. Revised as *Scholastic Journalism* with Clarence W. Hach, the book sold well year after year starting in 1950, supplementing English's salaried income.

Leaving Illinois, English earned a master's degree in journalism and a doctorate in psychology from the University of Iowa, where he simultaneously taught from 1937 until 1945, when he followed Mott from Iowa to the University of Missouri faculty.

English took a leave from campus life during 1946–1947 to serve as executive secretary of the American Council on Education for Journalism. In that job, he formulated accreditation standards; by visiting campus after campus, he accumulated so much information about journalism education that a deanship might have seemed inevitable. English became associate dean of the Missouri Journalism School in 1949, training for two years under Mott.

Before, during, and after his deanship, English contributed to the research/intellectual component of the Journalism School in many ways, including his interest in teaching general semantics for journalists. A course description said, "A new branch of empirical natural sciences as formulated by Alfred Korzybski dealing generally with the linguistic and semantic mechanisms which condition knowledge, activities and adjustment in life. Application is made to the journalist's problems of language-fact relationship, orientation, verifiability, evaluation, predictability and abstracting." Along with English's passion for the subject matter, he believed administrators "should teach in the classroom, if at all possible, in order to keep in touch with faculty-student problems."

English became renowned as a teacher and scholar of linguistics. As a result, he received inquiries such as this one from Celia Beshkin of Farrell, Pennsylvania: "I have been informed that your school sanctions the use of the word ain't in speaking, but not in writing. Is this so?" English replied, three days later, in full, "It ain't so."

Missouri newspaper publishers, always an important constituency, tended to warm up to English after expressing initial doubt about another doctorate holder winning the deanship. As Taft commented in his Missouri Press Association history, "Throughout his career at Missouri, English was closely involved with state papers, their publishers and editors. It was not unusual for English to drop in on a community publisher and eventually edge his way to the back shop, where he demonstrated his knowledge of the Linotype as well as other printing equipment. There was a time when the MPA supplemented English's salary to insure his continuation as Missouri's dean. To some publishers this developed a closer relationship with the school than through conversations with a nationally famous Pulitzer Prize winner."

English's solid support within the university administration and among Missouri news organization owners allowed him to weather the most sustained campuswide student unrest ever. The 1960s produced political and cultural protests across campus; some of the upheaval infiltrated the Journalism School. A substantial portion of the faculty warned students against direct involvement in campus politics, because it might compromise their reporting and editing for the *Missourian* and KOMU-TV and might complicate their job searches after graduation.

Occasionally, a journalism student protesting matters outside the school became part of the news. The highest profile case involved Barbara Papish. Papish began the master's program during 1963, proceeding slowly because of outside interests that spawned political activism and might have contributed to low grades. Visible on campus for years through the local chapter of a national activist group called Students for a Democratic Society, Papish nonetheless pretty much avoided the spotlight until February 16, 1969. On that day, police arrested her and three other students for distributing a publication called the *Free Press Underground* on a public sidewalk in front of the campus Memorial Union.

The newspaper included an editorial cartoon depicting police raping the Statue of Liberty. A separate item appeared under the headline "Motherfucker Acquitted," as it chronicled the trial of somebody belonging to a New York group calling itself Up Against the Wall, Motherfucker. Papish, then thirty-two years old, was expelled from the University of Missouri. She sued for reinstatement in U.S. District Court. After hearings and appeals, the Papish case reached the U.S. Supreme Court. During March 1973, a divided court ruled that Papish should be reinstated to her degree program because her First Amendment rights had been violated. William Rehnquist dissented, joined by Harry Blackmun and Chief Justice Warren Burger, who said the university had acted within its institutional rights. Although the Supreme Court ruling did not criticize the Journalism School, it seemed to suggest that a renowned bastion of free speech had allowed one of its daughters to be muzzled improperly.

No matter how intense the student unrest facing English, students recalled English's unflappable attentiveness to their personal situations. Tad Bartimus (BJ 1969), later a feature writer for the Associated Press, encountered the dean because she broke the rules by entering the Missouri Journalism School a semester early, hoping to save scarce tuition dollars. Furthermore, to help pay the bills she was reporting part-time at the *Columbia Daily Tribune*. English, though unhappy about Bartimus's activities, listened carefully, ruled strictly but fairly, and then benevolently monitored her performance until graduation. "Every time I would see him," Bartimus recalled, "he would inquire about my job, brother, courses, job prospects and [ask] 'are you getting enough rest?' He went out of his way to meet my parents when they came to the campus. . . . He honored me by choosing me to escort VIP journalists . . . when they came for visits. He helped me make contacts, and friends, who have lasted the rest of my life. When I was graduated . . . he was the first person to congratulate me. . . . He gave me my chance, and then he gave me his blessing. . . . In all the ensuing years, Dean English has cheered me on."

Faculty recalled English's attentiveness, too. Joye Patterson talked about her interactions with English during her MA and PhD studies at the Journalism School, as well as during her twenty years on the faculty. As a prospective graduate student, she said, "My first stop was the University of Missouri, my first choice based both on a review of the literature . . . and comments from professionals in the field. On arrival . . . I was amazed to find that Dean English had an open-door policy, first come, first served. He was very gracious, described the program briefly, and asked a few discerning questions of me. The unusual aspect of this interview was that in the midst of the discussion, he turned in his chair and looked out the window. I was considerably rattled by this response and began trying harder to make my case for entrance. Later, I would laugh with other graduate students who said they had experienced the same response. We decided this technique was part of his training in psychology. . . . I found him consistently gracious, accompanied by a delightful sense of humor and unpretentiousness."

English's overall decency, combined with the changing tenor of the times, led to the first sincere, sustained effort to welcome African Americans to the student body and the faculty. During the late 1960s, a few administrators, faculty, and staff at the Journalism School began paying nonstop attention to diversity. The Dow Jones Newspaper Fund provided money for minority journalism workshops aimed at high school print and broadcast journalism students, building on earlier summer workshops for high school journalism instructors. Tom Engleman at Dow Jones talked to Robert P. (Bob) Knight, a professor who agreed to lead an urban journalism workshop, with support first from English and then from English's successor, Roy Fisher.

The new dean moved to Columbia from Chicago and could not help but notice the lack of minorities in classrooms—just six blacks among the approximately twelve hundred University of Missouri journalism majors. Dorothy Jean Gaiter (BJ 1973), an African American student from Florida, noticed the whiteness, too. She recalls being on campus three days as a freshman before seeing another African American. Gaiter participated in the founding of *Blackout,* a student newspaper, because she sensed that the already established campus newspaper ignored race-related issues. Despite the challenging atmosphere, Gaiter not only remained for her degree but ended up as a widely recognized feature writer for the *Wall Street Journal.*

The long overdue outreach at the Journalism School to recruit minority students paid off, albeit gradually. In the first year of the urban journalism workshop, 1971, twenty high school students attended, all, by design, from St. Louis and Kansas City. A significant percentage of those minority high school journalists later attended the Missouri Journalism School. For example, D. Michael Cheers, a St. Louis high school student, attended the first workshop. He then enrolled at the Missouri Journalism School, graduated, and went on to a series of good jobs including one at *Jet* magazine. Cheers gave back by returning to the campus as a workshop instructor for a new generation of minority high school students.

Knight, his hardworking assistant Doris Barnhart, and, starting in 1990, broadcast faculty member Anna M. Romero took the lead in planning for and working with the youngsters. Beset by serious illness from a relatively young age, Knight, who joined the faculty during 1965 after earning two degrees from the University of Texas, pushed himself mercilessly to teach his regularly assigned classes effectively, as well as work closely with minority students, high school journalism teachers, and others generally ignored by the journalism establishment. In addition, Knight completed a doctorate at the Missouri Journalism School in 1968. Because of his penchant to say "yes" to everybody, Knight could seem disorganized. He knew it, and chose this inscription for his Post-It notepad: "A clean desk is the first sign of a misguided mind."

Reflecting the breadth of diversity, the Journalism School began terming its outreach effort the AHANA (African American, Hispanic American, Asian American, and Native American) Journalism Workshop. The students arrived not only from all over Missouri but also from other states. Knight located mentors such as Harry M. Williams, who earned a journalism degree from historically African American Lincoln University before working on a master's degree at the Missouri Journalism School. Mark Russell (BJ 1984), an African American student, recalled how Williams "served as a counselor to many. . . . He had more to do with the success of minority students, especially the many African Americans to come through Mizzou, than any other person at the time." Williams eventually left journalism, earned a doctorate in history, and joined the faculty of Carleton College in Minnesota.

The AHANA participants gained hands-on experience by writing and editing stories for the *Urban Pioneer* tabloid distributed within the Journalism School. In 2007, the AHANA workshop harked back to a previous name, the Missouri Urban Journalism Workshop, and opened enrollment to nonminorities as well as minorities. Such efforts earned justifiable applause but did not end the perception of racism at the Journalism School or across the University of Missouri campus.

When Robert L. (Bob) Terrell interviewed for a professorship at the Journalism School in 1976, he sensed institutional racism immediately. Terrell, an African American, had worked at the *New York Post* and *San Francisco Chronicle* and had taught while earning a doctorate at the University of California. He was employed at St. Mary's College in Moraga, California, when he agreed to travel to Missouri for an interview. Columbia looked to Terrell like "the racist Old South." Ready to say no to an offer, Terrell found University of Missouri officials ultimately persuasive when they told him the atmosphere might never change if every minority candidate refused to relocate. Terrell decided he would attempt to serve as an agent of change.

Shortly after his arrival, Terrell noticed racist graffiti about himself in the second-floor men's room in Walter Williams Hall. It remained there for years. Terrell doubted that graffiti about a white professor would have been treated as indelible. He wondered whether university administrators desired a racist atmosphere, creating an image to keep blacks away from campus. "Then they can say, 'Blacks just won't come here.'"

Impressed with many of the students and the opportunities for scholarship,

Terrell remained at the Journalism School ten years, eventually leaving for the University of Colorado. It never ceased to amaze him how the white power structure at the Missouri Journalism School perpetuated itself, even when that control seemed counterproductive in an increasingly multicultural world.

Toward the end of Terrell's tenure at the Missouri Journalism School, it appeared that at least some of the administrators had awakened to the essential truth of his critique about racism. On April 16, 1987, George Kennedy, the associate dean, wrote to the faculty about a meeting he had attended with a dozen black students. "A high proportion, perhaps all, of our black students seem to feel that the School of Journalism is a racist division of a racist university," Kennedy reported. The students said that "the ignorance and insensitivity of the journalism faculty undermines their self-confidence, erodes their self-esteem and leaves them frustrated and bitter."

After Terrell's departure, on March 9, 1990, Bob Knight wrote a letter in his role as chair of the Journalism School's Multicultural Development Committee. Knight had just spoken with Paulette Grimes, a campus equal rights monitor, and Gail Baker Woods, one of the few African Americans on the journalism faculty. Knight told newly arrived Dean Mills that "there continues to be a perception by some of our black students of attitudes and actions in the school that make them feel uncomfortable enough that they want to share those concerns. Those concerns are not extraordinary in nature but they do remind us we should always pay attention. . . . Gail strongly believes—with good reason, it seems to me—that we could be asking for trouble if we don't address the matter quickly. She reminds us that the numbers of AHANA in the school and as pre-journalism students are increasing rapidly (I say, thanks to her efforts) and suggests it's time for action."

Because of its overall reputation as a great journalism school, Missouri attracted minority faculty, despite apprehensions of many about whether they would feel welcome in Columbia. Retention proved to be a problem, however, partly because of actual and perceived racism and partly for reasons that also applied to white faculty: tenure and promotion difficulties, higher salaries offered by competing universities or media companies, a yearning to live in a major metropolitan area, personality clashes with administrators, and the desire to change career paths.

Because minority candidates could sometimes command higher than normal salaries due to the supply-demand equation, the dilemma of pay equity arose again and again. On January 8, 1990, Vernon Stone, chair of the Journalism School promotion and tenure committee, wrote Dean Mills about how much to offer Tim Gallimore. Gallimore, teaching at Indiana University while a doctoral candidate, was already earning more than the Missouri Journalism School salary structure would easily tolerate, Stone said.

Based on national statistics from journalism/communications programs and on local comparables, Stone said Gallimore should be offered no more than the amount being paid to already hired minority faculty member Lillian Dunlap, a well-regarded classroom teacher and television newsroom coach. "How much for affirmative action?" Stone asked. "The school needs minority faculty and should expect to pay a premium. Even so, in this case, the committee recommends a maximum of thirty-eight thousand dollars for an academic year appointment, which is roughly thirteen hundred dollars more for a year than a five percent increase would give him in his present position. More would tend to be racially patronizing toward the candidate and demoralizing to present faculty who make much less."

Gallimore accepted the Missouri Journalism School position, making his mark as a teacher with a reputation for vast knowledge, high standards, and extraordinary strictness. In 1996, with a tenure decision looming, Gallimore asked to be relieved of summer teaching to conduct additional research. Dean Mills granted the request, locating twenty-five hundred dollars to hire a summer course instructor. That extra summer of research was no panacea, however. After yet another wrenching tenure and promotion debate within the Missouri Journalism School, Gallimore departed the faculty in 1997.

Some minority hiring and retention sagas yielded happy endings. Cynthia (Cyndi) Frisby joined the faculty in 1998 after meeting Missouri Journalism School advertising professors Henry Hager and Frederick W. (Fritz) Cropp IV at a professional conference. Before starting graduate school at the University of Florida, Frisby had worked as a software company human resources director. At first, she did not think deeply about Hager's seeming offhand comment that "we've got to get you to come to Missouri." Then Hager called her at home in Florida. He "asked me to just come out to interview. What could I lose? I said, and the rest was history." Frisby presented a guest lecture; when she looked at the students, she could tell "that they were hanging on to every word I spoke. After the lecture, I was bombarded by students asking questions and to be quite honest I was blown away by their level of enthusiasm and interest. Coming from the University of Florida, where my class was simply an elective for most of the students, I was eager to work at an institution where the students really seemed to want to learn. I was also very impressed by the advertising faculty. I read articles by Dr. Esther Thorson. I was in awe of her work, and when we met for coffee I remember feeling like I was meeting a celebrity." A dynamic lecturer with a relentlessly upbeat personality, Frisby won tenure and promotion without difficulty.

The Missouri Journalism School never excluded women from the student rolls, and it hired women into staff and faculty positions from early in its history. Yet no woman received a PhD from the Missouri Journalism School until Mary Jane Rawlins in 1964. Over the years, gender grievances accumulated and sometimes boiled over.

Maurine Hoffman Beasley (BJ 1958) became a leading researcher on women in journalism as a professor at the University of Maryland journalism school. Her research demonstrated that because men froze women out of professional organizations, women often formed separate groups—sometimes enthusiastically, sometime reluctantly or downright angrily. The Woman's National Press Association, begun in 1882, and the League of American Pen Women, begun in 1897, eventually merged to become the National League of American Pen Women. Women hired into newsrooms usually found themselves limited to writing for the female portion of the audience. Helen Thomas of United Press International became highly visible as a Washington correspondent and pushed for gender walls to fall at the National Press Club. Closer to Columbia, the Missouri Women's Press Club, later called Missouri Press Women Inc., formed in 1937. It was an affiliate of the National Federation of Press Women, begun the same year.

The Missouri group initiated the Sara Lockwood Williams Scholarship and Loan Fund to help female journalism students. In 1941, Mary Margaret McBride (BJ 1919) became the first honorary member named by the organization. Born in Paris, Missouri, McBride worked for the Mexico, Missouri, newspaper before reporting for Cleveland and New York City newspapers as well as national magazines such as the *Saturday Evening Post, Cosmopolitan,* and *Good Housekeeping,* not to mention book publishers and radio programs.

"Women and the Media" emerged as an elective course at the Missouri Journalism School during 1980. The course suggested that the faculty cared about expanding the conversation on gender and partially counteracted the periodic accusations of sexism, usually initiated by female students against male professors.

On May 6, 1987, sixteen female faculty members at the Journalism School protested the underrepresentation of women and minorities there. Women held no administrative positions and for the most part were not paid equally with men. Of the fifteen full professors, only one was a woman. A faculty census during 1987 showed forty white males, twelve white females, two black females, two black males, one Asian American, and one Native American.

With the arrival of Dean Mills in 1989, the Missouri Journalism School made new progress toward gender equity. But it was too late to retain accomplished female faculty members—twelve of the sixteen female faculty members who had signed the 1987 petition departed sooner or later under less than contented circumstances.

Some of the female faculty who stayed expressed ambivalence—they did not feel powerless, but neither did they feel equal. Before Earl English's deanship, the number of women on the faculty was so small that a concerted movement seemed futile. As the number of women faculty members increased, they hoped that strength in numbers would bring positive results. It did, but only sporadically.

Karen Kuntz List, for example, became a popular, accomplished journalism history professor. Only three previous professors had taught the History and Principles course on a regular basis—Walter Williams, Frank Luther Mott, and William Howard Taft. When List reviewed the course content, she noticed a mention of only one female. List redesigned the course, focusing on "the notion of freedom of the press in America and how it played out over three centuries. When I talked about individuals," she said, "they included many women and people of color."

Although List respected many of the male faculty, she saw no diminution in the paternalistic attitude of the administrators. List decided the women should talk among themselves about how to alter the balance of power. "Some of us started having lunch together, and the men were very intimidated by that. They wondered what sort of revolution we were plotting," List said.

After Dean Atwater announced his departure date, List served on the search committee to replace him. The leading candidates were men, but many of them were outsiders who felt like "a breath of fresh air" to List. She left for a faculty position at the University of Massachusetts just before the new dean, Mills, arrived.

Mills, like Fisher and Atwater, was hired from outside the Missouri tradition. As he adjusted to his new position, he was dealing not only with problems brought about by a legacy of nondiversity but also with a confusing situation bound up with the shift from a school that had been almost purely vocational to one that was a hybrid of hands-on training and academic research.

Deans Mott and English, both holders of doctorates, certainly had not ignored the primacy of the Missouri Method and had not stopped hiring practitioners without PhDs and sometimes without master's degrees to direct the newsrooms. But they did hire an increasing number of faculty with advanced degrees and established credentials within academia. Then Deans Fisher and Atwater, without advanced degrees themselves, reversed course somewhat, more from inclination than from any animus toward academic research.

During the Mott-English era, perhaps the most conspicuous research hire arrived in 1958, in the person of William (Will) Stephenson. A psychologist with two PhDs from England, Stephenson, born in 1902, entered the United States during 1948 to join the psychology faculty at the University of Chicago and became an American citizen in 1955. Researchers the world over wondered what attracted the Missouri Journalism School to Stephenson and why he reciprocated the attraction. The short answer to the first part of the puzzle is that Earl English, himself a psychologist as well as a journalist, admired Stephenson's research. English approached Stephenson in New York City, where the longtime resident of Great Britain had accepted employment at a commercial firm.

From the Journalism School's perspective, Stephenson understood human communication subtleties in ways that had escaped other researchers. By importing theories and practices from psychology and other disciplines outside journalism, Stephenson helped advance the whole of communications research. Second, he realized how insights gathered from the research techniques he advocated could help corporations understand consumer likes and dislikes and could help the advertising agencies employed by those corporations find the most appropriate images and words to sell products.

Stephenson's Q methodology research technique permitted improved comparison of the relationships among human communication factors. Explained more colloquially, it allowed individuals to demonstrate their subjectivity along a coherent continuum. Within a journalism context, Stephenson would explain, "Researchers should be back-room boys for editors. Their job is to provide new insights that the editors can apply to their publications as they see fit." Stephenson believed that editors should devote attention to the enjoyment news consumers derived from reading, viewing, and listening. He developed his Play Theory of Mass Communications to drive home his contentions.

Keith P. Sanders, an Ohio newspaper sportswriter early in his career, joined the Journalism School faculty in 1967 from the doctoral program and part-time teaching at the University of Iowa. "I knew of Will Stephenson's work and was thrilled that he thought I could fit in," Sanders recalled. "Also, of course, I knew the J-School was the pinnacle of journalism education. In fact, I deliberately chose not to do my doctoral work [at MU] because colleagues elsewhere advised me that fairly universal attitudes about inbreeding would make it next to impossible to ever be hired at MU."

In a 1974 tribute to Stephenson, Sanders wrote that "he is a short, stocky man who bounces more than he walks. His walk, his energy, his productivity, his joy of life belie his seventy-two years of age. Of late he has taken more to wearing sweaters, but his trademark is a bowtie, which goes with his white hair, ruddy face and glasses like tea goes with crumpets. His overall appearance and manner, topped off by his accent, fit nicely with the stereotype most Americans have of the proper English gentleman. His interests include art, music, drama and film. He is particularly partial to Robert Burns and he is fond of wine and sherry."

Sanders acknowledged the critics of Q methodology and Stephenson personally. The critics saw Stephenson as "egotistical, showy, arrogant and impractical. Unlike most people, Stephenson does not beat around the bush, as many of his Missouri colleagues will attest. It is not unusual in a faculty or committee meeting for Stephenson to brand a colleague's argument 'utter nonsense.'"

Donald J. Brenner, another new PhD at the Journalism School, joined Sanders in working closely with Stephenson on Q methodology. Eventually, Brenner put together a consortium of journalism faculty, journalism graduate students, and faculty from other disciplines to study news media credibility using Q methodology. The proposal won a thirty-five-thousand-dollar grant in competition with other research requests coming from all four University of Missouri campuses. The Journalism School had never previously received money from that competition.

With Stephenson influencing so many Journalism School graduate students and faculty to move in a new direction, the hegemony of historical research at the school diminished. Arguably the biggest splash of post-Stephenson scholarship began in 1964, with the arrival of John Merrill. Merrill, born during 1924, lost several years of education to military service, earning his bachelor's degree in English and history from Mississippi Delta State University during 1949. He then completed a master's degree in journalism at Louisiana State University and his PhD in mass communication at the University of Iowa. He joined the Missouri journalism faculty after teaching at Northwestern State College of Louisiana and Texas A&M University.

Blessed with the ability for original thought, a willingness to combat the conventional wisdom, the certainty to engage his critics, and the facility to write groundbreaking theoretical books (such as *The Imperative of Freedom: A Philosophy of Journalistic Autonomy*) faster than most scholars, Merrill became one of the most prolific journalism academics in the life of the discipline. He wrote about the international press, ethics, and newsroom freedom coupled with professional responsibility. The Journalism School basked in Merrill's renown; any school with Merrill on the faculty had to be mentioned as a place where research mattered. When the Journalism School faculty approved one of several new course offerings from Merrill, the summary read in part: "Philosophy of Journalism. . . . Study of areas of philosophy especially related to problems of the journalist, with emphasis on ethics, aesthetics, symbolic logic, political theory and the theory of knowledge."

Merrill could captivate students in classroom lectures and in one-on-one conferences. His faculty colleague Ralph L. Lowenstein said, "John Merrill's distinction as a teacher is primarily based on an unusual ability to force students to think. He is a human catalyst, and he sets up a reaction that almost always leads in the direction of logical, innovative thought. . . . Teaching a student what is known is a quality of the best teachers. Teaching a student to test the old hypotheses and explore the unknown is a quality of a distinguished teacher."

Merrill left the Missouri faculty in 1980 to spend a year at the University of Maryland and then a decade directing the Louisiana State University journalism school. But he missed Missouri for professional and personal reasons and returned to the faculty in 1991. His successful affiliation with the Missouri Journalism School forever changed the atmosphere for hiring faculty members with doctorates. As of 2007, the faculty included twenty-seven professors with doctorates.

Still, finding a satisfying overall balance between teaching and research throughout the faculty remained more complicated than it should have been because of promotion and tenure conundrums. Some of the problems resulted directly from the individuals under consideration for tenure and promotion—they received unfavorable reviews within the Journalism School because of weak teaching, weak service to the greater journalism world, inadequate research, inability to get along with colleagues, misbehavior such as sexual harassment of students, and, occasionally, résumé fabrication or exaggeration.

Other promotion and tenure votes within normally tight-knit Journalism School department faculties could be difficult to fathom. On January 7, 1975, for example, the Editorial Department promotion and tenure panel met. It consisted of five white males—Ralph Lowenstein, Paul Fisher, Dale Spencer, Tom Duffy, and Phil Norman—because so few women had advanced to positions of authority within the faculty at that juncture. During that one meeting, the panel considered promotions for four professors and tenure for two professors. Jane E. Clark, who had specialized in editing a newspaper women's section before joining the faculty, won a recommendation for tenure by a four-to-one vote. Harold (Hal) Lister, who specialized in teaching about community newspapers, lost by a three-to-two vote. Two professors won promotion recommendations—Tom

Duffy (four to nothing) and Ernest Morgan (three to two). Two seemingly exemplary faculty members, Edmund Lambeth and Robert Knight, failed to win recommendations, Lambeth losing four to one and Knight three to two.

Just as nettlesome were cases when scholars on the promotion and tenure committee at the university level closed their minds to considering journalism education a legitimate academic discipline. As a result, the Journalism School faced difficulties with campus promotion and tenure authorities not experienced by other academic units.

On June 10, 1984, Russell C. Doerner, associate professor of advertising, decided to leave the faculty after three years, a stretch that included an ultimately successful but unpleasant tenure proceeding. Announcing that he would become creative director at Gardner Advertising in St. Louis, Doerner said, "It's probably hard for an academic to understand my walking away after having been given tenure, but the whole tenure issue and peer review might be something I can still help you with. Maybe I can be used as an example to make it a bit easier for you to attract and keep talented professionals. As you know, I wouldn't be leaving if the campus tenure committee hadn't turned down my application for tenure. I don't particularly care to have my destiny controlled by others, so I immediately made a few calls. . . . Peer review's fine, but am I the peer of a surgeon with thirty years of experience? Does a chemistry professor even begin to understand the subjective nature of advertising creativity and the inherent problems in trying to quantify the effects of nuances in written and visual persuasion? As for publishing, forget it. The *Journal of Advertising* is a non-publication as far as the advertising profession is concerned."

Doerner emphasized that he wanted to alleviate the tension over tenure and promotion decisions on his way out. "I hope my leaving can provide you with something to use with the provost to make sure it doesn't happen again with the next professional you hire. If his answer is, 'But we gave him tenure,' please remind him his campus committee didn't, at least not at first, because they didn't have the foggiest [idea] what I was about."

Doerner knew about the case of Dick Nelson, who joined the faculty in 1975 after four years at an Oklahoma City television newsroom. In 1982, Nelson, having become news director at KOMU-TV and an assistant professor, received a rejection from the campus promotion and tenure committee. Nelson's seven-year record at the university indicated little research, but then again he was not hired to conduct research given the full-time nature of his positions at KOMU. Furthermore, his classroom teaching load had increased since his hiring. Citing the Journalism School promotion and tenure guidelines in his appeal, Nelson said that if the criteria continued to be interpreted in a certain way by the campus committee, "I submit there will never be a faculty member serving also as a staff member at KOMU-TV who will be granted tenure." The campus committee rejected the appeal, despite vigorous backing of Nelson from Dean Roy Fisher and Associate Dean Roger Gafke. Elmer Lower, Fisher's successor for a year, took up the cause, and Nelson prevailed eventually. Again, however, the Journalism School's relationship with the larger campus had frayed.

Occasionally, those running the campus acknowledged the vagaries of the process that led to bitterness, as in the case of advertising faculty member Donald S. Walli. Walli earned his bachelor's degree from the University of Michigan during 1955, then worked at advertising agencies in Detroit, New York City, and Greenville, South Carolina, before earning a master's degree in 1975 at the University of South Carolina. He joined the Missouri Journalism School faculty later that year. In 1981, Walli received enthusiastic support from Journalism School associate dean Milton Gross as his tenure case ascended to the campus level.

On August 6, 1981, Provost Ronald F. Bunn wrote Chancellor Barbara S. Uehling about the Walli case. As it usually did, the dilemma revolved around scholarly research versus professional creativity. "Whatever differences the [Journalism] School and I might have about the place of disciplined, refereed original research in the intellectual development of those who teach journalism and in the obligations of journalism schools to the professional and scholarly communities, it is unreasonable to expect Mr. Walli to evidence a strong record of activity which he was led to believe to be incidental to his responsibilities," Bunn said. "These are matters that ought to be discussed and resolved as . . . policy."

About professional creativity, Bunn said, it "does not lend itself to precise meaning, not at all surprising given its subjective qualities. Presumably it requires minimally that something heretofore non-existing is done or made. It is not too fanciful also to presume that what is created is deemed to have relevance and merit, though in applying this requirement we enter the realm of considerable subjectivity."

So, Bunn wondered, "Where do we look in Mr. Walli's case to find evidence of creativity? In both his teaching in the curriculum and his service role as an advisor of students and as a supervisor of extracurricular learning he surely had opportunities, indeed obligations, to be creative. The evidence of creativity in his curriculum teaching is, for me, ambivalent. In his extracurricular teaching, evidenced for example by the record of the student team entries in the national marketing and communications competitions, there is a basis for concluding that

Mr. Walli has creative qualities which meet high standards of the professional marketing field."

Bunn conceded that "both Mr. Walli and I are confused as to what we should be looking for as a basis for judging him. For Mr. Walli's tenure to be denied as a result of this confusion is arguably unfair." Bunn told the chancellor he was inclined to reject the no-tenure recommendation: "In this particular case there are circumstances that could warrant an exception to my principled position."

Uehling could not be persuaded. Five days after receiving Bunn's letter, she denied tenure for Walli as "inappropriate. It is a time when we, on the campus, are engaged in significant budget reductions. . . . More than ever, it means that the choice of investing in a continuing salary and tenure appointment must be based on an assessment that the individual has the highest possible probability of making a significant contribution to programs as they develop in the future. I do not believe the case has been made, in the material presented to me, that to provide a tenured appointment to you would be consistent with these goals."

In addition to struggling with tenure and promotion cases, a succession of deans grappled with improving the advertising and public relations realm. Walter Williams had decided that courses teaching the business side of journalism belonged in the school, and that philosophy never changed. How to merge the different cultures successfully became the issue.

Dean Mott's decision to employ Milton E. Gross, somebody without a doctorate, to beef up the advertising curriculum became a turning point. Gross, a Pacific, Missouri, native (BJ 1939, MA 1941), had married classmate Juliet Mayfield (BJ 1940). They left Missouri but wanted to return. In 1942, Gross wrote Mott from the Department of Journalism and Publicity, College of Mines and Metallurgy, University of Texas–El Paso, about joining the Missouri faculty permanently. Mott replied that he wanted to hire a combination researcher and classroom instructor. Gross pointed out that during his graduate studies at the University of Missouri he had "worked with Mr. Martin, Mr. Johnston and Mr. Jones on a three-dimensional study of reader-listener interest in primary media," a research-oriented, sophisticated thesis. Mott took note. Gross was earning two thousand dollars at Texas on a nine-month contract, with another three hundred dollars for teaching summer school. Mott felt constrained by budget problems and offered less; Gross agreed on a pay reduction to join the faculty of his alma mater. He was not the first to accept a pay cut and would not be the last. The Missouri Journalism School, chronically underfunded given its reputation, frequently offered prestige in place of high salaries.

Gross joined Emery K. Johnston and Donald H. Jones on the small advertising faculty. Jones (BJ 1925, MA 1926) taught at the Missouri Journalism School briefly and then worked in the advertising field throughout Texas before entering academia permanently with his return to Missouri in 1937. He remained until his death in 1957.

Ruth Briggs Bratek became the first female member of the advertising faculty. Born in 1923, she graduated from high school in Macon, Missouri, in 1941, attended Central Methodist College for a year, then transferred to the Missouri Journalism School where her older brother, Eugene Briggs, had graduated and another brother, Thomas Briggs, had attended. Their father, Frank P. Briggs (BJ 1915), owned the Macon newspaper. Ruth Bratek, after earning her BJ in 1945, joined her father in Washington, D.C., where he was serving as a U.S. senator. After his electoral defeat, she worked for newspapers in West Plains and St. Joseph, married, and returned to Macon to help run the family newspaper. When she heard about the faculty opening at the Journalism School, she applied; Dean English hired her in 1956. Queen Smith, who joined the Journalism School faculty in 1947 after twenty-three years as society editor of the *Columbia Daily Tribune,* was the only other woman faculty member in 1956. But Bratek said she did not detect gender discrimination or suffer isolation.

While helping the *Missourian* improve the quality and quantity of its advertising, Bratek worked part-time toward a master's degree, completing it in 1964. Mixing quantitative research with commonsense precepts, Bratek concentrated the advertising sales lectures into the opening three weeks of her course, so students would be ready to sell *Missourian* space as quickly as possible. The grocery store advertising market had been untapped; Bratek sold the first grocery advertisement in the *Missourian* herself. She retired in 1985; in the interim, her daughter graduated from the Journalism School.

Achieving the optimum balance of research faculty, advertising/public relations faculty, and journalists at times seemed impossible given budget limitations, shifting student enrollments, and the predilections of each dean. At any given time at least one of the three realms seemed to feel discontentment. The advertising and public relations faculty began to feel ignored after the retirement of Dean English in 1970 (he was a vigorous sixty-five and would live another thirty years, but University of Missouri regulations mandated retirement).

The search to replace English—the first ever conducted by a faculty committee at the dean level—did not go well during the early stages. The search committee consisted of five white males. A preliminary list of desirable candidates contained thirty names—all white males. Roy Fisher's name did not appear on that list. No internal names appeared on the list, either. Chancellor John Schwada rejected the first list of nominees. The search committee members offered to resign. Schwada told them to continue.

As with every other search for a new dean, faculty weighed in on the most desirable qualities. Ruth Bratek raised the question, "Is this the time to break away from the concept of Walter Williams and convert the school into a School of Communications, a trend established in recent years by some other schools of journalism?" No, Bratek answered emphatically. The Journalism School should stick to the "nuts-and-bolts" approach. She seemed to get her wish with the hiring of Fisher. He appeared unlikely to advocate an abstract academic approach.

A 1940 Kansas State University graduate, Fisher had worked on Kansas and Nebraska newspapers early in his career. After serving in World War II, he joined the *Chicago Daily News* in 1945 as a reporter, then shifted to the editing/managing side of the newsroom. During 1949–1950, he spent a year at Harvard University as a Nieman Fellow. In 1959, Fisher left the newsroom for six years to serve as editorial director of the World Book encyclopedia operation, owned by the same Field family that published the newspaper. Fisher returned to the *Daily News* in 1965 as editor in chief. By 1970 he wanted to depart, partly because the future of the newspaper seemed precarious given its role as one of two afternoon dailies in a market dominated by the morning *Chicago Tribune*.

Although a Missouri Journalism School outsider, Fisher had dealt with the institution from time to time. For example, on June 28, 1961, Fisher wrote Dean English about Field Enterprises becoming "a partner in the effort conducted by the National Press Photographers Association and the School of Journalism toward encouraging improvement of photojournalism. As an erstwhile newspaperman and a staff member of the Medill School, I find this association a most natural one. I hope that Field Enterprises can make a constructive contribution to this worthwhile program, not only from the financial standpoint, but from other standpoints as well. It occurs to me that we may be able to use a number of the contest entries in our *Year Book,* which is published each spring. This would not only provide an additional outlet for the photographers who enter the contest, but also a publication fee for each of the pictures we are able to publish."

When Fisher learned during late 1970 that the search committee was considering his candidacy seriously, he faced a dilemma: should he pursue the Missouri job all-out or push for a quick wrap-up to negotiations at Northwestern University, where the campus president appeared ready to hire him as an executive assistant? On December 23, 1970, Fisher wrote newspaper publisher John S. Knight a letter in which he commented that the Missouri Journalism School seemed "beset with many problems. It would require some unusual measures to bring the school back to its former standard, and I am not yet certain that the administration at Missouri is willing to make the necessary commitment." A few months later, Fisher overcame his reservations about the administration's commitment.

Fisher received a congratulatory letter from Elie Abel, dean of the Columbia University Graduate School of Journalism. Like Fisher, Abel had not emerged from academia. "When you dropped your bombshell about leaving the *Chicago Daily News* for journalism education, that had its impact on me, I assure you," Abel said. "Suddenly I felt much less alone in the ranks of journalism deans, I mean the kind with PhDs and other academic credits."

On his first day at the Journalism School, April 1, 1971, Fisher found himself embroiled in a strike by the pressmen at the *Missourian*. He immediately recalled a conversation with acting dean Milton Gross from earlier in the year. "It usually takes two years to find a dean for Missouri," Gross had said. "The problem is finding anyone smart enough for the job who is dumb enough to take it."

Numerous constituencies besides the scholars with doctorates focused on Fisher's appointment, from a variety of perspectives. His relationship with Missouri Press Association members became complicated, for example, even though many of the publishers preferred Fisher's background to that of the deans with PhDs but limited newsroom/front office/back shop experience. Disagreement arose around Fisher's termination of the community newspaper sequence due to low enrollment. Missouri publishers advocating continuation of the sequence pointed out the large percentage of graduates owning newspapers within the state.

Fisher divided the Journalism School into departments—advertising, broadcast, news-editorial—for administrative purposes. That made sense to some faculty and staff. Others felt troubled that less collegiality would result and that Fisher, who possessed a details-oriented, controlling personality, meant to divide and conquer. All three of the initial department chairs were middle-age white males—Frank L. Dobyns in advertising, Edward C. Lambert in broadcasting, and Ernest C. Morgan in news-editorial. None could fairly be characterized as a compliant personality, but none seemed likely to challenge Fisher vigorously in public, either.

Despite his lack of an advanced degree—or maybe to compensate for that lack—Fisher appointed longtime professor William Howard Taft as the school's first associate dean for graduate programs and research. Taft (BJ 1938, MA 1939, and holder of a doctorate) had served as chairman of the school's graduate stud-

ies committee since 1970. In a news release dated August 18, 1980, Fisher noted that "the new position reflects the increased emphasis the school has placed
on graduate studies in recent years. Currently two hundred seventeen master's
and seventeen doctoral candidates are enrolled in its programs, including those
at off-campus centers in Jefferson City, Washington, D.C., London, Taipei,
Hong Kong and Jerusalem."

The faculty approved changes in master's degree requirements while Fisher
served as dean. Students had to complete thirty-six credit hours instead of thirty-
two. The core curriculum became the News and Editing Practicum for no credit (waived for students with certain experience levels), followed by Mass Media
Seminar, Newspaper Editing, Dynamics of Advertising, History of Mass Media,
Journalism as Communication or Research Methods, a graduate-level reporting
course, plus research hours needed to complete a scholarly thesis or a rigorous
but less academically oriented professional project. The new requirements beefed
up scholarship for master's degree candidates who thought they might become
professors in the future, while allowing those planning on newsroom or adver-
tising/public relations careers to make themselves as prepared and attractive as
possible to potential employers.

Those who criticized Fisher for his alleged lack of interest in scholarship certainly did not criticize him for any lack of interest in the physical plant of the
Journalism School. Gannett Hall became a reality during Fisher's administration,
as he helped raise money from the media company and other sources, worked
within the university bureaucracy to spend that money on a new building quickly rather than dawdling, then played a major role in the design and construction
of the building attached to Neff Hall. He termed it a scientific machine, with
"electronic marvels of modern education and modern broadcast communications—the most sophisticated film, videotape and sound equipment, new concepts of lecture hall construction."

Fisher enjoyed planning the building. It seemed as if he had memorized every
aspect of the architectural drawings. His ironclad memory for building details
surprised many who dealt with Fisher on a regular basis because of an irritating,
although almost certainly unconscious, problem he demonstrated regularly—
misremembering the names of faculty and staff. Those who came to know Fisher well usually forgave him his difficulties with names because they recognized
the generous spirit beneath the imperious exterior.

Some faculty members seemed irritated with Fisher on a regular basis. On
March 23, 1973, John Merrill complained to Fisher about the second-class treatment of faculty in the seating for the Journalism Week banquet. Fisher's well-

intentioned featuring of faculty awards during the banquet irritated Merrill, too: "It has hurt, not helped, faculty morale, and for some it has completely ruined the banquet, which used to be enjoyable for the faculty as a whole. The contest has made deep scars in our faculty, and certainly there is no evidence that it has stimulated better teaching—maybe more [classroom] showmanship or easier grading, etc. Anyway, I know I speak for most of the faculty when I say that it will be a wonderful day when the [awards] money runs out."

Six days later, Merrill wrote Fisher, "I am utterly flabbergasted by your blunt statement that I am disloyal to the School of Journalism because I wrote you the memo commenting on seating at the J-banquet and other ideas I had about J-Week. You said that I was not universally liked by the faculty (I hope not!), but I would be willing to bet that there are very few who think that I have not contributed at least my share to this school, and I doubt very seriously if they would impugn my loyalty."

Fisher's lack of patience with University of Missouri bureaucrats outside the Journalism School became well known. For example, during 1975 he was trying to achieve reclassification for Rosemary Ward, a staff member in the Journalism School dean's office. Fisher believed that the Personnel Services unit of the university was making the reclassification unduly difficult. After receiving a letter from L. F. Churchill, manager of wage and salary administration, Fisher replied that the ruling "extends a ridiculous situation into the realm of the absurd." Noting that three studies had led to contradictory conclusions about the reclassification, Fisher commented, "If you wish to make another study, please go ahead. I expect there will be still a fourth finding. . . . When you are finished playing games with your manual and are ready to discuss ways by which we can improve the efficiency of this office, I'd be glad to have you come over and talk to me about it."

After Barbara S. Uehling became chancellor of the Columbia campus during 1979, it looked as if Fisher would face difficulties because of his candor and his penchant for independence. She and Provost Ronald F. Bunn began detailed examinations of all the deans' performances. Fisher had enjoyed a comfortable relationship with Uehling's predecessor, Herbert Schooling. For example, when Journalism School faculty members Donald M. Ferrell, a *Missourian* editor with significant previous newsroom experience, and Daniel E. Garvey, a scholar in the broadcasting sequence with television network experience and a Stanford University doctorate, ran into difficulties at the campus committee level with their promotions to associate professor, Fisher persuaded Schooling to grant the promotions.

With Uehling, the personality clash seemed obvious, and rumors of shouting matches spread. Fisher did not deny those rumors to Art Kaul of the *Columbia Daily Tribune,* who reported an in-depth feature about the travails of the deans, with a focus on Fisher; the story appeared on April 12, 1981.

Advertising alumni and students seemed especially discontented, saying Fisher failed to understand their needs, did not care, and demonstrated clear partiality to newsroom operations. Sometimes, it seemed, they forgot Fisher's efforts to expand the advertising faculty and curriculum. During his first year as dean, for example, he labored to raise money for an endowed chair in international advertising. Braxton Pollard (BJ 1930) left a three-decade career in the international advertising department of Monsanto Company to fill the slot for a while. A generous gift from Irwin Vladimir (BJ 1924), who had directed the international advertising agency known as Gotham-Vladimir, paid Pollard's salary.

Fisher never found funding for a permanent endowed chair, however, despite discussions with executives from Monsanto, the multinational chemical company in St. Louis. Correspondence flowed and meetings occurred. Year after year, some detail stood in the way. The Monsanto initiative, in conjunction with the Public Relations Society of America, ended in frustration.

By the 1980s, Fisher seemingly could do no right in the minds of those in the advertising and public relations realms. Frank Waltrip, a doctoral student in advertising, wrote a complaint to the outside team visiting campus to accredit the Journalism School. The letter found its way into *Campus Digest,* a student newspaper, on March 6, 1981. Fisher told the editors that he would not dignify Waltrip's letter with a response.

When the visiting team from the American Council on Education for Journalism granted only probationary accreditation to the advertising curriculum, Fisher's detractors could not resist singing an I-told-you-so chorus. The accreditors pointed to flaws in the content of three classroom courses, too few hands-on selling and production opportunities for the students, minimal career preparation, inadequate laboratory equipment, and the dangers of hiring too many faculty with Missouri Journalism School degrees. The accrediting council granted full status the next year, after the Journalism School added two faculty members, among other changes. But the probationary period damaged morale; it would take a while before recovery could be called complete.

Linda Shipley tried to rectify the situation long-term. She had completed her master's degree at the Missouri Journalism School in 1969 and joined the faculty in 1974. A rare example then of a female faculty member with a PhD and tenure, Shipley became Advertising Department chair at Fisher's request upon the retirement of Frank Dobyns, who had joined the Missouri Journalism School faculty in 1968. When the school established departments in 1972, Dobyns had been the initial Advertising Department chair. He eventually tired of protesting what he considered inadequate staffing and classroom resources.

The timing did not work well for Shipley, because she had to deal with the fallout from the "accreditation fiasco," as she termed it. Shipley did manage to hire Russ Doerner and Gail Baker Woods to bolster the advertising faculty, which for a while had been concentrated in the newspaper world. For example, before arriving at the Journalism School in 1971, Dale L. Gaston's advertising experience came from editing and publishing small newspapers in Oklahoma. Doerner and Woods arrived with direct experience in advertising and public relations. Doerner had helped develop the "Weekends were made for Michelob" theme for a beer account at an advertising agency. Woods added valuable corporate public relations experience, an African American female presence, and a talent for recruiting minorities. Shipley departed in 1984.

Ratcheting up and refining the Missouri Method, the advertising and public relations faculty eventually instituted a campaigns course to expand real-world training beyond media-related work for the *Missourian,* KOMU, and KBIA. The course gave students the chance to interact with corporate, government, and not-for-profit clients such as Duncan Hines, the United Soybean Board, Edward D. Jones stockbrokers, Anheuser-Busch brewery, the Missouri Lottery, and Royal Canin USA pet food. A class working on behalf of Nokia, the cell phone manufacturer, designed television commercials so professionally that two ended up on the air.

Beth Ronsick (BJ 1989) demonstrated the thoughtfulness undergirding the Missouri Method for nonnews students. After graduation, Ronsick worked her way to Ogilvy and Mather in New York, where she developed branding for IBM, Reebok, American Express, Kodak, and Dove. She later moved to Ogilvy Hong Kong to develop talent in the Asia Pacific region. "There's a chicken-egg theory that was discussed during my years in J-School—in the end, don't the media just reflect what the people want? It is a fair question for students to turn over. But as professionals, we know better," Ronsick said. "I can honestly say that if we gave every client what they thought they wanted at the start of a project, then a good number of campaigns would have a giant logo, a shot of a smiling consumer, and a list of product benefits the R&D guys believe to be the Holy Grail. Clients and consumers need guidance to know what they really want."

At the Missouri Journalism School, she said, "you're trained to look at the big picture, to use your investigative and problem-solving skills to discern and address the core issues. Stop thinking about the bottom line and start thinking about what needs to be said. In doing so, you just might create a whole new voice and positioning that allows your work to stand out from the blur. If you really deem yourself an expert in journalism or communications, stand up and act like one, or you'll be nothing more than a vendor."

Fisher exited as gracefully as possible by becoming director of the school's Washington semester during 1983 after a year of working on various projects outside the university. Fisher's resignation letter to Chancellor Uehling said in part: "The school has prospered in many ways. . . . It pioneered programs for extending journalism education to minorities; it developed a revolutionary new curriculum for broadcast journalism; it extended its leadership in international programs; and it offered unique opportunities for professional reinforcement to mid-career journalists. The school handled a challenging enrollment crush in a responsible manner, and it completed the most expensive physical expansion program in its history, largely with private donations. . . . Most importantly, the school has attracted a student body and assembled a faculty that thrive under the severe requirements of the Missouri system—one that combines the best of both applied and theoretical education."

When he retired from directing the Washington semester, Fisher settled in the Chicago suburb of Glencoe. On June 30, 1997, he returned to the Missouri Journalism School with his family (two of his daughters graduated from the Journalism School) for the renaming of the largest classroom in Gannett Hall as Roy Fisher Auditorium. He died in 1999.

The search committee to replace Fisher as dean recommended outsiders Edward Bassett and Del Brinkman as its top choices, but both men—with management experience at other highly regarded journalism programs—withdrew. Faculty, staff, and students wondered why the process of hiring somebody to lead the self-proclaimed best journalism school in the world should run into such difficulty. Were hidden problems preventing a resolution?

Some frustrated faculty turned their attention to insider candidates. On April 20, 1983, Robert W. Haverfield, an advertising professor and the school's placement director, lobbied the campus chancellor for the appointment of Keith Sanders, who was serving on the search committee. "Many of us were disappointed when Dr. Brinkman withdrew from consideration," Haverfield said. "I know that we have scoured the nation for good candidates, and I believe that we have an excellent one right here." Haverfield called Sanders "a nationally known scholar" with an intimate knowledge of the Journalism School.

Suggestions for inside hires were futile. The campus provost and chancellor concluded that it would make sense to hire an interim dean, then start over on the national search. Alumnus Elmer Lower (BJ 1933), who had been employed as a television network news executive at ABC, CBS, and NBC after an early print career, agreed to serve as dean for the 1982–1983 academic year. Born in 1913 in Kansas City, Lower went to the *Trenton (Missouri) Republican-Times* immediately upon graduating, then found a reporting job at the *Louisville Herald-Post,* thanks to the newspaper's police reporter, who had graduated from the Missouri Journalism School a year before Lower. After Louisville, Lower worked for the *Flint (Michigan) Journal,* the United Press in Jefferson City and then Cleveland, and the Associated Press. During World War II he served overseas helping with a psychological warfare effort, then returned to journalism at *Life* magazine before reentering government during the early 1950s as chief of the Information Division in the Office of the United States High Commissioner for Germany.

Lower had never lost contact with his alma mater. He was awarded a Missouri Journalism School honor medal in 1959 and an honorary doctorate in 1975. Starting in 1978 until assuming the deanship, Lower returned to the University of Missouri campus to teach broadcasting courses each fall semester.

With Lower providing stability at the Journalism School, a revitalized dean search yielded James D. Atwater. Another Journalism School outsider, Atwater arrived from *Time* magazine. Missouri Journalism School alumnus Marshall Loeb, a Time Incorporated colleague, suggested that Atwater consider the deanship, a possibility that had not occurred to Atwater previously—although a temporary teaching position at Duke University during 1981 did lead him to think seriously about entering academia.

Atwater first tasted journalism as a high school student working a summer job at the *Springfield (Massachusetts) Union* newspaper. A 1950 Yale University graduate, Atwater obtained an entry-level editorial position at *Time.* The Korean War, during which he served in the Air Force psychological warfare division, interrupted his career. He left the military in 1953, working for *Time* in Washington and Detroit before going to the New York newsroom as a writer in 1957. Atwater shifted to the *Saturday Evening Post* in 1962 and remained there until the magazine folded in 1968. Atwater wrote occasionally for *Sports Illustrated, Esquire, Smithsonian,* and *Reader's Digest;* published a well-crafted novel with Viking; and worked in the Richard Nixon Republican White House, as a Democrat, on drug information programs. He returned to journalism during 1970, when *Reader's Digest* hired him for its London bureau. He rejoined the *Time* staff three years later. Unsurprisingly, the length of the search and the emergence of Atwater renewed the painful discussions about internal versus external candidates, about journalism practitioners versus academics.

Roy Fisher expressed satisfaction with his successor, writing in a private letter dated May 2, 1984, that Atwater "is a sensible man, has an easy understanding of students and what drives them, respect for our business and a determination to keep the Missouri Journalism School the best in the world. In my opinion, we could not have found a better person."

Because his arrival coincided with the Journalism School's seventy-fifth anniversary celebration, Atwater found himself immersed in the traditions, old and new. With great insight, he wrote, "The school is not remarkable simply because it was founded earlier than any other. As the new boy on campus, I soon discovered that the secret of this place is the fact that it is restless—that it is not content, that it worries a great deal about how it might improve what it is doing and what new projects it should be taking on. . . . So it seems to this newcomer that the school has done far more than endure; it has renewed itself without detaching itself from its moorings—no easy task."

Almost from his arrival in Columbia, Atwater unexpectedly suffered health problems that rarely relented. His poor health, combined with stingy budgets from the campus administration and the state legislature, made it difficult to administer the school smoothly. George Kennedy, serving as Atwater's associate dean, seemed to function as the de facto dean much of the time. Almost everybody liked Atwater as a human being, but some faculty members found him bumbling as an administrator, as well as a leader without a coherent vision. They worried that the Journalism School was drifting.

The deanship became Atwater's at a time when scholars at other universities who had earned their doctorates at the Missouri Journalism School were expressing dissatisfaction publicly. Max Utsler, who taught at Missouri from 1972 until 1983, warned Atwater about the continuing bad-mouthing that dated back to the Roy Fisher era. Utsler said, "The Missouri PhD grads are, for the most part, a rather renegade group from the school. They feel unwanted and unloved. They may be. In any case, the PhDs from the past several years have spent more time and effort criticizing the school than promoting it. I have a hard time understanding that. I want other people to know that I graduated from the best school of journalism, not one that was hampered by so many problems. Yet the fact remains—they will likely be your most outspoken and persistent critics. . . . My answer to them has always been, you can't be all things to all people and if we ever had to choose, we'd choose to continue a strong professional program and even disband the PhD program. While I hope it never comes to that, I always keep in mind that the professional experiences are what make the Missouri situation unique."

Atwater replied, "I have had some pressure from the PhDs, as you suggest." But Atwater mentioned facing greater pressure "from people who want to install a public relations sequence. My reply to them is that it is difficult to crank up something new when you are trying to strengthen what you have, but that I would listen to one and all proposals."

The Advertising Department faculty complained during the early years of the Atwater deanship, concerned that he cared about their program as little as Dean Fisher allegedly had. On December 6, 1984, Guy Tunnicliffe, chair of the Advertising Department, complained to the dean that less than full funding to replace two retiring faculty members would emasculate the program. Tunnicliffe had joined the faculty in 1983 after sales experience in private industry and a faculty position at Kent State University.

"These changes will disembowel the advertising curriculum," Tunnicliffe warned his faculty. "This move takes [away] any individuality that the program ever had. It produces a program that is no different than most others and inferior to the good ones. It really is difficult to justify making these enormous changes in a program that was to enjoy the full support of the School of Journalism. If you remember, Jim Atwater said this was to be the year for advertising. Now we are going to have a faculty of four people, two of professorial rank, one instructor and one part-time clinical instructor for approximately two hundred fifty students. The only word that describes this situation is tragic."

Eventually, new faculty joined the advertising ranks. Jim Albright (BJ 1957) joined the Missouri faculty in 1986 after teaching at Southern Methodist University. Before that, his career in the advertising agency realm included conceiving the Doritos snack chip promotion "They taste as good as they crunch." Albright had enjoyed the Missouri Journalism School as a student and felt excited about returning to teach. He introduced a broadcast advertising course that allowed students to write and produce radio and television commercials. He planned to stay for a long time, but university obstacles regarding tenure combined with what Albright perceived as a condescending news-editorial faculty attitude toward advertising caused him to return to Texas, which he had come to think of as home. Albright accepted a faculty position at the University of North Texas, received tenure, and never left there.

Birgit Wassmuth arrived about the same time as Albright and stayed fourteen years. Born in Germany, she arrived at the Missouri Journalism School with a

PhD, strong opinions inside and outside the classroom, plus a directness in her speech that did not always convey diplomacy. A graphics design specialist, with and without computers, Wassmuth tended to make a lasting impression on students. One of them, Tammy Cloutier (BJ 1999), recalled that whatever Wassmuth "was talking about—whether it was designing a logo, paper stock, how certain colors affect the advertisement—was truly represented on her person. She was a walking design. Birgit had a haircut with one side above her ear and one side below her chin. She wore purple every day because she believed that color affects a person. It was neat to see someone who personified everything she was teaching."

The Atwater administration scored a success in the realm of scholarship with the hiring of Robert Logan, who held his MA from the Missouri Journalism School. After obtaining his PhD at Iowa, Logan taught in California and Florida before joining the Missouri faculty during 1986. The opportunity to manage the new Science Journalism Center attracted Logan, as well as the freestanding nature of the school administratively and the chance to work with BJ, MA, and PhD candidates simultaneously. Besides helping the Science Journalism Center thrive, Logan obtained funding and staff for a related endeavor, the Missouri Arthritis Research and Rehabilitation Training Center. In addition, Logan built bridges to the rest of the campus by serving as chair of the Faculty Council, a prestigious and occasionally influential position.

Yet another Atwater administration success arrived with the hiring of Vernon A. Stone in 1987. With a PhD from the University of Wisconsin, Stone brought a modicum of research presence to the broadcast faculty. He had taught at the universities of Wisconsin, Illinois, and Georgia before Missouri. Throughout his academic career, Stone also served as research director for the Radio-Television News Directors Association, which meant that his studies permeated broadcast newsrooms and sometimes the popular media.

Jill Geisler of the Poynter Institute for Media Studies said in a eulogy after Stone's 2005 death that he had served as her professor at Wisconsin during the early 1970s: "We set about measuring something that hadn't received much attention—public attitudes toward women in broadcasting. . . . For me, this effort was a senior thesis. For Dr. Stone, it was the beginning of many years of focus on the progress of women and minorities in broadcast journalism. It mattered to him, so measuring it became his mission." Missouri Journalism School faculty member Rod G. Gelatt memorialized Stone with a tribute in the *Journal of Broadcasting and Electronic Media.*

Jo Ann Dickerson returned to the Missouri Journalism School faculty during the Atwater deanship. A Native American, Dickerson brought with her much-needed diversity, as well as considerable editing, research, and people skills. Dickerson had won numerous admirers during a previous presence on the *Columbia Missourian* faculty from 1968 to 1974. She departed for an editing position at the *Los Angeles Times,* then taught at the universities of Kansas, Nebraska, and Texas-Arlington. She won praise for her teaching from myriad students. David Zeeck, *Kansas City Star* managing editor in 1983 and one of her Missouri Journalism School students from the first go-round, said this in a support letter for a campus teaching award: "Jo Ann doesn't have to tell her students they're loved. It's obvious. It's one of the few facts I've run across that I don't have to double check." Atwater and numerous faculty wanted Dickerson to return to play a role in scholarship as well as newsroom administration. News-editorial professor Ernest Morgan wrote her, "God knows we need news people. The school is falling into the hands of the public relations folks." That assessment did not scare away Dickerson.

Atwater also played a role in attracting Edmund Lambeth back to the Missouri Journalism School faculty. Lambeth had lived in Washington, D.C., and directed the Missouri Washington Program from 1968 to 1978. In 1987, he became a professor on the main campus in Columbia. During the nine-year hiatus, Lambeth taught at Indiana University, founded an institute for training journalism professors in the teaching of ethics, and directed the journalism program at the University of Kentucky. Atwater placed Lambeth in the position of associate dean for graduate studies. Lambeth recalled, "In that position I worked hard to persuade administrators to give many faculty two-course loads, plus, with Dean Atwater's active support, expanded in-school financial assistance for faculty research and creative activities. Not least, we gained a sorely needed full-time administrative assistant in the graduate program as a condition of my coming to Missouri."

The Faculty Development Fund created by Donald Brenner while he directed the graduate program and strengthened by Lambeth distributed about thirty thousand dollars annually to both PhD and non-PhD faculty competing for small grants. Faculty members voted to remove money from their salary pool to create the fund. Although the grants did not exceed four figures, the concept and the faculty governance involved boosted morale during a time of tiny or nonexistent salary increases due to budget squeezes.

Lambeth said the fund "stimulated a new openness to the twin-emphasis approach within the school—that is to say an emphasis on research as well as professional education and creativity. The fruits of this effort could later be seen in the Community Knowledge Project, which was a professional research effort by KOMU, KBIA, and the daily and Sunday *Missourian* to use social science methods to test the impact on readers, viewers, and listeners of coverage that combined the strengths of those three quite different media."

As part of the struggle for increased funding, on August 17, 1987, Atwater wrote Chancellor Haskell Monroe and Provost Lois DeFleur about the school's strengths (including the return of Lambeth with his research agenda), weaknesses, and needs. "With the school's limited financial resources . . . it has been difficult to do everything equally well," Atwater said, after noting the school's number-one ranking by so many outsiders. "Take the subject of scholarship. Missouri has long prided itself on its academic work. Dean Frank Luther Mott was one of the giants among journalism researchers and authors. The first master's degree in journalism was awarded here in 1921, the first doctorate in 1934. The standards for accrediting journalism education were drafted by a Missouri faculty member in 1946. Kappa Tau Alpha, journalism's honor society, was founded at the school and its executive director is one of our professors emeriti. In the last decade or so, I think it's fair to say, the school did not pay enough attention to scholarship. We are trying to solve that basic problem by hiring the right people with new money made available by Jesse Hall."

George Kennedy said that, during the Atwater deanship, the campus administration's stinginess made governing the Journalism School difficult. "We were starved for resources and struggled to demonstrate to a skeptical administration the quality of the school. . . . [The administration] required every division to make a formal argument for its value. As I recall, at the end of that process, the Journalism School emerged along with one or two other units as preeminent. That didn't yield much additional budget, but at least we were able to hold on to what we had."

Atwater's ill health, the budget battles, and what could fairly be termed a coup led by some faculty members played a role in his stepping down. The *Missourian* of January 17, 1988, carried this headline: "Journalism Dean Submits Resignation." The opening paragraph noted, "The resignation . . . ends a long struggle between him and some faculty members who questioned his leadership. It also comes at a time when the school is facing a possible one hundred thousand dollar deficit."

The story related that Atwater had initiated faculty evaluations a year earlier of himself and Associate Dean George Kennedy. Of the fifty-eight faculty, twenty-three replied. Atwater's positives included his personal integrity and fund-raising ability. Negatives included lack of knowledge about academia and overreliance on a small group of faculty advisers. Kennedy won high marks for decisiveness but received criticism for arrogance and manipulativeness. Kennedy told a reporter that the evaluations were not representative and alluded to three unnamed faculty who spread dissent without widespread support.

Terry J. Hughes of the *St. Louis Post-Dispatch* dug deeper into the apparent coup after the official version came out. The reporting included Hughes's attendance at a January 20, 1988, meeting of Atwater with some of the faculty. Hughes portrayed Atwater in a February 1, 1988, feature as a leader trying to patch up a family feud: "Atwater listed what he felt were his accomplishments and talked about problems yet unsolved. He talked about pride, and recounted a speech he has given each of the last five Septembers at the school's annual banquet."

The recounting went like this: "'I always start out [the banquet] by saying "I have the best job in the world,"' the dean said, his voice quavering. He paused for several seconds. . . . The room was quiet. Voice still shaky, he went on, 'I am the dean of the School of Journalism at the University of Missouri. I intend to say that this September.' Most of the audience applauded. The others looked blankly at the door as Atwater gathered up his papers and hurried from the room."

Hughes's feature quoted supporters and detractors of Atwater's deanship. Quoted at greatest length was Don Ranly, chair of the magazine sequence, who provided perspective by saying the faculty as a whole contained fissures. "What we want is a very, very nice, nice king who will be pleasant and wonderful to everybody, who will inspire and lead us. . . . He's just a wonderful man, extremely bright, very nice, who got into some awfully deep things. But if we continue to hire people with a bachelor's degree who have never set foot in a university, we are going to continue to be in deep [trouble]. . . . I've been here for fifteen years, and I have never been so proud to be anywhere. We are clearly a stronger school than we were six years ago. We have better faculty, better facilities, better participation by faculty . . . we have a better grade of student. . . . Now, if you're going to tell me all that happened because of Dean Atwater, I'm not going to tell you that. It happened because everybody tried, together."

The campaign by some faculty members to depose Atwater as dean upset other faculty members. Louise Montgomery, for one, recalled leaving for the University of Arkansas rather than remain colleagues with the leaders of the Atwater opposition. "I don't like conflict that is not straightforward," she said. "That campaign was not open and clean. I will happily fight with the best of them in an open, aboveboard conflict. But not that kind."

Atwater remained on the Journalism School faculty, becoming a popular writing professor. His wife, Patty, who had disliked living in Columbia initially, made the best of the situation by earning a BJ at a relatively advanced age after taking the lead in rearing six children, plus watching one of her children graduate from the school and marry a fellow alumnus. Patty Atwater joined the faculty as a *Missourian* copyeditor, winning accolades for her teaching ability. She continued teaching and mothering students at Missouri after her husband's death on March 1, 1996.

When Atwater's successor as dean arrived in 1989, nobody knew that his length of service would be second only to that of Walter Williams and would result in unimaginable changes.

Ten

Reaching Out to the Profession
Midcareer Journalism Education

As a new dean prepared to arrive in 1989, he began to grasp that he would be presiding over more than current faculty, staff, and students. He would also be presiding over midcareer organizations with a significant impact on professional journalists and on the ambience of the Journalism School. Most of all, he would be presiding over a symbol.

Those realities, like so much else, could be traced back to the founder. Walter Williams had figured out during the first decade of the Journalism School's existence that serving only students would fail to satisfy him completely. He wanted to professionalize practices in newsrooms, advertising agencies, public relations firms, and anywhere else that came to mind. Williams's evangelism took him across the United States and to dozens of other nations.

Williams's successors reached out to professional organizations throughout the United States and to journalists in nations that did not even exist when Williams died in 1935. Most visibly, the Missouri Journalism School became home to professional organizations that chose a poorly accessible campus, in terms of travel, for their headquarters because of outstanding faculty, staff, and students.

The outreach began when Williams devised awards, themed weeks, and other events to entice journalists to Columbia, Missouri. Each visitor could rely on having one or more journalism students as guides during the stay, a move grounded not only in courtesy but also in Williams's desire to create opportunities for meaningful conversation between students and out-of-town professionals.

The Editors' Week of 1910 became an annual event, eventually known as

Journalism Week. Starting in 1930, the Journalism School awarded distinguished service medals to individual journalists and media organizations as part of the week's activities. The first medalists were the *New York Times,* publisher Arthur Hays Sulzberger accepting; Percy S. Bullen of the *London Daily Telegraph; La Prensa* of Buenos Aires, Jose Santos Gallon accepting; Ward A. Neff of the Corn Belt Dailies; and E. W. Stephens of the *Columbia (Missouri) Herald.*

On April 28, 1930, Williams wrote Herbert Hoover in the White House about the Journalism Week ceremony to be held on May 9, with the German ambassador to the United States as the keynote speaker. "The general theme of the banquet and of this year's program is Journalism in International Relations. The banquet itself will be a made-in-the-printing-office banquet, demonstrating the progress of journalism since Gutenberg's day." Williams asked Hoover to send a message to be read at the banquet. By telegram on the same date, Hoover replied, "Increasing interest in international affairs fostered by more complete journalistic reports and editorial discussion tends to improve international relations and reduce difficulties in the way of mutual good will. I wish you a most profitable discussion of your theme."

Professionals would make the sometimes arduous journey to Columbia, usually at their own expense or at their news organizations' expense, to receive a distinguished service medal. In 1964, winner Walter Cronkite of CBS News said, "This to me is a more meaningful award than the Pulitzer Prize. A Pulitzer is awarded for a single report or series, but this medal acknowledges the cumulative work of an entire life."

Graduates of the school invited to speak at Journalism Week often gushed about the opportunity to return to campus and their wonderful experiences once there. Inez Callaway traveled from Idaho to attend the school in 1921 and earned her BJ in 1922. She became a feature writer for the *Tulsa World,* then joined the *New York Daily News* in 1928 on the way to becoming a society writer (using the name Nancy Randolph) as well as a syndicated columnist. She married J. Addison Robb Jr. in 1929.

Before accepting an invitation to speak at the 1938 Journalism Week, Robb wrote Dean Martin, "I think it only fair to warn you that I am not a feminist. I don't know what the policy of the School of Journalism is, but I don't think that newspaper women should try to be good newspaper men. That is the idiotic goal of so many, who fall so far short. I am of the firm opinion that . . . women . . . should try to be good newspaper women. If nature hadn't intended the sexes to be different, it wouldn't have made them different. . . . The majority will be far more successful if they try to be skillful newspaper women—not, of necessity, sob sister or cooking editors—but newspaperwomen who know their job, who can make their niche or find it. The field is wide open."

Back in New York City after her Journalism Week speech, Robb wrote Martin, "Even if the boss doesn't know it, I can now tell myself I'm something of a success! The three days I spent in Columbia were among the happiest I've ever known. I dreaded coming back so much that my husband literally had to hound me to get me on the . . . train. The dread was all mixed up with a fear that I'd feel a million years old and that everyone would treat me with respect. Well, no one has ever treated me with respect in all my life, and I should have known that smart college students would see I was a fraud and treat me with no respect at all. Which they did, and it made me feel very young and gay again, instead of decrepit and cantankerous. . . . I came back to New York feeling ten years younger and fairly kicking up my heels."

About Journalism Week, Gilbert Grosvenor said, "Many tributes have been paid the *National Geographic* magazine, but, to my mind, one in particular seems to distill all that has been accomplished, expressed in only fifty-two words. I refer to the honor award for distinguished service in journalism, given to the magazine in 1954 by the University of Missouri School of Journalism. It read, 'To the *National Geographic* magazine in recognition of its matchless service over more than half a century as a teacher of geography and related sciences to the people of America, its consistently friendly attitude toward the peoples of the world and its extraordinary success in integrating popular interest with sound scientific fact.'" ·

The first long-standing professional relationship negotiated by Williams involved the Missouri Press Association. Although many Missouri newspaper editors and publishers at first opposed formalized journalism education, many of them ended up hiring graduates from the school. Journalism School faculty helped specific daily and weekly newspapers improve their operations by making site visits. Missouri editors and publishers started sending their children, nieces, nephews, and grandchildren to school in Columbia, hoping to ensure succession.

The relationship between the Missouri Press Association and the Journalism School was further cemented during the tenure of William (Bill) Bray, who served as the association's executive director from 1953 to 1989. Born in King City, Missouri, Bray started working on the small newspaper there while in high school. The publisher, Louis Bowman, paid Bray two dollars per week for sweeping the floor, melting lead for the printer, and stoking the furnace. Bowman, a Missouri Journalism School graduate, encouraged Bray to follow that path. Bray accepted Bowman's advice, receiving his BJ in 1948 and then purchasing the newspaper in Odessa with a business partner and running it for five years. After moving to Columbia to direct the Missouri Press Association, Bray taught the community journalism class and the newspaper management class at the Journalism School.

James (Jim) Sterling, the teacher of those courses after joining the faculty in 2000, studied under Bray. Sterling (BJ 1965 with an advertising major) worked part-time as a student at the Missouri Press Association, which used a portion of Walter Williams Hall for its office. Later, Sterling owned weekly newspapers. He redesigned the Bolivar newspaper using Garamond type, thanks to the influence of his Journalism School typography professor, Paul Fisher. Faculty member Dale Spencer performed legal work for Sterling's newspapers. While dean, Earl English subscribed to Sterling's Stockton newspaper because English kept a cabin on the lake there. "He was always critiquing the newspaper for me," Sterling recalled. In the mid-1980s, Sterling became Missouri Press Association president. Partly because of his political connections, Sterling ended up with a gubernatorial appointment to the University of Missouri Board of Curators. In that influential position, he could keep watch over his alma mater's budget.

When Sterling applied for a faculty opening at the Journalism School, he ended up in a field with other strong candidates. Some faculty members worried that he would receive the job based on his Board of Curators service and other political connections, rather than entirely on merit. Sterling indeed was hired. The grumbling stopped, however, when faculty colleagues saw his dedication to classroom teaching, his generous spirit, and his useful connections to professional journalists throughout the state. Shortly after joining the faculty, Sterling helped bring the National Newspaper Association headquarters to the Journalism School from the Washington, D.C., area. Sterling's career demonstrates not only the vitality of the linkage between the Missouri Press Association and the Journalism School but also how assistance has traveled in both directions, multiple times.

No snob and prescient about the need to educate youngsters about the craft of journalism before they applied to college, Williams labored as mightily to form relationships with high school journalists as with newsroom and counting room professionals. The Missouri Interscholastic Press Association originated in 1923 primarily through the efforts of student and faculty representatives from twelve high schools located in four cities (Boonville, Springfield, Hannibal, and Kansas City). Williams and E. W. Tucker of Kemper Military School (later Academy) of Boonville played prominent roles in the formation. From the start, the group forged ties to the Missouri Press Association, which offered internships and print-ing facilities for the high school newspapers, plus the Journalism School, which offered training to students and instructors. Williams and future deans hired cer-tain faculty—Granville Price and Otha C. Spencer are two examples—on the basis of their rapport with high school students.

The nexus between the Journalism School and professional journalists was ev-ident again during World War II, as the educators and the photographers formed a relationship. What became renowned as the Pictures of the Year International competition began at the Journalism School in 1944 under the appellation Fifty Print Exhibition, with newspaper photographers as the focal point. The Kodak company provided money for the competition. The Nikon company began con-tributing funds later, as did alumnus James Domke, inventor of a bag used by photographers to carry equipment. In 1983, when Nikon stopped contributing for a while, the Canon camera company agreed to help support the competition, which by then had achieved enough acclaim to qualify as an investment yielding considerable goodwill.

The photojournalism world heard about another new competition in 1945, with the unveiling of the College Photographer of the Year at the Journalism School. Simultaneously, a student photojournalist honorary society formed on campus as Kappa Alpha Mu. The Missouri chapter is credited as the first. By 1946, the honorary society had achieved national status, with chapters at six oth-er campuses. In 1947, the Encyclopedia Britannica company became a sponsor of College Photographer of the Year, abandoning its separate awards competi-tion.

In 1948, with the decision to include magazine photographers alongside newspaper photographers, the contest became known as News Pictures of the Year. The move spawned controversy, because awarding prize money to magazine photojournalists sapped the meager budget in a realm where newspaper photo-journalists dominated.

A different sort of territoriality reared up in 1952, when a series of misunder-standings mixed with incompatible egos led Encyclopedia Britannica to split from the Journalism School and cosponsor a separate contest endorsed by the National Press Photographers Association. In 1957, when the Journalism School and the National Press Photographers Association merged contests, Pictures of the Year became the new appellation.

Unity among sponsors reigned for a while. In 2001, though, the Journalism School and the National Press Photographers Association parted ways, leaving the Journalism School as the sole contest administrator, with financial assistance from Fujifilm, the Newseum, and National Geographic. The Journalism School administration decided to try to support the international competition by raising enough money for a five-million-dollar endowment. The competition had become massive—in one recent year, more than twenty-three thousand photographs arrived for judging. The upside of all those submissions was a digitized, searchable archive of entries spanning sixty years. The college photographer competition expanded to include more than five hundred young women and men from more than one hundred campuses.

A crowning piece of the mosaic fell into place during 1949 with the start-up of the Missouri Photo Workshop. The workshop brought together student and professional photojournalists in a small Missouri town to document everyday life; Columbia, naturally enough, served as the first locale to be documented.

Much of the workshop planning originated with Clifton C. Edom of the Journalism School faculty and his wife, Vi. Born in 1907, Edom joined the faculty during 1943. Vi Edom might as well have become a faculty member, because she labored at her husband's side while simultaneously holding a job down the street at the Missouri Press Association. Previously, Edom had taught at the Aurora, Missouri, School of Photoengraving. He had become a philosopher of photojournalism early in life. But until he joined the Journalism School faculty, he lacked a platform from which to spread his ideas across the nation and around the globe.

Arriving on campus, Edom recalled "rebelling at the brand of teaching being offered by colleges. . . . Certainly, I reasoned, there must be more to teach than mere mechanics. Without playing down the necessity for technical proficiency, I felt there was a demand for depth reporting, as opposed to the shallow flash-on-camera, stand 'em up and sit 'em down technique then in vogue."

Students found Edom's thinking enthralling. Alumnus Michael L. (Mike) Johansen recalled students gathering at the Edom home in the evening, "to go over the work for the *Missourian* magazine. We critiqued our work, he gave direction, we came up with story ideas and we were well treated by Clif and Vi. While he was very demanding of his students, he, and she, always cared for them a lot."

Edom oversaw the darkrooms, the mechanical room, and the drying room used by the expanding number of photography students. Enrollment in photography topped one hundred students in 1948. More than overseeing the physical plant, however, Edom wanted to promote storytelling through photography as well as through words; he wanted photographers to develop "sensitive" outlooks. Edom had viewed a range of Depression-era Farm Security Administration photographs in the 1940 book *Home Town: The Face of America,* which included text by novelist Sherwood Anderson. Farm Security Administration director Roy Stryker and photographer Russell Lee helped Edom organize the Missouri Photo Workshop, then traveled to the state to serve as faculty during the formative years. The initial workshop attracted twenty-three photographers. Accomplished photo editors, led by Stan Kalish of the *Milwaukee Journal* and John Morris of *Ladies' Home Journal,* helped shape the final look of the project.

In 1950, the workshop moved to Forsyth, Missouri; in subsequent years it continued to move around the state, with Columbia, Forsyth, and certain other locales doing duty more than once. As the workshop evolved, applicants learned that they had to submit a twenty-photograph portfolio and a reference letter from a professional. Each workshop began with a dinner to which townsfolk received invitations. At week's end, they could view a public exhibit of the photo stories.

In tune with Edom's philosophy of photojournalism, each workshop became an exercise in thinking as well as shooting. Photographers had to conduct research and interview townsfolk before any shooting occurred. The photographs themselves were not arranged by appointment but were spontaneous, the result of watching and waiting. They had to be taken with available light. Edom placed other constraints on the shooters—a maximum of ten rolls of film, for example. Later, in the digital era, that changed to four hundred frames.

Frank Van Riper, a *Washington Post* photography columnist, experienced the 2004 Missouri Photo Workshop in Hermann, a town of three thousand residents. He reported, "To make a photographic record of such a place that produces more than superficial images requires a boatload of research, a high level of technical skill, commitment, and not a little bit of luck. It also requires time, something that a flying squad of forty photographers and photojournalists did not have last month as part of the University of Missouri's storied weeklong workshop in documentary photography. That virtually every one of these mostly young shooters—many with scant professional experience—produced picture stories of warmth, depth, beauty, and intelligence by week's end is a testament not just to their own skill, but to the tough-love teaching of the professional photographers and editors who guided them through what for many may be the best week so far of their photographic lives."

Quoting Edom about "showing truth with a camera," Van Riper listed some of the truths shown in Hermann, including "the race-the-clock, beat-the-weather intensity of harvest time in a wine vineyard, where a whole year's success can depend on bringing in the grapes on time."

As the small-town workshop and the photography award competitions matured, they served as vehicles to attract some of the nation's best teachers to the full-time faculty at the Journalism School. Starting in 1955, the Edoms received much-needed assistance with the hiring of Richard (Dick) Cannon. Dean English, on a fishing vacation in Manitoba, Canada, sponsored by the provincial government, had taken a liking to Cannon, the government's photographer. English, a PhD, hired Cannon, who lacked a college degree, with a minimum of formality. Cannon remained at the Journalism School for the rest of his life.

With Edom reaching retirement age, Angus McDougall stepped into the leadership role during 1972. McDougall had altered his life after World War II. At the age of thirty, with two children and a wife, Betty, he walked away from a job teaching high school English in Wisconsin to enroll at the School of Modern Photography in New York City. Upon graduation, McDougall joined the *Milwaukee Journal.*

More experimental than the average newspaper photographer, McDougall more or less invented the "bled strobe" technique, making movement, such as a runner on an athletic field, seem in focus and natural. After McDougall left the newspaper to freelance, *Popular Photography* magazine featured his work for its innovations. When Edom approached McDougall to participate in the Missouri Photo Workshop, he was employed at *International Harvester World* magazine. McDougall enjoyed the teaching aspect of the workshop and opened his mind to a career as a professor.

Veita Jo Hampton was teaching high school journalism in St. Charles, Missouri, when she heard about McDougall's magic. She enrolled at the Journalism School, studied with him, and eventually joined the faculty. "Mac was articulate, passionate, usually good-humored, and always merciless with the truth," Hampton recalled. "More than once I witnessed the crushing effect on a fellow student or felt the pain of a critique that pointed out sloppy camera or darkroom work, errant assumptions, half-assed research, poor writing, and missed opportunities at covering a story." The best photojournalism students learned from the constructive criticism and often ended up idolizing McDougall.

Robert R. Mercer (BJ 1973) recalled, "Clif Edom and Angus McDougall constantly brainstormed what could be done with the media tools we had—slide projectors, etc.—besides the obvious television and newsprint. They set the intellectual attitude necessary for designing a convergence curriculum when computers became truly usable. They loved teaching. In one visual communication meeting at the Association for Education in Journalism and Mass Communications, there were seven professors presenting, all Angus McDougall–minted photojournalists."

David Rees, the eventual successor to Edom and McDougall, said of Mc-

Dougall, "More than anyone else I know, he has affected the visual reporting at newspapers in this country, by encouraging his students to take ownership of the whole journalistic process, to start at small papers where they could gain experience and create a reputation before moving on to the largest papers in the country."

After McDougall's retirement in 1982, Kenneth R. (Ken) Kobre filled the director's position for three tumultuous years. He had taught previously at Boston University, worked on a newspaper staff, coordinated a child development center, and shot pictures as a freelancer. No disciple of Edom or McDougall, Kobre tried to move photojournalism at the Missouri Journalism School in new directions. Some photojournalism faculty, students, and professionals in the field objected to the content of Kobre's plan. But his style might have caused more problems for him than his substance. Some of those who chafed at his directorship perceived him as dismissive of the Edom and McDougall legacy, to the point of rudeness.

A wave of superb photojournalists, some of whom were also superb writers, arrived on campus. Melissa Farlow and her husband, Randy Olson, made their presence felt during the Kobre years. Olson had been on staff at the *San Jose Mercury News,* Farlow at the *Louisville Courier-Journal.* Weary of a long-distance romance, they settled together in the middle at Missouri. Olson and Farlow felt privileged to pick the brains of Edom and McDougall, both semiretired but seemingly omnipresent. "It's pretty incredible to think that Clif invented the word 'photojournalist,'" Farlow said. "Angus followed in Clif's tradition, influencing photojournalists and enhancing Missouri's national reputation as a respected photographic school. Both men were driven, well-meaning tyrants who believed photographers are journalists and demanded high standards."

Kobre spawned loyalty, too. On November 25, 1985, three photojournalism students wrote to Dean Atwater, asking him to rescind the "requested resignation" of Kobre. The students mentioned Kobre's achievements, including obtaining new camera equipment, finding money for a new studio, improving inclusion of photojournalists in master's degree projects, and establishing first-rate internships. Atwater did not relent, and William (Bill) Kuykendall moved into the directorship.

After Kobre's departure, Atwater wrote the campus chancellor about the just-concluded Pictures of the Year events. "A number of the prizewinners and leaders in their profession made it clear to me how much our photojournalism sequence had improved since we brought in Bill Kuykendall to head the program. For three years, while the sequence was led by another person, the program had faltered badly, causing a great deal of worry among professionals who had long viewed our school as the best in the country."

Kuykendall, a McDougall protégé, turned out to be a good fit for the Journalism School. He had taught basic photojournalism at Missouri from 1972 to 1974, freelanced for eight years after that, then moved to the *Seattle Times* as photo director. Documentary photographer Dianne Hagaman followed Kuykendall to the Missouri Journalism School from Seattle. She, Farlow, and Olson, among others, inspired hundreds of students but eventually experienced restlessness.

Farlow and Olson departed for the *Pittsburgh Press* photojournalism staff, then began to freelance regularly for *National Geographic* magazine, carrying their cameras to remote portions of other continents. Their faithfulness to the Missouri Journalism School, however, led them to immerse themselves in a gigantic project—cataloging and preserving the entries from Pictures of the Year. "With no designated space to house the collection, we found prints stacked in the boiler room where janitors ate lunch on them," Olson recalled. "I turned over a photograph that had a shoe print on it and recognized a famous image by David Douglas Duncan, an iconic photograph published in *Life* magazine from World War II. We learned later that the negative was lost, so this was one of the few remaining prints from the original negative." Olson wrote a grant proposal, and the National Archives came through. The Journalism School designated a space as a combination workplace and storage area far more conducive to preservation than a boiler room.

After Kuykendall departed for a change of scenery, the steady David Rees, a Missouri alumnus, accepted the directorship. Before joining the faculty, he taught high school in small-town Nebraska and worked ten years at the *Columbia Daily Tribune* as a photographer. C. Zoe Smith, along with Rees, served in an administrative role to keep the photojournalism sequence on an even keel. Simultaneously, Smith's expertise attracted students to her photojournalism history classes. Faculty members such as Loup Langton, Rita Reed, Jacquelyn (Jackie) Bell, and Richard F. (Rick) Shaw maintained the impressive blend of classroom instruction and professional experience within the photojournalism sequence during the last years of the twentieth century and the early years of the twenty-first.

The midcareer programs that came to populate the Journalism School brought incalculable benefits. As it did with photojournalism outreach to professionals, the Journalism School played a groundbreaking role in the establishment of what became known as lifestyle journalism within newsrooms. The Penney-Missouri awards program to honor lifestyle journalism, thought of originally as women's interest journalism, arrived at the Journalism School in 1960, with a twenty-seven-thousand-dollar budget. Prizes for winners that initial year awarded one thousand dollars, five hundred dollars, and two hundred fifty dollars in each category.

The grant from James Cash Penney, a Missouri native and owner of the J. C. Penney Company, quite likely was intended to encourage traditional women's sections of newspapers to do what they had always done, but more effectively—to create a felt need that would indirectly sell household products, including clothing for females and children. Because of Missouri Journalism School involvement, however, lifestyle journalism became something more than that. Journalism School faculty took the lead in the judging; their willingness to choose innovative entries as winners helped alter the tenor of women's sections as well as spawn a legitimate niche that transcended family, fashion, food, and furnishings.

The Penney money paid for a new faculty position for the Missouri Journalism School, occupied initially by Paul Myhre, previously associate editor of the *Cleveland News*. After Myhre died in 1971, the *Missourian* commented in a September 19 editorial that his career did him proud. In his personal life, he showed devotion to the arts, especially music: "Like all of us, he also had his idiosyncracies, especially one which intrigued his colleagues. It was his lunch-time favorite, which became known as the Paul Myhre Special—one hamburger plus a dish of peppermint ice cream drowned in chocolate sauce. He rarely deviated in his noontime repast."

Accomplished feature writers and editors succeeded Myhre, including Robert Hosokawa, Ruth C. D'Arcy, Jean Cameron Thompson, George M. Pica, and Nancy Beth Jackson. Under D'Arcy's leadership, the Penney-Missouri program instituted "flying workshops," as Journalism School faculty members addressed state press associations. Those in attendance picked up useful professional tips and frequently found themselves so impressed that they became cheerleaders for the Missouri Journalism School.

The Penney-Missouri awards gradually expanded to include magazine and broadcast as well as newspaper journalism. Kent S. Collins, a Journalism School broadcast professor and author of a syndicated newspaper column about aging, took charge after Jackson's departure. Collins also assumed directorship of a smaller writing competition. The Darrell Sifford Memorial Prize in Journalism is named in honor of the *Philadelphia Inquirer* columnist "with the heart of a poet" who died in 1992. A Missouri Journalism School alumnus, Sifford used his column to "depict the personal struggles and triumphs that together make up the fabric of our lives." The prize honors newspaper writing "that illuminates the daily life of ordinary people and their everyday concerns."

After three decades of support, Penney sent signals that the lifestyle journalism money would dry up. On August 21, 1991, David H. Lenz, public affairs manager, wrote that the corporation's objectives had changed since initiating the journalism awards, shifting to support for public education, including dropout prevention and job-training programs. The Penney money ceased to arrive in 1993. The Journalism School changed the name of the competition to the Missouri Lifestyle Journalism award.

Lifestyle journalism cuts across all sorts of professional boundaries. The Journalism School became the headquarters as well to organizations with more targeted missions. A business and financial journalism group arrived on campus in 1963, then kept expanding. The presence began when the Independent Natural Gas Association of America decided to honor the best business and economic journalism with an annual competition, with the judging to occur at the Journalism School.

The expansion began in 1971 when Lyle E. Harris, working on his PhD, assumed leadership of the business journalism program. To help build the program, Harris hired assistant Doris Barnhart, who still worked at the Journalism School in 2008. Harris, a faculty lecturer with experience in business reporting at the *Washington (D.C.) Evening Star,* obtained a twenty-five-thousand-dollar grant from the Smith Richardson Foundation in 1974. The grant allowed creation of the summer Davenport Fellowships for midcareer journalists at the Journalism School. Journalism School professor James (Jimmy) Gentry and University of Missouri economics professor Steve Buckles, both superb classroom teachers, became closely identified with the summer Davenport Fellowships and business reporting in general.

The midcareer reporters and editors enriched the Journalism School as they arrived from newsrooms as varied as *American Banker, Minnesota Business Journal, Georgia Trend Magazine, Hawaii Business, Des Moines Business Record,* United Press International, and general circulation daily newspapers. Donors to the fellowship program included Ford Motor Company (which also gave the Journalism School scholarships for Detroit-area minority students), R. J. Reynolds Industries, Ameritech, Exxon, Conoco, Mobil, Dow Chemical, Sears Roebuck, Pfizer, Chase Manhattan Bank, American Cyanamid, E. I. du Pont de Nemours, Chevron, and others.

The donations from corporate America raised the obvious question of how much money the Journalism School should accept from private industry. At minimum, the corporate donors hoped to influence journalists to accept without severe questioning the benefits of capitalistic enterprise. Most of the faculty seemed content to let the dean and the program director guard against undue influence; open discussion about the donations barely occurred.

With the business and financial journalism curriculum expanding, Robert Hosokawa became involved in teaching those courses. An American citizen born in 1918 and imprisoned by the U.S. government during World War II simply because of his Japanese ancestry, Hosokawa arrived at the Journalism School during 1971, after ten years in the *Minneapolis Tribune* newsroom and another ten years with a public relations firm.

As Hosokawa eased toward retirement, Harris left Missouri in 1976 for a teaching position at Western Washington State University. William McPhatter, one of the rare African American faculty candidates willing to move to mid-Missouri at that juncture because of perceived racism, arrived as director of the business journalism curriculum. After several years, McPhatter left for a public affairs job at Amtrak in Washington, D.C.

A professional group known as the Society of American Business Editors and Writers (SABEW) paid increasing attention to the campus. The organization had formed in 1964, the brainchild primarily of R. K. T. (Kit) Larson, an editor at the *Norfolk Virginian-Pilot and Ledger-Star*. The Journalism School became the site of the society's headquarters in 1984; at that point, the organization served about 135 members. Jimmy Gentry, who had joined the faculty in 1976 as a *Missourian* editor, became director of the business journalism classroom curriculum in 1980 and simultaneously directed SABEW. Membership grew steadily until it topped three thousand.

Gentry departed in 1992 to become dean of journalism at the University of Nevada-Reno and later at the University of Kansas. SABEW continued to serve its members from the Journalism School. But none of the society's staff had attained the stature of Gentry in the realm of business and financial journalism. Business journalism courses slipped to a sporadic status in the Missouri curriculum. To remedy the slippage, the Journalism School and SABEW collaborated on finding a knowledgeable business reporter or editor to teach courses and play a role in the society's governance. Eventually, they raised enough money to create the Society of American Business Editors and Writers Chair in Business and Financial Reporting. Martha (Marty) Steffens, a thirty-year veteran of newspaper reporting and editing, became the first holder of the faculty chair.

Steffens quickly impressed faculty colleagues with her innovative classroom teaching, rapport with students, and high energy level. The proper role of the chair holder within the professional society caused some consternation, though. Rex Saline of the *Fort Worth Star-Telegram,* society president for 2004, wrote in the group's publication, the *Business Journalist,* about the endowed chair holder: "An early vision was to build on the Jimmy Gentry model, with the expectation that the chair might also serve as SABEW executive director. But as the organization grew and the relationship with Missouri matured, it became clear that model wouldn't work. Some folks thought the chair could serve as the academic voice of business journalism. Others envisioned a mid-career trainer. Missouri, for its part, had some interest in actually teaching students. . . . Truth be told, while we were worrying about the money and the accessories, we never really decided where the car should go. We never got a good fix on what the chair could and should do. Marty Steffens, as the inaugural chair, has been tested by SABEW's interests, Missouri's needs and other demands."

The society's directors decided to hire Carrie Paden, a nonjournalist, to oversee day-to-day operations, a different model than other midcareer programs at the Journalism School. A few years into the Steffens-Paden arrangement, SABEW consisted of about thirty-two hundred members; at least three-fourths of them derived from approximately two hundred institutional memberships. The staff produced a magazine and a Web site, offered a job bank, presented annual awards, and held an annual national conference as well as more targeted workshops, among other services.

Marty Steffens's husband, Brian Steffens, became the executive director of a professional organization that arrived on campus in 2002, the National Newspaper Association. Brian had edited *The Quill* magazine for the Society of Professional Journalists, directed coverage of the newspaper industry for *Editor and Publisher* magazine, worked in newsrooms, and operated a public relations firm.

The National Newspaper Association produced the tabloid monthly *Publishers' Auxiliary* and lobbied for its approximately two thousand members, mostly small dailies and weeklies specializing in community journalism. The group had begun in 1885 as the National Editorial Association. Walter Williams served as president eight years later. The group changed its name during 1964. It moved to the Missouri Journalism School from the Washington, D.C., suburb of Arlington, Virginia, maintaining a Washington-area office for lobbying Congress and tracking issues elsewhere in the federal government. When the organization relocated to Missouri, eleven employees needed to decide whether to relocate. One made the move. Steffens hired four new staff members from mid-Missouri.

The synergy between midcareer groups at the Journalism School and students benefiting from their presence is encapsulated by the case of Laura Sjurson and the National Newspaper Association. Sjurson undertook an assignment in a class taught by James Sterling to devise an advertising campaign for community newspapers. She chose the well-worn slogan "Think outside the box," placed the slogan on a television screen to give it a fresh meaning, then wrote copy that began "And get results from your advertising." Sjurson's idea led to promotional advertisements available to National Newspaper Association members on the group's Web site.

The Journalism School started its affiliation with Investigative Reporters and Editors (IRE) in 1978. The affiliation occurred with almost no planning on either side. It had appeared that IRE, in its third year of existence and growing faster than anticipated, would establish its headquarters at Ohio State University. But the premature death of faculty member Paul Williams, the instigator of the arrangement, led to the demise of the planned affiliation. Then it appeared that Boston University would become the headquarters site. The Missouri Journalism School ended up as the home of IRE only because of a hurried but persuasive sales pitch by media law professor Dale Spencer and Dean Roy Fisher.

After the IRE board of directors, consisting of volunteer journalists, said it would seriously consider the Missouri offer, Fisher collared John Ullmann, a doctoral candidate, and more or less ordered him to serve as IRE's first executive director. Ullmann had earned his bachelor's degree at Butler University and his master's degree at American University and had taught journalism for two years at the University of Alaska. He wanted to complete his doctoral studies; the IRE job would delay the completion date. It turned out that Ullmann warmed to the IRE opportunity, while Dean Fisher, the journalism faculty and students, and IRE's volunteer directors warmed to him. One of the most uninhibited, laughter-provoking, dynamic teachers ever to enter a Journalism School classroom, Ullmann probably never received an evaluation calling him boring.

At the IRE office, with no full-time professional staff but dedicated student workers, Ullmann spewed forth ideas at a dizzying rate. He also found time to collaborate with staff member Steve Honeyman to produce *The Reporter's Handbook: An Investigator's Guide to Documents and Techniques.* Published by St. Martin's Press, the book became a staple in newsrooms and classrooms around the nation and increasingly around the world. It included chapters from superb investigative journalists who contributed not only their expertise but also their precious time.

Ullmann kept IRE alive during a difficult time. Some of the difficulties stemmed from the normal pains of a fledgling not-for-profit educational organization. But the bulk of the trouble stemmed from libel litigation filed against IRE because of its high-profile Arizona Project, which began in the aftermath of the murder of Don Bolles, an early member of IRE. Bolles was conducting an investigation for the *Arizona Republic* when he was killed by a car bomb during June 1976. Members of IRE took leaves from their newsrooms to descend on Arizona, hoping to complete Bolles's investigation into linked and corrupt businesspeople, lawyers, and government officials—and thus send a signal that, while it is possible to murder a reporter, it is never possible to kill an investigation. The massive series appeared in various media outlets during 1977. IRE weathered the expense and stress of the litigation—barely.

Steve Weinberg became the second executive director in 1983, when Ullmann decided to join the *Minneapolis Star Tribune* as its investigative projects editor. Weinberg moved to Columbia from Washington, D.C., where he had been writing books and magazine features and serving as the director of the Missouri Journalism School's program in the nation's capital. Jan Colbert, a Journalism School graduate with a specialty in graphic design, joined the IRE staff as well. In 1990, Weinberg stepped aside from the executive directorship to spend more time with his family. He remained editor of IRE's magazine through 1999. Colbert left IRE soon thereafter to become a full-time classroom teacher at the Journalism School. She, too, continued her affiliation with IRE's magazine.

When a national search for a new executive director produced less than satisfactory results, Andy Scott, an experienced reporter with the Associated Press who had worked at IRE while a Journalism School student, agreed to serve as interim executive director. After a reconstituted national search, Rosemary Armao became executive director, leaving the *Norfolk Virginian-Pilot,* where she had earned a reputation as a supportive editor willing to champion daring projects. In an academic atmosphere, Armao's candor sometimes stood out. "I know that I am blunt and frequently give an impression of intensity and hostility that I don't intend," she wrote about herself in 1996.

Tracy Barnett, who had earned a master's degree from the Journalism School, became deputy director, leaving a reporting job at the *Columbia Daily Tribune.* Brant Houston arrived at IRE and joined the faculty at the same time as Armao, vacating a newsroom job at the *Hartford Courant.* Houston filled a new position, that of managing a computer-assisted reporting initiative. Therein lies a story that changed the face of contemporary journalism, in addition to placing IRE and the Journalism School on the cutting edge of midcareer training.

As the 1980s ended, Elliot Jaspin was looking for a new job. A superb traditional newspaper reporter with an intuitive grasp of how computers could improve the quality of journalism, Jaspin had completed groundbreaking projects at the *Providence Journal Bulletin.* He then honed his computer-assisted reporting skills during a journalism fellowship in New York City. Not wanting to return to the Providence newspaper, Jaspin contacted Weinberg to bat around possibilities. Although a Luddite, Weinberg somehow sensed the future. If the Journalism School and IRE could bring Jaspin to Columbia, who knew what marvelous advances for the profession might result?

Hiring Jaspin took the University of Missouri into uncharted territory. Although he had won a Pulitzer Prize early in his career, Jaspin lacked academic credentials and an advanced college degree. Furthermore, nobody had tried to teach computer-assisted reporting in a university setting quite like Jaspin planned to do, while simultaneously reaching out to newsrooms. Nonetheless, Missouri Journalism School administrators grasped the intriguing possibilities. On March 30, 1989, George Kennedy, associate dean, made a formal offer to Jaspin. The Journalism School would provide Jaspin "access to our IBM computers, software and other equipment; the services of our IBM program secretary and other clerical staff as necessary; one or more student assistants . . . paid during the first year from the school's budget; the expertise and cooperation of the director of professional programs [then Daryl Moen] in developing and implementing the mid-career training." Kennedy stated that it made sense to work with IRE as part of the outreach effort.

Like many pathfinders, Jaspin could be difficult to work with. Overall, though, students enjoyed learning from him. His outreach to newsrooms began to generate new kinds of stories that would have taken years to complete—or never even been initiated—without the power of computers to analyze massive amounts of data from government agencies. Working with the Journalism School administration and the journalists constituting the IRE board of directors, Jaspin created an entity eventually known as the National Institute for Computer-Assisted Reporting (NICAR).

Jaspin soon left mid-Missouri to join the Washington bureau of Cox Newspapers. His initiative did not die, however. NICAR became a vital part of IRE and the Journalism School under Houston's leadership. Training directors hired by IRE, but located away from Columbia, took computer-assisted reporting workshops into newsrooms across the nation. On the Journalism School campus, Jo Craven McGinty, hired from the *Washington Post;* Jeff Porter, hired from the *Arkansas Democrat-Gazette;* David Herzog, hired from the *Providence Journal;* as well as other cutting-edge journalists provided instruction in student classrooms and at weeklong "boot camps" for professionals traveling to mid-Missouri.

IRE had become an attractive asset for the Journalism School tree, made all the more valuable by the addition of the computer-assisted-reporting program. Naturally, other journalism schools coveted the asset. When the University of Maryland journalism school offered IRE-NICAR a new home during the mid-1990s, emotional discussions ensued. The possibility that IRE might leave the campus had been raised in 1989 because of overtures from other universities. At that point, Colbert and Weinberg had recommended to the IRE board of directors that the organization remain at Missouri for numerous reasons, the most compelling involving the quality and quantity of student workers. George Kennedy, a Journalism School administrator at that point, told newly arrived Dean Mills in 1989, "I don't think we have a crisis, but I do think IRE is far too important to the school for us to take a chance of giving the board an excuse to pull out."

During June 1996, the IRE board of directors decided in a close vote to remain at the Missouri Journalism School instead of moving to Maryland. Dean Mills promised to pay closer attention to the relationship between the school and IRE-NICAR. Armao departed shortly thereafter, accepting an editorship at the *Baltimore Sun.* Houston became IRE executive director while also retaining responsibility for NICAR operations and teaching the Journalism School's investigative reporting course. A second course aimed specifically at instructing students to use computers to report more effectively.

With its expanded reach, IRE-NICAR needed additional staff with management experience. In 1998, Len Bruzzese moved from the editorship of the Gannett newspaper in Olympia, Washington, to become IRE deputy director and a Journalism School faculty member. His wife, Anita, a syndicated columnist specializing in workplace issues, became involved, too, as editor of IRE's magazine.

After overseeing the hiring of an efficient staff, the growth of services, and the accumulation of a comfortable endowment, Houston announced in mid-2007 that he would leave IRE-NICAR to accept a prestigious investigative journalism chair at the University of Illinois. His enthusiasm for IRE had not dimmed. Meanwhile, his life partner, Rhonda Fallon, had lost her staff job at the Journalism School after more than twenty years as its manager of business and fiscal operations. Fallon's dismissal puzzled faculty, staff, and students alike, given her vast knowledge of school operations and her dedication to her job. Had Dean Mills or other Journalism School administrators taken the initiative to dismiss Fallon? Had the dismissal order come from somewhere higher in the University of Missouri hierarchy? Nobody in charge offered unambiguous answers. As Fallon challenged her dismissal in drawn-out proceedings inside and outside the university, her situation became a lightning rod. Numerous faculty and staff noticed morale plummeting due to the perception that the spirit of the Journalism School "family" had been violated.

Fortunately, such upheavals were the exception rather than the rule. In part because of a superb staff, the Missouri Journalism School continued to attract midcareer organizations in the twenty-first century. Len Bruzzese left the IRE deputy directorship during 2005 after being recruited to serve as executive director of another group moving to Columbia—the Association of Health Care Journalists. The membership included about nine hundred broadcast, online, and print journalists. Bruzzese helped plan the organization's departure from the University of Minnesota and hired new staff in Missouri.

The City and Regional Magazine Association administered its annual awards program through the Journalism School. The judging, and the planning of the awards presentation for the group's national conference, yields part-time jobs for Journalism School staff member Kim Townlain and for a student. The new alliance also allowed faculty judges to look systematically at city and regional magazines entering the awards competition. Such a systematic examination while judging sometimes led to valuable classroom teaching material. When the Journalism School hired John Fennell to teach magazine courses, his fit with the City and Regional Magazine Association felt perfect; Fennell had moved to Missouri from the editorship of *Milwaukee* magazine and had been active in the association. An accomplished painter in addition to being a skilled writer and editor, Fennell became the liaison between the Journalism School and the Meredith Corporation, the magazine giant based in Des Moines and New York City. Meredith had endowed a chair for a magazine faculty member, and Fennell was the newest occupant.

During 2004, Don Ranly, as he neared retirement from full-time teaching, formed the Missouri Association of Publications, open to magazines and newsletters, both print and electronic. At the outset, Ranly excluded daily and weekly newspapers, to avoid conflict with the Missouri Press Association. Interest grew quickly, based largely on Ranly's sterling reputation and well-known charisma. When Ranly fully retired from the faculty, the organization chose Dennis McDermott, previously vice president at the Missouri Association of Realtors but with a journalism background, to direct the annual conference and other events held in conjunction with the Journalism School.

The Center on Religion and the Professions entered the Missouri Journalism School mix during the twenty-first century, under the direction of faculty member Edmund B. Lambeth. Although the Journalism School had not previously offered a coherent curriculum on religion reporting and writing, it had considered doing so. For example, in 1958 Dean English exchanged letters with alumnus Roger W. Straus Jr. of Farrar, Straus, and Cudahy, a major New York City book publisher. English had heard from a third party about Straus's interest in religion journalism. English noted on October 7, 1958, that "Syracuse University has done some work in this field. . . . For several years I have explored with Dean Seth Slaughter, of the Missouri School of Religion here, the possibility of a cooperative arrangement to launch a teaching program."

Nearly half a century later, Lambeth told the Journalism School faculty and staff that "during its first year of existence the core faculty and fellows of the Center . . . worked to build an agenda of teaching, research and service that would reach both faculty and students at the University of Missouri and citizens of Columbia and the state of Missouri." Lambeth announced seven public lectures, one by Journalism School faculty member Geneva Overholser. The other speakers included a University of Missouri psychiatry professor about his assistance to persons traumatized by living in war zones; a University of Missouri women's studies professor on responding to domestic violence; a former insurance company executive addressing corporate ethics through the teachings of religions; a former member of the President's Council on Bioethics explaining that group's inner workings; a religious studies professor assessing creativity as a religious concept; and the codirector of Duke University Medical Center's Center for Spirituality, Theology, and Health on how religious belief affects well-being.

With Lambeth retiring, a search during 2006 for a new director yielded Debra L. Mason, holder of a master's degree in journalism from Northwestern University, a master's in theological studies from Trinity Lutheran Seminary, and a doctorate in mass communications from Ohio University. She moved to Columbia from Columbus, Ohio, where she had reported about religion for the local newspaper before becoming executive director of the Religious Newswriters Association. As part of Mason's relocation, that organization agreed to move its headquarters to the Missouri Journalism School. A few months later, Mason distributed a resource guide titled *Reporting on Religion: A Primer on Journalism's Best Beat*. She used it as a text for students in her Religion Reporting and Writing class.

Some but not all of the newly affiliated groups brought additional part-time faculty to the Journalism School. Some but not all of the new midcareer groups created a squeeze on office space. Sometimes old questions arose in new settings. For example, the addition of the Association of Health Care Journalists dredged up thoughts about the Journalism School's off-and-on attempts to improve health, environmental, and other science coverage.

During 1954, Dean English had addressed the American Medical Writers' Association about a plan to teach health reporting at the Missouri Journalism School, plus the journalism schools at Illinois and Oklahoma. The plan included two years of typical premedical school coursework, followed by two years of joint journalism and medicine courses. At the time, Missouri had one undergraduate student and one graduate student concentrating in medical journalism, with perhaps three prejournalism students in the pipeline. One student indeed earned the specialized degree during 1956.

After that, nothing much happened, until the addition of Joye Patterson to the Missouri Journalism School faculty. Despite her lack of newsroom experience, Patterson understood science journalism just fine. After graduating from the University of Texas with a bachelor's degree in 1947, Patterson taught high school briefly, became a medical researcher at the University of Tennessee briefly, then settled in Memphis, where from 1950 to 1960 she worked as a public information officer at a hospital. In 1960, she moved to Columbia for a fellowship at the University of Missouri Medical Center, also earning a master's degree and a doctorate from the Journalism School. She joined the Journalism School faculty in 1965. Until her retirement during the mid-1980s, Patterson's teaching skills drew undergraduate and graduate students to her science journalism classes. Many of her colleagues not only treasured Patterson for her teaching prowess but also considered her "the conscience" of the faculty, a role attributable to her unwavering common sense and high ethical standards.

Donald Brenner supplemented Patterson. A researcher rather than an experienced newsroom journalist, Brenner nonetheless added valuable knowledge to the health care portion of science writing courses. Brenner served on the University of Missouri faculty from 1966 to 1972 as a key figure in the Missouri Regional Medical Program. He left for employment elsewhere, then returned to the University of Missouri in 1977 as part of the Health Care Technology Center within the Medical School. In 1981, Brenner made his move to the Journalism School faculty.

Robert Logan replaced Patterson in the classroom and launched initiatives to further enhance the school's reputation. The Science Journalism Center organized by Logan assisted reporters and editors in performing their jobs. The science journalism program attracted outside contributors with a $225,000 challenge grant from Dow Chemical. Celanese, Rockwell, the MacArthur Foundation, and media companies—including Time Inc., the New York Times, and the Minneapolis Star and Tribune—added to the treasury.

The faculty began to split over the appropriateness of accepting donations from corporations and foundations that could be accused of buying favorable coverage in the present and the future. On the one hand, the Journalism School felt chronically underfunded; on the other hand, it seemed that acceptance of some corporate gifts created conflicts of interests, or at least the appearance of them.

The Health and Nutrition program, funded in part by a $113,000 grant from the Campbell Soup Company, drew about thirty journalists for an October 1986 workshop. Discussion ensued within the Journalism School about how much those visiting reporters and editors needed to be told about the source of the funding.

The off-and-on-again discussions broke into the open during 1991 when Kraft/Philip Morris/General Foods offered a $150,000 grant to the Science Journalism Center to initiate seminars about risk assessment, epidemiology, medical screening, and toxicology. Logan, not the funder, would have controlled the seminar sessions, including selecting the panelists. But the equation became complicated because tobacco is well established as a product that kills users. The question was obvious: should the Journalism School accept money from a corporation so closely associated with a deadly substance? The answer was less obvious.

Logan wanted to proceed, given the assurance of Philip Morris that its executives would refrain from trying to dictate the seminars' contents. He eventually decided against proceeding. "It became clear that very few science writers in large news organizations would come to a seminar sponsored by a cigarette manufacturer," Logan said. "Since there was no question about the responsibility to fully disclose the donor's identity, the acceptance of funds seemed to guarantee an unsuccessful series and significant criticism from some science and medical journalists."

Because so few corporate or individual donors are pristine, Journalism School faculty and staff could not establish a blanket policy rejecting all potentially tainted money. As a result, discussions about accepting or refusing outside donations continued on an ad hoc basis.

The Journalism and Women Symposium (JAWS) maintained a one-person headquarters at the Missouri Journalism School, starting in 1992, to plan an annual national meeting and anchor a network of female media workers. The organization grew out of a 1984 gathering at the Journalism School; faculty member Jean Gaddy Wilson had invited women journalists to campus to discuss their work and the issues they faced in their daily lives. Tad Bartimus, an Associated Press feature writer and Missouri Journalism School graduate, invited an expanded group to Estes Park, Colorado, in 1985. "Ever after, the fall JAWS session has been known as 'camp,' but we tell our bosses it's a symposium," member Kay Mills from the *Los Angeles Times* commented. At a different site in Estes Park during 1986, about twenty women attended. "Although we didn't realize it at the time, we had the nucleus of the current format—chats with people who make news or have covered the year's big stories as well as time to get advice from our pals," Mills recalled.

JAWS began to win outside financial support, starting with the Ms. Foundation for Education and Communications in 1990, then from foundations dealing with newspaper and broadcast news. When JAWS moved to the Missouri Journalism School, Wilson became executive secretary and hired Margie Meyer as part-time coordinator. Meyer became the primary JAWS staff member at Missouri. She stepped aside in 2001; at that point, JAWS hired a member away from the University of Missouri campus to keep the group on track; and the strong connection with the Journalism School diminished.

Jean Gaddy Wilson's role at JAWS played into her involvement with New Directions for News, a think tank for newspapers that called the Missouri Journalism School its home from 1987 until 2000. More specifically, New Directions for News identified itself as "a nonprofit organization fostering innovation in newspapers to make them relevant and useful in the service of democratic society." The organization's precursor originated in 1979, when Virginia R. Allan, the director of George Washington University's Women's Studies Program and Policy Center, decided to analyze whether press coverage played a role in the defeat of the Equal Rights Amendment to the U.S. Constitution. Dorothy Misener Jurney, a veteran newspaper reporter and editor, served as coauthor of the 1983 report about Equal Rights Amendment coverage, as well as coverage of pay equity, domestic relations laws, and treatment of women on campuses. Those studying the report decided that not only women's issues but other pressing social concerns could be covered more honestly if journalists focused increasingly on trends and less on breaking news without context.

The entrepreneurial Wilson (BJ 1964) decided that whatever grew out of Jurney and Allan's report ought to find a home at the Missouri Journalism School. Living in Marshall, Missouri, and teaching at a small college there, Wilson had returned to the Journalism School in 1981 to work on a master's degree. By 1982, Wilson had procured two outside grants, totaling thirty-five thousand dollars, to study the quantity and quality of women in the news media.

Ruth D'Arcy, who had joined the Journalism School faculty in 1975, collaborated with Wilson in recruiting prominent journalists to serve on various committees. A veteran newspaperwoman, D'Arcy had spent thirty-two years at the

Detroit News after starting there as a secretary. D'Arcy and Wilson's participation heightened the visibility, intellectualism, and prestige of the Missouri Journalism School inside the media world. Money arrived from a variety of sources, including the McCormick Foundation, related to the *Chicago Tribune.*

Some Missouri Journalism School faculty members believed New Directions for News would help rejuvenate ailing newspapers. Other faculty members found the results unimpressive, filled with generalizations and unsupportable projections about social conditions, economic solutions, and technology.

Wilson's combative personality made it difficult to retain staff. Her faculty appointment seemed precarious, too. In November 1991, twenty-two female students in her Women and the Media class filed a complaint with the dean, stating that Wilson had missed one-third of the classes without prior notice, had failed to return any of four assigned papers, was unavailable for individual conferences, did not appear to know the names of most students, and limited class discussion.

Wilson eventually left the faculty. New Directions for News lost its physical space inside the school, moving to a building off campus. Some of the distressed New Directions staff found employment elsewhere within the Journalism School. New Directions for News, in a different iteration, became affiliated with the University of Minnesota during 1999.

An attempt by the Journalism School to assume leadership in the multicultural newsroom movement did not always go smoothly, either. The Multicultural Management Program started with the goal of moving minorities into newsroom supervisory positions. The first conversation, in 1984, occurred between professor Robert P. Knight and Pam Johnson, the African American publisher of the *Journal* newspaper in Ithaca, New York. Knight shared his thinking early, in the February 1985 issue of the magazine of the American Society of Newspaper Editors. Here is part of his text:

"With backing from industry leaders, we at Missouri are on to a big idea—so simple it astounds us, so complex it awes us—to get and retain more minorities, get more minority managers and more white managers who are multicultural. Together they can improve newspapers for staffs and readers. For nearly fifteen years, we'd been searching for a powerful idea to link our sincere but relatively small minority efforts to a program of industry-wide impact. . . . Can multicultural management be taught? That's what we're setting out to test in a national experimental model for experienced minority and nonminority journalists on the management fast track."

Knight's account ran alongside a piece by Ellis Cose, the African American president of the Institute for Journalism Education, based at the University of California–Berkeley. The Institute directed professional programs for minority journalists. Cose announced that his institute would soon start a management training program in cooperation with the journalism and management schools at Northwestern University, using seed money from the Gannett Foundation.

At Missouri, the early vision focused on a one-year or two-year degree program combining business administration and media management. But the brainstormers realized that the type of journalists the program most wanted to attract, and to whom the program would be most attractive, would rarely receive a year or two years away from their newsrooms. Thus, the plan changed to a concentrated four-week course, with two hours of graduate-degree credit awarded to those who desired that option.

The Journalism School hired Ben Johnson as executive director and his wife, Mary Bullard-Johnson, as associate director of the Multicultural Management Program. African Americans, the Johnsons moved themselves and their children to a venue with a reputation for being sometimes inhospitable to minorities. Ben Johnson had attended one of the 1985 brainstorming sessions in his role of assistant to the managing editor of the *Detroit Free Press*. "As far as I'm concerned, Providence intervened," Ben Johnson said. "I had wanted to do something different and something important, and this was it."

Gail Baker Woods, one of the few African Americans teaching at the Missouri Journalism School in 1985, felt conflicted about the hiring of the Johnsons. She had arrived at Missouri during 1983 as a PhD candidate, after earning a journalism degree from Northwestern University in 1976, spending three years in the *Chicago Daily Defender* newsroom, obtaining a master's degree in marketing communications from Roosevelt University, and serving as an information representative for International Business Machines. While completing her Missouri doctorate, Woods taught in the Advertising Department, coordinated recruiting of minority graduate students, worked with minority high school and University of Missouri undergraduate students, plus served as faculty adviser to the Public Relations Society of America student chapter and the Minority Journalism Association.

"I give the school credit for recognizing and acting on a need to diversify newsrooms," Woods said in retrospect. "It was appropriate to have the Multicultural Management Program located at Missouri, and I was personally proud to see my school take the lead in addressing a national problem. With that said, the selection of Ben Johnson was controversial. He certainly had the credentials on paper, but his management style was disconcerting. I was uneasy about the decision, but was reluctant to deny anyone an opportunity to grow at the university—the same opportunity the institution had given me. . . . My complaint was that the school did not look far and wide for the absolute best person to run the program, and that by choosing an African American who was convenient or available, they did not give the Multicultural Management Program the same respect as other high-profile programs at the school. . . . People of color can, do, and should compete and earn positions in universities. In the case of the Multicultural Management Program, I believed there were other qualified people who did not come with the same issues Ben brought to the program. By not making every effort to find individuals who met all the standards—and they were out there—and who also had the temperament to handle a university culture, the school missed an opportunity to launch and sustain a program with tremendous impact for change."

After arriving on campus, Johnson pushed to raise awareness. On February 16, 1986, he wrote Journalism School administrators, "I was very impressed with the credentials for this year's judges of our Pictures of the Year competition. But there's a point I'd like to make about an omission. There seems to be no diversity in this stellar lineup. Might I suggest that this year be the one when we attempt to include a diverse representation in everything we do? That ranges from students participating on a panel to judges for our many contests to speakers for our program. If we are to communicate the message to those around the country that we are leaders in the multicultural approach to journalism, we must convey that message here at home. I think it makes good sense and it's the fair and just thing to do."

The Multicultural Management Program's board of directors met in Columbia on May 19, 1986. "The challenge was how to make the Multicultural Management Program special," Mary Bullard-Johnson said after the meeting. "How do you get at that touchy-feely thing we came to call multiculturalism? Would tough editors see that as sandbox journalism? . . . Other management programs offered classes on time management and stress management, performance evaluations and budget analysis. The Multicultural Management Program had to do something more. In putting together a jam-packed four-week schedule, the administrators planned to shuttle in some of the industry's top leaders. They added sessions on executive style and newsroom humor. They added daily homework sessions and evening discussion groups. And overlapping all of the classwork, homework and evening work was an ever-present case study. The fellows had to complete a five-year strategic marketing plan on a major newspaper market. The case study was not unlike the ones assigned over a semester by top business schools. But this one had to be done within four weeks by a group of strangers who knew little about the business side of a newspaper."

Seeking additional funding, Dean Atwater shared his vision for the Journalism School's role with Ford Foundation executives in a June 19, 1986, letter. Why should the Ford Foundation commit money to training meant to increase the number of minority managers in newsrooms? Because, Atwater said, "Journalism is of particular importance to minorities and the life of the United States. . . . We are rapidly becoming a pluralistic and multicultural society. . . . But the press . . . has been slow to report on these sweeping changes in American society. That's not only bad journalism, that's bad for the country. . . . Our Multicultural Management Program . . . seeks to attack this problem at its point: the fact that so few minorities in the nation's newsrooms have the power to decide, or to influence, what is covered by their publications. . . . The bedrock reason for all this is not that minorities lack the talent or the experience to be managers. The reason is a lack of communication and understanding in white-dominated newsrooms that often make it difficult for a minority with a different cultural background, a different style and a different viewpoint to fit into the system."

The first group of journalists, all with at least three years of professional experience, arrived on campus on September 7, 1986, remaining until October 3. Some responded to an advertisement carrying the headline "The Missouri Way: Newsroom Managers Are Not Born; They Are Created." Initially, the program seemed to be viewed throughout the industry as something solely for black management trainees. Only one white could be found among the original class of fifteen. But improving cross-cultural communication was among the goals all along, and eventually the diversity of the classes grew. A census of the forty-nine participants through 1989 showed thirty African Americans, nine whites, five Hispanic Americans, three Native Americans, and two Asian Americans.

Ben Johnson departed as executive director of the program in late 1987 to become managing editor of the *Columbia Missourian*. His wife became the executive director. Many of the journalists who attended under her direction sent positive reports to their supervisors back home. But complaints about disorganization and unpleasantness arose from journalists sent to the workshops by the *Miami Herald, Wall Street Journal, Newsday,* and *Seattle Times,* among other news organizations. Questions arose, too, about how much the Johnsons charged for newsroom workshops they conducted elsewhere, and how much they should be entitled to keep as personal income. Simultaneously, two Multicultural Management Program employees complained about Bullard-Johnson's alleged verbal harassment. She resigned as executive director, effective May 1, 1990.

Carolyn A. Dorsey, chair of the University of Missouri Black Faculty and Staff Organization, defended the Johnsons, telling Dean Mills, "This matter, which you might perceive as one only affecting the School of Journalism, affects all black faculty and staff on this campus. The institutional climate in which we work affects us and one which is biased or unfair, as this matter seemingly is, affects our professional comfort and growth." The *Columbia Daily Tribune* published news stories about the controversy.

On May 3, 1990, Gail Baker Woods weighed in with Journalism School administrators: "I must bring to your attention the far-reaching and unfortunate effects of the recent negative publicity surrounding the Multicultural Management Program and the Johnsons. Within the past two weeks, my office has fielded numerous questions from concerned parents, civic and religious leaders, high school teachers and current students regarding the 'lynching' of these two black members of our faculty. Because it is my responsibility to maintain the most positive image possible for the school with minority communities, this type of publicity is particularly damaging to the recruiting effort.

"I find myself caught between a rock and a hard place—unable to defend either the Johnsons or the School of Journalism. Parents of students who have been accepted to the university are wondering whether their children can survive in an environment they perceive as hostile to black professionals. The article in Thursday's *Missourian,* which I assume will be picked up by the St. Louis and Kansas City press, only perpetuates the belief that the school is racist. . . . While I certainly do not subscribe that the school is racist because it 'picked on' the Johnsons, I am concerned that this matter lasted as long as it did and, to date, has not been resolved satisfactorily.

"In my seven years at the university, I have never witnessed a nastier, more undesirable situation. This is a public relations nightmare and it is most unfortunate that it is centered on a minority program. The poor handling of the matter and the subsequent waffling and backpedaling in the press reflects badly on the school, on faculty, on the Minority Recruiting and Retention Program, and on anyone attempting to make any positive changes. If the School of Journalism is not prepared to make a concerted effort in the future to maintain the same standards for minority programs as it does for others, then perhaps the administration should consider not conducting any such programs here. The ill effects of this situation are more damaging to the school's overall image than if it had done absolutely nothing in minority relations. The newspaper articles make it appear that the school is willing to take the most expedient route available when it comes to handling minority matters rather than seriously considering what is best for the entire program.

"While I realize that it is impossible to prevent negative publicity from appearing in the press, it is possible to seek qualified and committed minority representatives to be members of this faculty and, thus, minimize the probability of racism being used as an excuse for incompetence. If this is not possible, then perhaps the school and the university should reconsider the viability and sincerity of its affirmative action policies. If the school is to be manipulated by thin and unsubstantiated claims of discrimination and racism, then what are the chances that any legitimate claim will be recognized and taken seriously? I deeply resent, after years of working diligently to make this program attractive to minority students and faculty, being placed in a situation that causes me to question my purpose at this institution. As soon as we are able to take one step forward in terms of race relations, we are forced to take two steps backward—and over what?

"Why should any minority educator consider working at the School of Journalism? If the university has unfairly treated the Johnsons, then what is to prevent this from happening to someone else? If these are the best representatives the school could find for high-profile positions, then why should any self-respecting minority educator join a faculty that promotes such mediocrity and grandstanding? Is this school so desperate for minorities that it chooses to disregard its own high standards? Are minority programs not deserving of the same level of professionalism as other programs? Unfortunately, I don't know the answers to these questions. But I assure you, they are being asked."

The Johnsons left the university with some matters unresolved. On May 2, 1991, Ben Johnson wrote campus chancellor Haskell Monroe from St. Petersburg, Florida. Johnson felt a "rapport" with Monroe and hoped the chancellor would overrule Dean Mills regarding a disputed $6,750 in separation pay. Johnson said he had agreed to leave without a thorough public airing of his grievances in exchange for certain conditions, one of which involved money. "More than anything, Mills did not want it to seem I was being forced out or that it was happening because I'm black. I'm still trying to sort that one out."

Later in the letter, Johnson alluded to "the ugliness with my wife and the dispute over who should benefit from our consulting . . . that was used as a wedge to drive my wife away from [the Multicultural Management Program] that she and I had worked hard to make nationally recognized. It was also used to sully my name and reputation." On May 10, Monroe sent Mills the Johnson letter with a note saying, "Please give me your help in drafting [a] response." Mills on

May 21 sent a suggested draft denying Johnson the money. Mills commented, "Ben certainly is creative in his recall of the facts."

The Multicultural Management Program became a memory at the Journalism School. Other valuable professional programs survived budget shortfalls and personnel disputes.

The Freedom of Information Center opened during 1958 to serve faculty, students, professional journalists, and citizen activists. Its extensive files of newspaper and magazine clippings, congressional hearing and executive agency reports, and judicial rulings could not be matched anywhere in the world. Neither could its own publication program, which yielded up-to-date studies of almost every access issue imaginable.

Paul Fisher served as the center's initial director, with assistance in the formative years from Edwin Moss Williams, son of Journalism School founding dean Walter Williams. The strengths and problems at the Freedom of Information Center derived in part from Fisher's personality. Popular with students in seminar settings, Fisher could come across as reclusive or shy or impatient in larger forums. Faculty colleague John Merrill once wrote about Fisher, "He doesn't talk much unless he is enticed into a serious conversation about the state of our nation. Also, he is willing to expound on the dangers to a free press in the United States or to explore the intricacies of typography, both subjects in which he excels. He is not in the least anti-social, but believes that there is too much shallow and insipid chatter in the world."

Born in Fairhaven, Massachusetts, during 1918, Fisher received a bachelor's degree in English, married, became a father, served in the military during World War II, then settled in Columbia while earning his BJ in 1946, MA in 1947, and PhD in 1950. His dissertation was titled "Modernism in American Typography, 1925–1934." Before earning the PhD, Fisher taught courses in the Linotype School, part of the Journalism School complex, as well as pioneering graphic design classes.

Demonstrating his broad professional interests, Fisher devised a two-semester sequence called Controls of Information that broke new intellectual ground within journalism education. Faculty colleague George Kennedy said Fisher "in his own self-deprecatory way was a giant in the movement to open American government to its citizens."

With Fisher spread thin, staff members including Jeanni Atkins, James Lumpp, and Kathleen Edwards did their best to keep the Freedom of Information Center on an even keel. In 1971, Roy Fisher (no relation to Paul), beginning to place his mark on the Journalism School as dean, found an annual deficit at the Freedom of Information Center approaching ten thousand dollars. As a result, Roy Fisher hired Dwight E. Sargent, age fifty-five, as director of the Freedom of Information Foundation, the fund-raising arm of the center. Sargent had served as director of the Nieman Fellowships at Harvard University and could demonstrate significant newsroom experience. Roy Fisher expected Sargent to provide higher visibility for the Freedom of Information Center inside and outside the journalism world. That visibility would probably lead to larger donations, Roy Fisher calculated. Money did arrive, from specific news organizations as well as from trade groups such as the National Association of Broadcasters and the American Newspaper Publishers Associations.

Unfortunately, Paul Fisher and Sargent clashed over the mission and direction of the center. Further complications arose when the other members of the center's small staff, devoted to Paul Fisher, decided they could not work well with Sargent. Atkins wrote to Roy Fisher on April 24, 1974, about Sargent's inadequacies as a manager, adding about Paul Fisher, "It is as if he no longer exists." Later that year, the discord became public in the *Columbia Daily Tribune.* Then former student staff member Daniel Epstein, who had graduated and was employed at a Virginia newspaper, complained to University of Missouri President C. Brice Ratchford.

Roy Fisher told Ratchford that Epstein "and the rest of the clique were very loyal to Dr. Paul Fisher, who is a fine teacher but a completely impractical administrator who asked to be relieved of all fundraising responsibilities. We have cleaned out the entire team and hope to be rebuilding the center on a practical basis."

Paul Fisher outlasted both Sargent and Roy Fisher but felt dispirited. On a 1980 Journalism School form he wrote, "Recognition comes from two sources— the students in their respect, the institution in the salary. I have the respect. I have had no recognition from the institution in the past ten years."

Eventually, Paul Fisher resumed leadership of the Freedom of Information Center operation. By then, however, staff morale had plummeted and disorder had reached into the center's elaborate filing system and its publication program, the backbones of its usefulness to journalists and other patrons. All that, combined with funding shortages, caused the operation to lose not only effectiveness but also visibility.

With Paul Fisher's retirement in 1986, control of the center bounced back and forth between the Journalism School and the University of Missouri library system. Everybody seemed well intentioned. The jurisdictional uncertainty, however, did not abate for many years, leading to a bunker mentality among staff members even as they labored as mightily as ever to provide efficient service.

Following Paul Fisher's retirement, several faculty members did their best to teach the Controls of Information course and to stabilize the Freedom of Information Center's budget. Nobody succeeded, however, quite like Charles N. Davis, who joined the faculty in the late 1990s from Southern Methodist University. Already well versed in access issues because of his newsroom experience and his doctoral research at the University of Florida, Davis earned a reputation as an excellent classroom teacher and an inspiring executive director of the center. One of his innovations was a regular online newsletter. A typical issue included coverage of a ruling by the Texas attorney general about the openness of hospital records despite a federal law that had been used to shield information from public scrutiny; a federal Department of Homeland Security publication of rules sealing off data under the Critical Infrastructure Information Act; a United States Transportation Security Administration request that a company providing transcripts of congressional hearings to news organizations expunge two pages of testimony from its archives; a federal appeals court ruling denying the constitutional right of journalists to accompany U.S. military troops to Afghanistan; the refusal by the U.S. Supreme Court to hear a case involving secrecy surrounding the detention and deportation of an Algerian immigrant; a summary of a General Accounting Office study regarding federal agency compliance with online FOIA requests; developments in a variety of state executive branch agencies, courts, and legislatures; international developments; and a roundup of editorial commentary from the mass media.

In 2005, Davis helped engineer the relocation of the National Freedom of Information Coalition to the Missouri Journalism School from its Texas headquarters. In many ways, the Missouri Journalism School Freedom of Information Center had always been the touchstone of the access movement. With the national umbrella organization merging into the center, it seemed as if all the pieces finally fitted perfectly.

The Freedom of Information Center and the other resources for professionals clustered at the Journalism School found additional synergies as endowed chairs expanded the faculty. The professionals hired to fill the endowed chairs received not only a substantial annual salary, an administrative assistant, and a travel stipend but also program money to improve reporting or editing or writing or quantitative research about the profession.

The relative plenty available to faculty members holding endowed chairs caused bitterness among some Journalism School professors who lacked such resources. Objectively, the creation of the endowed chairs meant a two-tiered faculty. Subjectively, however, most Journalism School faculty and staff seemed to adjust to the two-tiered system without bitterness. After all, the endowed chairs helped the Journalism School budget as a whole. Furthermore, those hired to fill the endowed chairs tended to be extraordinarily talented women and men.

When the Missouri Journalism School gained its first endowed chair in 1986, such endowments were unusual for a journalism school. The Meredith Corporation magazine conglomerate of Des Moines donated $1,100,000 to be paid over a five-year span for a service journalism specialist and a separate agricultural journalism teacher.

Byron Scott taught and promoted service journalism as the Meredith chair's first occupant. The purpose of the endowed chair generated some grumbling: service journalism seemed like a soft niche within a news-oriented curriculum. Should the Journalism School be training students how to write and edit features about buying a new refrigerator as opposed to covering the police beat? That interpretation of service journalism felt unfairly narrow, however, to those who taught it. Most faculty members seemed content with the Meredith chair, understanding that service journalism and police coverage do not need to exist at odds in an either/or environment.

In 1995, the Journalism School hired Danita Allen to replace Scott as holder of the endowed chair, as he became increasingly immersed in international programming. Allen (who sometimes used her married name Wood) had graduated from the University of Missouri in 1977 with an agriculture degree, later earning a master's degree from the Journalism School in 1993. From 1977 to 1980, she performed technical editing for the University of Missouri College of Agriculture. From 1980 to 1989, she worked for *Successful Farming,* a national magazine. Then, shifting to Meredith, she founded the rural lifestyle magazine *Country America,* which grew to a circulation of a million and paid her well.

Allen left the high-pressure world of national magazines to join the Journalism School faculty at a substantial salary reduction. Like so many other journalists, she found the thought of a professor's life at Missouri enticing enough to accept prestige in lieu of a big salary.

A proponent of service journalism, Allen, with her husband, Greg Wood, decided to revive a nearly moribund travel and culture magazine called *Missouri Life* as a venture outside the Journalism School. Allen worked simultaneously on *Missouri Life* while retaining the endowed chair. Discussion swirled around whether her faculty responsibilities meshed appropriately with owning a for-profit magazine. Eventually, Allen chose the magazine as her full-time occupation, leaving a secure faculty position for something more risky. She hired interns and full-time staff from the Journalism School student body.

John Fennell replaced Allen as the Meredith chair, moving to Missouri from his editorship of a highly regarded city magazine in Milwaukee. Like Allen, Fennell understood production inside and out. Like Allen, Fennell believed in service journalism. Unlike Allen, Fennell also felt comfortable dealing with investigative reporting and other edgy stories, thus expanding the Meredith chair beyond the perception that service journalism meant soft features.

Under a short-term funding arrangement approved by the state legislature, the Journalism School gained a spate of endowed chairs to supplement the Meredith initiative. The windfall from the state legislature seemed almost too good to be true; Dean Mills and other Journalism School administrators capitalized on the windfall beautifully before the opportunity expired. Eventually, private donations to supplement the legislative appropriations paid for large portions of some endowed chairs, lesser portions of others. As of 2008, the line-up looked like this:

Curtis B. Hurley Chair in Public Affairs Journalism, filled by Geneva Overholser. Dean Mills informed the campus chancellor on March 23, 1998, "We now have in hand one million two hundred twenty-five thousand dollars from the estate of E. A. McLaughlin, a wonderful alumnus of the school who left the money to establish an endowed chair in the name of one of his early newspaper mentors, Curtis B. Hurley." Mills asked approval for "the state matching fund program at the one million one hundred thousand dollar level."

Mills wanted to hire a high-profile journalist, preferably from the East Coast. He identified Overholser quickly as a good fit. Previously an editorial writer at the *Des Moines Register* and *New York Times,* editor in chief of the *Des Moines Register,* a nationally syndicated columnist, and ombudsman at the *Washington Post,* Overholser lived in Washington, D.C. An extraordinary thinker within the often intellectually pedestrian world of journalism, Overholser found herself focusing on the implications of how media ownership by companies traded on stock exchanges compromised journalistic quality, as corporate executives placed profit margins above thorough reporting and writing. Mills hired her with the understanding that she would assist with the Journalism School's Washington semester and commute to mid-Missouri as deemed necessary. A caring faculty colleague, Overholser made that journey without complaint multiple times each year. Overholser's columns, speeches, books, and conferences raised the level of discourse within the journalism realm and increased the visibility of the Missouri Journalism School, especially in East Coast media centers.

Houston Harte Chair in Journalism, filled by Dorothy Judith (Judy) Bolch. Starting as a reporter for daily newspapers, Bolch earned a master's degree in English from the University of North Carolina in 1970, then taught journalism at North Carolina State University part-time while employed at the *Raleigh News and Observer.* She rose to the managing editor's position there. In 1978, she cowrote one of the first textbooks on investigative journalism. As a newsroom editor, Bolch interviewed hundreds of job applicants. "Although I hired some Mizzou grads who were ordinary, I never hired one who was a dud. I did not see that consistency from any other university, much less any other school of journalism."

Bolch had also formed a positive impression of the Journalism School during the early years of the Penney-Missouri awards, while laboring as a "young lifestyle editor trying to change the world of features. . . . Most journalists couldn't see beyond the city council. . . . [Penney-Missouri] gave features validity that indeed meant much to those of us struggling in the trenches. I actually tear up when I think of how much Penney-Missouri meant to some of us."

In her classes at the Missouri Journalism School after joining the faculty in 1997, Bolch showed students how to place a hard edge on lifestyle features. Reaching out to the profession in the name of the Texas newspaper publisher whose family contributed the endowed chair, Bolch preached innovation in daily coverage.

Knight Chair in Journalism, filled by Jacqui Banaszynski. While seeking funding to create the endowed chair, Dean Mills cited the tradition of the newspaper editing course at the Journalism School, which pioneered a stylebook during the first few years of the *Missourian's* existence. Robert S. Mann (BJ 1913), a faculty member beginning in 1916, served as keeper and reviser of the stylebook well into the 1920s. Mills named skilled editing professors such as William Bickley, Robert Neal, Dale Spencer, Jo Ann Dickerson, Brian Brooks, Don Ranly, Daryl Moen, and Ann Brill in his funding pitch. Mills also named graduates holding major newsroom editing positions, including Richard S. (Rich) Holden, a former *Wall Street Journal* news editor serving as executive director of the Dow Jones Newspaper Fund.

Winner of a Pulitzer Prize for feature writing before becoming a newspaper editor, Banaszynski was working at the *Seattle Times* when she accepted the Knight Chair. Her original thinking, outsize personality, undeniable physical presence, and lively presentation skills made her an unforgettable classroom and newsroom teacher. In addition to spreading the gospel of compelling editing and writing in newsrooms and classrooms, Banaszynski made a special point of reaching out to assigning editors, "those forgotten folks in the middle who make it happen," as she said. As part of that effort, each year Banaszynski chose and supervised two Knight editing fellows who helped at the *Missourian* and shared their knowledge in Journalism School classrooms.

Maxine Wilson Gregory Chair in Journalism Research, filled by Glen T. Cameron. Gregory, a University of Missouri graduate who became a book editor, died during 1995 in New York City, leaving money to the Journalism School. Cameron was teaching at the University of Georgia and serving as research director at the Cox Institute for Newspaper Management there when hired for the Gregory chair in 1998. After a few years at Missouri, Cameron, a rugged Montana-bred outdoorsman who often bicycled to campus, outlined his impressive accomplishments as the endowed chair holder. They included "bolstering the doctoral program and research productivity coming from our faculty, including new media research; helping to reinvent the Advertising Department with the strategic communication model; generating about one million seven hundred thousand dollars for the school which funds doctoral students, helps cover costs in programs around the school and basically enables us to depend minimally upon state dollars." Having developed a "contingency theory of strategic conflict management," Cameron ranked as the most productive public relations scholar in the world over the past ten years. Defining his chair duties broadly, Cameron worked closely with two newly created institutions that cut across academic disciplines—the Center for the Digital Globe and the Health Communication Research Center.

Lee Hills Chair in Free-Press Studies, filled by Stuart Loory. Loory attended the Columbia University journalism school in the late 1950s and then launched a career that included reporting and editing on newspapers in New York City, Los Angeles, and Chicago. He also taught journalism at Ohio State University. In 1980, he made an unusual move by shifting to television, opening the CNN Moscow bureau; when Loory applied for the Lee Hills Chair in 1997, the application arrived from Moscow. He arrived in Columbia to begin teaching at the Missouri Journalism School along with his Muscovite wife, Nina, a professional ballet dancer. Students, staff, and faculty quickly realized that Loory knew just about everybody of importance in journalism spanning decades.

Missouri Community Newspaper Management Chair, filled by James Sterling. A first-generation college graduate when he left the Missouri Journalism School with his degree, Sterling became a small-town newspaper publisher.

Later, his daughter Stephanie received her BJ and married Jim Lawrence, a Journalism School classmate. Stephanie's mother, Charlotte, received a master's degree from the Journalism School. Sterling's sister Diane graduated with a Home Economics Journalism degree. "This school has meant so much to me and my family," Sterling said. In his chair position, he worked tirelessly to build bridges to small-town Missouri journalists and also seemed to know those practicing community journalism well in every other state.

Society of American Business Editors and Writers Chair in Business and Financial Journalism, filled by Martha (Marty) Steffens. Steffens stepped into the position from the *San Francisco Examiner.* She revived business journalism classes at the Journalism School, which had become sporadic in scheduling and spotty in content. Steffens also worked closely with the Society of American Business Editors and Writers, headquartered within the Missouri Journalism School.

Goldenson Chair in Local Broadcasting. Leonard H. Goldenson headed ABC News. In 1988, Charles (Charlie) Warner became the first Journalism School faculty member to fill the Goldenson position, which had been donated six years earlier, technically making it the first endowed chair at the Journalism School. Warner, a brash, confident, extroverted man who had excelled on the business side of broadcasting, offered his sales and marketing expertise to KBIA and KOMU.

He also sparked controversy about the mission of the endowed chair. On June 8, 1993, Martin Umansky wrote Warner and Journalism School administrators. Umansky (BJ 1940), a television veteran, had helped establish the chair in meetings with Dean Roy Fisher and had remained involved. Umansky commented, "It is my belief that the Goldenson mission has been altered, without any discussion with an advisory board (which does not exist at this time) as directed by the program, and has become narrowly focused on building Charlie's, as he says, 'national reputation as a sales and management expert [to] build credibility for the Goldenson program . . . ' My opinion has some backing in the comments of a number of broadcasters that 'Charlie is doing his own thing.'"

In addition, Umansky raised questions concerning Warner's "personal ventures," including news management seminars offered at the Missouri Journalism School. The personal ventures, part of Warner's "own thing," seemed to Umansky to detract attention from the missions of the endowed chair.

Warner believed he was accomplishing plenty. He emphasized a management seminar for news executives recently attended by thirty-four paying participants and three minorities on scholarship. The Goldenson program had surveyed television community affairs directors, using the data to inform a book, *The One*

Hundred Best Community Service Project Ideas. Warner felt pleased about building a relationship with the community affairs liaisons at broadcast stations. "Unfortunately," Warner said, "television station managers do not put community service in a high priority in reality. They will give lip service to it, but they are evaluated more and more on the bottom line, so that is where their priorities are. . . . Community service is more considered to be part of a marketing and promotion effort than the primary reason for existence."

After Warner retired from the Journalism School faculty, the Goldenson chair remained unfilled for years. That changed during 2006, with the hiring of Jeffrey Dvorkin from National Public Radio. Dvorkin, based in Washington, D.C., doubled as the executive director at the Committee of Concerned Journalists, which had just negotiated an affiliation with the Missouri Journalism School. Dvorkin and the Committee of Concerned Journalists staff moved to the Washington, D.C., office of the Missouri Journalism School in the National Press Building.

The Journalism School had received a $2,228,000 grant from the John S. and James L. Knight Foundation to establish a partnership with the Committee of Concerned Journalists to help train professional journalists and conduct research about improving news programming for a broad audience. The Committee of Concerned Journalists' trainers began with personal visits to newsrooms, then followed up with interchangeable modules that allowed sessions tailored to individual needs. The training menu included a dozen options, including covering politics, journalism in a time of national crisis, and accuracy and verification in the age of twenty-four-hour news. Dvorkin found, however, that his thinking did not fit well within the hierarchy of the Committee of Concerned Journalists. He departed in late 2007, leaving the Goldenson chair to be filled again.

The changes in the Journalism School lineup—especially with the influx of endowed chairs—brought to mind the baseball cliché that you cannot tell the players without a scorecard. Yet amid the comings and goings, one element remained constant: faculty, staff, and students—current and former—bound by their loyalty to Walter Williams's creation. That loyalty created such close ties that the term Missouri Mafia came into being.

Eleven

The Missouri "Mafia"

The term *Missouri Mafia* has nothing to do with organized crime and every-thing to do with journalists organizing to help one another in classrooms and in the job market. From the early years of the school, faculty went to extraordinary lengths to help students professionally, and students after graduation helped those who earned their Missouri Journalism School degrees later.

Enough newsrooms, advertising agencies, public relations firms, high schools, and other universities wanted Missouri Journalism School graduates that, start-ing with the first class in 1910, degree holders have generally experienced little trouble finding the types of jobs they wanted. By 1928, on the twentieth an-niversary of the Journalism School, the number of its graduates had reached 916. Older graduates started hiring or recommending newer ones, creating a network that has never dissipated.

Formal organization bolstered informal networks. A 1923 gathering of grad-uates at the Daniel Boone Hotel in Columbia led to formation of the Journal-ism Alumni Association. J. Harrison Brown, a 1914 graduate, became the first president. Until then, no other school or college at the University of Missouri had formed an alumni association.

It certainly seemed as if Missouri Journalism School graduates were every-where. NBC News anchor David Brinkley, not an alumnus, noted when he vis-ited campus during 1960, "I have not been to Columbia before, and until tonight I felt like the Arab who had never been to Mecca. I mean that quite sincerely, be-cause of all the [journalists] I have known, it seems to me at least half of them were products of this campus."

Evidence of the special bond among Missouri Journalism School graduates, surpassing the norm in other academic disciplines, is overwhelming. One example of many documented in various archives is typical. On March 10, 1925, from his employment at the *Dallas Morning News* as business editor, Alfonso Johnson wrote Walter Williams about an informal alumni dinner at the Jefferson Hotel. "We talked more about Dean Williams and the School of Journalism than anything else. . . . By standing vote we acknowledged the debt we owe you for having given us a good start in the right direction and for the wonderful influence you have been and always will be in our lives. We have found it necessary to curb somewhat our desire to tell the world that we are from your school, as our co-workers are jealous of us and feel that Mr. Dealey [the publisher] favors the Missouri boys too much."

The omnipresence of Missouri Journalism School graduates gave rise to letters such as the following, written to Dean English on March 3, 1961, by Leslie Slote (BJ 1947), an aide to the New York City mayor: "I think you will be amused to know that last Tuesday I ran a meeting for the mayors of the tri-state New York metropolitan region in Stamford, Connecticut. . . . The meeting was held at Pitney-Bowes Inc., whose public relations director is Jim Turrentine, BJ 1940. Covering the meeting for United Press International was Jack Fox, BJ 1939. We had great fun comparing notes."

Those who graduated often returned to Columbia to meet students in person, thus giving back and simultaneously strengthening the network. For example, Robert W. (Bob) Charlton (BJ 1974) returned to campus thirty years after his graduation. He had just retired from Dow Chemical Company, where he rose to the position of global vice president of public affairs. Early in his career at Dow, while editing the employee magazine, Charlton sent copies to Paul Fisher, his former professor. Fisher marked up the copies with constructive feedback and returned them to Charlton. During the visit to Columbia in 2004, Charlton taught a one-hour seminar in public affairs that included a mock meeting with students playing the roles of eight key stakeholders. The class then devised a communications plan for corporate executives based on the needs of the stakeholders.

Sometimes the bonds among Journalism School graduates linked generations not only within the same professional discipline but also within the same biological family. The examples are numerous of parents with degrees from the Missouri Journalism School watching their children graduate from there.

"Both of my parents graduated from the Journalism School in the late 1930s," Sanford J. Kornberg recalled. "Thus, my interest in the University of Missouri, and all that the Journalism School offered . . . had been deeply and positively instilled in me during my formative years." Kornberg said that, while attending classes during 1963–1964, he "was positively touched by the knowledge, professionalism, and spirit of Dean Earl English, Milton Gross, Robert Haverfield, William Taft, and William Stephenson, both inside the classroom and across all other associated activities. It has remained with me until now." An advertising major, Kornberg spent thirty years employed by the Interpublic Group of Companies, including twenty-five years with McCann-Erickson in Asia.

Laetitia (Tisha) Thompson graduated at the beginning of the twenty-first century, following the path of her grandmother Cornelia Linerieux Rice Hopkins, a newspaper major; her grandfather Stephen Hopkins, an advertising major who became Cornelia's husband; and Stephen Fenton Hopkins, their son, a magazine major. Tisha's mother, Lea Hopkins Thompson, did not attend Missouri but did become an NBC News correspondent and end up with an invitation to speak at a Missouri Journalism School commencement. Tisha also became a television journalist after earning her master's degree at Missouri.

Of the faculty as 2008 began, Brian Brooks, Kent Collins, George Kennedy, Edmund Lambeth, Keith Sanders, James Sterling, Esther Thorson, and Steve Weinberg counted children with Missouri Journalism School degrees.

Literal blood brothers bonded, too. Morris E. Jacobs arrived in Columbia from Omaha during 1914 to major in advertising at the Journalism School. He departed to work at newspapers in Des Moines and Omaha, then started Bozell and Jacobs, an Omaha advertising agency. Morris's younger brother, Nathan E. Jacobs, graduated from the Journalism School before joining Bozell and Jacobs. After hosting a Missouri Journalism School class that had traveled to Omaha, Morris Jacobs wrote Walter Williams, "Graduates and former students of the School of Journalism, every one of them, are boosters for you and the school. How could they be otherwise? . . . Both my brother and myself sense a keen obligation to that school and what it has given us. We hope as the future rolls on to be able to give it something." The Jacobs brothers realized that hope, donating cash and other resources again and again.

Lifelong friendships have abounded as well. Todd Donoho and Dan O'Brien, both broadcast majors who graduated in 1977, worked for television stations and networks in a variety of cities but never lost touch. Football served as one of their bonds. In 2004, Donoho and his wife, Paula, whom he had met at the University of Missouri during their undergraduate studies, decided to return to Columbia permanently. In conjunction with the move, Donoho and O'Brien, who was living in Greenwood, Indiana, began discussing authorship of a coffee table book to commemorate Missouri Tiger football history. The book came to fruition in time for the 2004 Christmas gift-giving season.

Marriage bonds have expanded and strengthened the Missouri Mafia again and again. Based on anecdotal research, marriages between graduates of the Missouri Journalism School probably total several hundred. One of those weddings, in 2006, brought together my daughter, Sonia Weinberg (BJ 2002), and Wright Thompson (BJ 2001). The best man and a maid of honor in the wedding party came from a long list of Journalism School friends, and many of the guests who had graduated from the Journalism School traveled long distances to Columbia to attend the ceremony.

Journalism students Doug Halonen and Pamela Grainger met in 1979, as they swam at the strip-mining pit near campus. A few weeks after they met, they found themselves together in Don Ranly's magazine editing class. "I think we might have been assigned seats together in the front row. . . . She was the last G while I was the first H. But maybe we just sat together because we liked each other," Doug recalled. They both earned their degrees and moved back East to accept journalism jobs. Twenty-five years later, their daughter entered the Missouri Journalism School after growing up in the Virginia suburbs of Washington, D.C. Emily Halonen graduated from the magazine sequence in 2007. I taught her in two separate classes—twenty-five years after I taught her father during the Washington semester. Her parents traveled from Virginia to Columbia to watch her graduate.

Robert E. (Rob) Davis recalled working as a graduate teaching assistant at KBIA-FM during 1974. "I was supervising the early morning shift of students who would prepare and deliver newscasts. I would get there about 4:30 a.m. and get things ready for students who began arriving around 5 a.m. This was the first morning of the summer semester. I'm looking out the window and this campus police car drives up and out pops a young lovely. She comes into the newsroom and introduces herself as one of my new students, Patricia Boddy. Why are you driving up in a police car? [I asked]. She says, Well, the officer saw me walking over here and told me there had been a report of an assault on campus overnight and he didn't want me walking in the dark by myself. Bingo—a news story had just walked in the door." They married a year later.

Deborah Hacker (BJ 1975) married James D. Serra (BJ 1976), and they began their broadcast journalism careers together in Lake Charles, Louisiana. He was not the only man in her student life during Journalism School coursework. Because so few women chose broadcasting back during the early 1970s, Hacker recalls that "most of my friends were guys, and I was just one of the guys. Al-

though we were competing for very few jobs open at that time, we weren't over-
ly cutthroat with one another. . . . Many of us still get together, either in Columbia or for other events."

William C. (Bill) Price (BJ 1963) and Mary Beth Sandlin (BJ 1971) met at a
Journalism School alumni gathering in Chicago. Each of them had succeeded in
the advertising world. They eventually married, reared children in Cincinnati,
and continued their careers. They also decided to give back to the Journalism
School, where Bill's father had taught advertising sales. When the Prices learned
about the creation of MoJo Ad, a Journalism School student-operated business
with real-world clients, they sent Stephanie Padgett, a staff member of Bill's in
Cincinnati, to Columbia to serve as a consultant. "We're doing this partly out of
enlightened self-interest," Bill Price said. "We hire about fifteen graduates a year.
This allows us to scout new hires and interns."

Beyond marriages, extraordinary circumstances led to loyal graduates who became prominent within the informal network. During 1935, the year of Walter
Williams's death, the Missouri Journalism School offered admission to Louisiana
State University students censored on the Baton Rouge campus. The students
worked on the school newspaper, which planned to publish a letter mildly critical of U.S. senator and former governor Huey Long. Before the newspaper
reached the presses, Long heard about the letter and moved to halt its publication. The students faced expulsion after refusing to cave. In response to an inquiry from United Press, Dean Martin said he would "be glad to have those
journalism students expelled from LSU come to Missouri to complete their education, provided, of course, they meet the necessary requirements for entrance.
At this school these students will find instruction based on the cardinal principle of a free, untrampled press and the right to comment upon or criticize public acts, restrained only by a common sense of decency. Without freedom of the
press, the sovereign people cannot retain or exercise their sovereignty."

One of the seven Louisiana students was Samuel A. Montague, who graduated from the Missouri Journalism School after the unusual reason for admission.
Montague never lost touch. He wrote Dean Martin on May 29, 1939, from Ford
Motor Company, where he worked as a publicist and photographer. On February 14, 1949, Montague wrote Dean Mott from his post as director of information, United States section, Mexican-American Commission to Eradicate Foot
and Mouth Disease in livestock. On July 9, 1959, Montague wrote Dean English from Kansas City, where he served as director of special projects at the Hallmark Foundation. Through the decades, Montague helped current and former
Missouri Journalism School students in the job market. He also devoted huge

amounts of time to helping plan the Journalism School's fiftieth anniversary celebration.

Earning a degree from the Missouri Journalism School could carry emotional significance for a variety of reasons, as the Gartner family can attest. Michael
Gartner presented the Journalism School's commencement speech on May 16,
1993. The former editor in chief of the *Des Moines Register,* page-one editor of
the *Wall Street Journal,* president of NBC News, and Pulitzer Prize–winning editorial writer was not a Missouri alumnus. His connection came through his father, Carl, who enrolled at the Missouri Journalism School in 1921 but did not
quite complete his degree for economic reasons. Decades later, Michael Gartner
started lobbying the dean to grant the degree and finally prevailed. In his commencement speech, Michael Gartner said, "Not many sons, I suspect, speak at
their father's graduation. At least, not many 54-year-old sons. . . . He enrolled at
the university . . . in 1921, so it has taken him 72 years to get through the
place. . . . When you die, I told my father the other day, the obituary will say
'Born in 1902, he was a 1993 graduate. . . . People might think you were kind
of slow.' [My father replied] 'That's not my problem. If it's my obituary, I'll be
dead.'"

One bonding point for the graduates came through the honor society Kappa
Tau Alpha, with its admission based on grade-point average. Walter Williams had
become miffed when national honorary society Phi Beta Kappa, with its liberal
arts tradition, overlooked outstanding journalism students because of their so-
called professional/vocational orientation. So Williams played a role in starting
an alternative to honor high-achieving students. After the Kappa Tau Alpha
chapter took root at Missouri, the concept spread to the University of Illinois
journalism program and eventually to more than one hundred other campuses.
Williams carried on a spirited correspondence with alumnus and building donor
Ward Neff about whether the Missouri Journalism School should push to build
Kappa Tau Alpha as a national society. Williams felt inclined to do so. Neff, who
served as Sigma Delta Chi president, asked him to refrain; Neff wanted to promote Sigma Delta Chi as a journalism honorary society instead. Williams bowed
to Neff's desires.

Journalism clubs related to majors within the school tended toward selfless-
ness while building community among current and former students. Henry H.
Kinyon, while a student, served as president of the Ad Club, for advertising majors within the Journalism School. "The club was organized," he recalled, "principally for the purpose of promoting the university back in the students' home
communities. . . . We tried to coordinate the activities of the various county clubs

to some extent and assist them in financing some of their promotion programs—sending out students and faculty members as speakers, distributing pictures, publications, and other material to high schools. . . . Such limited funds as we had were derived principally from the Ad Club Carnival, held in the gym, a dance–street fair sort of thing."

Jobs abounded through the informal Missouri Mafia network, as well as the more formalized route of the Journalism School's placement apparatus. The *Journalism Alumni News* of January 1960 mentioned the record of the Placement Bureau, directed at that juncture by Frank Rucker of the faculty. For the 1958–1959 academic year, the Placement Bureau posted 448 jobs brought to the attention of staff there. Of the jobs filled, 48 percent involved newspapers, 15 percent magazines, 7 percent broadcasting, 4 percent teaching, 15 percent advertising, and 8 percent public relations. Almost every graduate received at least one job offer.

I am proof. When I received my BJ in 1970, I accepted a reporting job at a newspaper, the *Metro East Journal* of East St. Louis, Illinois, where Thomas Duffy, one of my faculty mentors, had served as editor in chief. The first time I moved to Washington, D.C., I joined my then wife, Janet L. Hopson, who had received a master's degree from the Journalism School that led to a writing job on a weekly science magazine. While living in Washington that first time, I won magazine freelance assignments partly because of Journalism School connections, then accepted a staff job as a Washington correspondent offered by a New York City editor who had graduated from Missouri and heard about me through the network. When I departed Washington for an investigative reporting opening at the *Des Moines Register,* the editor who made the unsolicited offer, James O'Shea, had earned a master's degree from the Journalism School. Three years later, I returned to Washington to direct the Journalism School's reporting and writing semester there. Many of my freelance reporting, writing, and editing assignments since then—for newspapers, magazines, book publishers, and online sites—have involved a Journalism School connection.

The Internet era gave rise to mizzoumafia@topica.com, a daily listserv exchange with at least one thousand current and former Missouri Journalism School students involved. Job openings, jobs wanted, orientations to geographic and workplace locales, discussions of journalism ethics, and other controversies—the flow never ended. Early in the Internet era, the Journalism School mounted a Web site that has made job networking and networking in general even more pervasive. Hundreds of Journalism School graduates have written and posted profiles about themselves and their jobs that serve as both inspiration and points of contact for current students.

Specialized placement efforts organized by Journalism School faculty and staff often yielded results. Natalie Hammer Noblitt (BJ 2000) served as editor in chief of a specialized trade magazine, *Fancy Food and Culinary Products,* as of 2007. "I landed my first job in trade publishing through an internship I found during a Magazine Club job fair while at Mizzou," she recalled.

When students succeed in the job market or in any other way, the word often radiates on the Web and through internal listservs from proud department chairs, associate deans, and the like. On March 29, 2004, Brian Brooks, associate dean for undergraduate students, transmitted this email: "It has been a great couple of days for our broadcast news department. Mike Hall, a senior, won a national competition at ESPN for a one-year contract as a Sports Center anchor, complete with a ninety-five thousand dollar salary and a Mazda. Way to go, Mike! You've made us proud. . . . Broadcast News junior Kyle Palmer has been named as one of ten students campus wide selected for early membership in Phi Beta Kappa, the most prestigious academic honorary. Great work, Kyle!"

Individual attention to star students and troubled students alike became part of the package because of fierce faculty loyalty to those in the network. Denny Jay Walsh (BJ 1962) almost left the Journalism School during his first semester to resume driving a cab in Los Angeles. "I petitioned out of all my courses and was in the last stages of quitting the campus when Professor [William Howard] Taft . . . let me know that he didn't see me as a career cabby. I told him he was wrong, but he talked me into sticking around and proving it." After graduation, Walsh won a Pulitzer Prize for investigative reporting at the *St. Louis Globe-Democrat* and later won accolades for his investigative reporting at *Life* magazine and the *Sacramento Bee.*

Those members of the Missouri Mafia who ended up teaching journalism to high school and college students closed the circle beautifully. Of all those professors, one of the best known outside the realm of academic journalism is Samir Husni. Born in Lebanon, Husni earned his doctorate while in residence at the Missouri Journalism School during the early 1980s. Married with children, Husni lived in a small, subsidized university apartment crammed from floor to ceiling with magazines. He tracked start-up magazines, and dead ones, obsessively. After joining the University of Mississippi faculty, he began publishing annual guides to magazine start-ups and deaths, took the name Mister Magazine for himself, persuaded journalists to use that name repeatedly until he became a human brand, and won lucrative consulting contracts. Casual readers of general-circulation newspapers and general-interest magazines would see Mister Magazine quoted over and over.

Some of the early Missouri graduates helped establish journalism programs at other universities. Then a later generation of Missouri journalism graduates helped bring the programs to prominence. Examples include Joseph Willard Ridings, who earned a master's degree in 1928 and taught on the Missouri faculty before starting the journalism program at Texas Christian University, and Ralph Lowenstein, who earned a doctorate in 1967 and taught on the Missouri faculty before moving to Gainesville to become dean at the University of Florida.

At the annual meetings of the Association for Education in Journalism and Mass Communication, dozens of Missouri graduates on the faculties at other universities show up year after year as presenters, moderators, and award recipients. The 2007 meeting in Washington, D.C., included presentations by forty-seven current Missouri faculty and students, plus another forty-seven from other campuses all around the United States who had graduated from or taught at the Missouri Journalism School.

The influence of the Missouri Mafia has played out in special and sometimes unpredictable ways within the Journalism School faculty. The magazine faculty (my home base as of 2008) provides a case study. Jan Colbert, the magazine faculty director, holds both of her degrees from the Missouri Journalism School. So do I.

Another magazine faculty member, Jennifer Moeller Rowe, earned her master's degree at the Journalism School and then received an immediate faculty appointment because of her competence in multiple professional realms. She had served as Don Ranly's teaching assistant in the Magazine Editing course, which was feared by many students during the semester in the classroom, then praised by many in retrospect when they realized how much they had learned. "Although I heard similar material from semester to semester," Rowe recalled, "Don always made the content fresh, with new examples, different insights and fresh angles. Then I spent my last semester under Don's guidance working on a new textbook for the class. In 1998, I started teaching the class." As Rowe found out, Ranly's Magazine Editing course carried cachet in magazine and newspaper newsrooms throughout the nation, helping those who completed it successfully to win job competitions.

During her graduate studies, Rowe became friends with Amanda Hinnant, who was also earning a master's degree from the Journalism School. Hinnant left Columbia to help edit magazines in New York City, then earned a doctorate at

Northwestern University. With the doctorate secured, she joined the Missouri faculty. Magazine faculty members Mary Kay Blakely, John Fennell, Michael Grinfeld, Berkley Hudson, and Stuart Loory did not earn their degrees at Missouri. Their fresh perspectives contributed mightily to the positive growth of the magazine curriculum from the time they arrived on campus. But those fresh perspectives could be seasoned just so by the faculty who had grown up professionally with the Missouri Method.

Every sequence within the Journalism School has served as home to well-known teachers, scholars, and those providing service to professional organizations. Perhaps the best-known Missouri faculty members within the larger academic realm as of 2008 were Brian Brooks, George Kennedy, Daryl Moen, and Don Ranly, known collectively as the Missouri Group. Their textbook *News Reporting and Writing* had sold well through nine editions as of 2008, educating students and faculty at universities around the nation and increasingly around the globe. They collaborated on other books emphasizing writing and editing, as well as writing books independently of each other. Their collective name, the Missouri Group, seemed saleable, apt, and maybe even a bit presumptuous in a positive way. Journalism professors collaborating at another journalism school and calling themselves, for instance, the Illinois Group, would quite likely have lacked comparable cachet.

Twelve

Present and Future
The Dean Mills Era

Rilla Dean Mills entered the candidate pool for the top position at the Missouri Journalism School with an October 6, 1988, letter of application. (Mills usually dropped the first name altogether in favor of his middle name; occasionally he signed his name R. Dean Mills.) "The University of Missouri School of Journalism is rich in both tradition and promise, and from all I hear, good things are happening there," Mills said in his letter.

After growing up in small-town Iowa where he met the woman he would marry, Mills earned a BA from the University of Iowa in journalism and Russian during 1965, plus an MA from the University of Michigan in journalism during 1967. His newsroom career began in 1967 at the *Baltimore Evening Sun,* where he covered Baltimore County politics. In 1969, he shifted to the Moscow bureau, then in 1972 to the Washington bureau. Leaving the newsroom to pursue an academic career, Mills served as a visiting lecturer at the University of Mississippi in 1976, then taught at the University of Illinois while working toward his doctorate in communications, which he received in 1981. From 1979 to 1983, he taught at California State University–Fullerton. From 1983 to 1986, Mills served as director of the Pennsylvania State University School of Journalism. In 1986, he returned to Fullerton as a professor and coordinator of graduate studies in communications.

Despite Mills's accomplishments as a newspaper journalist early in his career, by 1989 he was primarily a communications researcher with a PhD. Other journalism programs had moved toward communications studies. Many Missouri faculty members, especially those without doctorates, wondered whether Mills, if hired, would move away from vocational education grounded in the hallowed Missouri Method.

Mills impressed those who interviewed him for the position of dean. On the other hand, internal candidate Edmund B. Lambeth came forward as a known quantity with enthusiastic backers. Many of those who admired Lambeth found themselves impressed by Mills, too, complicating the search. At least one shouting match occurred in a public space, involving a Mills backer on the faculty and another faculty member who thought Lambeth deserved more serious consideration than he appeared to be receiving.

Pleased with both Lambeth and Mills as candidates, faculty member Steve Weinberg protested a lack of information in a December 2, 1988, letter to faculty member Keith Sanders, focusing on the "mindless secrecy" of the search committee. Three days later, committee chair Sanders replied in writing, promising better communication with faculty and staff who did not sit on the search panel.

After Mills received the offer and accepted, Lambeth acknowledged the division within the faculty that had occurred. Congratulating Mills in a March 31, 1989, letter, Lambeth said, "I for one intend to do what I can to work for healing. Certainly, retrospectively, we all should learn as much as we can from that painful experience. Because I want my colleagues to know how I feel about these matters, I am sharing my letter to you with them. We all have a stake in your success and, perhaps more importantly, so does the practice of journalism."

Thus Mills began his direction of the Journalism School; his tenure as dean has lasted longer than that of anybody except Walter Williams. That is a fact, but trying to interpret the significance of that fact leads to difficulties. The wisdom of making any book about an academic institution dean-centric is open to debate. Should the Missouri Journalism School be examined from the top down? When I started researching the centennial history, I thought not. In important ways, I have changed my thinking. For readers who approve of the top-down approach to institutional history, this chapter will not offend. For readers who disapprove, consider the "Mills era" a convenient term rather than an encapsulation of philosophy.

Another problem in writing the story of an ongoing institution is achieving perspective. It is especially difficult to discuss the "Mills era" before it has ended. To determine which initiatives during the Mills era qualify as the most significant is impossible, because the answer depends upon the perspective of the arbiter.

Mills never intended to serve as a status quo dean, no matter the Journalism School's legendary status. He wanted to turn a great but somewhat flawed institution into an even greater one with less pronounced flaws. Furthermore, Mills knew that increased competition for students, staff, and faculty loomed. After all, other venerable journalism education programs planned improvements, with additional challenges arising from new programs at locales such as Yale University, New York University, City University of New York, and State University of New York at Stony Brook.

Like most who attain power, Mills ended up as the subject of endless conversations among students, staff, faculty, and alumni. Many of those conversations centered on the view of Mills as a dean who found it difficult to make decisions quickly, partly because of a desire to avoid conflict. During the reaccreditation of the Journalism School in 1998, the accrediting team found that "he wants to build consensus and avoid conflict: however, in some cases tough personnel decisions may be delayed in an effort to avoid a problem."

Mills disagreed with that evaluation. In a letter dated November 9, 1998, he wrote, "Build consensus, yes. But I think it fairer to say that I've worked hard to manage, not avoid, conflict. In the time that I have been dean I have:

*fired a managing editor of the *Missourian* and forced the resignation of his wife, the director of the Multicultural Management Program

*fired a political science faculty member who was head of our Center for Advanced Social Research

*fired a longtime non-producing member and former chair of the Advertising Department, and fought, successfully, the subsequent grievance

*worked with the faculty to develop a controversial professional practice track [as an alternative to the tenure track] that has since become widely accepted

*worked quietly to persuade a number of [Journalism School] administrators that they should return to the faculty.

This is not to say I regard myself as a tough guy. I certainly don't. But I don't think I have avoided any problem that I thought would stand in the way of the [Journalism School's] progress. It is true that I try to avoid public conflict, because it often causes internal strife that lasts for years. And I know some faculty would like me to fire this or that faculty or staff member because they don't agree with the way they do their jobs. But the second-guessing faculty sometimes don't have all the facts. In short, I think there's too much evidence to the contrary to say I try to avoid conflict or to avoid a problem."

One Journalism School administrator who departed in part because of disagreements with Mills was Robert Logan, associate dean for undergraduate studies. In 2003, Logan joined the National Library of Medicine staff in Bethesda, Maryland. Despite his difficulty in meshing with Mills, Logan remained a cheerleader for the Journalism School. He said that it "remains by far the most multidimensional of any program in the United States or globally. It remains the only journalism school to offer student access to a general-circulation newspaper and a commercial television station, plus other media, and simultaneously has a leading doctoral program and a thriving intellectual tradition. It is one of the few graduate programs that simultaneously challenges graduates to elevate professional skills with an understanding of media scholarship and its role in society. . . . The school provides the best blend of pragmatism and thoughtful inquiry."

Mills certainly paid attention to the pragmatic side—that is, vocational training via the Missouri Method. Any Missouri Journalism School dean would have, given the approach's entrenched nature. During the early years of his deanship, however, Mills focused more heavily on the "thoughtful inquiry" side of the school—that is, the academic research. He inherited a faculty research effort more vigorous than in the past. Still, the Journalism School's reputation within the scholarly realm of higher education seemed weak, if for no other reason than cultural lag. Until Lambeth's arrival in 1987, at certain junctures only a handful of faculty members possessed the qualifications to advise doctoral students, "a travesty for a major program such as ours," according to Keith Sanders.

A hiring decision made by Mills altered the nature of research at the Journalism School and the perception of the school in the scholarly world. At first, however, quite a few faculty members wondered if Mills had taken leave of his senses. The center of attention was Esther Thorson, trained as a nonjournalist.

Holder of a PhD in psychology from the University of Minnesota, Thorson headed the psychology department at Denison University, then taught psychology at the University of Wisconsin. Her connection to journalism came when she moved within the University of Wisconsin campus to direct the journalism/mass communications graduate program there.

Thorson arrived at the Missouri Journalism School in 1993 as associate dean for graduate studies. She had accepted what she considered a challenge, given her perception that the Missouri Journalism School, despite its fame, had "marginalized itself at the PhD level by choosing highly descriptive, mostly theory-free dissertations, laughable to most outside scholars. . . . My colleagues at Wisconsin said 'Esther, we'll never hear from you again, you're going into the abyss.'"

By the time Thorson arrived, Mills had hired Betty Winfield from Washington State University, Lillian (Lee) Wilkins from the University of Colorado, C. Zoe Smith from Marquette University, plus other mature scholars with teaching credentials and doctorates from well-regarded mainstream programs. Wilkins moved into the position of associate dean for undergraduate studies. Smith became Editorial Department chair. Thus Mills quickly demonstrated his commitment to hiring female administrators as well as PhD holders with considerable academic experience. The previously tiny doctoral faculty, overwhelmed with student dissertations and non-PhD teaching loads, began to feel less beleaguered. A later wave of hiring yielded PhD holders who also possessed significant newsroom experience, including Stephanie Craft, Charles N. Davis, and Earnest Perry. Yong Volz, another newly minted PhD, bolstered the teaching of journalism history and also helped renew Chinese connections with the Journalism School because of her personal background and her research specialties.

At the master's degree level, Thorson realized the Missouri Method prevailed over theoretical research; she saw her mission as showing the professional project (nonthesis) students the relevance of quantitative research—how it could combine with journalism and how the mixture could be applied to improve traditional practices in print news, broadcast news, advertising, and public relations. "The key to being a researcher is not just to be good at it, but to do lots of it," Thorson said. "For years, the faculty didn't publish very much, and the students hardly at all. Then, we ramped up the research component of everything."

To grasp the changes that occurred because of Thorson's arrival, it is necessary to know more than her academic pedigree. It is also necessary to understand the force of her personality. Around the school, Thorson worked as hard or harder than anybody else, setting an example that even the most accomplished, energetic scholars wondered if they could match. Sometimes she put on her "Dr. Thorson" face to make sure the members of the graduate faculty and graduate students understood she would not suffer fools or tolerate missed deadlines. Away from campus, however, "Dr. Thorson" could easily transform herself into "Esther," an extrovert with an infectious smile. She smashed stereotypes within the Journalism School about nonjournalists on the faculty, about women fearing statistics, and about female leadership.

Placing emphasis on faculty and graduate student productivity in the research realm, Thorson pushed for a record number of presentations at the annual meetings of the International Communication Association and the Association for

Education in Journalism and Mass Communications, as well as at other gatherings of scholars. Not so incidentally, faculty researcher Wayne Wanta, whom Thorson helped attract to the Missouri Journalism School, won election as president of the Association for Education in Journalism and Mass Communication. With his term in 2006–2007, Wanta became just the second president of that high-visibility group elected from the Missouri Journalism School; the first was Earl English in 1953.

Every month, the newsletter distributed by the Journalism School Graduate Studies Center provided evidence of Thorson's push for research eminence, a push assisted by longtime, hard-working staff members attuned to her agenda, such as Amy Lenk, Martha Pickens, and Ginny Cowell. As of 2008, Lenk had served on the staff of every graduate studies director in the Journalism School's history. Graduate students appreciated her vast knowledge of the rules, her accessibility, and her seemingly bottomless patience.

Seeking to define diversity broadly in the realm of research, Thorson spoke out against what she saw as an unwise amount of inbreeding on the faculty. She discouraged hiring new faculty who had earned terminal degrees from the Missouri Journalism School.

Bonnie Brennen, a PhD history professor and nonalumnus who joined the faculty during 1999 from Virginia Commonwealth University, applauded Thorson's campaign: "We have tradition, we have history and we have a huge number of sacred cows. That makes us different than most journalism schools. We have the name and reputation which allows us to do some wonderful things here. However, I think the fact that most faculty were once students is a problem; it lessens students' access to different approaches and ways of thinking. Most journalism schools do not make it a routine practice to hire their own."

Thorson also became involved in various matters in which university policy and Journalism School needs clashed. She made the case with university officials for the remission of tuition and fees for certain graduate students, thus allowing them to complete their degrees without dropping out because of limited financial resources. She negotiated with the campus Institutional Review Board so that graduate students asking questions of human subjects would be allowed to proceed as journalists, rather than having to submit questions for prior approval because of some vague concern about harm to the interviewees.

Assuming an especially thankless role, Thorson wrestled with the questionable management of the Center for Advanced Social Research, intended as a profit center for the Journalism School through income generated by clients such as news organizations, government agencies, charities, and for-profit nonmedia businesses. What became the center began in 1984 as the Media Research Bureau, mostly conducting public opinion polls about local concerns for Missouri newspapers. Before Thorson joined the faculty, a political science professor with research experience had been imported to manage the Media Research Bureau. The budget deficit had become alarming. Thorson helped remove the political science professor, then worked overtime to devise an ultimately successful plan to move the organization into profitability. She helped design survey instruments for more than a dozen large-scale projects, then helped market those projects to clients.

Not at all incidentally, Thorson's membership within the advertising/public relations (later strategic communication) faculty helped stabilize what had looked like an unstable program within the Journalism School.

When Henry Hager arrived at the Journalism School during 1985 after a career at the Young and Rubicam advertising agency, he found a curriculum in disarray. Several faculty from what Hager considered the "old school" of advertising had retired. They had been replaced by individuals with strong professional experience, Hager said, but poor collegiality. Three of them departed amid tension, disciplinary actions, and talk about lawsuits. Throughout the tense period, Hager helped revise the curriculum so that it included a backup elective course for each advertising/public relations core course.

Hager rode out turnover in the Advertising Department until Suzette Heiman assumed the management of the department. Heiman (BJ 1973) gained experience in the advertising and public relations fields, earned a master's degree, then joined the Missouri Journalism School faculty during 1989. She and administrative assistant Kathy Sharp helped stabilize the day-to-day atmosphere.

Glenn M. Leshner bolstered the quantitative research component within the strategic communication realm, as well as the broadcasting curriculum, when he arrived during 1994 with his doctorate from Stanford University. With support from the dean, Heiman found money to build on a promising foundation, hiring two young PhD researchers, Fritz Cropp and Cynthia Frisby; a more experienced PhD researcher, Margaret Duffy, who had worked in private industry for GTE (Verizon); plus two big names from the advertising agency business, Stephen C. Kopcha and Jack Smith.

When Heiman shifted jobs within the Journalism School to handle alumni and public relations along with staff member Billie Dukes, Kopcha became advertising chair, hiring newly minted PhD scholar Shelly Rodgers and advertising agency owner Larry Powell. Then Duffy became chair, hiring young PhD researchers Paul Bolls, Maria Len-Rios, and Kevin Wise. As of 2007, the attitude had changed from a feeling of second-class citizenship within the school to the belief that Missouri's strategic communication program deserved a number-one ranking within journalism education.

Glen T. Cameron from the strategic communication faculty, who had been hired into one of the endowed chairs funded during the Mills era, took an especially entrepreneurial approach to research. He turned idea after idea into income for the Journalism School, including the Missouri Health Communication Research Center, established in 2003 with Jane Armer at the university's Ellis Fischel Cancer Center. The Journalism School formed a partnership with St. Louis University to create the Center of Excellence in Cancer Communication Research. St. Louis University received $10 million from the National Cancer Institute; the Missouri Journalism School received $850,000 of that amount. Another initiative spawned a five-year, four-hundred-thousand dollar grant to the Journalism School's Missouri Arthritis Research and Rehabilitation Training Center for developing "a media relations plan to increase journalists' and the general public's awareness of disability issues."

Outside grant makers tend to encourage interdisciplinary research. Missouri Journalism School faculty became deeply involved in that realm. Professor Wayne Wanta served as director of the Center for the Digital Globe, an interdisciplinary research and teaching effort begun in 2002 that involved the Journalism School, School of Law, School of Business, College of Human Environmental Sciences, Department of Political Science, and School of Information Science and Learning Technology.

A separate liaison between the journalism and law faculties led to joint courses, joint degree programs, and joint research projects. The Journalism School hired Michael Grinfeld, a lawyer turned journalist, specifically to feed the partnership. The law school hired a counterpart lawyer-journalist to collaborate with Grinfeld.

During 2007, the law school on the University of Missouri–Kansas City campus made the liaison a three-way one. The law schools in Kansas City and Columbia plus the Journalism School announced the Innocence Project, providing a mechanism for wrongly imprisoned defendants to receive investigative services from students, staff, and faculty that might lead to overturning an injustice.

During 2004, the Journalism School began a collaboration with the College of Education allowing practicing secondary teachers to earn journalism certification. The joint effort built on nearly a century of Journalism School assistance to high schools. "We've been hoping for a long time to help high school teachers earn journalism certification," said Brian Brooks, Journalism School associate dean for undergraduate studies. "This program makes it possible for a teacher to earn a master's degree while completing certification requirements. And all of it will be offered online. . . . The Missouri Department of Elementary and Secondary Education requires thirty hours of college credit beyond the bachelor's degree for certification in journalism. When we looked at that, it made sense to design the program with a master's degree option because obtaining a master's almost always gives a teacher a pay increase."

Innovations for the Journalism School's own students appeared. An online master's degree with a thesis requirement attracted newsroom professionals who did not want to surrender their jobs. They included Dan Dennison, news director of KHON-TV, Honolulu; Christine McNeal, photo editor of the *Milwaukee Journal Sentinel;* and Tom Stultz, president of Gray Television, Lawrenceville, Georgia. The degree could be completed with a media management or a strategic communication emphasis.

Another graduate studies innovation involved a five-year bachelor's/master's program for those with a Missouri BJ. This cut a year off graduate study by allowing up to six credit hours of master's degree coursework during the final semester of bachelor's degree studies. The program offered nine areas of concentration from which to choose: broadcast management, in-depth public affairs reporting, magazine design, magazine editing, magazine writing, computer-assisted reporting, newspaper design, arts/entertainment reporting, and strategic communication.

Graduate and undergraduate students alike benefited from a dizzying expansion of Journalism School opportunities overseas. An internationalist his entire career, Mills encouraged the expansion of the Journalism School's already considerable overseas legacy. As of 2007, one of every four undergraduates studied abroad as part of their BJ programs. A high percentage of graduate students earned credit hours overseas, too. In fact, such a high percentage of graduate students arrived in Missouri from other nations that the country-of-origin list of the new graduate students each semester resembled a United Nations roster.

Faculty from the Missouri campus traveled as needed to supervise for-credit courses in London, Sydney, Buenos Aires, Paris, Hong Kong, and Guadalajara. Furthermore, students who wanted to earn credits in cities other than those could frequently arrange temporary supervision from professional journalists agreeing to serve as adjunct faculty.

Given the rapid expansion, Mills appointed Byron Scott as international programs coordinator in 1994. Scott had taught at Ohio University before moving to Missouri. The quick-witted, garrulous, bearlike Scott (called "Scotty" by just

about everybody, and a highly visible actor-director within the Columbia ama-
teur theater community) traveled tirelessly back and forth across the international dateline. Informally, faculty and staff referred to him as the "international czar." Scott, a former newspaper and magazine journalist, eventually worked
directly with journalists in forty-three nations. He achieved conversational skills
in Russian, Spanish, and Bulgarian.

Before his appointment, Scott recalled, "The international program had no
formal locus or coordination. . . . There had been scholars like John Merrill
teaching international journalism and [the school] had always sent faculty abroad
to lecture and . . . consult. But it was not an integral part of the program. The
international program was kind of a ghetto for international students. It was
where the international students who came over took their courses. Whereas now,
half to two-thirds of any international journalism class is domestic students."

Besides the arrival of Mills at Missouri, "a number of things came together all
at once in the late 1980s," Scott said. "The fall of communism, which opened
up central and eastern Europe and a great demand for work—teaching workshops and so on . . . globalization and the whole growth of international news
networks such as CNN. . . . State Department and foundation funding became
available. . . . A big break was we got a large State Department grant . . . so there
were a lot of us going into Eastern Europe and Russia as sort of journalistic missionaries, with the same spotty success that other missionaries have had. At that
time, the American University in Bulgaria was getting started, the first Western-
style university in the former Soviet bloc. They wanted to do journalism; they
came here and asked if the University of Missouri could help them out."

Scott took up residence in Bulgaria for three full semesters and a summer, with
other Missouri journalism faculty coming and going, an undertaking made possible in part by a two-hundred-thousand-dollar grant from the International Media Fund. Offering guidance to Missouri faculty entering territory previously unknown to them, Scott advocated that visiting professors explain what they knew
about journalism in a democracy, then let the hosts build something appropriate for their own culture. Some fundamentals are translatable, Scott said, such as
the obligation to tell the truth. Still, telling the truth is not always a central concept for media outlets in nations such as Bulgaria that have been controlled
by government or for those essentially independent of government control but
advocacy-oriented according to a news organization's agenda.

Spreading his personal influence and the Missouri Method beyond Bulgaria,
Scott collaborated with Corina Cepoi, who traveled from Eastern Europe to
study at the Missouri Journalism School, then returned to her country to open

the Independent Journalism Center of Moldova. The one-year course of study in Moldova would be conducted primarily in Romanian, with English taught to, at minimum, help students conduct effective Internet research. Cepoi and other Moldovan journalists studied pedagogical techniques at Missouri, while Missouri faculty conducted workshops in Chisinau as part of what Cepoi called the "Moldova-Missouri shuttle."

Missouri Journalism School faculty member Fritz Cropp IV worked with Cepoi to distill her master's project into a proposal that secured $220,000 from the U.S. Department of State to help the center develop a degree-granting program in Moldovia. Scott and Cropp attended the official opening of the Moldovan journalism school.

When Scott stepped aside as international czar in 2001, the dapper Cropp replaced him. Cropp had been employed at Hewlett-Packard as a marketing communications specialist early in his career. He studied for his master's degree at California State University–Fullerton, enrolling while Mills coordinated the graduate program there. Then Cropp entered the Missouri Journalism School to earn his PhD. Mills, who had since become journalism dean at Missouri, wanted to retain Cropp on the faculty with the doctorate completed but felt obliged to observe the sometimes hard-to-grasp convention of schools not hiring their own PhDs. Cropp accepted an assistant professorship to teach public relations at Syracuse University but soon returned to the Missouri Journalism School.

As international coordinator at Missouri, Cropp inherited the arrangements instituted by Scott and added more. As of 2008, he oversaw seventeen study-abroad programs. Furthermore, structured opportunities for students and/or faculty directed largely by the host existed with Moscow State University; Imperial College–London; European Journalism Academy–Vienna; American University of Blagoevgrad, Bulgaria; Danish School of Journalism of Aarhus, Denmark; Institut d'Etudes Politiques–Paris; Napier University of Edinburgh, Scotland; the University of Navarra, Pamplona, Spain; and Nanyang Technological University, Jurong, Singapore.

Mills had established relationships with Moscow State University faculty before moving to Missouri. As dean of the Missouri Journalism School, he, with Cropp, oversaw administration of a four-year, one-million-dollar grant aimed at integrating the Missouri Method into the curriculum there. From the Missouri faculty, Scott, Stuart Loory, and Martha (Marty) Steffens spent full semesters at the Moscow campus, while more than a dozen additional faculty made short-term teaching trips.

During the summers, travel by Journalism School faculty to train and learn from journalists in other nations reached astounding proportions. A partial list from one recent summer includes: Jacqui Banaszynski, Singapore; Kent Collins, Albania; Michael Grinfeld, South Africa; George Kennedy, Mexico; Zoe Smith, Serbia; Byron Scott, Montenegro; Stuart Loory and Daryl Moen, Russia; Roger Gafke, India; Reuben Stern, Jennifer Moeller Rowe, Rita Reed, Stacey Woelfel, Dan Potter, Clyde Bentley, Margaret Duffy, Tom Warhover, and Ken Fleming, China.

Fleming, born and reared in China, Americanized his name after arriving at the Journalism School in 1990 to study for a doctorate and supervise staff at the Center for Advanced Social Research. Because of his Chinese language skills and his familiarity with the geography, he served as interpreter and travel guide for some of the visiting faculty. As the Journalism School connections throughout the vast nation multiplied and Fleming became overwhelmed, Cropp hired Ernest Zhang as coordinator of China programs.

Mills boosted the Journalism School's international visibility when the International Press Institute magazine *IPI Report,* later renamed *Global Journalist,* arrived at its new home of Columbia, Missouri, during 1999. Loory, active in the International Press Institute, played a significant role in the magazine's move after he joined the Missouri faculty. Journalism School faculty members Danita Allen, a former Des Moines and New York City magazine editor, and Pat Smith, a longtime Missouri magazine editor, adapted *Global Journalist* to its new environment. Students participated in the writing, editing, and design for academic credit, while professional journalists, including some from the faculty, made freelance contributions. By 2007, the magazine counted readers in 127 nations. Loory also created the *Global Journalist* radio program, produced by students and broadcast weekly on KBIA-FM, with transcripts available for print outlets. When the program reached its fifth anniversary during 2005, Loory could enumerate more than one thousand on-air guests, mostly journalists, from seventy-nine countries, commenting on topics that included the outsourcing of jobs from the United States, modern-day slavery, and the spread of AIDS.

Initiatives involving Spanish-speaking nations developed, too, some of them built around *Adelante,* a bilingual monthly magazine distributed with the *Missourian.* Tracy Barnett, a part-time Journalism School faculty member, served as founding editor of *Adelante.* Students flocked to help, given Barnett's editing skills and sweet disposition. Eventually, though, she became discouraged at the lack of money and other resources coming from the Journalism School. Barnett departed during 2004 to work for Mexamerica, a Texas-based start-up company publishing Spanish-language newspapers in a variety of U.S. locales.

The future of *Adelante* became doubtful. Michael Ugarte, a Spanish-language professor at the University of Missouri and an *Adelante* advisory board member, questioned the commitment of the Journalism School to the enterprise. Mills replied that he lacked resources to support every venture he would like to support. *Adelante* survived, but when Katherine Reed began to serve as the editor in chief, dissatisfaction arose—partly because Reed was already overworked as a *Missourian* city editor, partly because she was not a Spanish speaker. Reed juggled the *Missourian* and *Adelante* assignments, overseeing a publication of continuing high quality. Students who were native Spanish speakers, Anglo Americans who had learned the language, and non-Spanish speakers served together on the staff.

Adelante received a boost when the Journalism School announced the Argentina Schifano (Tina) Hills Fellowship for Latin American Journalists, providing tuition and a five-thousand-dollar annual stipend. The recipient worked as a part-time instructor at *Adelante* while completing master's or doctoral degree coursework at the Journalism School. Hills, born during 1921 in Italy, had served as president of the Inter-American Press Association, as had her husband Lee Hills, former chief executive officer of Knight Ridder newspapers.

Marina Walker, an Argentinean student, was the first Hills fellow. While at the Journalism School working for *Adelante* and earning a master's degree, Walker wrote an exposé of environmental degradation in the mining town of La Oroya, Peru. The town's main employer was Doe Run Company of St. Louis, the largest lead producer in America. The exposé won international attention.

Unsurprisingly, the growth of international programs at the Missouri Journalism School led to language conundrums. Roy Fisher wrote about one of the conundrums while dean in 1972; he could have written the same words in 2007, given their continuing relevance: "What should we expect of a foreign student who comes to this country to study journalism but who will probably have a relatively poor command of English? We have traditionally had here what we called a 'China B,' meaning that we'd give a Chinese student his degree and forget about his clumsy English if we thought he was going to be working in Chinese. But our faculty wants to get tough with the foreign language student."

Because so many international students sought employment as graduate teaching assistants, the Journalism School staff developed training to help with English fluency. Master's degree candidates became eligible to apply for teaching assistantships after one semester on campus and demonstration of proficiency.

Doctoral candidates went through a different process. As staff member Martha Pickens noted in the Journalism School graduate studies newsletter, "Our goal is that graduates of our doctoral program will be fully equipped to teach and do research at any university upon graduation, whether in the United States or abroad. Towards that end, we expect a high level of fluency in both spoken and written English from our doctoral students, as well as demonstrated abilities in the classroom." Doctoral candidates completed informal language screening before arrival on campus. Their fluency level after arrival on campus determined whether English language instruction would be unnecessary, recommended, or required. If a doctoral student became certified as a teaching assistant or, one step up, as an instructor, he or she would be "encouraged to participate in the classes offered as part of the teaching minor on campus" through the College of Education.

Year after year, newly minted Missouri Journalism School PhDs from other nations found full-time faculty positions in the United States. During 2005, for example, Yan Jin obtained a position teaching at Virginia Commonwealth University; Yoonhyeung Choi, at Michigan State University; Sooyoung Cho, at the University of South Carolina; I-Huei Cheng, at the University of Alabama; and Anca Micu, at Sacred Heart University.

Internationalism is an affirming, vital kind of diversity. Mills pushed to achieve domestic diversity, as well. The Journalism School, with funding from the Ford Foundation, published a 142-page booklet, *Guide to Research on Race and News,* largely due to the initiative of Mills, Thorson, and project director Ron Kelley, an African American who had taught broadcast journalism at Missouri before earning a doctorate in higher education administration and becoming a full-time staff member dealing with alumni relations. Maria Len-Rios, one of ten graduate assistants working on the project, later joined the Missouri Journalism School faculty. Another, Teresa Lamsam, an American Indian from an Oklahoma tribe, earned her PhD at the Journalism School and accepted a faculty position elsewhere. A third, Hilary Hurd, became editor of *Black Issues in Higher Education* magazine.

The foreword of the booklet says, "We gather here the results of a comprehensive survey of academic research to date on how the United States media cover issues of ethnicity . . . the study covers scholarly research from the beginning of the twentieth century, with most of it clustering in the last three decades. Looking for and summarizing scholarly efforts in this area have been much more difficult than members of the team anticipated. Like news coverage of issues involving race and minorities, research has been episodic, scattered and, often, taken on with no reference to earlier work on the subject." Kelley supplemented the annotated bibliography with interviews of twenty pioneering journalists.

Another approach to becoming a leader in diversity issues involved adding a course to the curriculum. Mills devised and pushed adoption of a required cross-cultural journalism class. When the proposal reached the faculty, almost everybody liked the concept but worried about the specifics. Mills's proposed course listing said, "Cross-cultural journalism provides journalistic tools for the coverage of diverse ethnic, gender, ability and ideological groups inside and outside the United States. The critical role of diverse voices in a democracy will be discussed." Ideally, students would enroll concurrently with the practicum course in their major sequence, such as reporting for KOMU. After the requirement became a reality, however, lots of students unexpectedly delayed enrollment until their final semester, reducing the course's value as a learning tool and causing an enrollment logjam. The faculty revisited enrollment requirements, hoping to ameliorate the problem.

Anna Romero became the first co-instructor of the cross-cultural course with Mills. Romero joined the faculty from KTEP-FM, El Paso. "I was attracted to the hands-on approach at the Missouri Journalism School and wanted to be in a newsroom and classroom at the same time," she said. "I was also interested in living in an area where Hispanics/Latinos were still not a large population. I wanted to see the population explosion and issues that come with it firsthand."

When students complained about being required to sit through a course they saw as boring and politically correct, Romero felt the brunt of the criticism. Mills stood firm. "It's not a class about political correctness," he said. "To be a good journalist, students need to know how to relate to different cultures and races." A textbook for the course came from the faculty; *Journalism Across Cultures* listed Mills, Cyndi Frisby, and Fritz Cropp as coeditors. The teaching of the course focused on five fault lines impeding cross-cultural understanding—race/ethnicity, class, gender, generation, and geography.

Jacqui Banaszynski, a dynamic teacher, became directly involved to enliven the classroom sessions. A veteran newsroom writer and editor, Banaszynski discussed the importance of diverse sourcing for both factual and contextual accuracy. No matter who the instructor, some students, especially those who had grown up in homogeneous communities, found the course content, including the frank discussions about conscious and unconscious bias, uncomfortable. The process of figuring out how to satisfy the majority of students in the course seemed riddled with difficulties. If the instructor was Caucasian, some students grumbled, understandably, about whether somebody never targeted by bigots could bring the necessary empathy to the course. If, on the other hand, an African American instructor taught the course, some students whispered about tokenism and political correctness.

When Earnest Perry, a former *Missourian* city editor, returned to the faculty after finishing his doctorate and teaching at Texas Christian University, he grappled with improving the class as an African American professor. "For many of our students, their first experience with people from different cultures occurs when they arrive here," Perry said. "Even those experiences are often in sheltered environments and can't be translated to the real world, but exposing them to some of what they will experience in their professional careers is part of what we do at the Journalism School."

Managing the Journalism School with technology in mind became just as central to the deanship as managing with diversity in mind. With computers permeating the profession—in print and broadcast newsrooms, advertising agencies, public relations firms, throughout the production process, and, later, via the Internet—the Missouri Journalism School served as part of the vanguard. In order to do so, it needed to move a long way from the typewriter era remembered vividly by older graduates and quite a few still-employed faculty. A typical Journalism School announcement from the past (in this instance, 1948) quoted Dean Mott on the installation of forty-eight new typewriters, bringing the number for student, staff, and faculty use to more than one hundred.

As part of the transition, an arrangement with IBM Corporation allowed the purchase of about three hundred computer terminals, with linkages to each other and mainframes through a fiber-optic network. During 1993, Mills could report to the University of Missouri hierarchy, "We have equipped four computer classrooms with advanced teacher workstations. These permit teachers to use the instructor's computer and attached projection equipment to substitute multimedia-based instructional solutions for more traditional overheads and slides. The machines also have the capability of playing full-motion video and digitized audio both from hard disk and CD-ROMs."

Mills explained how the new capability "led to the production of our first multimedia-based classroom exercise this year. Students are presented a situation in which there has been a train wreck, and they must make decisions about whom to interview. Once the selections are made, students see and hear the interview and write their stories. When papers are returned, interviews they did not select are played. As a result, students receive excellent instruction in the editorial decision-making process."

Computer innovation cut across all Journalism School sequences, Mills said. "We are making extensive use of spreadsheets and specialized programs in our media planning class. Our advertising department has become the national leader in teaching students to make media-buying decisions. Nielsen ratings and other databases are used to help students make good decisions about where to place advertising. Such skills are now essential for students to find employment in large agencies, yet few schools provide such instruction."

Year after year, John S. Meyer led the technical team that kept the computer hardware maintained and installed new software as mandated, maintaining patience with faculty, staff, and students as they bombarded the crew with informed questions and uninformed questions alike.

Within photojournalism, the faculty worked with students and those in newsrooms who wanted to understand electronic imaging, using software commercially available for personal computers. As early as 1990, photojournalism faculty member Bill Kuykendall was spreading the message that "if you're just interested in the video-still cameras, you're neglecting some powerful tools for enhancing detail and definition."

Almost every new technology, no matter how much of a blessing, was accompanied by problems, often unanticipated. At the end of 1994, Journalism School administrators were trying to figure out how to pay for maintenance of about three hundred and fifty IBM machines and about fifty Apple Macintoshes after scrapping a commitment to minicomputers in favor of personal computers. At least one-fifth of the computers would need replacement each year, a seemingly overwhelming task with a budget that didn't even include enough personnel to care for the existing hardware and software.

Faculty members Brian Brooks and Phill Brooks (not related to one another) led the technology revolution within the Journalism School during the IBM era. Both veterans from the typewriter era who taught themselves how to adapt computerization to the classrooms, laboratories, and news operations, the so-called Brooks Brothers demonstrated the outer reaches of flexible minds mixed with persistence.

Another spectacular early adapter turned out to be broadcast faculty member Mike McKean. He had arrived in 1986 from Houston, where he was working as a survey research analyst after KTRH news radio had laid him off as managing editor. McKean (BJ 1979) accepted an offer to return to Missouri to serve as managing editor of KBIA-FM. As technology drove Journalism School course offerings, McKean kept up with seemingly every development, then instructed less facile faculty as well as students about searching the Internet for information, designing Web pages, and presenting stories via multiple media instead of just one medium.

One of Mills's computer-savvy hires was Clyde Bentley. He joined the faculty after twenty-five years as a newspaper reporter, editor, advertising manager, and general manager and the acquisition of a late-in-life doctorate. A convert to using advanced technology in newsrooms, Bentley played a major role in conceiving and implementing MyMissourian.com. As he explained, the purpose was to give "mid-Missourians a new way to share their own stories about life in their communities" through a Web site available free to anybody. Bentley told area residents, "You will be the reporter, and students from the School of Journalism will be the editors—guiding the writers, suggesting topics and tuning the grammar." Anybody wanting to contribute could sign up at MyMissourian.com, then "report your club news, argue for your favorite politician or share a photograph you think is special."

MyMissourian.com expanded the scope of what could be considered news, much as did public access television. "We don't presume to have the staff and expertise to make sure every opinion is informed," Bentley said. "We can, however, make sure that the presenters of those opinions are identified and that others in the community have ample opportunity to refute or support those opinions." Students in a class taught by Bentley and Curt Wohleber served as editors. Wohleber programmed the software for the site.

Bentley spread the word about the Journalism School experiments by writing in the winter 2005 issue of *Nieman Reports*. He started his essay in the Harvard University journalism magazine by echoing the skepticism he weathered: "Traditional journalists are wracked with fear about untrained 'civilians' dabbling in their domain. How could we have credibility without fact checkers? Citizens won't have a clue about the Associated Press stylebook or standard spelling. This is a college town, so count on a lot of swearing. What if they want to write about trivial events or tabloid trash?"

Conceding that "I was equally nervous," Bentley explained how the Journalism School "approached the challenge with a balance of cold-blooded research and warm-hearted humanism. . . . In the public's eye, newspapers are a world of 'no.' Our space constraints, high 'quality' standards and often inexplicable traditions create more reasons for not accepting material than John and Jane reader can imagine. Format and timeliness rules may be forgivable, but try explaining why we don't publish Little League results. Or why we will publish a twenty-fifth wedding anniversary but not a twenty-seventh. We're leery of any story that might 'promote' a business, and we don't allow authors to show emotion about anything—even the death of a loved one. As we resolved to eliminate most of the 'no' in the *Missourian,* we bumped into a few longer words like decency, literacy, commercialism, and outright banality. . . . We require original work from our citizen writers, but we managed to cut our litany of 'no' to just four—no profanity, no nudity, no personal attacks, no attacks on race, religion, national origin, gender, or sexual orientation."

Convergence, an offshoot of new technology, became a mantra of Mills and much of the faculty. Combined coverage by previously separate news media became a reality within the Journalism School. At a debate of U.S. Senate candidates from Missouri, reporters from the *Missourian,* KOMU, and KBIA asked the questions. A faculty member/editor from each of those newsrooms co-produced—Catherine Welch for radio, Stacey Woelfel for television, and Scott Swafford for the newspaper. The two broadcast stations covered the debate live; the *Missourian* covered it later. All three of the media-related Web sites carried accounts. C-SPAN, with its national video presence on cable television, received a feed from the Journalism School.

Sarah Ashworth, KBIA news director in 2006, explained her convergence routine: "Every afternoon I leave KBIA and walk across the Quad to the *Missourian.* First, I check in with each editor and see if she has a story that would work for radio. I look for stories that will appeal, and have significance to KBIA's listening area, which is huge. Once a reporter is selected, we sit down together at two computers and talk about the story: what's necessary to know, how would you sit down next to a stranger and tell them your story? Then the student sets out to write the radio script and I follow along and make corrections. They then read the piece out loud, and at that point I hand the student the microphone and they read through their story. Oftentimes we'll do it two or three times. Then I quickly edit the audio and send it off to the KBIA morning anchor. . . . We take a story that's inches long and turn it into about an eight-sentence story. The sentences become shorter and more direct, as well as more conversational. The story becomes much simpler out of necessity, in order to boil it down to a piece that can be read in about 45 seconds."

Ashworth said most of the print students "are reluctant at first, mainly because they're trying something new and stepping out of their element and they haven't had any real preparation. It's a different style and there's a certain talent needed to read aloud smoothly and in a conversational tone." Some print students accepted broadcast story assignments for independent credit. One, Aaron Kessler, "ended up winning an Edward R. Murrow award for his coverage of the tornado damage to Pierce City, graduating with an honor most broadcast students never receive in their lifetime," Ashworth commented.

At KOMU, Martin L. (Marty) Siddall, the general manager, hoped to generate enough income to keep up with frequently changing broadcast technology. The Channel Eight Web site began to carry video, and thus began to attract paid advertising. Content sent to cell phones would come next, and perhaps could provide advertising income, too, Siddall figured. "We need to think of ourselves as video content providers for computers and mobile telephones, not just for television sets."

Mills asked McKean to develop a convergence sequence. Two years later, McKean and broadcast faculty member Lynda Kraxberger became the first two appointments in the new sequence, followed soon by Bentley and Wohleber.

As the computing landscape changed, Apple technology started to play a significant role in the day-to-day culture of the Journalism School, with IBM fading out. Faculty received Apple computers free of charge, and journalism students learned that access to an Apple computer would be mandatory for coursework.

Kraxberger explained the possibilities of combining new hardware, new software, and a convergence journalism mentality: "It's the first day of the semester. A student walks into his journalism class and his teacher opens up a software program and says, 'we'll be starting class today with my theme song.' A funky bass blares, followed by a full rhythm and blues section, a Motown drum kit, and finally, frighteningly, the teacher's own voice singing scat. It's probably one of the riskiest steps I've taken as a teacher and begs the question, what does this have to do with journalism?" Kraxberger answered the question by saying, "I designed Digital Audio and Visual Basics for Journalists to teach print journalists how they might use audio and video online and in converged news environments to enhance our reporting. . . . For instance, students used iPods to interview people and create audio biographies. They learned that some of the interview techniques that work well for written stories aren't always effective in an audio story. They learned ways to focus their questions and the ethics of pre-interviewing people before they begin recording audio. They also learned that hearing someone's own story in his or her own words can often be more powerful than a written description. . . . By creating their own theme songs in GarageBand, a music editing software, students learned how music can subtly or overtly change the mood of a story. If the teacher's introduction was backed by the familiar *Jaws* soundtrack, that might have influenced the mood of the class differently than the classic 1970s Mary Tyler Moore theme song. GarageBand also helped introduce the concepts of copyright and licensing—important issues discussed in real news-rooms."

Roger Fidler, who joined the Journalism School technology effort during 2005, brought a star's presence and bold ideas to campus. Fidler developed a portable flat-panel reading device called a tablet to display a newspaper electronically as early as 1981. He conducted applied research to make the device affordable as a Freedom Forum media studies fellow at Columbia University during the early 1990s. Later, he obtained funding from the *Los Angeles Times* and Adobe Systems and served as director of new media for Knight Ridder Incorporated.

The applied research yielded something tangible for Missouri—the twice weekly eMprint (Electronic Media Print) edition of the *Columbia Missourian*, available every Wednesday and Sunday from March 2005 through May 2007. Fidler explained eMprint as "bringing together the familiar qualities of printed newspapers with the interactivity of the Web. . . . The editions are designed specifically for downloading and reading offline on a computer screen. The result is a visually rich, comfortable reading experience with no page scrolling. . . . The eMprint format also makes it possible to embed sound and video clips into the newspaper, turning traditional reading into a complete multimedia experience." Loyal readers abounded, but advertisers did not. As of 2008, the eMprint model was activated only for occasional special sections.

An insert in the hard-copy *Missourian* carried the heading "Important Advancements in the History of Communication." It mentioned the printing press in the year 1450, radio in 1895, television in 1927, and a Web browser in 1992, then introduced eMprint. *Missourian* general manager Dan Potter noted in a September 16, 2005, memorandum that the Marketplace pages of eMprint had gained sixteen new advertisers during one week, with fourteen of the sixteen buying companion advertising in the broadsheet *Missourian* or its Thursday magazine, *Vox.* One advertiser purchased the ultimate 24/7 package of eMprint, the *Missourian* daily, the giveaway *Missourian* (also known as the TMC edition, for total market coverage), and columbiamissourian.com.

Starting in September 2005, the Wednesday food coverage in the *Missourian* taste section could be found only on eMprint, irritating some readers who preferred holding newsprint in their hands but pleasing a new generation of readers who preferred going online. Another exclusive of eMprint was a new section called PlugIn, covering technology, especially the way human beings relate to it.

The *Missourian,* the backbone of the Missouri Method since day one, served as a constant in the maelstrom of technology by commanding the dean's attention for good and ill. At times, Mills found his déjà vu battles with publisher Hank Waters at the *Columbia Daily Tribune* irritating because they consumed precious resources. In the electronic era, Waters tried a new angle of attack on the *Missourian.*

It started with the Digital Missourian and its initial target audience of Columbia public school sixth graders during the early 1990s; would an online daily newspaper attract young readers and turn them into lifelong newspaper consumers? The preliminary results looked promising. Faculty members Jeff Adams and Kurt Foss, the digital newspaper hands-on experts, could actually monitor usage by the sixth graders.

At the *Tribune,* the Digital Missourian caused consternation about unfair competition, just as the print *Missourian* had caused consternation for decades. University of Missouri Provost Edward P. Sheridan told Mills on February 5, 1996, that, as a result of a *Tribune* complaint, the Digital Missourian could not accept paid advertising or promote subscriptions while using the campus MOREnet computing link. In a letter eight days later, Mills dissented but said the Digital Missourian would separate from MOREnet and pay extra from its budget to implement a "purist approach."

"Please allow me to add a personal note of frustration," Mills told Sheridan. "I was recruited to Missouri with four chief expectations: I would find a way to raise funds to build Lee Hills Hall; rebuild a doctoral and research program that was in shambles; improve the climate for women and minorities; and work with the administration to improve the Missourian's financial situation."

Mills told campus administrators repeatedly, "The *Missourian* is not guilty of predatory pricing or unfair competition. The *Missourian* does compete aggressively but within the bounds of both procedure and pricing that board members experience in other competitive markets. The *Missourian* Board reaffirms its intention to get out of commercial printing as soon as that can be done without undermining the very existence of the newspaper. However, with the current level of university funding for the Journalism School and with the current stagnation of the advertising market, the board sees no alternative to an active program of commercial printing. . . . The most important source of Hank Waters' economic distress may very well be not the *Missourian* but his own business decisions. The debt burden imposed by his huge new printing plant and the relative inefficiency of that plant have undoubtedly raised his costs of doing business. . . . To fulfill its teaching mission, the *Missourian* must remain an independent, daily, community newspaper. Everything else is negotiable."

After grappling with the removal of Ben Johnson as the *Missourian's* top editor almost immediately upon becoming dean, Mills became accustomed to Johnson's sometimes prickly successor, long-time faculty member and administrator George Kennedy. The hiring of Kennedy had not helped the Journalism School's diversity record, although diversity had been an issue. Mills wrote campus chancellor Haskell Monroe, with copies to campus provost Lois DeFleur and four-campus president Peter Magrath, "Thank you for your forbearance on the matter of our *Missourian* managing editor search. George Kennedy accepted the position today. . . . I enclose the list of women journalists around the country whom Jane Clark, chair of the search committee, telephoned in an effort to increase the disappointing initial pool of twelve candidates for the job, and women journalists who we thought might be candidates for the job. We could not convince them to come in, even for an interview, with the kind of money we were offering. I can understand that a search in which we interviewed only two finalists, both inside, might seem, on the surface, flawed. But the fact is, we tried harder to find good people, particularly from the outside, than the *Missourian* has ever tried. We simply didn't reel any in on the managing editor search, although, as you know, we hired, as the result of the same search, an excellent new general manager. She happens to be a woman."

A mid-Missouri native, Kennedy earned his BJ and PhD from the Missouri Journalism School and his master's in political science from the University of Pennsylvania. He joined the faculty in 1974 after three years at the *Wilmington (Delaware) News Journal* and seven years at the *Miami Herald.*

When Kennedy decided to apply for the managing editorship, he was serving as the Journalism School's associate dean. "I was looking for something interesting to do," Kennedy said. "Faculty editors [in the wake of Johnson's dismissal] had largely turned the day-to-day operations over to graduate students. Faculty were angry and frustrated, as were students. The paper was in a shambles. . . . I had to reassert the authority of the faculty, reassert the authority of the managing editor to the faculty, instill some new sense of creativity and esprit de corps, and, of course, get the paper out. It helped that the most disgruntled faculty mainly left in the first eighteen months or so of my tenure, and I was able to hire some eager and creative people."

During Kennedy's reign at the *Missourian,* some students and faculty believed a drill-sergeant boot-camp mentality took root among some of the city editors and became counterproductive. Kennedy's sarcastic outward demeanor upset some students, even those who came to respect him because of his high standards, dedication, and professional experience.

Kennedy produced a daily critique of the newspaper, mentioning students by name as they succeeded or failed, assignment by assignment. Some students embraced the praise and welcomed the criticism, usually constructive even when sometimes tinged with sarcasm. Other students lived in fear of being mentioned negatively by Kennedy in the Second Guesses bulletin.

Kennedy became the public face of the newspaper by writing a column on local politics, business, and personalities filled with his trademark humor. Some students, staff, and faculty thought it unseemly for an editor in chief to write front-page commentary that might be perceived as affecting news coverage. Others found the column the highlight of the *Missourian* and believed that the gain outweighed the pain in terms of journalism ethics. Mills, caught in the middle, told Kennedy during 1995 to end the column. Unsurprisingly, some free press absolutists accused Mills of censorship, suggesting that Kennedy's views—including a statement that Wal-Mart retail stores in Columbia had diminished the quality of life—caused problems the dean disliked confronting.

Wal-Mart and other potential advertisers sometimes rejected the *Missourian* as an effective vehicle to reach customers given the *Tribune*'s larger circulation. Like Mills, Kennedy rarely stopped worrying about the *Missourian*'s financial troubles. "When Patti Hoddinott was hired as general manager, I told her that every *Missourian* GM gets the chance to save the paper, and this was her chance. Ed Heins did it by creating the free weekly. Patti did it by enforcing numerous efficiencies, strengthening the sales effort, and just imposing her remarkable skills and strength on the commercial side of the operation," Kennedy said.

Patricia B. (Patti) Hoddinott moved from Kentucky to run the business side of the *Missourian*. Her brisk efficiency and candid manner of speaking did not always win her friends, but many who worked with her over the long haul marveled at her tirelessness in a thankless job and enjoyed her company. On July 30, 1991, Hoddinott wrote Mills about her first year: "One month prior to my arrival at MU, we lost our largest commercial printing customer, to the tune of approximately one million dollars a year in gross sales. Two weeks after my arrival, the grocery wars with the *Tribune* began, and by October we were engaged in all-out warfare. We managed to maintain half of the accounts and regain the other half which we had lost, but at a dear price. By January 1, 1991, we had regained all the lost lineage, at half the original dollar value."

After overcoming such obstacles, Hoddinott still found her plans to achieve financial stability criticized by the *Tribune*. On February 23, 1997, Hank Waters contacted other Missouri newspaper publishers, hoping to organize a concerted campaign against the *Missourian*'s free-circulation shopper. The campaign should include letters of protest addressed to the campus chancellor, the system president, and a curator named Fred Hall appointed by the Missouri governor, Waters said. "You can simply say you agree the shopper is unfair and that the relationship between the school and private enterprise Missouri newspapers can only be enhanced if blatant competition with the private sector is lessened," Waters told his publisher colleagues.

On March 11, 1997, Mills backed Hoddinott's strategy, reiterating the educational benefits of the free-circulation newspaper, as opposed to the *Tribune* serving as a vehicle to generate "wealth for private individuals." In a separate communication, Mills commented, "Hank's transparently greedy machinations become tiresome."

Simultaneously, the *Missourian* felt a revenue squeeze from the *Maneater* and other student publications. Founded in 1955, the *Maneater* appealed to some advertisers because of its focused circulation on the University of Missouri campus. Many advertisers will spend at just one newspaper per town, putting the *Missourian* at a disadvantage on campus as well as off-campus.

Bright moments appeared through the cloudy forecasts. In a memo of November 16, 1993, campus chancellor Charles A. Kiesler told Mills much of what the dean hoped to hear: "We agree, in principle, that the *Missourian* represents an important and central feature of the journalism educational experience at the university. . . . Every graduate of the school involved in newspaper reporting and editing . . . I have met has not only described the *Missourian* as the central feature of their experience at MU, but also as the critical feature that makes MU the number one journalism school in the country. . . . We both agree that the *Missourian* is to be considered quite properly as a laboratory of the School of Journalism. As such, there is no reason to expect it to break even, although that would be appreciated. With that in mind, what is currently being regarded on an annual basis as a deficit will in the future be seen as an appropriate investment in a university laboratory, and subject to the same sort of review process that other university laboratories are."

When university administrators seemed to be considering reneging two years later, Mills wrote to the campus provost that perhaps discussions needed to restart: "While the *Missourian* debt is a serious problem, the *Missourian* balance sheet is, in a macro sense, positive. Lee Hills Hall came about solely because of the *Missourian*. The Knight Foundation challenge grant was specifically for a building for the *Missourian*. That means nearly six million dollars in private funds that would otherwise never have come to this campus."

Furthermore, Mills said, "You'll recall that Lee and Tina Hills decided to give one million one hundred thousand dollars for a chair because of the relationship we developed during planning and fund-raising for the building. That's two million two hundred thousand dollars more, if you count the state matching funds. The nine million dollars of IBM funding also was a direct result of the *Missourian,* whose pioneering work in the use of networked personal computers persuaded IBM officials to locate their journalism education demonstration here. E. A. McLaughlin, one of our alums, decided to leave a one million dollar–plus estate to us to establish another endowed professorship in public affairs reporting—because of his fond memories of working at the *Missourian.* The Harte brothers gave five hundred fifty thousand dollars, to be matched by the state, for an endowed professorship specifically to be attached to the *Missourian* teaching laboratory. In short, the school, and the campus, are several million real dollars better off as a direct result of the *Missourian.* . . . While I know the school has given the campus some financial headaches, I also believe that we have contributed to the campus' financial well-being far out of proportion to our size."

Hoddinott communicated with campus administrators, too. Why did University of Missouri units place so much classified advertising with the *Tribune,* Hoddinott wondered; a change of policy could increase *Missourian* revenue by about one hundred seventy-five thousand dollars. Purchasing items such as newsprint, copy paper, and ink through the university system instead of retail would save the *Missourian* money as well. Workers' compensation insurance premiums could be lowered by as much as eighteen thousand dollars annually if funneled through the university, Hoddinott suggested.

When Hoddinott retired in 2002, Mills and other Journalism School managers worried about being able to replace her with somebody as talented. W. Edward Wendover received the offer. He served as general manager for only about six months, by which time the bad fit seemed obvious to many who interacted with Wendover. Nobody said publicly that the misguided hiring of Wendover would sink the *Missourian.* But morale, often low in previous years because of precarious newspaper finances and weak circulation, sank lower. Daniel S. (Dan) Potter (BJ 1976), who had run the newspaper in Blue Springs, Missouri, turned out to be a much better fit as general manager, doing his best to pick up where Hoddinott had left off, hoping not only to keep the *Missourian* alive but also, somehow, to help it thrive.

A devotee of the Missouri Method from his student years, Potter partnered with James Sterling's media sales class to fill the Homecoming section of the newspaper. "As appreciative as I am of the revenue, there is something more important at work here—the Missouri Method," Potter commented. "It has long been one of my top goals to have more students from sequences other than news,

magazine, and photojournalism learn by doing *Missourian* projects. . . . Selling
advertising is about more than generating dollars. It is about building relationships, conducting needs assessments, overcoming objections, learning to really
listen, and ushering a general idea through to creative design and execution.
Though I hope some of our student partners in advertising go on to careers at
newspapers, those are important skills whatever their career path."

With change occurring on the business side of the newspaper, Kennedy decided to step aside on the news side as he neared retirement age. A national search
began for Kennedy's replacement. It seemed like a propitious time for the *Missourian* to hire its first female editor. For those seeking newsroom diversity, the
search result yielded mixed feelings; neither the female alumna nor the female
nonalumna in the finalist pool became the first woman editor in chief. Instead,
Tom Warhover was hired. Warhover, the only Missouri Journalism School alumnus among the finalists interviewed on campus, represented the least diversity.
He arrived from the *Virginian-Pilot* newspaper, where he had spent his entire career after graduating from the Journalism School.

From his *Missourian* student shifts during the mid-1980s, Warhover recalled
city editor Bob Gassaway "blowing into the newsroom, larger than life; he was a
big guy physically, but big also in the way he swept into the room; [city editor]
Jeanne Abbott and her birdlike hand movements while editing; [investigative reporting teacher] John Ullmann, who could never tuck in a shirt but whose lessons
in project editing and management I still use today."

As Warhover filled city editor and copyeditor positions, he did not need to
worry about tenure battles involving newsroom faculty within the Journalism
School or at the campus level. That particular kind of unpleasantness, historically so troubling, had ended for the newsroom faculty. During the 1990s, Dean
Mills and other administrative faculty collaborated with university administrators to adopt a nontenure track modeled on the School of Medicine clinical pro-
fessorships. Adoption of a professional practice hiring track, based on three-year
renewable contracts, worked well from the start.

Those familiar with Warhover felt he would preside over substantial changes
in the look and feel of the newspaper, given his cerebral nature and reputation
for experimenting with concepts such as citizen journalism. They predicted correctly. Warhover served as the front man while the Sunday *Missourian* experi-
mented with a tabloid page size, other format changes, and revised content.

The first new prototype appeared on April 4, 2004. Warhover evaluated the
feedback, then shared it with readers. On April 18, he announced that the "second draft" would appear May 2. A follow-up from April 4 indicated, "People

who spent more time reading the . . . edition found more stories and features to like." Warhover reported, "They liked the positive community focus. They liked the in-depth reporting. They found *New Sunday* to be useful and relevant. In other words, there's hope. In my first letter, I said we began this experiment with an assumption that Sunday is a half-step slower and a whole stride more thoughtful—a day for reading the newspaper. The research suggests that editors gave you something worth spending your time on. Now, don't get me wrong—the research also left my backside a little sore from the not-so-positive findings. With the exception of format (some absolutely hated the size of the *New Sunday* edition), most of the negatives were things editors can improve."

New Sunday debuted on September 19, 2004, with a letter from Warhover: "*New Sunday* aspires to provide the background for more informed public conversations. Giving you . . . the information necessary to make democracy work is one of our main goals. But we know how important your personal lives are as well. Newspapers over the years have gotten better at things like providing phone numbers or Web sites for an upcoming event. But what about things you can use as you interact with your neighbors, family and friends? A story about a new cancer treatment should include enough detail to help you decide whether someone in your family needs to know more. A piece about a drunk driving conviction should provide the context that explains how likely you are to face a drunk driver on the road. *New Sunday* aspires to be unabashedly local. That's what the Missourian does best and should do best. Even in our national and world coverage, editors should provide local context where appropriate, or at least explain why a story may be locally meaningful. The reverse works, too: Missourian editors and reporters should report the global implications in local events. But, in almost all things, local trumps. *New Sunday* aspires to celebrate and inspire. *New Sunday* will bring you more stories of people doing good in our community. There's an old saw in journalism: Newspapers cover the community, warts and all. We need to expose the warts. We must also recognize the size of the warts in relation to the size of the hand. We must be fearless in our pursuit of wrongdoing while being equally courageous in recognizing things well done."

The reconstituted *Missourian* published significant breaking news stories, as always. Students working directly with editors or with classroom teachers funneling stories to the newsroom enlightened readers with in-depth projects. During summer 2006, for example, a series by student Anya Litvak on how public schools deal with sex education provided candid insights from the perspectives of students, classroom teachers, professional sex educators, ministers, and parents.

By 2007, Warhover had shifted to a newly created position: executive editor for innovation. He left day-to-day management of the *Missourian* to brainstorm about transforming the daily newspaper and its satellite publications into newsrooms of the future. Because the traditional print edition continued to need a managing editor, Reuben Stern replaced Warhover. Stern received his degrees from the Journalism School, a BJ in 1993 and an MA in 2006. Primarily a graphics editor who worked at the *Los Angeles Daily News* before returning to Missouri, Stern tended to view the news package from a different perspective than did city editors without such a pronounced visual emphasis.

No matter what changes occurred for the better, rumors about the demise of the *Missourian* continued to arise. In his column of May 21, 2006, Warhover called the rumors false: "There are plenty of legitimate questions, including the best use of print publications in the new world of digital. . . . I have no idea where these conversations will take us. The 'how' of it all remains cloudy to me. I know the 'what,' though—make the *Missourian* journalistically excellent and economically viable. Serve the people of mid-Missouri. Train tomorrow's best journalists today. The rest will take care of itself."

On March 3, 2007, the *Missourian* showed up in another incarnation, guided by professionally experienced editors specializing in news, features, sports, grammar, design, photography, and typesetting such as John Schneller, Scott Swafford, Elizabeth Brixey, Katherine Reed, Brian Wallstin, Greg Bowers, Grant Hodder, Margaret Walter, Mike Fulhage, Mary Lawrence, Joy Mayer, Rie Woodward, and Ron Jensen. A Saturday newspaper filled with in-depth features appeared at homes and offices of paid subscribers and nonsubscribers alike. It carried the title *Weekend*. Printed on Friday morning, it used features from the previous Sunday's *Missourian*, original stories by student journalists, and content from the citizen journalism product MyMissourian.com. The newspaper Web site became the place to go on Saturday for breaking news. The Sunday newspaper, thinner than before, carried fresh reportage and sports coverage.

As opposed to the *Missourian*, KOMU-TV's finances rarely worried anybody. Marty Siddall succeeded Tom Gray during 1999. Gray had solidified KOMU's profitability during his twenty-five years as general manager. Siddall knew that improving on Gray's performance would be difficult but undertook the challenge vigorously.

After earning a business administration degree in his native New York State, Siddall ended up employed by the television station arm of McGraw-Hill, a diversified corporation. Before moving to mid-Missouri, he spent thirteen years running the business operations of an Indianapolis television station. Not a University of Missouri alumnus, not a journalism school graduate, Siddall heard about the KOMU opening from an executive recruiter hired by the University of Missouri. After visiting Columbia, Siddall felt attracted to the concept of a locally owned station, with the owner doubling as the largest employer in the market. Siddall also liked the precedent set by Gray for becoming deeply involved in town/gown relations.

Broadcasting department chair Kent Collins noted the difference in management styles between Gray and Siddall. "Marty has a casual personality, but a much more formalized style of management. He is rigorous in his pursuit of input from his department heads before he comes to a final decision," Collins said. "Lines of authority, and responsibility, are clear."

The revenue generated by a professional sales staff that could brag about the station's number-one market ranking allowed KOMU to keep up technologically and sometimes show the way for the industry. As of 2007, according to Collins, KOMU enjoyed "one of the most modern newsrooms in the country."

KBIA-FM's original news programming bounced back in both quality and extent of coverage starting in 2001, and professional broadcasters outside the Missouri Journalism School noticed. During 2006, KBIA won five awards in the regional Edward R. Murrow competition, apparently the most in the station's history. The winning entries came in the categories of hard news, news documentary, newscast, sports reporting, and use of sound.

All the possibilities for students to use the Missouri Method kept the quality of applicants high, a good sign for the Journalism School in the competition for hegemony. Perhaps the most sweeping change in the competition for students occurred when the Journalism School decided to guarantee freshmen a place if they achieved a certain level in high school.

The Journalism School had been on the verge of turning away sophomores with 3.2 grade point averages (on a scale of 4.0) who met prejournalism requirements while officially enrolled in the Arts and Science College because not enough teachers, classrooms, and course openings existed to accommodate everybody. "We have students coming in from all over the country, all over the world actually, [who] in some cases rack up good but not stellar GPAs, but then are told sorry, we can't accept you into the school," Mills said. Freshmen admitted for fall 2004 included forty-three high school valedictorians. Sixty percent of the freshmen arrived from outside Missouri, and 13 percent were minorities. By fall 2007, the average ACT score reached 28.8 (out of 36), compared to 25.5 for all MU freshmen and 21.5 for all Missouri high school graduates with reported results. That meant the average freshman journalism major was eligible for the University of Missouri Honors College, something achieved by only 15 percent of the university's total student population.

As part of the quest for hegemony, the Journalism School invented other new inducements. Although not every student received money to ameliorate financial need, scholarships donated by individuals, institutions, and professional associations abounded throughout the academic sequences. Some of them went unclaimed amid the largesse. Others attracted intense competition and jump-started professional careers. For example, a bequest from the estate of O. O. McIntyre—a Missouri-born syndicated newspaper columnist who died in 1938—led to the McIntyre Fellowship, a ten-thousand-dollar award to a just-graduated student for an in-depth reporting project. In 2007, student Jennifer Price bested the competition. She proposed to use the money for travel to Sudan, where she hoped to document the problems of child soldiers and other refugees in that war-ravaged African nation.

A Journalism Scholars Program assisted high-achieving freshmen. Those designated scholars became automatically enrolled in the Honors College and could participate in a Freshman Interest Group, live in a residence hall set aside for future journalists, and attend social events designed specifically for them.

The highest achieving Journalism Scholars (with a minimum ACT score of 33 and often in the top 1 percent of their high school graduating class) attained the designation of Walter Williams Scholars, which included a one-thousand-dollar award for studying abroad or in the school's Washington, D.C., or New York City semesters any time before graduating. Each of the scholars received advice from a faculty mentor. A subset of Walter Williams Scholars were named by the university as Discovery Fellows, assisting research faculty, for pay, while still freshmen. In 2004, the university designated twenty-five students as Discovery Fellows; ten came from the Journalism School admissions.

The high-achieving students almost all grew up with computer technology; most adapted without anxiety to the frequent upgrades integrated into their university experience. Some of the faculty, however, found the emphasis on technology at the Journalism School not only anxiety producing but also disconcerting. Mills, on the other hand, embraced the rapid pace of change.

Some of the technology research and applications would find a new home within the Journalism School during its centennial year because of a thirty-one-million-dollar donation from the Donald W. Reynolds Foundation, based in Las Vegas. Never had the Journalism School, or any other unit of the university, received a larger gift.

After Donald W. Reynolds graduated from the Journalism School in 1927, he worked at newspapers in Kansas City, Indianapolis, and Austin. Fascinated with the business side of the daily miracle, by 1931 he had become a publisher of newspapers in Massachusetts and New Jersey. He retained his Journalism School connections on the path to wealth. On September 24, 1933, for example, Reynolds wrote Frank Martin with a question about opportunities to buy small daily newspapers with his ten thousand dollars in savings as a down payment. Martin made inquiries, then wrote Reynolds three days later about newspapers available for purchase in Colorado and Missouri.

Reynolds eventually built a newspaper chain with about fifty properties. The newspapers received little praise from the profession; journalists generally viewed them as profit centers that skimped on newsroom budgets. The criticism might have stung Reynolds, but he remained a proud Missouri journalism alumnus.

At first, Reynolds directed money to another part of the campus, rather than to the Journalism School; in 1992, the University of Missouri Reynolds Alumni Center opened, built with a nine-million-dollar donation from the newspaper magnate. After Reynolds died in 1993, those in charge of his legacy agreed to open discussions with Journalism School representatives, led by Roger Gafke and Dean Mills. Gafke was a savvy fund-raiser, having left the Journalism School faculty for a while to seek donations for the entire campus. Mills, like most deans, had learned a lot about fund-raising on the job. He also learned about it at home; his wife, Sue, worked for the university as a professional fund-raiser. After becoming Journalism School dean, Mills expanded the fund-raising staff until, as of 2008, it included three full-time field professionals—Colin Kilpatrick, Catey Terry, and Kimberly Lakin Mize—and an office assistant, Helen Pattrin.

The conversations with the Reynolds Foundation staff obviously paid off. Much of the thirty-one-million-dollar gift would pay for renovating the former Sociology Building on the campus Quadrangle to serve as the newly conceived Reynolds Journalism Institute. A much expanded, high-technology journalism library would consume part of the space. The Reynolds money would also pay for construction of a new building between the Journalism Institute building and Walter Williams Hall, plus a complete overhaul of the interior of Walter Williams Hall.

Pam Johnson (BJ 1969) became the Journalism Institute's first executive director. She moved to Columbia from the Poynter Institute for Media Studies; before that, she had worked as an editor at the *Arizona Republic/Phoenix Gazette* and *Kansas City Star*. Mills said that Johnson would "oversee the Institute's three areas of emphasis—the Fellows and faculty projects aimed at improving the practice and understanding of journalism; the experiments using new technologies for journalism and advertising; and the forums, workshops, lectures, and other programs in which journalists, citizens, and academics work together to strengthen the quality of journalism in democratic societies."

Then, in the middle of 2007, Mills surprised just about everyone by announcing he would take a year's break from the day-to-day business of the deanship to become even more deeply involved in the Journalism Institute. Esther Thorson became acting dean, with the consent of campus Provost Brian Foster.

A clearer sense of what the nascent Reynolds Journalism Institute might be about emerged gradually. Thorson and faculty member Margaret Duffy signed a research contract with the Newspaper Association of America to explore applying digital technologies to improve information collection and presentation in local journalism. As part of the research, the Journalism Institute paid a consulting team led by Merrill Brown, the first editor at MSNBC.com; two Missouri Journalism School graduates constituted part of the consulting team.

Missourian editor Warhover began collaborating with the Journalism Institute to lead the way in reporting/presenting the news across previously distinct media. The *Missourian,* KOMU, and KBIA would serve as the testing locales. Warhover hoped to mesh the Missouri Method—joining theory and practice—with a new formulation that might become known as the Missouri Model.

In a memo of March 18, 2006, Warhover said, "This project attempts to find a bunch of new tools to do new journalism, or at least preserve old journalistic values in a new media landscape. . . . Roger Fidler, the director of technology for the Reynolds Journalism Institute, told me something that rings true here. He said it's easy to envision media fifteen or fifty years out; you don't have to actually see it come to fruition. The Missouri Model project says we need to find things we can actually put into practice, and then do it. . . . [We hope] to produce a set of new digital tools that can be used by our industry. That may mean software, content, marketing, advertising, newsroom structure, or pieces of all of them and more. And if it doesn't have a reasonable chance of making money, it doesn't get done."

The Journalism Institute constituted a journey into the mostly unknown reaches of the profession. At the Journalism School, with everything up for grabs, even the nomenclature to describe various corners of journalism seemed uncertain. Brian Brooks, associate dean for undergraduate studies, asked faculty and staff in a June 7, 2006, memo to stop using the term *sequences* and start using *emphasis areas.* He noted that the six current emphasis areas consisted of newspaper journalism, magazine journalism, radio-television journalism, convergence journalism, photojournalism, and strategic communication. That seemingly innocuous memo opened a debate about the accuracy of those terms.

"Just as we are preparing to change the Missourian to a 24/7 newsroom where everyone gathers and distributes news over a variety of media—print, Web, eM-print, text messaging, etc., we are proposing to change the name [of one emphasis area] to Newspaper Journalism," former *Missourian* editor Daryl Moen complained. "That doesn't accurately describe what we do, nor does it offer any encouragement to students who want to take advantage of new media nor does it say to our profession that we know we are in the midst of change. You could make the same case for Radio-Television Journalism. They also report for the Web and send information out through other media. In a sense, all media is converged."

Professor Jacqui Banaszynski wondered whether the faculty would "consider defining our focus around what we do, not the platform we do it on," suggesting reporting/writing, visual journalism, and multimedia journalism as potential terminology. Professor Phill Brooks said that, as he looked at the school through the filter of content, he saw four categories of course offerings and faculty interests: journalism (reporting, editing, photography), public communication (advertising, public relations), management, and research and theory.

John Merrill, viewing the Missouri Journalism School and sister institutions from his emeritus professor perch, sounded off in an essay published by *Media Ethics*. As usual, Merrill did not hold back. Merrill found the drift from practice to theory unsurprising, given the "growing numbers of graduate students, beginning in the 1970s . . . increasingly lack[ing] substantial professional journalism experience. Some PhDs now teaching in communications and journalism programs have no real practical experience at all. They consider themselves communications specialists, not journalists. And most of their own academic work has been in . . . areas such as psychology and sociology. And then there are the advertising and public relations faculty members that have entrenched themselves solidly in the old journalism programs. Students enrolled in their courses have rapidly increased, due to the promise of public exposure and better salaries."

The convergence of journalism and communications within the same institution, Merrill worried, might end up with a program dominated by theory-based PhDs "teaching research and theoretical courses that assume no real knowledge of how the real media work. What is happening, naturally then, is that the old concept of journalism education is disappearing into a new convergence curriculum of something called 'communication.' The new student in this area will be a product of theory, research and technology. Maybe a new degree will be needed—TRT (Technical Research Theorist). The new TRTer will, of course, face the same old foundational problem in public communication—the morality issue. Will his or her post-modern education make for more ethical communication? I doubt it very much. Not what can I do, but what should I do? That is still the foundational question."

As Merrill's words appeared in print, heavy machinery dug up the University of Missouri Quadrangle to expand the Journalism School physically beyond recognition. Whether it would change intellectually beyond recognition during a digital era remained uncertain as its centennial year opened.

Walter Williams had left a remarkable legacy, but perhaps not one remarkable enough to last in perpetuity.

Sources and Acknowledgments

No narrative history of the Missouri Journalism School has been published in book form until now.

This book benefited from material never seen by previous researchers. The material has been scattered throughout Missouri Journalism School buildings—some of it held for nearly one hundred years, some of it for just a few years. Many of those uncataloged pieces of paper, pamphlets, and reports are in superb shape, while others are partially crumbled or worse. Such a situation constitutes a nightmare for a professional archivist; the material should have been turned over to climate-controlled archives but for whatever reasons was not. Presumably, it will be archived soon.

For a historian writing about the Journalism School, the uncataloged documents are welcome, although occasional illegibility and gaps in the record are maddening. The largest trove of such material consists of personal correspondence, business correspondence, newspaper and magazine clippings, manuscript drafts, expense vouchers, photographs, budget documents, official and unofficial meeting minutes, and hard-to-describe miscellany mixed together within folders labeled with the names of individuals—students, staff, faculty, outsider donors, and a variety of others in the realms of news gathering, news editing, photojournalism, advertising, and public relations. The folders appear to have originated in the dean's office, starting with Walter Williams.

Fortunately, large amounts of material relating to the history of the Journalism School have been carefully archived. Walter Williams's personal papers are cataloged at the Western Historical Manuscript Collection, in a wing of the University of Missouri campus library, where the archivists are learned, efficient, and available. Also there are the papers of Sara Lockwood Williams, Frank Luther Mott, Earl English, Robert P. Knight, and KOMU-TV.

The official archives of the University of Missouri, located in Lewis Hall, yielded papers from the Journalism School dean's office, including faculty meeting minutes and all manner of correspondence. Every dean is represented. Faculty members including Edward Lambert, Joye Patterson, and Dale Spencer also sent papers to the Lewis Hall archives. The helpfulness and knowledge of the Lewis Hall staff—especially Kristopher Anstine, Gary Cox, and Michael E. Holland—impressed me during each visit.

Additional archives in Columbia at the State Historical Society of Missouri held some useful documents.

Unarchived material from the papers of Maurice E. Votaw came to me from Fred G. Moore of Boulder, Colorado, a descendant of Votaw's.

Time and budget considerations prevented me from checking every archive in Missouri and other states housing personal and official papers that might have contained relevant material. One site I did explore was the Harry S. Truman Presidential Museum and Library in Independence, Missouri, which is home to a Mary Paxton Keeley oral history that provided insights.

Material came directly from each of midcareer and other affiliated programs at the Journalism School, especially the Missourian Publishing Association, Investigative Reporters and Editors, Society of American Business Editors and Writers, National Freedom of Information Coalition and its precursor Freedom of Information Center, National Newspaper Association, Journalism and Women Symposium, New Directions for News, City and Regional Magazine Association, Pictures of the Year, JC Penney–Missouri Lifestyle Journalism Awards, Committee of Concerned Journalists, Missouri Interscholastic Press Association, International Press Institute, Missouri Association of Publications, Kappa Tau Alpha, plus the Center on Religion and the Professions.

A small number of books helped significantly. Two mostly upbeat biographies of Walter Williams provided accurate details about his life and pointed me in productive directions for learning about the life of the Journalism School through 1935. Frank W. Rucker, who knew Williams and who taught at the Journalism School, weighed in first with *Walter Williams* (Missourian Publishing Association, 1964). Ronald T. Farrar, born the year of Williams's death, followed, from his faculty office at the University of South Carolina, with *A Creed for My Profession: Walter Williams, Journalist to the World* (University of Missouri Press, 1998). Farrar is also the author of *Reluctant Servant: The Story of Charles G. Ross* (University of Missouri Press, 1969).

After his retirement as dean of the Journalism School, Earl English compiled faculty meeting minutes, rosters of graduated students, snippets from press releases, news reports, and his own reminiscences, placing the resulting stew between covers with the title *Journalism Education at the University of Missouri–Columbia* (Walsworth Publishing, 1988).

William H. Taft, who taught history at the Missourian Journalism School, wrote numerous books before and after his retirement. One of them, *Missouri Newspapers and the Missouri Press Association: 125 Years of Service, 1867–1992* (Heritage House Publishing, 1992), proved especially helpful. Taft collaborated with Kent M. Ford of the Missouri Press Association staff to compile *The Missouri Honor Medal for Distinguished Service in Journalism: Its First Seventy-Five Years, 1930–2005* (Heritage House Publishing, 2005). Various other publications and documents issued by the Missouri Press Association headquarters in Columbia contributed details to the text.

Particulars about newspapering in Columbia during Williams's lifetime can be found in *Ed Watson: Country Editor, His Life and Times,* by Leland Francis Pike (Walsworth Publishing, 1982).

The *Columbia Missourian* served as a secondary source over and over. For some of the years since 1908, I or a research assistant skimmed each day of publication, looking for news reports about Journalism School developments or features about students, staff, and faculty. Back issues of the *Columbia Daily Tribune* plus student newspapers such as the *Maneater* and *Campus Digest* served that function as well. The financial operations of the *Missourian* are detailed to some extent in *Business Management History: University Missourian Association, Publisher of the Columbia Missourian, 1908–1952.* The compiler of the twenty-six-page pamphlet, printed in 1952, is J. Harrison Brown.

During his lifetime, both before and after his Missouri Journalism School deanship, Frank Luther Mott published numerous volumes that helped place education for the craft in perspective. One textbook surveying the professional landscape, *American Journalism: A History, 1690–1960* (3d ed., Macmillan, 1962), yielded much in the way of context.

Sara Lockwood Williams—Walter's student, staff assistant, faculty member, wife, stepmother of his children, and widow—wrote an unpublished biography of him, which eventually landed at the Western Historical Manuscript Collection on the University of Missouri Columbia campus. It is not always reliable; she wrote it after his death while understandably emotional, and she seemed to idolize her late husband, or at least wanted others to idolize him. Before her marriage to Williams, Sara Lockwood began to compile material for what became *Twenty Years of Education for Journalism* (E. W. Stephens Publishing, 1929). As Sara Lawrence Lockwood, she compiled *Written by Students in Journalism: Selected Articles Written by Students in the School of Journalism, University of Missouri, as Part of Their Class Work During 1926–1927,* then found money to publish it through the university during 1927.

Some journalism organizations have published their own histories. *Talent, Truth, and Energy: Seventy-Five Years of Service to Journalism,* by Bert N. Bostrom (1984), is an example from the Society of Professional Journalists/Sigma Delta Chi.

"Walter Williams: Spokesman for Journalism and Spokesman for the University of Missouri," by Helen Brookshire Adams (PhD diss., University of Missouri, 1969) provided valuable information, as did numerous master's theses done for the University of Missouri Journalism School. These include "The Life and Teachings of Frank Lee Martin," by Sandy Kay Baer (1971); "KOMU-TV: The First Ten Years," by Joan Berk (1964); "Twenty-Three Years [of] Development of the *Columbia Missourian,*" by Frances Ethel Gleason (1931); "The University of Missouri and [the] Journalism of China," by Wei San Lau (1949); "A Biography of David R. McAnally, Jr.," by Leon William Lindsay (1956); "A Socio-Economic Study of the Currently Active Alumni of the University of Missouri School of Journalism," by Lyman S. McKean (1949); "E. W. Stephens: Preparer of the Way," by Carrol Jean Mills (1970); "An Analysis of Journalism Curricula," by Vernon Nash (1928); "A Historical Survey of Broadcasting in Missouri," by James H. Porchey (1969); "A Study of the Curriculum of the School of Journalism of the University of Missouri Based on the Opinions of Four Hundred Alumni and Other Former Students," by Helen Jo Scott (1929); and "A Study of the *Columbia* Missouri *Herald,*" by Sara Lockwood Williams (1931).

Histories of the University of Missouri and the state of Missouri provided useful context. They include *A History of Missouri: Volume IV, 1875 to 1919,* by Lawrence O. Christensen and Gary R. Kremer (University of Missouri Press, 1997); *The University of Missouri: An Illustrated History,* by James and Vera Olson (University of Missouri Press, 1988); *A History of the University of Missouri,* by Frank V. Stephens (University of Missouri Press, 1962). Back issues of the *Missouri Historical Review,* a scholarly journal now more than one hundred years old, provided enlightenment again and again. I found extremely helpful a ten-part series by Walter B. Stevens titled "The New Journalism in Missouri" that started in the April 1923 issue and ended in the July 1925 issue. "A Century of Journalism in Missouri," by William Vincent Byars, appeared in the October 1920 issue of the *Missouri Historical Review.*

The University of Missouri alumni magazine and the Missouri Journalism School alumni magazine in their various incarnations with their various titles yielded useful material. For example, the *Journalism Alumni News* of May 1966 devoted its pages to a remembrance of Charles G. Ross, sixteen years after his death. The remembrances by his former students supplemented information published during his years of teaching at the Journalism School (1908–1918) and available in Ross's own publications.

In addition, the Journalism School published a *Bulletin* from time to time, starting in 1912 and dealing primarily with issues relevant to the profession. After Walter Williams's death, an eighty-page booklet styled the University of Missouri Bulletin (volume 37, number 5, Journalism series number 75) appeared with the title *In Memoriam: Walter Williams, 1864–1935*. It carried the date of February 10, 1936, and listed Roscoe B. Ellard as editor. Press releases spanning the decades from the University of Missouri Office of Public Information, later called the News Bureau, helped nail down dates and places.

For context about journalism education, publications from the organization currently known as the Association for Education in Journalism and Mass Communication helped. The association is based in Columbia, South Carolina. Regularly issued publications include *Journalism Quarterly, Journalism Monographs,* and *Journalism and Mass Communication Educator.*

The full run of the magazine *Columbia Journalism Review,* published at Columbia University in New York City, helped with context as well. So, to a lesser extent, did *The Quill,* the magazine of Society of Professional Journalists/Sigma Delta Chi; *Editor and Publisher; Broadcasting and Cable; Advertising Age; Nieman Reports,* published at Harvard University; *American Journalism Review,* published at the University of Maryland; *American Society of Newspaper Editors Bulletin; Presstime,* the magazine of the American Newspaper Publishers Association and its later iteration; *News Photographer,* the magazine of the National Press Photographers Association; and public relations professional publications. Among nonjournalism magazines, the *Chronicle of Higher Education* yielded useful contextual news features and opinion pieces.

Scattered reports about sequences within academic journalism proved useful. For instance, "Advertising Education: Yesterday, Today, Tomorrow" provided context. It is a collaborative study published during 2006 by professors at Louisiana State University, Texas Tech University, and the University of Texas. Billy I. Ross is the lead author.

Histories of other journalism schools proved useful, especially *Pulitzer's School: Columbia University's School of Journalism, 1903–2003,* by James Boylan (Columbia University Press, 2003).

I interviewed past and current Missouri Journalism School students, staff, and faculty in person, by telephone, and via email. All deserve gratitude.

Rhonda Fallon, Journalism School fiscal officer, helped smooth a number of hurdles on the way to completion.

Former journalism student Pam Cooper, a researcher at the University of Missouri Nursing School, is also a leader in local gay/lesbian organizations. Her generosity in sharing her research about Emery Johnston is deeply appreciated.

Student researchers helped locate information for this book, in return for academic credit or cash payment. Angie Vo searched the broadest and dug the deepest over the longest stretch. Others making significant research contributions included MacKenzie Allison, Maura Dunst, Gwyneth Gibby, Holly Hacker, Meghan Lyden, Anastasia Masurat, Ginger McFarland, Sara Morrow, Chip Stewart, and Rachel Williams.

In the *Missourian* newspaper library, Steve Clayton and Nina M. Johnson provided research assistance. Now retired Journalism School librarian Pat Timberlake demonstrated unbounded enthusiasm from the start. Journalism School librarian Sue Schuermann is the most knowledgeable, most accommodating information gatherer I have ever known.

Index

Abbott, Jeanne, 49, 248
Abbott, Stanley E. (Stan), 49
Abel, Elie, 160
Accreditation of journalism schools, 77–81, 91, 143, 163, 224–25
ACT college entrance examination, 251–52
Adams, Helen Brookshire, 260
Adams, Jeff, 243
Ad Club, 217–18
Adelante, 233–34
Admission standards for the Journalism School, 15, 57, 59–61, 73–76, 78, 116, 251–52
Adobe Systems Incorporated, 242
Advertising Age magazine, 64, 261
Advertising classes at the Journalism School, ix, xi, 23–24, 33–36, 68, 79, 141, 160–69, 224, 228–29, 238, 247–48, 254–55
"Advertising Education: Yesterday, Today, Tomorrow" report, 261
Affirmative action, 198–203. *See also* Race relations
Agricultural journalism. *See* Rural journalism
AHANA Journalism Workshop (African American, Hispanic American, Asian American, Native American), 147
Air Force, U.S., 109–10, 166
Albania, 233
Albright, Jim, 168
Aldridge, Mahlon, 98
Alfred I. DuPont–Columbia broadcasting awards, 77
Allan, Virginia R., 196
Allard, Winston, 42
Allbaugh, R. R., 29–30
Allbee, Roger, 100
Allen (Wood), Danita, 206–7, 233

Allen, Ethelbert, 27
Allen, Herman R., 64
Allen, Spencer M., 130–31
Allison, MacKenzie, 262
All the President's Men (Woodward and Bernstein), 44
All the President's Men (movie), 44
America-Japan Society, 124–25
American Agricultural Editors Society, 72
American Journalism: A History, 1690–1960 (Mott), 2
American Association of Schools and Departments of Journalism, 72, 77–78, 135
American Association of Teachers of Journalism, 77–78
American Banker, 185
American Broadcasting Company (ABC), 45, 94, 101, 104, 166, 210
American Council on Education for Journalism, 78, 143, 163
American Cyanamid Company, 185
American Express Company, 164
American Journalism: A History, 1690–1960 (Mott), 2, 137–39, 259
American Medical Writers' Association, 194
American Newspaper Publishers Association, 78, 204, 261
American Red Cross, 98, 121–22
American Society of Newspaper Editors, 60, 77–78, 136–37, 197, 261
American Telephone and Telegraph Company (AT&T), 76
American University, Washington, D.C., 128, 188
American University of Bulgaria, 232
Ameritech Corporation, 185
Amtrak railroad system, 186

"Analysis of Journalism Curricula, An"
    (Nash), 260
Anchorage Daily News, 49
Anchors of television newscasts, 105–6
Anderson, Sherwood, 180
Anheuser-Busch Company, 35, 164
Anti-Semitism, 134
A. P. Green Fire Brick Company, 33
Apple computers, 238, 241
Archibald, John J., 64
Archibald, Sam, 128
Argentina, 132
Arizona Project, 189
Arizona Republic, 189, 253
Arkansas Democrat-Gazette, 190
Armao, Rosemary, 189–91
Armer, Jane, 229
Armstead, George B., 78
Armstrong, Orland K., 64
Army, U.S., 60–63, 100
Arnold, Charles, 24
Arts journalism classes at the Journalism
    School, 67, 230
Asbile, Robert A., 64
Ashland, Missouri, 24, 54
Ashworth, Sarah, 240–41
Asian Wall Street Journal, 127
Associated Press, 40, 61, 64, 121, 145, 166,
    189, 195
Association for Education in Journalism
    and Mass Communications, 181, 220,
    226–27, 261
Association of Health Care Journalists,
    192–93
Atkins, Jeanni, 203–4
Atwater, James D., 37, 48–50, 94, 107,
    114, 127, 151, 166–73, 182–83, 200
Atwater, Patricia (Patty), 173
Aurora, Missouri, School of Photoengrav-
    ing, 179

Baer, Sandy Kay, 260
Bailey, Angie, 106
Baltimore Evening Sun, 222
Baltimore Sun, 127, 191, 222
Banaszynski, Jacqui, 208–9, 233, 236, 255
Barnard, Charles, 64
Barnett, Tracy, 189, 233–34
Barnhart, Doris, 146, 185
Bartimus, Tad, 145, 195
Bassett, Edward, 165

Beard, Charles A., 140
Beasley, Maurine Hoffman, 150
Beetle Bailey comic strip, 60–61
Bell, Jacquelyn (Jackie), 183
Belleville, Illinois, Community College, 110
Beloit College, 73
Bent, Silas, 20–21, 28
Bentley, Clyde, 233, 239–41
Berk, Joan, 103, 260
Berk, Philip E., 100, 102–3, 116
Bernstein, Carl, 44
Beshkin, Celia, 143
Beshore, George Warren, 64
Best, Albert, 64
Between the Lines radio program, 110
Bickel, Karl, 125
Bickley, William B., 44–45, 209
"Biography of David R. McAnally, Jr., A"
    (Lindsay), 260
Black Issues in Higher Education magazine,
    235
Blackmun, Harry, 145
Blackout campus newspaper, 146
Blakely, Mary Kay, 131, 221
Blanton, H. J., 8
Bleyer, Willard G., 76
Blue Book magazine, 42
Blue Springs, Missouri, 247
Bluford, Lucille H., 74–75
Blumenshine, Philip B., 112–13
Bolch, Dorothy Judith (Judy), 208
Bolivar (Missouri), Herald-Free Press, 177
Bolivia, 126
Bolles, Don, 189
Bolls, Paul, 228
Book reviewing class at the Journalism
    School, 42
Boone County Journal, 5
Boonville, Missouri, 4–6
Boonville Advertiser, 6, 69
Boonville Topic, 5
Boston University, 81, 182, 188
Bostrom, Bert N., 76, 260
Bowers, Gregory Glenn (Greg), 250
Bowman, Georgia, 98
Bowman, Louis, 176–77
Boylan, James, 261
Boyle, Hal, 64
Bozell and Jacobs Incorporated, 214
Brandt, Raymond, 64
Bratek, Catherine (Cathy), 158

Bratek, Ruth Briggs, 52, 158–59
Bray, William (Bill), 176–77
Brennen, Bonnie, 227
Brenner, Donald J. (Don), 153, 170, 194
Briggs, Eugene, 158
Briggs, Frank P., 158
Briggs, Thomas, 158
Brill, Ann, 209
Brinkley, David, 212
Brinkman, Del, 165
British Empire Press Union, 125
Brixey, Elizabeth K., 250
Broadcasting classes at the Journalism
    School, ix, 79, 82, 98–116, 130, 160,
    230, 254–55
Brookman, Laura Lou, 64
Brooks, Brian S., 46–48, 50, 209, 214,
    219, 221, 229, 238, 254–55
Brooks, Phillips R. (Phill), 129–30, 238,
    255
Brooks, Stratton D., 68
Brooks, Tom, 38
Brown, J. Harrison, 33, 212, 259
Brown, Jim, 51
Brown, Merrill, 254
Brown, Penny, 38
Brown, Walter B., 29
Browning, Norma Lee, 64
Bruce, Betsey Barnett, 104
Brussels, Belgium, semester of the Journal-
    ism School, 127, 132
Bruzzese, Anita, 191
Bruzzese, Len, 191–92
Bryan, Wright, 64
Buckles, Steve, 185
Buenos Aires, Argentina, semester of the
    Journalism School, 230
Bulgaria, 231
Bullen, Percy S., 175
Bunn, Ronald F., 156–57, 162
Burger, Chester, 99
Burger, Warren, 145
Burns, Robert, 153
Business journalism, 185–87
Business Journalist magazine, 187
*Business Management History: University
    Missourian Association, Publisher of the
    Columbia Missourian, 1908–1952*
    (Brown), 259
Butler University, 188
Byars, William Vincent, 260

Cable News Network (CNN), 209, 231
California State University–Fullerton, 222,
    232
California State University–Long Beach,
    105
Cambodia, 112
Cameras in the courtroom, for television
    news, 101
Cameron, Glen T., 209, 229
Campbell Soup Company, 195
Campus Digest student newspaper, 163, 259
Canada, 125
Canada, Stanley W., 74
Canadian Broadcasting Corporation, 110
Cannon, Clarence, 65
Cannon, Richard (Dick), 103–4, 181
Canon Incorporated, 178
Cape Girardeau, Missouri, 58
Capper's Farmer, 64
Carleton College, 147
Carnahan, Mel, 111
Carnegie Foundation, 78
Carr, Robert Spencer, 75
Cauley, John, 64
CD-ROMs (compact disks), 237
Celanese Chemicals, 194
Cellular telephones, 241
Center for Advanced Social Research, 224,
    227–28, 233
Center for the Digital Globe, 209
Center of Excellence in Cancer Communi-
    cation Research, 229
Center on Religion and the Professions,
    192–93, 258
Central Methodist College, 158
Central State University, 111
Cepoi, Corina, 231–32
Chang, Eva, 71
Chang, Won Ho, 126
Channel Eight. *See* KOMU-TV
Charlton, Robert W. (Bob), 213
Chase Manhattan Bank, 185
Chasnoff, Joseph Edwin, 24
Cheers, D. Michael, 146
Cheng, I-Huei, 235
Chevron Petroleum Company, 185
Chicago Daily Defender, 198
Chicago Daily News, 37, 65, 94, 126, 159–
    60
Chicago Record, 22
Chicago Tribune, 3, 64, 159, 197

Childers, Elihu Root, 33
Childers, Henry F., 56
Chillicothe, Missouri, 38, 67
China, 27, 70, 73, 88, 117–25, 226, 233
China Weekly Review, 119–20, 124
Cho, Sooyoung, 235
Choi, Yoonhyeng, 235
Christian, Dick, 81
Christian Science Monitor, 107
Churchill, L. F., 162
Circuit Court, Boone County, 74
City and Regional Magazine Association, 192, 258
City News Bureau of Chicago, 29
City University of New York, 224
Civil War, U.S., 2, 4
Clark, Champ, 11
Clark, Jane E., 154, 244
Clayton, Stephen P. (Steve), 262
Cleveland News, 184
Cleveland Plain Dealer, 7, 64
Cloutier, Tammy, 169
Cloyd, Patricia A., 73
Coast Geodetic Survey, U.S., 125
Coday, Reed, 51
Colbert, Jan Louise, 43–44, 189, 191, 220
College Photographer of the Year competition, 178–79
Collier's magazine, 29
Collier's Weekly, 22
Collins, Corrice, 106–7
Collins, Kent S., 103, 111, 116, 184, 214, 233, 251
Colman, Norman J., 5
Colman's Rural World, 5
Columbia Broadcasting System (CBS), 45, 64, 99, 101, 109, 166, 175
Columbia (Missouri) Daily Tribune, 16, 18–19, 39, 41, 44, 46, 49–55, 98, 113, 141, 145, 158, 163, 183, 201, 204, 243, 245–47, 259
Columbia Herald, 6–7, 11–12, 16, 20, 24, 68, 175
Columbia Journal, 7
Columbia Journalism Review, 77
Columbia Missourian. See Missourian
Columbiamissourian.com, 242
Columbia Savings Bank, 69
Columbia Statesman, 5, 16, 23
Columbia Theater, 32

Columbia University, 9–10, 76–78, 109, 134, 160, 242
Columbus Dispatch, 193
Commencement ceremonies, 214, 217
Commerce Bancshares Incorporated, 43
Committee of Concerned Journalists, 129, 211, 258
Communications education, 79
Community journalism, 79, 160, 177, 209–10
Community Knowledge Project, 171
Computer-Assisted Reporting, 189–91, 230
Computers in classrooms and newsrooms, 237–40
Confidential Survey of Administration, Problems and Function of the St. Louis Post-Dispatch (Housman), 134
Confucius, 124
Congress, U.S. *See* House of Representatives; Senate
Conoco Incorporated, 185
Constitution, U.S., 13, 145, 196
Controls of Information class at the Journalism School, 203, 205
Convergence journalism classes at the Journalism School, xi, 82, 130, 240–43, 254–55
Conwell, John O., 101
Cooper, Pam, 262
Copyright issues, 242
Corbin, Carl McArn, 64
Corn Belt Dailies, 175
Cornell University, 3, 11
Correspondence class at the Journalism School, 19
Cose, Ellis, 197–98
Cosmopolitan magazine, 150
Council on Education for Journalism, 77
Country America magazine, 206
Country Editor magazine, 8
Courts: federal, 144–45; state, 130
Covitz, Randy, 38–39
Cowell, Ginny, 227
Cox Institute for Newspaper Management, 209
Cox Newspapers, 190
Craft, Stephanie, 226
Creed for My Profession: Walter Williams, Journalist to the World, A (Farrar), 258
Crichton, John, 64

Critical Infrastructure Information Act, federal, 205
Cronkite, Walter, 109, 175
Cropp, Frederick W. IV (Fritz), 149, 228, 232, 236
Cross-cultural studies, 236–37
C-SPAN cable television channel, 240
Cure, Pansy Riley, 73
Curtis B. Hurley Chair in Public Affairs Journalism, 207–8, 247
Cutlip, Scott M., 141
Cycle of the West, A (Neihardt), 101

Daniel Boone Hotel, 212
Dallas Morning News, 20, 213
Danish School of Journalism, 232
D'Arcy, Ruth, 46, 184, 196–97
D'Arcy Advertising Company, 64
Darrell Sifford Memorial Prize in Journalism, 184–85
Dartmouth College, 109
Davenport Fellowships for business journalists, 185
Davidson, Sandra Scott (Sandy), 39–40
Davis, Charles N., 205, 226
Davis, Patricia Boddy, 215
Davis, Robert E. (Rob), 215
DeFleur, Lois, 171, 244
DeKalb, Illinois, 47
Dell Publishing Company, 61
Denison University, 225
Dennison, Dan, 230
Design classes at the Journalism School, 47, 250, 255
Des Moines Business Record, 185
Des Moines Register, 49, 64, 129, 207, 217–18
Detroit Free Press, 48, 59, 64, 198
Detroit News, 64, 197
Dickerson, Jo Ann, 169–70, 209
Digges, Sam Cook, 64
Digital Audio and Video Basics for Journalists class at the Journalism School, 241
Digital Missourian, 243
Dobyns, Frank L., 160, 164
Doctorates in journalism. *See* Graduate studies
Doerner, Russell C., 155, 164
Doe Run Company, 234
Domke, James, 178
Donaldson, Sam, 129

Donald W. Reynolds Foundation, 97, 252–53
Donoho, Paula, 214
Donoho, Todd, 214
Dorsey, Carolyn A., 201
Dove company, 164
Dow Chemical Company, 185, 194, 213
Dow Jones Newspaper Fund, 146, 209
Dressler, Robert, 103
Duffy, George Thomas (Tom), 40–42, 154–55, 218
Duffy, Margaret, 228, 233, 254
Dugan, W. David (Dave), 109
Duke University, 166, 193
Dukes, Billie, 228
DuMont, Allen B., 99
DuMont television network, 99, 101
Duncan, David Douglas, 183
Duncan Hines company, 164
Dunlap, Lillian, 106–8
Dunn, Michael W. (Mike), 111
Dunst, Maura, 262
Dvorkin, Jeffrey, 129, 211
Dynamics of Advertising class at the Journalism School, 161

Early Montana Territorial Journalism as a Reflection of the American Frontier in the New Northwest (Housman), 134
Eastern European nations, 127
Eastgate supermarket, 53
Eckhardt, Willard L., 142
Edgar Snow Fellowships for Chinese journalists, 120
Edgell, Holly, 115
Editor and Publisher magazine, 107, 187
Editorial writing, 23, 26, 36–37, 46
Editors' Week, 174
Edom, Clifton C., 57, 179–81
Edom, Vi, 179
Edson, Arthur, 64
Edward D. Jones and Company, 164
Edward R. Murrow journalism award, 240–41, 251
Edwards, Clark, 116
Edwards, Kathleen, 203
Ed Watson: Country Editor, His Life and Times (Pike), 259
Egypt, 125
E. I. DuPont de Nemours and Company, 185

Elections, coverage of, 45, 115
Electronic Media Print (eMprint) technology, 242, 255
Elementary and Secondary Education, Missouri Department of, 230
Ellard, Roscoe B., 70, 76–77, 125, 261
Ellis, Elmer, 65
Ellis, Lorraine, 101
Elm Street, 57–58, 96
El Salvador, 127
Elwood, Charles, 22
Encyclopedia Britannica Incorporated, 178
Endowed chairs for faculty at the Journalism School, 205–11
Engleman, Tom, 146
English, Ceola Bartlett, 143
English, Earl, 36–37, 75–76, 79–81, 91, 99, 103–4, 110, 113, 122, 128, 142–46, 151, 158, 177, 181, 193, 213–14, 216, 227, 257–58
Enrollment at the Journalism School. *See* Admission standards
Environmental journalism, 36
Epic America television program, 101
Epstein, Daniel, 204
Equal Rights Amendment, 196
ESPN sports network, 219
Esquire magazine, 166
Ethics classes at the Journalism School, 40
Eureka, Missouri, 133
European Community, 128
European Journalism Academy, Vienna, 232
Evans, E. R., 20
Exercises in High School Journalism (English), 143
E. W. Stephens Company, 22
"E. W. Stephens: Preparer of the Way" (Mills), 260
Exxon Corporation, 185

Facts Are, The (Seldes), 140
Faculty Development Fund of the Journalism School, 170–71
Fair Practices Committee of the Journalism School, 107
Fallon, Rhonda, 191–92, 261
Fancy Food and Culinary Products magazine, 219
Farlow, Melissa, 182–83
Farm news. *See* Rural journalism

Farm Security Administration, U.S., 179–80
Farrar, Ronald T., 258
Farrar, Straus and Cudahy book publisher, 65, 193
Feature writing classes at the Journalism School, 23, 32, 40–42, 67–68
Federal Communications Commission, 99–100, 103, 108, 113
Feldman, Chester, 64
Fennell, John, 192, 207, 221
Ferguson, John Donald, 64
Ferrell, Donald M., 162
Fidler, Roger, 242, 254
Field, Eugene, 17
Field Enterprises Incorporated, 159
Fiftieth anniversary celebration of the Journalism School, 63–65
Financial journalism. *See* Business journalism
Fisher, Paul, 42–43, 109, 154, 177, 203–5, 213
Fisher, Roy, 37–39, 43, 45–46, 51, 53–54, 94, 106, 109, 113–14, 129–30, 146, 151, 156, 158–63, 165, 167, 188, 203–4, 210, 234
Fleming, Kenneth (Zhi G. Sun), 233
Flint Journal, 166
Flynn, Donald R., 139–40
Flynn, Doral, 51–52
Flynn, F. M., 64
Food coverage. *See* Health and nutrition reporting
Ford, Kent M., 259
Ford Foundation, 200, 235
Ford Motor Company, 185, 216
Foreign correspondents, 222
Formosa, 125–26
Forsee, Joe, 54
Forsyth, Missouri, 180
Fort Worth Star-Telegram, 187
Foss, Kurt, 243
Foster, Brian, 254
Fox, Jack, 213
France, 62, 125
Francis, David R., 6, 9
Franklin, Benjamin, 136
Frank Luther Mott: Scholar, Teacher, Human Being (Long), 135
Freedom Forum, 40, 242
Freedom of Information Center, 128, 203–5, 258

Free Press Underground, 144
Frisby, Cynthia (Cyndi), 149–50, 228, 236
From Missouri to the Isle of Mull (W.
    Williams), 27
Froug, William, 64
Fuji Photo Film, 179
Fulbright Fellowships, 126
Fulhage, Mike, 250
Fulton (Missouri) Gazette, 26–27

Gafke, Roger, 109–10, 156, 233, 253
Gaiter, Dorothy Jean, 146
Gallimore, Tim, 149
Gallon, Jose Santos, 175
Gannett Foundation, 58, 198
Gannett Hall, 55, 58, 95, 161, 165
Gannett Newspapers, 58, 128, 191
Gardner Advertising Company, 155
Gartner, Carl, 217
Gartner, Michael, 217
Garvey, Daniel E., 104–5, 162
Gassaway, Robert (Bob), 248
Gaston, Dale L., 164
Gay rights. *See* Homosexuality
Geisler, Jill, 169
Gelatt, Rod G., 103–6, 112–14, 116, 169
Gender relations. *See* Sexism
General Accounting Office, U.S., 205
General Foods Corporation, 195
Gentry, James (Jimmy), 185–87
George Washington University, 196
Georgia Trend Magazine, 185
Gerald, James Edward, 62, 75
Germany, 74, 117, 125, 166, 175
Gibby, Gwyneth, 262
GI Bill of Rights, 62
Gibson, Rodney David, 42
Gibson, Thomas Duffy, 42
Gilpin, Barbara, 51–52
Gleason, Frances Ethel, 260
Global Journalist magazine, 233
Goldenson, Leonard H., 210
Goldenson Chair in Community/Local
    Broadcasting, 129, 210–11
Good Housekeeping magazine, 150
Gotham-Vladimir Advertising Incorporat-
    ed, 163
Gould, Robin, 29
Governor of Missouri, 8, 38, 101, 130, 246
Graduate studies at the Journalism School,
    xi, 47, 128, 132–73, 225–28, 243

Graduate Studies Center of the Journalism
    School, 160–61, 170, 227
Grand Junction (Iowa) Globe, 134
Graphics. *See* Design
Gray, Thomas R., 103, 250–51
Gray Television Incorporated, 230
Greeley, Horace, 139
Greenblatt, Mark, 115
Greenlease Motor Company, 33
Gregory, Maxine Wilson, 209
Grigsby, Gary, 115
Grimes, Paulette, 148
Grinfeld, Michael, 221, 229, 233
Grinstead, Frances Dabney, 62, 68
Griswold, Glenn, 112
Groff, Samuel D., 123
Gross, Juliet Mayfield, 157
Gross, Milton E., 34, 51, 157–58, 160, 214
Grosvenor, Gilbert, 176
Grosvenor, Melville Bell, 57
GTE/Verizon, 228
Guadalajara, Mexico, semester of the Jour-
    nalism School, 230
Guatemala, 117–18
Guide to Research on Race and News, 235
Gutenberg, Johannes, 175
Guy, Harry D., 32

Hach, Clarence W., 143
Hacker, Holly, 262
Hagaman, Diane, 183
Hager, Henry, 149, 228
Hahn, John Riley, 75
Hailey, Foster B., 30, 64
Hall, Fred, 246
Hall, Mike, 219
Hallmark Foundation, 216
Halonen, Doug, 215
Halonen, Emily, 215
Halonen, Pamela Grainger, 215
Hampton, Veita Jo, 181
Hannibal (Missouri) Courier-Post, 134
Hannibal Morning Journal, 16
Hapgood, Norman, 22
Hardin College, 6
Harding, Warren G., 32
Harper's Weekly, 15
Harris, Lyle E., 185–86
Harrison, Kenneth, 98
Harry S. Truman Presidential Museum and
    Library, 258

Harte, Houston, 50–51, 208
Hartford Courant, 189
Harvard University, 159, 204, 239
Harvey, George, 15
Haverfield, Betty Luker, 81
Haverfield, Robert W., 34, 81–82, 165, 214
Hawaii Business magazine, 185
Health and nutrition reporting, 195, 242
Health, Education, and Welfare, U.S. Department of, 108
Heiman, Suzette, 228
Heins, Edward, 53–54, 245
Hendin, David, 131
Herbert, H. H., 78
Hermann, Missouri, 180
Herzog, David, 190
Hewlett-Packard Company, 232
Higgins, Flora J., 76
Higginsville, Missouri, 29
High school journalism education, 91, 143, 146, 177–78, 181, 198, 229–30
Hill, Albert Ross, 10, 14–15, 17–18, 28
Hill, Sarah, 106
Hills, Argentina Schifano (Tina), 234, 246
Hills, Lee, 59, 64, 96, 209, 234, 246
Hinnant, Amanda, 220–21
"Historical Survey of Broadcasting in Missouri, A" (Porchey), 260
History and Principles of Journalism class at the Journalism School, 24–26, 62, 68, 138–41, 151
History of American Magazines, A (Mott), 135
History of Mass Media class at the Journalism School, 161
History of the University of Missouri, A (Stephens), 260
Hodder, Grant H., 250
Hoddinott, Patricia B. (Patti), 245–47
Holden, Richard S. (Rich), 209
Hollins College, 28
Holtzman, Elias, 75
Home economics journalism, 79, 210
Homeland Security, U.S. Department of, 205
Home Town: The Face of America, 179–80
Homosexuality, 141–42
Honduras, 127
Honeyman, Steve, 188
Hong Kong semester of the Journalism School, 127, 161, 230

Honolulu, 67
Honolulu Star-Bulletin, 67
Hoover, Herbert, 68, 175
Hopkins, Cornelia Linerieux Rice, 214
Hopkins, Stephen, 214
Hopkins, Stephen Fenton, 214
Hopson, Janet L., 218
Hosokawa, Robert, 184, 186
House of Representatives of Missouri. *See* Legislature of Missouri
House of Representatives, U.S., 11, 65
Housman, Robert Lloyd, 133–34
Houston, Joseph Brant (Brant), 189–91
Houston Harte Chair in Journalism, 208, 247
Howard, Margaret (Meg), 110
Hubbard, Jack, 110, 116
Hudson, Fraser Berkley (Berkley), 221
Hughes, Dorothy Belle Flanagan, 64
Hughes, Terry J., 172
Humphreys, J. Robert (Bob), 51–53
Hurd, Hilary, 235
Hurley, Curtis B., 207
Husni, Samir, 219

IBM Corporation, 164, 198, 237, 241, 247
Imperative of Freedom, The (Merrill), 153
Imperial College, London, 232
Independence (Missouri) Examiner, 33, 117
Independent Natural Gas Association of America, 185
Independent Television News, 127
India, 125, 233
Indiana University, 129, 149, 170
In Fact newsletter, 140
Inland Daily Press Association, 78
In Memoriam, Walter Williams, 1864–1935, 70, 261
Institut d'Etudes Politiques, Paris, 232
Institute for Journalism Education, 198
Institute of Journalists, 27
Inter-American Press Association, 234
International Circulation Managers Association, 54
International Communication Association, 226
International Harvester World magazine, 181
International Media Fund, 231
International Press Institute, 233
International Relations television program, 101

Internships in journalism. *See* Placement
    Office
Interpublic Group of Companies, 214
Investigative journalism, 37–39, 114–15,
    188–92, 208, 230
Investigative Reporters and Editors, ix, 129,
    188–92, 258
Iowa State Teachers College, 143
Iowa State University Press, 143
IPI Report magazine, 233
Iran, 126
Ireland, 27
Italy, 234
I've Got a Secret television program, 64

Jackson, Nancy Beth, 184
Jacobs, Morris E., 214
Jacobs, Nathan E., 214
Japan, 62, 66, 73–74, 117, 125
Japan Advertiser, 27
Jaspin, Elliot, 189–90
Jay H. Neff Hall, 32, 55–57, 86–87, 125,
    137, 161
Jay H. Neff Hall Annex, 57–58
J. C. Penney Company, 184
Jefferson, Thomas, 65
Jefferson City semester of the Journalism
    School, 39, 110, 116, 129–30, 132,
    161
Jeffries, Nellie, 81
Jensen, Ronald V. (Ron), 250
Jerusalem semester of the Journalism
    School, 161
Jesse, Richard Henry, 9–11, 14
Jet magazine, 146
Jin, Yan, 235
Jobs in journalism after graduation. *See*
    Placement Office
Johansen, Michael L. (Mike), 179
John S. and James L. Knight Foundation.
    See Knight Foundation
Johnson, Alfonso, 27–28, 213
Johnson, Ben, 48–50, 198–203, 243–44
Johnson, Joseph French, 3
Johnson, Mary Esther Bullard, 48–50,
    198–202
Johnson, Nina M., 262
Johnson, Pam (newspaper publisher), 197
Johnson, Pamela Jean (Pam), 253–54
Johnston, Emery Kenney, 68, 141–42,
    157–58, 262

Joint Council of Schools of Journalism and
    Newspaper Groups, 78
Jones, Donald Hugh, 157–58
Jones, J. Carleton, 10
Journal of Advertising, 155
*Journal of Broadcasting and Electronic Me-
    dia,* 169
Journalism Across Cultures, 236
Journalism Alumni Association, 212
Journalism Alumni News, 61, 218, 260
Journalism and Women Symposium, 195–
    96, 258
Journalism as Communication class at the
    Journalism School, 161
*Journalism Education at the University of
    Missouri–Columbia* (English), 258
Journalism Placement Center. *See* Place-
    ment Office
Journalism Quarterly, 80, 135
Journalism Scholars Program, 252
Journalism Students Association, 42
Journalism Week, 34, 61, 75, 161–62,
    175–76
Journalist's Creed, v, 71–72
*Journalist's Library: Books for Reference and
    Reading, The* (Kane), 22
Jurney, Dorothy Misener, 196

Kahle, Louis, 101
Kalamazoo Gazette, 143
Kalish, Stan, 180
Kane, Charles E., 22
Kansas City Call, 74
Kansas City Journal, 15
Kansas City Post, 29
Kansas City Star, 8, 21–22, 48, 64, 121,
    170, 253
Kansas State Agricultural College, 3
Kansas State University, 159
Kapel, George, 100
Kappa Alpha Mu, 178
Kappa Tau Alpha, 171, 217, 258
Karsch, Robert, 101
Karwoski, Roger, 110
Kaul, Art, 163
KBIA-FM, Columbia, Missouri, 37, 40, 55,
    92, 107–12, 114–15, 164, 171, 210,
    215, 233. 238, 240–41, 251, 254
KCGM-AM, Columbia, Missouri, 108
Keeley, Mary Paxton. *See* Paxton, Mary
    Gentry

Kelley, Ron, 235–36
Kemper Military Academy, 177
Kennedy, George, 46, 49–50, 148, 167, 171–72, 190–91, 203, 214, 221, 233, 244–45, 248
Kent State University, 168
Kessler, Aaron, 240–41
KFRU-AM, Columbia, Missouri, 98, 108–9
KHON-TV, Honolulu, 230
Kiesler, Charles A., 246
Kilpatrick, Colin J., 253
King City, Missouri, 176
Kinyon, Henry H., 77, 217–18
Knight, John S., 159–60
Knight, Robert P. (Bob), 146–48, 155, 197–98, 257
Knight Chair in Journalism, 208–9
Knight Foundation, 58, 211, 246
Knight Ridder Newspapers, 48, 59, 234, 242
Kobre, Kenneth R. (Ken), 182–83
Kodak Company, 164, 178
Koelling, Bettie, 73
KOMU-TV, Columbia, Missouri, xi, 37, 40, 55, 57–58, 76, 90, 92, 98–116, 144, 155–56, 164, 171, 210, 236, 240–41, 250–51, 254, 257
"KOMU-TV: The First Ten Years" (Berk), 103, 260
Kopcha, Stephen C. (Steve), 228
Korea, 125–26
Korean Media Research Center, 126
Korean War, 63, 166
Kornberg, Sanford J., 213–14
Korzybski, Alfred, 143
Kraxberger, Lynda, 241–42
KSD-TV, St. Louis, 99
KSMU-FM, Springfield, Missouri, 111
KTEP-FM, El Paso, 236
KTRH Radio, Houston, 238
Kung, H. H., 124
Kuomintang, 119
Kuykendall, William (Bill), 182–83, 238
KWMU-FM, St. Louis, 111
Kyle, Greeley, 108

Ladies' Home Journal magazine, 64, 180
Lambert, Edward C., 90, 99–101, 103–4, 160, 258
Lambeth, Edmund B., 40, 128–29, 155, 170–71, 192–93, 214, 223, 225
Lamsam, Teresa, 235

Langton, Loup, 183
La Prensa of Buenos Aires, 26, 175
Laramie (Wyoming) Daily Boomerang, 29
Larson, R. K. T. (Kit), 186
Lathrop, William H., 68
Lau, Wei San, 260
Law classes at the Journalism School, 39–40
Law for the Newsman (Spencer), 39
Lawrence, James (Jim), 210
Lawrence, Mary H., 250
Lawson, John D., 19
League of American Pen Women, 150
Lebanon, 219
Lee, Robert E., 2
Lee, Russell, 180
Lee Hills Chair in Free-Press Studies, 209, 246–47
Lee Hills Hall, 55, 96, 243, 246
Legislature of Missouri, 18, 56–58, 115, 130, 207
Lenk, Amy, 227
Len-Rios, Maria, 228, 235
Lenz, David H., 185
Leshner, Glenn M., 228
Let's Write a Feature (Duffy), 41
Letterpress printing, 51
Liberal arts instruction, 79, 93
Library at the Journalism School, 56, 93, 253, 262
Library of Congress, 137
Life magazine, 166, 183, 219
"Life and Teachings of Frank Lee Martin, The" (Baer), 260
Lifestyle journalism, 183–85
Lincoln, Abraham, 139
Lincoln University, 48, 74–75, 147
Lindsay, Leon William, 260
Lindsay, Malvina, 28, 64
Linguistics, 143–44
Linotype printing, 42, 46, 144, 203
Lipman, David, 48
List, Karen Kuntz, 138–39, 151
Lister, Harold (Hal), 154
Literature of Journalism class at the Journalism School, 138
Litvak, Anya, 249
Lockwood, Sara Lawrence. See Williams, Sara
Loeb, Marshall, 166
Logan, Robert (Rob), 169, 194–95, 225

London Daily Telegraph, 175
London, England, semester of the Journalism School, 126–27, 132, 161, 230
Long, Howard Rusk, 135–38
Long, Huey, 216
Look magazine, 64
Loory, Nina, 209
Loory, Stuart, 209, 221, 232–33
Los Angeles Daily News, 250
Los Angeles Herald-Examiner, 126
Los Angeles Times, 170, 196, 242
Louisiana State University, 153–54, 216
Louisville Courier-Journal, 65, 182
Louisville Herald-Post, 166
Lowenstein, Ralph L., 154
Lower, Elmer, 94, 156, 166
Lu, David C. H., 123
Lucas Brothers publishing, 41
Luebke, Barbara, 47
Luehrs, M. E., 109
Luehrs Broadcasting Company, 109
Lumpp, James, 203
Lyden, Meghan, 262

MacArthur Foundation, 194
Macintosh computers. *See* Apple computers
Macon, Missouri, 121, 158
Madden, Frances L. Gorman, 104
Madden, Sarah, 104
Magazine classes at the Journalism School, ix, xi, 19, 42–44, 68, 79, 96, 220–21, 230, 254–55
Magazine Club, 219
Magazine Publishers Association, 79
Magrath, Peter, 244
Malaysia, 107
Management instruction for journalists, 79
Maneater campus newspaper, 246, 259
Mangan, Frank, 139
Mann, Robert S., 208
Mansbarger, Roberta, 70
Marcou, David J., 126
Marengo (Iowa) Republican, 134
Marine Corps, U.S., 48
Marken, Edith C., 68, 73
Markham, James W., 36
Marquand School for Boys, 135
Marquette University, 226
Marsh, John David, 43
Marshall, Missouri, 196
Martin, Frank Lee, 21–22, 34, 68–76, 88, 119, 123–25, 133–34, 157, 175–76, 216, 253
Martin, Frank L. (Sonny), 61
Martin, Martha Marie Hall, 21, 72
Mason, Debra L., 193
Masons fraternal order, 27
Mass Media Seminar class at the Journalism School, 161
Master's degrees in journalism. *See* Graduate studies
Masurat, Anastasia, 262
Maxine Wilson Gregory Chair in Journalism Research, 209
Mayer, Joy Mathis, 250
McAnally, David Russell, 3
McBride, Francelle (Fran), 107
McBride, Mary Margaret, 64, 150
McCann-Erickson agency, 214
McCarthy, Catherine, 75
McCormick Foundation, 197
McDavid, F. M., 70
McDearmon, Mary Irwin, 17
McDermott, Dennis, 192
McDougall, Angus, 181–82
McDougall, Betty, 181
McFarland, Virginia (Ginger), 262
McGinty, Jo Craven, 190
McGraw-Hill Company, 250
McIntyre Fellowship, 252
McIntyre, O. O., 252
McKean, Lyman S., 260
McKean, Michael L. (Mike), 110, 238–39, 241
McKinney, Fred, 101
McLaughlin, E. A., 207
McNeal, Christine, 230
McPhatter, William (Bill), 186
McQueen, Marion Duncan, 64
McReynolds, Jill, 82
Media Ethics magazine, 255–56
Media Research Bureau. *See* Center for Advanced Social Research
Meet the Press television program, 101
Memphis Press-Scimitar, 38
Mercer, Robert R., 181
Meredith Corporation, 192, 206–7
Meriwether, Heath, 41–42
Merrill, John C., 40, 153–54, 161–62, 203, 231, 255–56
Metro East Journal, East St. Louis, Illinois, 218

Mexamericana publications, 234

Mexican-American Commission to Eradicate Foot and Mouth Disease, 216

Mexico, 117, 233

Mexico (Missouri) Ledger, 16

Meyer, John S., 238

Meyer, Margie, 196

Meyer, Vernon, 70

Miami Herald, 42, 59, 200, 244

Michigan State University, 235

Micu, Anca, 235

Midcareer programs at the Journalism School, 174–211

Mid-Missouri Weekly Shopper, 52–53

Middlebush, Frederick A., 70, 73–74, 140–41

Middle East, 129

Millard, Thomas Franklin Fairfax, 119–20

Mills, Carrol Jean, 260

Mills, Kay, 196

Mills, Rilla Dean (Dean), ix, xi, 50, 54, 58–59, 97, 111, 115, 127, 148–49, 151, 173–74, 191, 201–3, 207–8, 222–26

Mills, Sue V., 222, 253

Milwaukee magazine, 192

Milwaukee Journal, 64, 180–81

Milwaukee Journal Sentinel, 230

Minneapolis Star and Tribune, 65, 194

Minneapolis Tribune, 186

Minnesota Business Journal, 185

Minorities. *See* Race relations

Minority Journalism Association, 198

Minority Recruiting and Retention Program at the Journalism School, 201

Misselwitz, Henry F., 59–60

Mississippi Delta State University, 153

Missouri Alumnus Magazine, 44

Missourian (newspaper), xi, 14–19, 23–24, 31–54, 56–58, 66, 69–70, 76, 90, 92, 96, 98, 100, 102, 107, 109, 111–13, 141, 144, 158, 160, 162, 164, 170–71, 173, 179, 186, 200–201, 208–9, 224, 237, 242–50, 254, 259

Missourian Magazine, 32

Missourian Publishing Association, 33, 51, 258

Missouri Arthritis Research and Rehabilitation Training Center, 169, 229

Missouri Association of Publications, 192, 258

Missouri Association of Realtors, 192

Missouri Community Newspaper Management Chair, 209–10

Missouri Editor magazine, 7–8

Missouri Forum television program, 101, 104

Missouri Group, 221

Missouri Health Communication Research Center, 209, 229

Missouri Honor Medal for Distinguished Service in Journalism: Its First Seventy-Five Years, 1930–2005, The, 259

Missouri Interscholastic Press Association, 177, 258

Missouri Life magazine, 206–7

Missouri Lottery, 164

Missouri Mafia, 211–21

Missouri Medal, 75, 175–76

Missouri Method, 13–14, 34, 36, 89, 91, 98, 102, 116, 131, 133, 151, 164, 221, 225–26, 242, 247, 251, 254

Missouri Model, 254

Missourinet reporting service, 111

Missouri Newspapers and the Missouri Press Association: 125 Years of Service, 1867–1992 (Taft), 259

Missouri Photo Workshop, 179–81

Missouri Power and Light Company, 81

Missouri Press Association, 5–6, 8, 16, 51, 61, 109, 135, 144, 160, 176–78, 192, 259

Missouri Press Women Incorporated, 150

Missouri Student (campus newspaper), 77

Missouri Today magazine, 43

Missouri Urban Journalism Workshop, 146–47

Missouri Women's Press Club, 150

Missouri-Yenching Journalism Foundation, 72, 123

Mitchell, Ernest L., 16

Mize, Kimberly Lakin, 253

Mizzoumafia@topica.com, 218

Mobil Oil Corporation, 185

Modernism in American Typography (Fisher), 203

Modern Maturity magazine, 42

Moeller, Jennifer L. (Jennifer Rowe), 43, 220, 233

Moen, Daryl R., 45–47, 190, 208, 221, 233, 255

MoJo Ad, 216

Moldova, 232

Monroe, Haskell, 58, 114, 171, 202–3, 244
Monsanto Company, 163
Montague, Samuel A., 216–17
Montenegro, 233
Montgomery, Louise, 172–73
Moore, Fred G., 258
Moore, Horatio Booth, 20
Morelock, Thomas Cecil, 34, 61–62, 68
Morgan, Ernest C., 39, 155, 160, 170
Morris, John, 180
Morris, Mackie, 115
Morrow, Sara, 262
Moscow State University, 232
Mosley, Janice Ann (Thomas), 102
Moss, John, 128
Mother Earth News magazine, 42
Mother Teresa, 126
Mott, Frank Luther, 2, 36–37, 61–63, 73, 75, 89, 91, 133–42, 151, 157, 171, 216, 237, 257, 259
Mott, Vera Ingram, 135, 138
Ms. Foundation for Education and Communications, 196
MSNBC.com, 254
Multicultural Development Committee of the Journalism School, 148
Multicultural Management Program, 48–50, 197–203, 224
Murdock, Hazel, 73
Murrow, Edward R., 240, 251
Muskie Fellowships, 126
Myers, Vernon C., 64
Myhre, Paul, 184
MyMissourian.com, 239–40

Nanyang Technological University, Singapore, 232
Napier University, Edinburgh, 232
Nash, Vernon, 70–71, 123, 260
National Advisory Commission on Civil Disorders, 76
National Archives, U.S., 183
National Association of Broadcasters, 204
National Association of Radio and Television Broadcasters, 79
National Broadcasting Company (NBC), 45, 64–65, 101, 104, 166, 212, 214, 217
National Cancer Institute, 229
National Council on Professional Education for Journalism, 78

National Council on Research, 80
National Editorial Association, 6, 187
National Federation of Press Women, 150
National Freedom of Information Coalition, 205, 258
National Geographic magazine, 57, 176, 179, 183
National Institute for Computer-Assisted Reporting, 190–91
National League of American Pen Women, 150
National Library of Medicine, 225
National Magazine Awards, 77
National Newspaper Association, 78, 177, 187–88, 258
National Press Building, 129, 211
National Press Club, 150
National Press Photographers Association, 159, 178
National Public Radio, 110, 129, 211
National Workshop on the Teaching of Ethics in Journalism, 40
Navy, U.S., 99
Neal, Robert M. 44, 208
Neff, Jay Holcomb, 56
Neff, Kevan, 81
Neff, Ward A., 56, 86, 175, 217
Neff Hall. *See* Jay H. Neff Hall
Neihardt, John G., 101
Neill, Betty Ann Peterson, 61
Nelson, Richard (Dick), 116, 155–56
New Directions for News, 196–97, 258
New Orleans Item and Morning Tribune, 30
New Orleans States-Item, 64
News and Editing Practicum class at the Journalism School, 161
New School University, 131
Newsday, 200
News directors of broadcast stations, 105–6
Newseum, 179
Newspaper Association of America, 254
Newspaper Blue Book rating service, 7
Newspaper classes at the Journalism School, ix, 19–20, 23, 79. 133, 160–61, 177, 220, 230, 254–55
Newspaper Enterprise Association, 131
Newspaper Guild, 50
News Pictures of the Year competition, 178
News Reporting and Writing (Missouri Group), 221
Newsweek magazine, 42, 64

New York City semester of the Journalism School, 116, 131–32
New York Daily News, 64, 175
New York Herald Tribune, 70
New York Post, 147
New York Sun, 122
New York Times, 30, 64, 175, 194, 207
New York Tribune, 2
New York University, 224
New York World, 9
Nichol, David, 126
Nieman Fellowships, 159, 204
Nieman Reports magazine, 239
Nikon Incorporated, 178
9/11. *See* September 11, 2001
Nixon, Richard M., 123, 166
Noblitt, Natalie Hammer, 219
Nokia Incorporated, 164
Norfolk Virginian-Pilot, 186, 189, 248
Norlander, Everett C., 29, 65
Norman, John Philip (Phil), 40–41, 45, 56, 154
North Carolina State University, 208
Northwestern State College of Louisiana, 153
Northwestern University, 75, 78, 81, 159, 193, 198
"Notes on Sensitivity" in Journalism School newsrooms, 107
Not in Our Stars television program, 101
Nowell, Jack, 52, 54
Nowell's supermarkets, 46, 52, 54

O'Brien, Dan, 214
Odessa, Missouri, 177
Office Equipment class at the Journalism School, 19
Office of War Information, U.S., 61
Offset printing, 51
Ogilvy and Mather advertising agency, 164
Ohio State University, 188, 209
Ohio University, 193, 230
Oklahoma City Times, 59
Olenyik, Richard, 112–13
Olson, James, 260
Olson, Kenneth E., 75, 78
Olson, Randy, 182–83
Olson, Vera, 260
One Hundred Best Community Service Project Ideas, The, 210–11
Online information classes at the Journalism School, ix, xi

Open meetings, 130
Opportunities for Women in Journalism class, 70
Oregon State University, 126
Organization and Administration of Television Programming for School Systems and Institutions of Higher Learning, The (Lambert), 99
Orr, Edwin C., 142
Orr, Warren H., 20
O'Shea, James, 218
Overholser, Geneva, 193, 207–8
Ownership of media, 207–8
Oxford University, 22

Paden, Carrie, 187
Padgett, Stephanie, 216
Pakistan, 126
Palestine, 27
Palmer, Kyle, 219
Pan-Pacific International Exposition, 118
Papish, Barbara, 144–45
Pardee, Mark A., 107
Paris, France, semester of the Journalism School, 230
Paris (Missouri) Appeal, 8
Park, Jaeyung, 126
Park College, 119
Parry, Thomas W., Jr., 118
Patterson, Don Denham, 120–21
Patterson, Joye, 45, 131, 145, 194, 258
Patterson, Ruth, 121
Pattrin, Helen Marie, 253
Paxton, Mary Gentry (Keeley), 28–29, 67, 84, 258
Pegler, Westbrook, 37
Peking University, 120
Penney, James Cash, 184
Penney-Missouri journalism program, 183–85, 208, 258
Pennsylvania State University, 138, 222
People You Should Know television program, 107
Perry, Earnest, 226, 237
Persian Gulf War, 63
Pett, Saul, 65
Pfizer company, 185
PhDs in journalism. *See* Graduate studies
Phi Beta Kappa, 217, 219
Philadelphia Evening Public Ledger, 66
Philadelphia Inquirer, 184

Philip Morris USA, 195
Philippines, 117
Philosophy of Journalism class at the Jour-
    nalism School, 40, 154
Photography classes at the Journalism
    School, ix, xi, 19–20, 24, 34, 57, 79, 96,
    178–83, 238, 255
Pica, George, 184
Pickens, Martha, 227, 235
Pictures of the Year competition, 178–79,
    182–83, 199, 258
Pictures of the Year International, 178–79
Pierce City, Missouri, 241
Pike, Leland Francis, 259
Pippert, Wesley G., 129
Pitney-Bowes Incorporated, 213
Pittsburgh Press, 183
Placement Office of Journalism School,
    81–82, 218–19
Platte City, Missouri, 27
Play Theory of Mass Communications,
    152
Policy Committee of the Journalism School,
    107
Pollard, Braxton, 163
Popular Photography magazine, 181
Porchey, James H., 260
Porter, Jeff, 190
Potter, Daniel S. (Dan), 233, 242, 247–48
Potter, Mary Frances, 73
Powell, John Benjamin, 62, 68, 74, 120, 124
Powell, Larry, 228
Poynter Institute for Media Studies, 108,
    169, 253
Practice of Journalism, The (W. Williams and
    Martin), 22
Presbyterian faith, 5, 8, 70
President's Council on Bioethics, 193
Price, Granville, 178
Price, Jennifer, 252
Price, Mary Beth Sandlin, 216
Price, R. B., 51
Price, William C. (Bill), 216
Priddy, Bob, 110–11
Principles of American Journalism class at
    the Journalism School, 40
Professional practice track of the Journalism
    School, 224, 248
Promotion and Tenure Committee of the
    Journalism School, 148–49, 154–57
Protestant faith, 117, 120

Providence Journal, 190
Providence Journal Bulletin, 190
Psychology as an academic discipline, 80
Public relations classes at the Journalism
    School, ix, xi, 34–36, 79, 141, 160–69,
    228–29
Public Relations Society of America, 163,
    198
Public Service Employees Union, 114
Publishers Auxiliary, 187
Pulitzer, Joseph, 9–10
Pulitzer Prizes, 47, 77, 135, 175, 190, 217,
    219
*Pulitzer's School: Columbia University's
    School of Journalism, 1903–2003*
    (Boylan), 261

Q-methodology research, 152–53
Quarderer, John, 116
Quill magazine, 187
Quinn, Cannie R., 20, 67

Race relations, x–xi, 48–50, 73–76, 107–
    8, 145–50, 197–203, 235–37, 243
Radio classes. *See* Broadcasting classes
Radio-Television News Directors Associa-
    tion, 169
Raleigh News and Observer, 208
Ralston-Purina Company, 101
Randolph, Nancy. *See* Robb, Inez Callaway
Ranly, Donald P. (Don), 40, 43, 172, 192,
    208, 215, 220–21
Ransom, Richard, 104
Ratchford, C. Brice, 114, 204
Rau, Rene Collins, 73
Rawlins, Mary Jane, 150
Raziq, David, 115
Reader's Digest magazine, 64, 166
Reebok International, 164
Reed, Katherine Trimarco, 234, 250
Reed, Rita, 183, 233
Rees, David, 181–83
Reeves, Jennifer Lee, 115
Reeves, Randy A., 115
Rehnquist, William, 145
Reid, Marion, 101
Reid, Whitelaw, 2
Religion journalism, 192–93
Religion Reporting and Writing class at the
    Journalism School, 193
Religious Newswriters Association, 193

Reporter's Handbook: An Investigator's Guide to Documents and Techniques, The, 188
Reporting on Religion: A Primer on Journalism's Best Beat, 193
Research Methods class at the Journalism School, 161
Reuters, 122
Reynolds, Donald W., 51, 252–53
Reynolds Journalism Institute, 253–54
RFD 8 television program, 100–101
Rhodes scholars, 71, 123
Ricchiardi, Sherry, 49
Ridings, Harry E., 33
Ridings, Joseph Willard, 220
Riggs, Robert, 65
R. J. Reynolds Industries, 185
Robb, Inez Callaway, 175–76
Robb, J. Addison, Jr., 175
Robichaux, Mark, 38
Rock Port, Missouri, 66
Rockwell Corporation, 194
Rodgers, Shelly, 228
Roe, Dorothy, 65
Rolla, Missouri, 142
Romania, 232
Romero, Anna M., 146, 236
Romero, Donald G., 42
Ronsick, Beth, 164–65
Roosevelt University, 198
Ross, Billy I., 261
Ross, Charles G., 18, 20, 22, 28, 59, 127–28, 258, 260–61
Round Table Club, 24
Royal Canin USA company, 164
Rucker, Frank W., 33, 72, 218, 258
Rural journalism, 23, 32–33, 45, 56, 68
Russell, Mark, 147
Russia. *See* Soviet Union

Sacramento Bee, 219
Sacred Heart University, 235
Sadiwskyj, Lena, 110
St. Bonaventure University, 109
St. Charles, Missouri, 181
St. John's University, 120–21
St. Joseph (Missouri) Gazette, 66, 158
St. Louis Cardinals baseball team, 72–73
St. Louis Globe-Democrat, 3, 219
St. Louis Post-Dispatch, 9, 20, 48, 59, 64, 124, 127–28, 134, 172
St. Louis Presbyterian, 8

St. Louis Republic, 7
St. Louis semester of the Journalism School, 39, 129–32
St. Louis Star, 15–16
St. Louis University, 229
St. Martin's Press, 188
St. Mary's College, 147
St. Paul's Cathedral, 125
Saline, Rex, 187
Salt Lake City, 67
Samuels, Alice, 41
Sampson, Julia, 56
San Angelo Standard-Times, 50
Sanders, Keith P., 45, 152–53, 165, 214, 223, 225
San Francisco Chronicle, 147
San Francisco Examiner, 210
San Jose Mercury News, 182
Sara Lockwood Williams Scholarship and Loan Fund, 150
Sargent, Dwight E., 204
Saturday Evening Post magazine, 150, 166
Saunders, James Allen, 76
Schneller, John T., 55, 250
Scholarship for journalism students, 252
Scholastic Journalism (English), 143
Schooling, Herbert, 162
School of Modern Photography, 181
Schott, Henry, 22
Schuermann, Sue, 262
Schwada, John, 112–13, 159
Science journalism, 79, 131, 169, 193–95
Science Journalism Center, 169, 194–95
Science News magazine, 131
Scott, Andy, 189
Scott, Byron T., 48, 206, 230–33
Scott, Frank W., 3
Scott, Helen Jo, 260
Scott, Naomi, 42
Scott, Walter D., 65
Scripps-Howard newspapers, 59
Sears Roebuck and Company, 185
Seattle Times, 183, 200, 208
Second Guesses bulletin at the *Missourian,* 244–45
Seldes, George, 140–41
Semantics class at the Journalism School, 43, 143
Senate of Missouri. *See* Legislature of Missouri
Senate, U.S., 65, 240

Sengsavanh, Phousavanh, 82
September 11, 2001, terrorist attack, 115–16
Serbia, 233
Serra, Deborah Hacker, 105–6, 215–16
Serra, James D., 215–16
Service journalism, 206–7
Sexism, x–xi, 47–48, 150–51, 226, 243
Sharp, Eugene W., 33, 41, 68, 92
Sharp, Kathy, 228
Shaw, Richard F. (Rick), 183
Shen, James C. H., 123
Sheridan, Edward P., 243
Shipley, Linda, 163–64
Shippey, Lee, 29
Showcase television program, 101
Siddall, Martin L. (Marty), 241, 250–51
Sifford, Darrell, 184–85
Sigma Delta Chi. *See* Society of Professional
    Journalists
Simpson College, 134
Singapore, 233
Sjurson, Laura, 187–88
Slaughter, Seth, 193
Slote, Leslie, 213
Smith, C. Zoe, 183, 226, 233
Smith, Herbert Warren, 19, 59
Smith, Jack, 228
Smith, Patricia N. (Pat), 233
Smith, Queen, 158
Smith, Rodney, 49
Smith Richardson Foundation, 185
Smithsonian magazine, 166
Snow, Edgar, 119–20
Society news, 32
Society of American Business Editors and
    Writers, 186–87, 210, 258
Society of American Business Editors and
    Writers Chair in Business and Financial
    Journalism, 186–87, 210
Society of Professional Journalists, 61, 76,
    187, 217, 260–61
"Socio-Economic Study of the Currently
    Active Alumni of the University of Mis-
    souri, A" (McKean), 260
Soderstrom, E. A., 33–34, 72–73
South Africa, 233
Southern, William, 117
Southern Illinois University, 110
Southern Methodist University, 168, 205
Southern Newspaper Publishers Associa-
    tion, 78

Soviet Union, 122, 127, 132, 222, 231
Sowers, Edward W., 69
Spaulding, Harvey D. (Dan), 115–16
Spaulding, Patricia Gorman, 115
Spencer, Dale R., 39, 44–45, 154, 177,
    188, 208, 258
Spencer, Otha C., 178
Sports Center television program, 219
Sports journalism, 32, 38–39, 219
Sports Illustrated magazine, 166
Springfield, Missouri, 177
Springfield (Massachusetts) Union, 166
Stanford University, 81, 104, 162, 228
Staples, George R., 72–73
State Department, U.S., 231–32
State Government and Administration televi-
    sion program, 101
State Historical Society of Missouri, 258
State University of New York at Stony
    Brook, 224
Statue of Liberty, 144
Steffens, Brian, 187
Steffens, Martha (Marty), 186–87, 210,
    232
Stephens, Edwin William, 5, 7, 16, 175
Stephens, Frank V., 260
Stephens, Lon V., 8
Stephens College, 99, 108
Stephenson, William (Will), 152–53, 214
Sterling, Charlotte Butler, 210
Sterling, Diane, 210
Sterling, James (Jim), 177, 188, 209–10,
    214, 247
Sterling, Stephanie, 210
Stern, Reuben Joseph, 233, 250
Stevens, Walter B., 260
Stewart, Chip, 262
Stewart, Norm, 38–39
Stockton, Missouri, 177
Stone, A. L., 134
Stone, Vernon, 148–49, 169
Strategic communication classes at the Jour-
    nalism School, xi, 97, 209, 228–30, 255
Straus, Roger W., Jr., 65, 193
Strong, Charles M., 16
Stryker, Roy, 180
Students for a Democratic Society, 144
"Study of the *Columbia,* Missouri, *Herald,*
    A" (S. Williams), 260
"Study of the Curriculum of the School of
    Journalism of the University of Missouri

Based on the Opinions of Four Hundred Alumni and Other Former Students, A" (Scott), 260
Stultz, Tom, 230
Successful Farming magazine, 206
Sudan, 252
Sulzberger, Arthur Hays, 175
Sunday Times of London, 127
Supreme Court of Missouri, 74
Supreme Court, U.S., 144–45, 205
Sutherland, Jack, 65
Swafford, Scott Cunningham, 240, 250
Swan, Joyce A., 65
Swartz, John Thomas (Jack), 53
Sweet, Nathaniel A., 73–74
Switzler, William F., 5, 23
Sydney, Australia, semester of the Journalism School, 230
Symington, Stuart, 65
Synor, Paul, 36
Syracuse University, 193, 232

Taft, William Howard, 139, 144, 151, 160–61, 214, 219, 259
Taiwan semester of the Journalism School, 119, 161
Talent, Truth, and Energy: Seventy-Five Years of Service to Journalism (Bostrom), 260
Television classes. *See* Broadcasting classes
Terrell, Robert L. (Bob), 147–48
Texas A&M University, 153
Texas Christian University, 220, 237
Textbooks (writing and publishing of), 221
Text messaging, 255
Theory and Practice of Journalism class, 68
Theta Sigma Pi, 67
Thilly, Frank, 11
Thomas, Helen, 129, 150
Thompson, Jean Cameron, 184
Thompson, Laetitia (Tish), 130, 214
Thompson, Lea Hopkins, 214
Thompson, Paul J., 25–26
Thompson, Walter Wright II (Wright), 215
Thorson, Esther, 120, 149–50, 214, 225–28, 235, 254
Timberlake, Patricia (Pat), 262
Time Enough: Essays in Autobiography (Mott), 135
Time Incorporated, 94, 166, 194
Time magazine, 37, 127, 166
Times of London, 26

Today Show, 106
Tong, Hollington K., 27, 119
Topeka Daily Capital, 126
Townlain, Kimberly (Kim), 43, 192
Townsend, Newton I., 126
Training for Journalism as a Profession (W. Williams), 13–14
Transportation Security Administration, U.S., 205
Trenton (Missouri) Republican-Times, 166
Trinity Lutheran Seminary, 193
Troy (Missouri) Free Press, 56
True magazine, 42, 64
Truman, Harry, 20, 128
Tucker, E. W., 177
Tulsa Times and Democrat, 66
Tulsa World, 175
Tunnicliffe, Guy, 168
Turkey, 125
Turner, Edwin, 38
Turner, Ralph H., 34
Turrentine, Jim, 213
Typewriters, 237
Typography, 33, 43, 177
"Twenty-Three Years of Development of the *Columbia Missourian*" (Gleason), 260
Twenty Years of Education for Journalism (Lockwood), 259

Uehling, Barbara, 54, 156–57, 162, 165
Ugarte, Michael, 234
Ullmann, John, 188–89, 248
Umansky, Martin, 210
United Nations, 230
United Press (later United Press International), 17, 33–34, 45, 65, 70, 98, 125, 129, 150, 166, 213
United Soybean Board, 164
United States Department of Health, Education and Welfare. *See* Health, Education and Welfare, U.S. Department of
United States House of Representatives. *See* House of Representatives, U.S.
United States Information Agency
United States Senate. *See* Senate, U.S.
United Way, 50
University Missourian. See Missourian
University Missourian Association, 19
University Missourian magazine, 17
University of Alabama, 235
University of Alaska, 188

University of Arkansas, 172
University of California, 147, 198
University of Chicago, 28, 134, 152
University of Colorado, 34, 40, 120, 148, 226
University of Florida, 149, 205, 220
University of Georgia, 141, 169, 209
University of Illinois, 3, 169, 191, 194, 217
University of Iowa, 3, 42, 79, 91, 126, 135, 142–43, 152–53, 169, 222
University of Kansas, 62, 124, 170, 186
University of Kentucky, 40, 170
University of Maryland, 154, 191
University of Massachusetts, 151
University of Michigan, 81, 156, 222
University of Minnesota, 40, 62, 197, 225
University of Mississippi, 219, 222
University of Missouri: Academic Department, 10; Academic Hall, 22; Admissions, 15, 23; Adult Education and Extension Service, 102; Agricultural Extension Division, 100; Agriculture College, 14, 18, 22–23, 206; Alumni Association, 18, 44; Alumni Center, 253; archives, 257; Art Department, 22; Arts and Science College, 5, 10, 23, 251; athletics, 22, 50; basketball, 38–39; Biological Sciences Department, 15; Black Faculty and Staff Organization, 201; Board of Curators, 5, 8–11, 16–18, 27, 38, 57, 61, 69–70, 100, 102, 114, 130, 141–42, 177, 246; budgets, 131, 157, 170–71, 245–47; Business School, 229; Center for the Digital Globe, 209, 229; chancellor's residence, 112–13; Concert Series, 111; Discovery Fellows, 252; Economics Department, 15, 185; Education College, 10, 14, 22, 229–30, 235; Ellis Fischel Cancer Center, 229; Ellis Library, 204–5, 257; endowed chairs, 205–11; Engineering College, 14, 22; English Department, 3, 15; Faculty Council, 169; Fine Arts Day, 69; football, 18, 34, 38, 67, 214–15; foreign language instruction, 10, 15; fraternities, 50; Freshman Interest Groups, 252; fundraising, 253; gay rights, 141–42; general counsel, 114; History Department, 10; homecoming, 247; Honors College, 252; Human Environmental Sciences College, 229; Information Science and Learning Technology

School, 229; Innocence Project, 229; Institutional Review Board, 227; Jesse Hall, 28, 55, 58, 108, 112, 125; Law School, 10, 14, 22, 39–40, 58, 132, 229; Lewis Hall, 257–58; liberal arts, 15; Mathematics Department, 15; Medical Center, 194; Medicine School, 10, 14, 22, 132, 194, 248; Memorial Union, 100, 144; Mining faculty, 22; Music School, 22; News Bureau, 261; Office of Public Information, 34, 261; Personnel Services, 162; Philosophy Department, 15; police, 144; Political Science Department, 15, 101, 224, 228–29; purchasing policies, 247; Psychiatry Department, 193; Psychology Department, 15, 101; Quadrangle, 23, 58, 65, 85, 95, 97, 240, 253, 256; racism, x, 73–76, 141, 201; Regional Medical Program, 194; registrar, 73–76; Religion School, 193; sexism, x, 141; Sociology Building, 253; Sociology Department, 15, 22; Switzler Hall, 23, 26, 56, 85; system president, 114; teaching assistants, 234–35; tenure and promotion cases, 20, 149, 154–57, 162, 248; Theatre Department, 22; tuition, 227; Veterinary Medicine College, 38, 58; Western Historical Manuscript Collection, 257, 259; Women's and Gender Studies, 193
University of Missouri: An Illustrated History, The (Olson and Olson), 260
University of Missouri and the Journalism of China, The (Lau), 260
University of Missouri Bulletin, 22, 70, 261
University of Missouri–Kansas City, 229
University of Missouri–St. Louis, 131
University of Montana, 134
University of Navarra, Pamplona, Spain, 232
University of Nebraska, 21, 170
University of Nevada-Reno, 186
University of North Carolina, 208
University of Oklahoma, 78, 194
University of Oregon, 42
University of Pennsylvania, 3, 244
University of Pittsburgh, 24
University of Rhode Island, 138
University of South Carolina, 156, 235
University of Southern California, 126
University of Tennessee, 194

University of Texas, 25–26, 34, 146
University of Texas–Arlington, 170
University of Texas–El Paso, 157
University of Wisconsin, 76, 81, 138, 141, 169, 225–26
University of Wisconsin–Eau Claire, 45
Up Against the Wall, Motherfucker, 144
Urban journalism, 129–32, 146–47
Urban Pioneer, 147
U.S. News and World Report magazine, 65
Utsler, Max, 106–7, 167–68

Van Riper, Frank, 180
Vermont, Missouri, 7
Vibrations magazine, 43
Vietnam War, 44, 63
Virginia Commonwealth University, 227, 235
Vladimir, Irwin, 163
Vo, Angie, 262
Vocational education, xi, 1–12
Volz, Yong, 226
Votaw, Maurice, 36–37, 119–22, 133
Vox magazine, 43, 242

Wade, Duke, 116
Walker, Marina, 234
Walker, Mort, 60–61
Walli, Donald S., 156–57
Wallstin, Brian John, 250
Wall Street Journal, 146, 200, 217
Wal-Mart stores, 245
Walsh, Denny Jay, 219
Walter, John, 4
Walter, Margaret Rose, 250
Walter Williams (Rucker), 258
Walter Williams Hall, 55, 57, 87, 93, 124, 177, 253
Walter Williams Memorial Journalism Foundation, 71–72
Walter Williams Scholars, 252
"Walter Williams: Spokesman for Journalism and Spokesman for the University of Missouri" (Adams), 260
Waltrip, Frank, 163
Wanta, Wayne, 120, 227, 229
War Department, U.S., 63
Ward, Rosemary, 162
Warhover, Thomas A. (Tom), 233, 248–50, 254
Warner, Charles (Charlie), 210–11

Washington, D.C., semester of the Journalism School, 110, 116, 128–29, 132, 161, 165, 170, 189, 207, 211, 215, 252
Washington and Lee University, 2
Washington correspondents, 59, 127, 222
Washington Evening Star, 185
Washington, George, 140
Washington Post, 28, 123, 180, 190, 207
Washington Post and Times-Herald, 64
Washington State University, 226
Washington University, St. Louis, 70
Wassmuth, Birgit, 168–69
Watergate political scandal, 44, 46
Waters, Henry J., 16
Waters, Henry J., III (Hank), 50, 54, 243, 245–46
Watson, Edwin Moss, 16, 18
Watson Place, 58
Wayne State University, 48
WCBS-TV, New York City, 64
WDAF-TV, Kansas City, 99
Weekly Review of the Far East, 121
Weinberg, Sonia, ix, 215
Weinberg, Steve, ix–xi, 189–91, 214–15, 223
Weise, Duane M., 100
Welch, Catherine, 240
Wellman, Walter, 22
Wells, Campbell, 27
Wendover, W. Edward, 247
Western Michigan University, 143
Western Washington State University, 186
West Plains, Missouri, 158
WFRV-TV, Green Bay, Wisconsin, 115
Whale, John, 127
White, Carolyn, 39
White House, 129, 175
WIBV radio, Belleville, Illinois
Wilkins, Lillian (Lee), 226
Williams, Edwin Moss, 7, 69, 203
Williams, Harry M., 147
Williams, Helen (Mrs. John F. Rhodes), 7, 69
Williams, Hulda Harned, 6–7
Williams, Marcus, 4
Williams, Marcus Walter, Jr. (Walter), ix–xi, 1–30, 56, 59–60, 65–72, 81, 83, 87–88, 117–24, 132–34, 157, 159, 173–78, 187, 203, 211, 213–14, 217, 223, 256–61
Williams, Mary Jane Littlepage, 4

Williams, Paul N., 188
Williams, Rachel, 262
Williams, Sara Lawrence Lockwood, 34, 66–71, 83, 150, 257, 260
Williams, Susan Ann, 4
Williams, Walter, Jr., 70
Williams, Walter Winston, 7
Williams, William (Billy), 11
Wilmington News Journal, 244
Wilson, Dale, 22
Wilson, Jean Gaddy, 195–97
Wilson, Leigh, 116
Wilson, Lyle C., 65
Winfield, Betty, 120, 226
Winsor Newspapers, 52–53
Wise, Kevin, 228
Wise, Rick, 52
WLW-AM, Cincinnati, 98
WMC-TV, Memphis, 108
Woelfel, Scott, 115
Woelfel, Stacey, 115–16, 233, 240
Wohleber, Curt, 239, 241
Woman's National Press Association, 150
Women and the Media class at the Journalism School, 150, 197
Women's pages in newspapers, 67
Wong, Hin, 71, 123
Woo, Elizabeth Hart, 123–24
Woo, Ky Tang, 123–24
Woo, William F., 123–24

Wood, Greg, 206
Woods, Gail Baker, 148, 164, 198–99, 201–2
Woodward, Anne-Marie Sullivan (Rie), 250
Woodward, Bob, 44
World Book Publishing, 159
World Press Congress, 118
World's Journalism, The (W. Williams), 118
World War I, 59
World War II, 59–61, 178, 186
World Wide Web, 239–43, 250, 255
Wright, Guy, 42
Wright, Jackson A., 114
Writing of News, The (Ross), 22
Written by Students in Journalism (S. Williams), 34, 259
Wyman, Scott, 49

Yale University, 15, 166, 224
Yates, Thomas L., 68
Yenching (Peking) University, 70–71, 123
Yonhap News Agency, 126
Young, Virginia, 49
Young and Rubicam Incorporated, 228
Young Men's Christian Association (YMCA), 71

Zabowsky, Stanley, 134
Zeeck, David, 48, 170
Zhang, Ernest, 120, 233